A New Approach to Synch

This book offers an up-to-date handling of C. G. Jung's Theory of Synchronicity and the more mainstream paranormal phenomena known as extra-sensory perception (ESP) and psychokinesis (PK), collectively referred to as 'psi'.

Author Lance Storm re-works various aspects of synchronicity, traditionally marginalized by parapsychologists, to bring about a paradigm shift in the field. Most often seen as fundamentally different, the book draws parallels between psi and synchronicity and equates the two, arguing that psi was all along a form of synchronicity—just as Jung had anticipated. To achieve this, Storm necessarily modifies both the parapsychologist's views about psi, and Jung's views about synchronicity, enabling a satisfactory merger of the two paranormal phenomena.

Based on rigorous scientific research and written in an easy-to-understand style, this book is an important resource for specialists such as anomalistic psychologists, parapsychologists, philosophers, paranormalists, and theologians.

Lance Storm is a Visiting Research Fellow at the School of Psychology, University of Adelaide, Australia. He has over 20 years of post-doctoral research experience as a theorist and designer of funded experiments in parapsychology. Storm has published in major journals including *Psychological Bulletin, Journal of Parapsychology*, and *Journal of Scientific Exploration*. He is a full member of the AIPR, and Chief Editor of the *Australian Journal of Parapsychology*.

A New Approach to Synchronicity

A Re-Appraisal of Jung's Acausal Connecting Principle with a Focus on Psi

Lance Storm

Routledge
Taylor & Francis Group
LONDON AND NEW YORK

Designed cover image: Connected [Oil on canvas, 76cm x 102cm] by Bernard Palchick. Used with permission.

First published 2025
by Routledge
4 Park Square, Milton Park, Abingdon, Oxon OX14 4RN

and by Routledge
605 Third Avenue, New York, NY 10158

Routledge is an imprint of the Taylor & Francis Group, an informa business

British Library Cataloguing in Publication Data
A catalogue record for this book is available from the British Library

ISBN: 978-1-032-91099-4 (hbk)
ISBN: 978-1-032-90238-8 (pbk)
ISBN: 978-1-003-56133-0 (ebk)

DOI: 10.4324/9781003561330

Typeset in Times New Roman
by Taylor & Francis Books

To the memory of a true pioneer, Alice Johnson (1860–1940)

Dedicated to truth-seekers everywhere

Special thanks to Laurence Browne for his encouragement

Contents

Preface

> "Synchronicity is … an intellectually necessary principle"
>
> Carl Gustav Jung (1952/1969, para. 960)

As a researcher, I believe I have come a long way since 2002, which was my first year as a funded post-doctoral research psychologist specializing in parapsychology (the science *beyond* psychology). Having come this far, I now make the following declaration: C. G. Jung's synchronicity theory goes a long way towards describing and even explaining many paranormal phenomena. I say "many" because there are some effects that should not be considered paranormal, which means "outside the realm of human or animal capabilities as presently conceived by conventional scientists" (Thalbourne, 2003, p. 83). I will provide more detail on synchronicity in later chapters, but for now it suffices to define synchronicity as a "coincidence in time of two or more causally unrelated events which have the same or a similar meaning" (Jung, 1952/1969, para. 849). The subject of synchronicity does not come up as often in parapsychology as does the word "psi", which is used either as "a noun or adjective to identify paranormal processes and paranormal causation" (Thalbourne, p. 92). Thus, psi works as a short-hand term for extrasensory perception (ESP) and psychokinesis (PK) as *processes*, but the word is also descriptive (e.g., a *psi* effect). ESP and PK are considered paranormal because ESP is defined as the "acquisition of information about, or response to, an external event, object or influence (mental or physical; past, present or future) otherwise than through any of the known sensory channels" (Thalbourne, p. 40); PK is defined as "the direct influence of mind on a physical system that cannot be entirely accounted for by the mediation of any known physical energy" (p. 98). There are of course those parapsychologists who feel the word "paranormal" has outgrown its use.

Jung (1968a) equated synchronicity with meaningful coincidence, and regarded psi as a form of synchronicity because of its meaningful elements: "These [ESP] experiments and the whole experience of ESP are sufficient proof that meaningful coincidences do exist" (para. 1198). Like Jung, when I use the term "meaningful coincidence", I mean synchronicity *as well as psi,* although I allow for the broader context in which the term *meaningful coincidence* may be used to mean "serendipity" (i.e., an accidental but fortuitous event), "seriality" (i.e., an objective series of related events), and "simulpathity" (i.e., a shared emotional experience; see Beitman, 2022, pp. 13–21).

In equating psi with synchronicity, I must exclude from the synchronicity category some phenomena thought to be paranormal, though I will refer to them on occasion. I include life after death (LAD), and any kind of non-physical entity, be it an apparition, ghost, poltergeist, cryptomorph, xenomorph, extra-terrestrial, extradimensional being, or visitor from the twilight zone, as well as unicorns, leprechauns, elves, dwarfs, pixies, and so on, *except* on those occasions when any or all of these may be mental products induced, by means known or unknown, in the experient's mind during any kind of altered state of consciousness (ASC), including the dream state. These exceptions, like any fantasy or dream content, might attain special significance in the synchronistic sense. However, since science has not settled the post-mortem survival vs. living-agent psi (LAP) debate,[1] though many punters will advise that the matter is settled (I will not be naming names; nor will I discuss the issues in any great detail), I will leave open the possibility that synchronicity may well explain *other* LAD phenomena insofar as some of these may in fact actually be cases of LAP.

For those readers unfamiliar with the debate, there are two schools of thought: On the one hand, there are those who believe in an afterlife (a.k.a. post-mortem survival); on the other hand, there are those who regard so-called afterlife communications (e.g., from mediumship) as examples of LAP—that is, some person still living (still physically incarnate) has the sought-after information about the deceased, and the medium merely tunes into that person via "super-psi", which is naively described as more sophisticated variants of telepathy, clairvoyance, and precognition. Needless to say, there are arguments for and against both theories.[2] Here I will introduce a few more definitions: Telepathy refers to the "paranormal acquisition of information concerning the thoughts, feelings or activity of another conscious being" (Thalbourne, 2003, p. 125). Clairvoyance is defined as "paranormal acquisition of information concerning an object [or symbol] or contemporary physical event; in contrast to telepathy, the information is assumed to derive directly from an external physical source" (Thalbourne, 2003, p. 18). Precognition is defined as "a form of extrasensory perception in which the target is some future event that cannot be deduced from normally known data in the present" (Thalbourne, 2003, p. 90).

It is noted that special conditions or contingencies apply in the case of synchronicity, whereas psi is thought to be an unexplained form of psychological perception or physical perturbation, yet both are regarded as not only anomalous but paranormal because synchronistic conditions or contingencies concern controversial assumptions about how the universe might operate, and what is possible in that universe, whereas psi perceptions and perturbations concern how the organism might function in extraordinary ways. Or at least, that is how we are given to understand the two. In fact, the distinction is not so clear if we consider that sufficiently self-aware organisms, as part of the universe, may find that these special functions are crucially intertwined with certain principles of nature, as are vision and light, hearing and sound, and communication and neural processes.

I hasten to add that I regard the synchronicity/psi parallel as valid only if and when both are re-envisioned, which I will attempt in this book. Here (as in Storm, 2025), I aim to cover as much as I can that is currently known about synchronicity and psi, in their parallel and seemingly disparate forms, in order to dispel as much doubt as possible about what each means in terms of the other. And to do that adequately, I must question the worth of some long-held assumptions that do no more than impede parapsychology's progress towards unification.

Conceptually, work on this book began in 2008 with an anthology I edited called *Synchronicity: Multiple Perspectives on Meaningful Coincidence* (Storm, 2008c)—I will be referring to chapters from that anthology quite often throughout this book. I thank again those who contributed to that anthology. Some of them are no longer with us: Victor Mansfield (1941–2008) passed away suddenly only months before the anthology's release, Berthold Eric Schwartz (1924–2010) passed away two years after publication, William Braud (1942–2012) passed away four years after publication; James Hall (1934–2013) passed away five years after publication; and both F. David Peat (1938–2017) and Lila L. Gatlin (1928–2017) passed away nine years after publication—my posthumous thanks go to those magnificent scholars. No doubt the works they leave behind are seeds from the past growing in the present and into the future. I also extend my posthumous thanks to two contributors Kenower Bash (1913–1986), and John Beloff (1920–2006), both of whom had passed before I had given even the slightest thought towards compiling a collection of synchronicity articles that became the *Synchronicity* anthology. I must also thank the other contributors Robert Aziz, Joseph Cambray, Marialuisa Donati, George Hogenson, Roderick Main, John Palmer, Sally Rhine-Feather, Shantena Sabbadini, and Charles Tart. Influences from all these authors are apparent in my three summing-up chapters in *Synchronicity*; indeed, the works of these same authors will quite often be cited in the pages to follow.

In practical terms, as far as producing the manuscript that became this book, I did not actually start tapping away on the keyboard until 2017. My thanks go to all those just mentioned, as well as my newfound colleagues, students, and friends who, in many discussions on the topics of psi and synchronicity, set me thinking that it was time for another *look* (at the psi problem), and another *book* (on synchronicity), even when none of us expected it at the time. Those people include Laurence Browne, Tony Jinks, Madeline Kretschmer, Colin Mitchell, Dominic Gill, and Robb Tilley.

—Lance Storm
2024

Notes

1 Readers interested in fairly unbiased treatments of the debate can see Braude (2003), Rock (2013), and Sudduth (2016).
2 For a debate on post-mortem survival and living-agent psi, see "Do We Survive Death?" in the *Journal of Parapsychology* (Volume 80, Issue 2). The books which triggered the debate are *Beyond Physicalism* (Kelly, Crabtree, & Marshall, 2015), and *The Myth of an Afterlife* (Martin & Augustine, 2015).

Introduction

> "... meaningful connections between events allows reality to display its concrete character that we experience in our everyday life"
>
> Fotini Pallikari, Emil Boller, & Holger Bösch (2000, p. 220)

At this critical juncture in the sciences, where shifts are occurring everywhere, could it be such a bad idea to resurrect a theory from the past as a strategy that is better than a hope for something new? That proposition seems reasonable in spite of the fact that the American philosopher Thomas Kuhn (1962) out-rightly stated that replacement paradigms would have to be novel and innovative simply because the old paradigms fail. Yet Kuhn's theory is *in itself* a revolutionary and paradigmatic shift in sociological and scientific thinking, so it too might be subject to replacement or "*ad hoc* modifications" (p. 78)—an observation Kuhn rejected, but unjustifiably to my way of thinking. So perhaps it is not unreasonable to hold the notion that old ideas are worth revisiting. By that I mean some old ideas may not have been fully developed or explored as thoroughly as they might or should have been.[1]

One theory from the not-so-distant past is C. G. Jung's Theory of Synchronicity, though that theory itself borrows from ideas going back centuries (see Jung, 1952/1969, para. 916–946). Synchronicity is defined as a "coincidence in time of two or more causally unrelated [acausal] events which have the same or a similar meaning" (para. 849). In other words, synchronicity does not describe the "casual coincidence" (to use John Stuart Mill's term) or "ordinary, expectable coincidence" (Colman, 2011)—it has to be meaningful; hence, synchronicity is also known as "meaningful coincidence" (see Chapter 1 for examples). Also, the word 'acausal' should not be taken too dogmatically for Jung actually said *causal* explanations for meaningful coincidences were merely impossible to think. As Jung explains,

> ... it is impossible, with our present resources, to explain ESP, or the fact of meaningful coincidence, as a phenomenon of energy. This makes an end of the causal explanation as well, for "effect" cannot be understood

DOI: 10.4324/9781003561330-1

> as anything except a phenomenon of energy. Therefore it cannot be a question of cause and effect, but of a falling together in time, a kind of simultaneity.
>
> (para. 840)

In this regard, Jung has been accused of thinking in terms of *mechanical* causality, but the word "simultaneity" already indicates a different (archetypal) process at work based on "contingence" rather than "causality" (see Chapter 1). In other words, there are events that occur together based on psychophysical parameters and patterns that do not emulate cause-and-effect relations. The notions of information transmission and energy transfer or exchange are also undermined in synchronicity theory, though I suggest Jung did not address either of these adequately for both psi and synchronicity. The idea of contingence also seems to defeat the argument some might make that "intention" has causal properties, yet it would seem proper to make a place for it at some specifiable level without it necessarily violating synchronicity as a so-called "principle". Oddly, there are experimental findings suggesting psi effects can arise counter to what is consciously intended or expected (Carpenter, Cannard, Wahbeh, & Radin, 2021; Storm, 2022).

Only occasionally has synchronicity been comprehensively and unsparingly reviewed for its viability as a parapsychological theory (e.g., Beloff, 1977; Braud, 1983; Stokes, 1987), and even less so has it been tested, to the extent that only one prominent parapsychologist (Braud, 1983) in the 20th century, besides Jung himself, went to the effort of publishing his results on tests of meaningful coincidence. I might add that there was some dabbling in experimental *I Ching* in that century (see Chapter 2), which I consider a step in the right direction (see Rubin & Honorton, 1971, 1972; Thalbourne, 1994), and set the ball rolling for similar research (Storm & Thalbourne, 1998–1999).

While there are also a few key books in the 20th century focusing purely on synchronicity as a theory and approach to paranormal goings-on (e.g., Combs & Holland, 1996; Mansfield, 1995; Peat, 1987; Progoff, 1973; von Franz, 1980), matched by others in the 21st century (e.g., Beitman, 2016, 2022; Browne, 2017; Cambray, 2009; Main, 2004, 2007), there has only been slight interest in empirical (observational or experimental) research into synchronicity in this new century (e.g., Coleman & Beitman, 2009; Coleman, Beitman, & Celebi, 2009; Pallikari, Boller, & Bösch, 2000; Palmer, 2016; Storm, 2008a; von Lucadou, Römer, & Walach, 2007).[2]

While synchronicity does raise occasional theoretical interest (Colman, 2011; Yiassemides, 2011), Grattan-Guinness (1983) noted decades ago the long-running inattention it has received, and little has changed (for similar comments, see Yiassemides, 2011).[3] Why the disinterest? The most obvious answer is that the greater majority of mainstream researchers remain unconvinced about synchronicity, as they do psi, and a host of alternative explanations (mainly statistical) have been furnished as "evidence" explaining away those effects. While some remain unconvinced, those same people should note that such explanations are often useful if appropriately applied, but I will argue that genuine synchronicity escapes the net each time (see Chapter 1).

It is crucial at this juncture to point out that another obstacle blocking the acceptance of synchronicity, especially in its broader sense that embraces a holistic view of the world,[4] is that it is impossible to think how it can come about other than by chance and outside causal factors. Colman (2011) explicitly identifies the hair-splitting tedium the synchronicity concept invokes:

> It is this "contributing in" of the material world that creates the sense of non-human intentionality at work in the universe characteristic of "strong synchronicity". And, in turn, it is much more difficult to see (at least for me) how such coincidences might be connected in any conceivably measurable system, no matter how complex.
>
> (p. 480)

That connection is meaning, but it seems the "difficulty" for Colman is how meanings ("qualitative states of mind" or "emergent properties") can be factored into an objectively measurable system, and be accounted for in that system, and thereby be given scientific status, all of which exemplifies just how much synchronicity can be impossible to conceptualize in causal terms. This impossibility stifles any hope of seeing how synchronicity actually can have a unifying aspect (or has unifying power), but this stifling effect more than likely has its source in the false sense of autonomy (even isolation) we build *for* and *around* ourselves. If one is not able to see how we could be interconnected with our world at many levels, subtle and not so subtle, then synchronicity, and psi for that matter, would naturally be impossible to conceptualize in causal terms. Biologically, living, breathing, consuming, and moving freely and independently in the Earth's biosphere is largely responsible for that sensibility, but ironically it is actually the biosphere that not only sustains us, and keeps us alive, but accounts for our symbiosis. And we must even acknowledge the disconcerting notion that an immense number of bacterial forms contribute sizeably to our body mass.[5] These facts put a question mark over our false sense of autonomy. And psychologically, Jung's Collective Unconscious is a phylogenetic or inherited factor in our make-up that enables archetypal experiences and these, as we shall see, can also break our false sense of autonomy (see Jung, 1959/1968). In short, we are far too dependent and too locked into a manifold of interacting systems to be making overtures about how autonomous we are, and any reflection on meaning should take this fact into consideration.

Yet science as an objectifying enterprise has naturally emerged from our sense of autonomy, to the degree that Jung's idea that meaning might have equal status with such concepts as spacetime and causality is repudiated, purely because meaning seems such a subjective concern. However, spacetime and causality provide frameworks for *relatively* objective views of reality only and, more to the point, it can be argued that meaning can also be relatively objective (see Chapter 1). Not allowing for these concessions, we can see how the ambitious idea that "non-human intentionality" is behind synchronicity might be proposed since it satisfies the need for a cause that is both intelligent *and* independent of human machinations. Such a view, however, stems from the failure to realize that archetypes (the contingent factors underpinning synchronicity) give only the *impression* of intelligent behaviour. The ancients, of course, thought the same way about their gods, though these days we more likely see that worldview as the result of the innate psychological tendency to project our own inner functions into some other dimension where they exist as anthropomorphized human-like entities. More correctly, archetypes are like collating and correlating forces, or more accurately, ground-plans or blue-prints for normal cognitions and actions, but also for synchronicity, and their overall effects will carry with them characteristic pre-defined meanings. The collective unconscious in all of us enables these commonalities of archetypal experience. These not only break our false sense of autonomy, they can result in shared experiences and meanings as is evident from synchronicity, psi, and even collective visions.[6] (For an exemplary review on synchronistic meaning, see Main, 2014.)

Archetypes are many and varied (far too numerous to count but not unlimited), and they constitute the sum of all human encounters, experiences, and even life choices having been built into the very fabric of life over time (see also Jacobi, 1973). So much so that they have been viewed in older societies as acting like forces, albeit by other names, that stand behind the fates of mankind. We see that our intentions have some part to play, with freewill seeming to have a hand, but as most people can attest, our "choices" so often and obviously seem to be the correct ones (they are 'the right thing to do'), but we could not really tell if something "other" also had a hand in it, as if each of us is a jigsaw piece with only one right place in the whole. Unlike jigsaw pieces, however, we might just be able to move about the whole. Only the most skeptical among us would want to deny that the effects of "our" decisions extend beyond our existential bounds, and that things almost seemed planned, no matter how they turn out.

Failure to elicit and identify archetypal situations in the laboratory, or even assume their presence, may be at the root of the *main concern*, which is the sporadic nature of psi in experimental parapsychology (these issues will come up in Chapter 3). However, testing synchronicity should not be any more difficult than testing ESP and PK. Indeed, I suggest throughout this text that experimenters are already doing that, but do not realize it—for example, they only need to consider the content of their targets in terms of their numinosity (e.g., their emotional charge) and their relevance to participants. John Palmer (2008), although a parapsychologist with a long history of following the Rhinean paradigm, nevertheless suggests as quite feasible the possibility of creating laboratory-based situations where archetypes and archetypal situations may be invoked.

Annoyingly, some (maybe many) skeptics seem to think it is not so much a lack of theory about psi that is the problem; it is the lack of evidence. Unfortunately, that misinformed claim leads to other dubious claims, prompting skeptics like Robert Carroll (author of *The Skeptic's Dictionary*) to proclaim that he "isn't convinced that there is anything to be explained" (Carroll, 2009). I do not intend to give much voice to dismissive skeptical (even *pseudo* skeptical) positions because there is sufficient research proving time and again that these statistical anomalies exist, but I *will* take pains to find out whether our understanding of psi could be better informed, requiring at the very least that I heed Everton Maraldi's (2017) words: "… much of the evidence available is not sufficiently understood or is merely suggestive of certain paranormal claims" (p. 900). I will argue that Jung did not have the whole story on psi, and he occasionally veered off track, so that the theory of synchronicity might only fill the void in our parapsychological knowledge if it gets a little help from the sidelines. In Chapter 3, I try to re-envision synchronicity from that perspective.

In Chapter 4, I will present an example drawn straight out of our synchronistic world that reaches beyond the confines of the laboratory and the theoretician's mind, into the lives of everyday people. But again, heeding Maraldi's (2017) words, it will be seen that while some anomalous effects *do* deserve to be called paranormal (whether they be called psi or synchronicity), others have over-stayed their welcome. Chapter 5 will feature many of these phenomena. That final chapter will also come to far-reaching conclusions about synchronicity and what it means to live in a synchronistic world.

Can a single volume on psi and synchronicity offer insights that might illuminate the way ahead and lead us down a new path, or a better-lit old path? Insights are one thing, whether they are reached by consensus or are merely the speculative thoughts of a single person, but it is certainly never an easy task convincing a skeptical society, or even a community entrenched in their beliefs. After all, look at what one is up against: The following experience was reported by clinical psychologist and parapsychologist, James Carpenter, after the release of his somewhat controversial book *First Sight* (Carpenter, 2012):

> A couple of years ago I gave a reading of my book, *First Sight*, at a local bookstore …. [A] flood of [questions] started, from about 7 or 8 people scattered through the audience. The first man asked why I had written a book defending creationism. This set me back, since my book has nothing to do with creationism, but I tried to respond thoughtfully. Then I was scolded for not understanding scientific method. I pointed out the large body of scientific work that my book treats. I was told that J. B. Rhine cheated in his research and was careless to boot. I gave personal

> stories about Rhine (I knew him fairly well) illustrating his remarkable honesty and self-critical integrity. I was told that I did not understand the mind's capacity to deceive itself by seeing illusory patterns in random data. I pointed out places in my text in which I dealt usefully with just that possibility. And so on it went, all from people who clearly had not read a word in my book and had no idea what it contained.
>
> (Carpenter, 2014)

In this one quote, I spotted at least half a dozen pseudo-problems conjured up by these critics of Carpenter's book (mainly the machinations of a group calling themselves the Research Triangle Atheists), and I think that kind of uninformedness (or shall I just call it ignorance?) describes a large proportion of the populace opiated by the hegemony of the other competing disciplines—until such attitudes change, parapsychology has a long and arduous road ahead. It will not be otherwise unless and until we (i) can defeat these intolerances, inside and outside the field; (ii) win a broader public and academic acceptance by way of (say) a handful of profound and solid ideas that befit a mature science; and (iii) deliver substantial results from our research efforts (even better if they come from reputable and highly regarded sources). In point of fact, we are slowly making gains in all three areas.

To gain further ground, I hope the ideas in this book serve to illuminate the way ahead so as to lead parapsychology down a better-lit path (old or new). May they also help clear up some doubts about psi, and make a little more sense of synchronicity than before.

Notes

1 This notion is not new (see Collins & Pinch, 1982). See also Storm (2005) for comments.

2 In his Fibonacci Life-Chart Method, psychotherapist and independent researcher Robert G. Sacco claims that certain life events (e.g., spiritual experiences, synchronicity experiences) occur at peak moments (ages) in a person's life determined by algorithms using the Fibonacci series, thus making the coincidences synchronistic. For example, at 11, 18, 30 years of age, only age 18 showed a significant peak in spiritual experiences (Sacco, 2017). In another study, only one effect in ten was significant, suggesting synchronicity experience could be predicted (Sacco, 2019). I suggest such effects are not psychophysical, but are psychophysiological (they are normal age-specific maturational effects) and are therefore not synchronistic (on this differentiation, see Chapter 5).

3 Over the three-decade period up to 2010, the number of journal articles and books on synchronicity increased fivefold compared to the three decades before that, with 25 new articles and books coming out per decade since the 1970–80s (Beitman, Celebi, & Coleman, 2010). However, this figure is disconcertingly constant when contrasted with the consistent growth in number of general research articles over the same period (Plume & van Weijen, 2014).

4 I take "holistic" to mean "intimately interconnected and explicable only by reference to the whole" (https://www.lexico.com/definition/holistic). The word "holistic"

also means "dealing with or treating the whole of something or someone and not just a part" (https://dictionary.cambridge.org/dictionary/english/holistic).

5 Sender et al. (2016) find that "the number of bacteria in the body is actually of the same order as the number of human cells" (p. 1). A "reference man" of 70 kilograms (age 20 to 30 years old, 1.7 meters tall) contains about 30 trillion human cells and 39 trillion bacteria. That can be up to 3 kg. of bacteria.

6 Archetypes may constellate *en masse* as community effects (i.e., collective visions), such as the well-documented archetypal apparitions of the Virgin Mary and other entities in Garabandal, Spain, 1961 to 1965 (Perez, 1998) and Fatima, Portugal, 1915 to 1917 (De Marchi, 1952). A modern equivalent is the 1994 case in Ruwa, Zimbabwe, when 60+ school children witnessed UFO landings and alien beings on the school grounds (Dunning, 2020). As in all these cases, however, many who were present on those occasions witnessed nothing at all. Rather than being cases of mass hysteria, such experiences reflect psychological realities (not physical realities), as they depend entirely on the relevant archetypes constellating.

Chapter 1

Defining Synchronicity

> "… one person's profoundly meaningful synchronistic experience may be another's probability calculation, or a third's causal analysis"
>
> Laurence Browne (2017, p. 114)

What is synchronicity? Since nature always presents phenomena first, and only then do we theorize, it might be best to start with examples of synchronicity, and follow up with a formal definition. In this first chapter, I describe synchronicity (meaningful coincidences) using examples, and contrast those with meaningless chance groupings. I define various synchronicity-related concepts, offer ways of identifying meaningful coincidence, and close with discussions on various alternatives put forward to explain synchronicity.

Examples of Synchronicity

The first example I shall give, and also the most commonly cited, is the scarab case given foremost treatment twice by C. G. Jung in his *Collected Works*; first in his essay 'Synchronicity: An Acausal Connecting Principle' (1952/1969), and then in his short paper 'On Synchronicity' (1951/1969). A female patient of Jung's could not make progress during analysis due to her intellectual resistance. Jung hoped for something unexpected. During analysis, the woman told Jung about her dream of a golden scarab in the form of a costly piece of jewellery. As she spoke, something tapped on the window-pane behind Jung—a large flying insect was knocking against the window-pane from outside. It was a common *rose-chafer* (a beetle of the *Scarabaeidae* family). The beetle was gold-green in colour resembling the golden scarab in the woman's dream. Jung said: "Here is your scarab" (1951/1969, para. 982).

This synchronistic experience cracked the woman's rationalistic mindset, and the treatment continued successfully. Jung writes: "Any essential change of attitude signifies a psychic renewal which is usually accompanied by symbols of rebirth in the patient's dreams and fantasies" (Jung, 1952/1969, para. 845).[1] However, for this therapeutic moment to have been successful, the experience had to be *meaningful* to the woman, as well as to Jung, who noted

DOI: 10.4324/9781003561330-2

the so-called *archetypal foundation* in the woman's dream that facilitated the breakthrough process. Specifically, the archetype of rebirth was constellated (formed or triggered) in the dream—the scarab is a classic example of a rebirth symbol—and since archetypes (defined later in this section) are ubiquitous and timeless (seemingly not bound—i.e., unbounded—by the barriers of time and space), the *numinosity* (i.e., the profundity and emotional power) of the experience was amplified by the apparent paranormal components of the woman's synchronistic experience. Essential to synchronicity is its "numinosity" (implying a fundamentally important experience), which breaks the mental inertia: Mishlove and Engen (2007) describe numinosity as "a mysterious, cognitively jarring, awe inspiring quality" (p. 227).

Thus did Jung realize the potential therapeutic value of meaningful coincidences, and while many of his colleagues might have been happy to exploit the fortuitous and serendipitous nature of such coincidences as they would any other timely event for the sake of therapeutic progress, Jung had the presence of mind to label the phenomenon "synchronicity", and see it as a more objective, even scientific phenomenon of empirical worth. Given its value is so extensive (a kind of philosophical gold), and noting synchronicity is not a modern invention (merely Jung's *discovery*), it is perhaps not surprising that the concept has precursors, ranging from the Chinese philosophy of *Tao* (which underscores the principles of "meaning", "purpose", and "balance"), to the medieval doctrine of *correspondentia* (where "all things are in sympathy"), the alchemical ideas of Paracelsus and Agrippa von Nettesheim ("all things are in all"), the philosophies of Kepler, Leibniz, and Schopenhauer, and finally the seriality of Paul Kammerer. Thus is psychotherapist Carolin S. Keutzer (1984) accurate in describing synchronicity as "a modern derivation of the archetypal belief in the fundamental unity of all things transcending mechanical causality" (p. 90).

This ability of Jung's to spot the parallels between the "inner" and the "outer" no doubt came from Jung's decades of experience interpreting clients' dreams and fantasies that contained meaningful imagery, often in symbolic form. A therapeutic approach to synchronicity was inevitable. Jung saw the external component of the inner/outer parallel acting as an objective cue, a substantive bridge, a means of accessing the mental landscape, and a wake-up call to the experient.

The second example of synchronicity—the Stockholm fire—also comes from Jung (1952/1969, para. 912, 915). In 1759, at a dinner party in Gothenburg, Swedish religious leader, scientist, philosopher, and mystic, Emanuel Swedenborg (1688–1772), while in an agitated state, had a vision of houses on fire nearly 500 kilometres away in Stockholm. Jung writes:

> When … the vision arose in Swedenborg's mind of a fire in Stockholm, there was a real fire raging there at the same time, without there being any demonstrable or even thinkable connection between the two.
>
> (para. 912)

An account of this fire, including such details as the time of the fire, and when it was put out, was given by Swedenborg to guests at the party held by a Mr. William Castel. Though the fire had consumed 300 houses, Swedenborg was relieved that the fire had stopped three doors from his own house (a fact which was confirmed later). The same account was given later to the Gothenburg city authorities. It took two to three days for news from Stockholm to reach Gothenburg by courier. Jung makes the point that this fire "was in a sense, burning in him [Swedenborg] too" (para. 912), and he hails this psychological fact as being a prime ingredient of the synchronistic event. This revelation of Jung's is derived from details in Swedenborg's biography in which is indicated the likelihood of a psychological state Jung describes as an "inner fire"—an inner manifestation or representation of fear and anxiety.[2] The archetype of fire is often taken to be symbolic of intense emotional affect, frustration, turmoil, and so on. Therefore, Swedenborg's "inner" (or spiritual) fire is of particular meaningful (i.e., psychological) significance. As an aside, C. A. Meier (2001) relates a similar event involving inner and outer fire which took place outside the Café Odeon in Zurich where physicist Wolfgang Pauli was seated, "pondering over his inferior function (feeling-color red)" (p. xviii):

> There was a large, unoccupied car parked outside the café. [Pauli] could not take his eyes off it, and then it suddenly caught fire and burst into flames.
> (p. xviii)

This example gives further evidence of the psychological (inner) link of the experient to the physical (outer) event without the need to assume the link is causal, which is to say, Pauli did not *cause* the car to catch fire, which can be explained in any number of normal ways. In fact, relatively speaking, acausality *per se* is not the mystery; the real mystery is how Pauli managed to get himself into these situations! (For more on Pauli's synchronicities, see Storm, 2025.)

My third key example—discovered just before writing this section—describes a situation which makes salient the closeness-of-fit (i.e., the approximating nature or "fuzziness")[3] of many synchronicities, and has important repercussions on the conventional understanding of synchronicity theory (but more on that later). In the mid-1980s, a long-time colleague of mine, the late Michael A. Thalbourne (1955–2010), in the early stages of his post-doctoral career, conducted research at the McDonnell Laboratory for Psychical Research at Washington University, St. Louis, Missouri. He worked with a fellow researcher Linda Evans. She related to Candace O'Connor, journalist and editor of the magazine *St. Louis* (O'Connor, 1985), the case of a bridge accident involving her fiancé. Alone in her apartment one night (as her fiancé was driving to an out-of-town conference), Linda thought she heard the word "Chappaquiddick" during a TV evangelical crusade. She then had the overwhelming image playing out in her mind of Edward Kennedy's 1969 bridge accident on Chappaquiddick Island, Massachusetts. It was the emotionality of this event that gripped her. About 20 minutes later, her fiancé called to tell her "he'd driven onto a flooded road and his car had sunk in the Mississippi River" (p. 128). The crisis moment associated with a bridge or river crossing is an archetypal situation that is repeated throughout history (e.g., Julius Caesar at the Rubicon, or Washington at the Delaware). Jung (1977) says of this crisis situation:

> It's an important moment, a risk. There is danger in the water, on the banks. Not for nothing did Christianity invent great St. Christopher, the giant who carried the infant Jesus through the water. ...; one feels that one's destiny—human destiny, almost—is at stake.
>
> (p. 415)

I will return to the issue of closeness-of-fit later, but here we can see that the archetypal image lacks alignment (e.g., Kennedy vs. Linda's fiancé), but fundamentally what is key is that a certain situation, once entered into, constellates an age-old archetypal theme of *crisis at a decisive moment*, which we can modify and refer to as *decision at a critical moment*. When an archetype constellates like this, we observe a kind of regularity in nature that even speaks to human activity. It is an ancient, higher order or pattern that governs the general situation particular to a moment, and though it may lack exacting detail, and cannot be expected to provide it, we see the advantage because the archetype draws into its sphere those who happen to be attuned (or are able to attune) to that moment irrespective of their time and place. This attunement would be underpinned by a compensatory need or some kind of outer stimulus.

Apart from the fact that there seems to be a kind of "observing" or "knowing" in synchronicity that comes without the aid of the five senses, and there seems to be no causal connection between "inner" and "outer", the reader can identify in these three cogent examples, the overwhelming presence of affect (i.e., emotional tone) in the three experients; Jung's female client, Emanuel Swedenborg, and Linda Evans. Generally speaking, then, we might infer that synchronicity triggers or evokes certain feelings in the experient. Jungian scholar Aniela Jaffé (1967) refers to the emotional component as a 'secondary symptom' that may be "present in the person who perceives the event, or it may be connected with the happening that is extra-sensorially observed" (p. 276). (Note how Jaffé cannot avoid positing an extra-sensory psi component in synchronicity.) More important is the archetype, whereby emotion is a "determinant" that brings the unconscious and the archetype to the foreground, thus giving rise to associated factors, such as simple and complex responses and thoughts, including the affective and cognitive components of belief and disbelief or, related to issues of belief, reconciling oneself with seemingly impossible (acausal) facts and factors, as in the case of the woman who had the scarab dream. But more importantly, in most cases of synchronicity, which do seem to call for crisis management in extreme cases, psychological healing, or change in outlook, or the birth of new ideas or options may result, especially if a certain shiftless form of single-mindedness is present that is to be ameliorated or resolved.

Any or all of these factors may be present to varying degrees, according to the numinosity of the experience (see Jung, 1921/1971, para. 681, 1951/1969, para. 982). Ultimately the result is a transformation of personality in some way, which Jung saw as the embodiment of the individuation process, "having for its goal the development of the individual personality" (Jung, 1921/1971, para. 757). Of course, to assert objectively that healing, or transformation, or individuation, etc., do actually transpire, or are underway, after a given synchronistic experience requires adequate knowledge of the case, which is not always available. It does appear, though, that experients are capable of making judgements about their own experiences, and they can and do discern meaningfulness (see Beitman & Shaw, 2009; Coleman & Beitman, 2009; Meyer, 1989).

I suggest too that the scarab case, the Swedenborg case, and the Evans case, are not typical paranormal (i.e., 'psi') cases in the conventional parapsychological sense which would see these three examples tagged as precognition, clairvoyance, and telepathy, respectively. Although it is a fact that Jung believed ESP and PK share similar phenomenology as synchronicity (1951/1969, para. 977–979; 1952/1969, para. 840, 863), we shall see later such apparent differences (such as the scale and scope of events, context, details, elements, etc.) suffice for some to call out theoretical and phenomenological differences between synchronicity and psi, while others will nevertheless try to reduce synchronicity to psi. This struggle with nomenclature and process is persistent: For example, Colman (2011) describes the scarab case as "an uncanny event in the world, as if the world 'knows' something it could not possibly know", whereas he describes Swedenborg's vision as "an uncanny event in the psyche as if the person experiencing the synchronicity knows something they could not possibly know" (p. 474).

Colman's (2011) demarcations couch synchronicity in limited egoic terms that see something or someone doing something, especially if it is on a grand scale. But synchronicity can be seen as other than that. Thus, there is, or can be, much dispute over the conceptual differences between synchronicity and psi (see especially, Mansfield et al., 1998), based on the phenomenology of both. I have covered much of this material elsewhere (Storm, 2008b; 2025), and will not go into any great detail in this chapter, but I will necessarily revive some of those issues in Chapter 3. For now, I raise a fundamental point for the reader's sake—the key to synchronicity is the seemingly paranormal inner/outer link; the link between the psychological and the physical, or between "psyche and physis" as Jung (1952/1969, para. 948) calls it, and this link is considered meaningful. While there are other forms besides the psyche/physis link, I will cover those later (see "Forms of Synchronicity" in Chapter 2). Nevertheless, for every form, meaningfulness is tied in with the transcendent/

transpersonal realm of archetypes; the experient unknowingly taps into an activated archetype and is instrumental in the event, though they may not realize that the resultant "inner" and "outer" manifestations are archetypal, which is often taken for information, seemingly for good reason. From these examples we can see that synchronicity comes across as coincidental in nature, usually comprised of an inner and an outer event that parallel each other in a meaningful way, and is thus seen as a principle of nature in action.

In conceptualizing synchronicity, Jung provides a deceptively subtle but crucial defining detail for he tells us synchronicity rests on the "*simultaneous occurrence of two different psychic states*"—the one as a "normal, probable state (… causally explicable)", while the other is the "critical experience" that "cannot be derived causally from the first" (para. 855). The external event, regardless of when and where it occurs, is the image that will constitute the normal psychic state, and the individual aligns that image with the critical experience (whether it was a dream or vision, a thought or an idea, an insight or intuition). The term synchronicity does not only imply the events have to be *synchronous* (as in the scarab case), for earlier and later events, not being together in real time, are also synchronicity (as in the case of the Stockholm fire). Jung wants us to recognise the *simultaneity* in two different psychic states (the vision of the fire which is held constant *and* Swedenborg's later synchronistic realization when he learns about the actual fire), yet he does not mention that the vision and the physical event in Stockholm were actually synchronous, which is true in general of pure telepathy and pure clairvoyance. And since there are such cases, I propose the term *synchronous synchronicity* later to describe those forms of synchronicity (again see "Forms of Synchronicity" in Chapter 2). However, insofar as the events do show that the components of a given synchronicity can appear to be separated in time, they are *asynchronous synchronicity.* In both cases, they are "experienced as psychic images *in the present*, as though the objective event already existed" (Jung, 1952/1969, para. 855). In fact, I would argue that the apparently "already existing objective event" is prefigured in the form of a relevant constellated archetype and it is that pivotal event made conscious that constitutes (is the defining element of) the synchronistic experience.

We have seen that the humble dream can be a launch point for synchronicity, but it can fully occur in fantasy or waking life, as the above examples show. While the standard synchronicity usually consists of two elements—one mental, one physical—Main (2007, pp. 18–20) notes that the elements can be two or more mental (internal) events only (e.g., shared dreams or fantasies similar in content and meaning), or two or more physical (external) events (e.g., coming across a rare but meaningful item more than once in a short space of time).[4]

Given its sporadic nature, synchronicity seems to occur as if by chance (i.e., randomly), but it is not "pure chance" (Jung, 1952/1969, para. 967). I prefer the term 'chance-like'; a term Jung never uses in his essay (see Storm, 1999), and it would have been helpful if Jung did make the distinction given his other comments about chance (e.g., para. 823 & 964; for further comments, see the section below in this chapter "Alternative Explanations of Synchronicity: I. Chance").

Examples of Meaningless Chance Groupings

In the previous section, I stated that, for the more common type of synchronicity to be effected, we need (a) an inner *and* outer condition (not causally connected), and (b) meaningfulness (i.e., an *equivalence of meaning*, or a meaningful parallel). If we do not have these two conditions (a) and (b), we only have a meaningless coincidence, or a cluster of meaningless coincidences, which Jung calls "meaningless chance groupings" (1952/1969, para. 846).[5] While a person might glean something ostensibly "meaningful" from chance groupings, it is not, by definition, "synchronistic meaning" which is a special case of meaningfulness. It should be clear that this special case is defined by certain other criteria, including two touched on earlier (i.e., archetypes and numinosity), but (a) and (b) are the two defining conditions.

The following is an example of a meaningless chance grouping from Harry Wilmer's (1987) book *Practical Jung*:

- A wife gives a man a new pipe for his birthday;
- He takes a walk and sits under a tree in a park;
- Sitting next to him is a man smoking the same kind of pipe;
- He tells the man his wife gave him his pipe for his birthday;
- The man says, "Mine did too";
- It turns out that they both have the same birthday;
- They introduce themselves. They have identical first names.

We can argue that condition (a) was not met. In order to satisfy the conditions of synchronicity, an inner psychic (psychological) experience would be required from at least one of the men directly relating to the events at hand that would be of a paranormal or acausal nature. We have an event comprised of a series of coincidences only. Wilmer (1987) says, "This is not a synchronistic event because there is no simultaneous, inner-meaningful, subjective event" (p. 169). That is, not only was condition (a) not met, but condition (b) was not met (the pipe-smoker parallels can be spoken of as chance correlations only). We might arguably see this example as synchronicity in the light of Main's (2007) more flexible view, but Wilmer's exemplar comprises superficial outer elements only (no psychic state) to drive home his point. In fact, real-world examples will probably always have a psychic component (see the personal "origami" example given by Main, 2007, p. 18). I shall comment further on this issue later (see "Forms of Synchronicity" in Chapter 2). We must look for meaningfulness as a pivotal requirement of synchronicity, and as the cases show, *archetypal meaning* (e.g., "rebirth" symbolism in the scarab case) is needed. Thus we only have meaningless chance groupings in the idealised pipe-smokers case.

To clarify, Jung (1952/1969) notes a difference between synchronicity and synchronism: "synchronicity" is "the simultaneous occurrence of two meaningful but not causally connected events" whereas "synchronism ... simply means the simultaneous occurrence of two events" (para. 849). Also, as indicated by the scarab example, synchronistic events can manifest as if *temporally displaced*. We note that Jung uses the word "simultaneous" twice to describe synchronicity *and* synchronism. Main (2004) criticizes Jung on his loose application of the word "simultaneous" "to sets of events that are not conspicuously simultaneous" (p. 39), as if the time gap undoes the simultaneity. Main notes that "simultaneity" is *not always* "immediately obvious", though Jung thinks it is in the scarab case (para. 850). Jung argues that the simultaneity lies phenomenologically *at the very moment* the individual mentally "encounters" the contingent component that is otherwise missing (i.e., unconscious to the individual), regardless of the fact that it may only be identified at a later time in physical space. I note the field of parapsychology makes exactly the same premise—under the psi hypothesis, there are those events that are, for a given time, beyond sensory awareness (outside our personal spacetime framework or field of consciousness), and these exist either "now" or "later" (or "in the past"), but as soon as they become conscious to the experient, those events align simultaneously with the prior *idea* (mental image) of them.

Having evaluated Wilmer's (1987) birthday example *qualitatively*, it would be appropriate to demonstrate *quantitatively* how such a stream of events may be the mere play of chance, and we can show that statistically in the instance of two people having the same birthday.[6] It might be thought that finding two people by chance with the same birthday (i.e., same day and month) in a roomful of people (or a public park for that matter) is unlikely, no matter how many people are present. However, the probability is high (99% probable in a room of only 57 people, and effectively guaranteed 100% in a room of about 60 people or more). Figure 1.1 shows other probabilities for differently-sized groups—the example given shows that we can find two people with the same birthday about 50% of the time amongst a mere 23 people. (The formula for calculating the exact probability is given in Appendix A.)[7]

In trying to find a solution to the so-called 'birthday problem', the lay person tends not to think counter-intuitively and assumes, since there are 365 possible birthdays, that a very large number of people (in excess of 365, and maybe twice as many) is needed to find a match because all birthdays have to be covered to be on the safe side. However, it is *not one particular birthday* that is being sought (one out of 365); in fact, a considerably larger number of all possible pairs are probabilistically screened with the aim of finding a match. In our example of 23 people, there are not 23 different birthdays all being sought for a possible match, but 253 pairs to consider (i.e., $23 \times 22/2$), which increases the probability of a match and leads to a 50% chance of finding one.

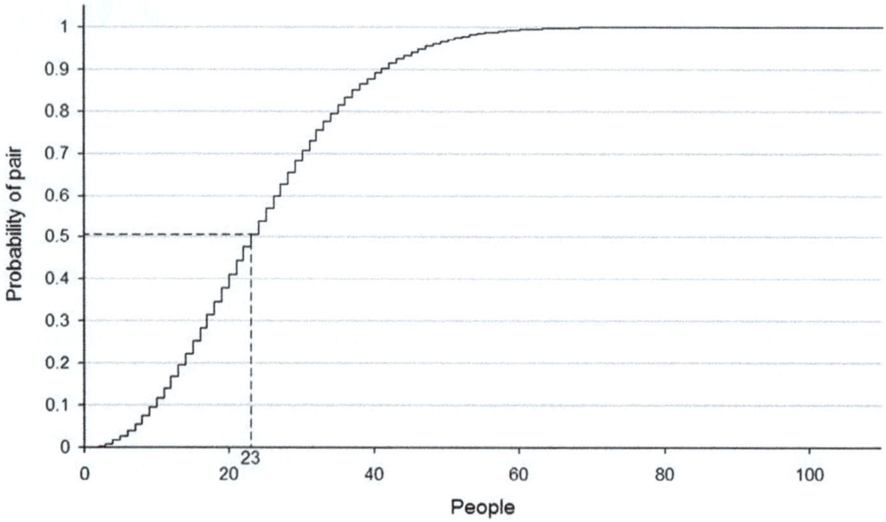

Figure 1.1 The probability that there is at least one pair of people with the same birthday amongst a certain number of people. (*Source*: © 2010, Wikimedia Commons/ Rajkiran-g. Creative Commons)

Synchronistic matches are quite different: a match (actually a correspondence) with something internally or psychologically unique to oneself is being sought in some other (say, physical or psychological) experience. That is why statistically modelling the birthday problem speaks more to chance groupings than to synchronicity, the latter of which is a comparatively rarer event that cannot be *qualitatively* modelled to a sufficient or satisfactory degree for the individual using a statistical framework. However, I argue that *quantitative* modelling can help establish the viability of the synchronicity concept, and has been demonstrated (discussed later in this chapter). From Jung's perspective, the individual synchronistic case "cannot be repeated experimentally" (1952/1969, para. 965) if one's focus is on specific meaning, whereas statistical modelling gives a general picture. But again I would argue there can be a hint that the individual outcome is not necessarily random, but may be uniquely synchronistic (this effect can be seen, for example, in the meaningful readings produced in the *I Ching* procedure first used by Storm, 2008a; see also the subsection *The Two Spatial Forms of Synchronicity* in Chapter 2).

In short, the birthday problem answers the general question, How many people must be in a group for at least two to share a birthday? I must add that in a demonstration of the birthday problem in my undergraduate years, the psychology professor failed to find a single match the first time for a specific birthday (day and month) that was called out from an audience of many hundreds of students. But on the second call-out, a different nominated birthday yielded not one, but two matches. Looking at Figure 1.1 again, when failure like this occurs the first time, one wonders where that 100% guarantee went. To this, Beitman would add:

> When someone asks "What are the odds?" odds are they aren't asking "What are the odds that a coincidence of this nature would have happened to anyone in the room?" but more like "What are the odds that this specific thing would happen to *me,* here and now?" And with anything more complicated than a birthday match, that becomes almost impossible to calculate.
>
> (as cited in Beck, 2016)

Of course, there is no question that determining the single probability of a cluster of events (or groupings) can be quite complex. Each event in cases of multiple correlations or correspondences has its own probability, and it is a mathematical fact that the cumulative (overall) probability will decrease as the required number of individual events increases (e.g., getting three Heads in three separate coin tosses is less probable than getting two Heads in two separate coin tosses). The task, however, of calculating a complex probability is made easier by the fact that some events tend to happen together causally. Thus, there is another factor at play when we attempt to resolve the difference between synchronicity and meaningless chance grouping, and Jung (1952/1969, para. 826–827) helps here. In this second example of meaningless chance grouping, Jung gives an example of his own (a series of related events having a fish theme that recurred six times in 24 hours) to show how meaningless chance groupings can fall "within the limits of probability" (para. 827), primarily on the basis of social context, which can be regarded as a more sophisticated form of "common cause" (a term coined by German philosopher Hans Reichenbach, discussed in more detail shortly).

Jung had been studying the history of fish symbolism for several months, so that fact alone created a window of opportunity for similarly themed motifs to manifest. In that period, on Friday, April 1st, he had fish for lunch (typical on a Friday in Europe); someone mentioned making an "April fish" (i.e., April fool) of someone (bound to happen on April 1st); a former patient showed Jung some of her fish paintings; someone else later that day showed Jung a piece of embroidery featuring fish-like sea-monsters (perhaps both parties held out until the special day); and the following day (April 2nd) a patient told Jung about a fish dream she had (easily sparked by the prominence of the previous day).

By Jung's own admission, there was a certain "numinosity" to the fish series, and it made a "considerable impression" on him as it would, no doubt, on others (1952/1969, para. 827). Astrologer Maggie Hyde (1992), for example, was convinced that synchronicity was in full swing for Jung during the fish series. However, Jung was bound to run into former patients on occasion and, in Jung's analytical psychology, the fish motif often appears as a symbol of unconscious contents, so the symbol can be expected to come up often in

Jung's circle. Jung therefore sees all these interlinked events as being largely attributable to the prevailing circumstances—"there is no possible justification for seeing in this anything but a chance grouping" (para. 827).

What is at odds here is that Combs and Holland (1996) also classify the fish series as another one of Jung's "remarkable instances of synchronicity" (pp. 66–67). Cambray (2009), Colman (2011), Hyde (1992), Peat (1987), and Winther (2012) all make the same assumption, yet Jung pointed out the "causal chains" and dismissed the fish account as a "fortuitous coincidence" (para. 827). I see these "chains" as largely generated by social context, which might also be characterized by an overarching "common cause". Purely from Jung's account, I find I must agree with Jung because he has not responded to the series as one would expect of someone who had just had an encounter with the *numinosum* (something ethereal, nebulous, intangible, and even spiritual or divine). Either Jung was in denial, or the personal relevance of the symbolism escaped him, which is unlikely given Jung's character, his expertise, and his approach to life. More likely, the causal chains were so obvious to Jung that a ruling principle of synchronicity—namely, its acausality—could not be undermined.

A third case of meaningless chance grouping is that of two girls going by the same name, Laura Buxton. One Laura Buxton (an only child) from Milton Lilbourne, near Marlborough UK, celebrated her grandparents' 50th wedding anniversary by setting loose a helium balloon with a message that included the line: "please return to laura buxton" (her address was enclosed). When the balloon finally came to rest in a hedge, a farmer found it and took it to his neighbours, Peter and Eleanor Buxton, who lived in the Midlands, 140 miles away from Milton Lilbourne. They also had a daughter named Laura (also an only child). This second Laura Buxton (ten years old) followed the instruction on the balloon tag. The first Laura (almost ten years old) then phoned the second Laura. The girls discovered they shared more than a name. When they first met, they were roughly the same age, both wore jeans with pink jumpers, they were the same height, had the same build, the same eye and hair color, and both were year-five primary school students. Each had a three-year-old black female Labrador dog, a rabbit, and a guinea pig. But is all this matching so unusual? The name Laura is not so unusual, and girls of roughly the same age will tend to be roughly the same height and build, be at the same year level in school, and if they come from the same regions, they may even tend to have the same hair and eye colouring.

The Buxtons' case is placed firmly within the range of statistical likelihood due to social context so there is a degree of causation that affects the consistent matching. As Diaconis and Mosteller (1989) note, the likelihood of multiple matching can be quite high based purely on circumstance. While we do need to be careful of such assertions, the Buxtons' case does bear similarities to the multiple matching in Wilmer's (1987) "pipe-smokers" scenario. Arizona State University professor in probability and statistics, Jay Koehler (2009), presented his explanation of the Buxtons' coincidences in an episode of the radio show *Radiolab*. He reminds us that there has been some cherry-picking (i.e., selective reporting) whereby only the matches are reported and the mismatches are ignored (e.g., one girl's favourite colour is blue, the other pink; they did not study the same subjects at school, and so on).

These points have ramifications on twin telepathy reports, not simply because there may be cherry-picking (for reviews, see Playfair, 2002; Powell, 2009). Guy Lyon Playfair warns about "coincidences of purely genetic origin" (p. 151), conservatively excluding them as *not* being paranormal in the telepathic sense ("people who are virtually identical are likely to have the same tastes and abilities"; p. 66). Identical (monozygotic) twins often do "predictable" things because they are like two identical (synchronized) watches that even stop at the same time (assuming they are fully wound up at the same time). So while it is argued that there may be a relatively strong psychic (telepathic) connection between twins—bearing all the hallmarks of synchronicity—we have to distinguish matching life choices made by twins (even those raised apart) that are probably meaningless chance groupings from those events that indicate a *possible* psychic connection, as evinced by so-called "crisis telepathy" where one twin "knows" when the other experiences pain or accident, and even duplicates the same psychological and/or physical conditions without the same cause. The genetic factor extends to similarity of thought, better known as "thought concordance" (TC). Blackmore and Chamberlain (1993) found that twins benefited from TC significantly more than non-twin siblings, but no superiority in ESP was demonstrated. The authors concluded that thinking alike is not the same as "meaningful coincidence ... telepathy or some other form of ESP" (p. 96). (These problems are considered further in Chapter 5.)

Still on the subject of the clustering of events that suggest meaningful coincidence, the so-called *principle of the common cause* (a.k.a. "concurrence") mentioned above (Reichenbach, 1956) can be invoked for cases where there is a confluence of similar or seemingly related events which have a common cause underlying them (e.g., light bulbs all blowing out at the same time because a single fuse burned out). We can dispense with acausal explanations once we have good evidence that our cluster has a common cause. This point is implied in Reichenbach's argument: "If an improbable coincidence has occurred, there must exist a common cause" (p. 157). I suggest this assumption, known as *Reichenbach's Inference*, is a little too doctrinaire—Reichenbach means the cause and the correlated events cannot be *simultaneous*—but it does follow logically from the standard understanding made clear in *Causal Inference*, whereby cause must *precede* effect, though Reichenbach does not rule out chance. What is also problematic is the term "improbable coincidence"—how a coincidence can be *improbable* is anybody's guess; if it happened, it is not and never could be improbable.

Using the word "simultaneous" in the same sense, my colleague Laurence Browne (2017) gives many examples of "simultaneous or near simultaneous inventions" (p. 43)[8] that follow the principle of the common cause: "six inventors of the thermometer, five for vaccinations, four for the isolation of adrenalin, three for the hypodermic needle, three for decimal fractions, three for logarithms, four for photography, five for the telegraph" (p. 43). But one of the more impressive cases of common cause is the relatively simultaneous arrival at the theory of natural selection by Charles Darwin and Alfred Russel Wallace. To Wallace's essay on the subject (sent by Wallace from the Dutch East Indies and received by Darwin in 1858), a stunned Darwin responded:

> "I never saw a more striking coincidence," .... "If Wallace had my MS sketch written out in 1842 he could not have made a better short abstract!"
>
> (J. Browne, 2003)[9]

However, L. Browne (2017) points out how Charles Darwin and Alfred Russel Wallace had both read Thomas Malthus's *Essay on the Principle of Population* (Malthus, 1798/1998), and both clearly caught on to the idea of the ever-present struggle for survival in society—Darwin and Wallace merely extended the Malthusian principle to an evolutionary schema. The coincidences do not end there: In one particular incident, Scottish botanist, Patrick Matthew (1831), had earlier written about the "natural process of selection" in his book *On Naval Timber and Arboriculture.* According to J. Browne (2003), Darwin denied Matthew's book influenced his *On the Origin of Species* (Darwin, 1859/2004), even though there are impressive similarities between Darwin's and Matthew's theories (though there are also differences).

None of this intrigue gets to the more important point I wish to make here, which is that Darwin and Wallace and Matthew and Malthus (and indeed others) were all raised and educated in the same socio-cultural (historical and scientific) milieu, which increased the likelihood of the same ideas, principles, and theories, arising independently. In 1859, Darwin even said:

> It is rather a singular instance of the manner in which similar views arise at about the same period, that Goethe in Germany, Dr. [Erasmus] Darwin in England, and Geoffroy Saint-Hilaire … in France, came to the same conclusion on the origin of species in the years 1794–5.
>
> (p. 528)

In other words, a shared social context can set up the conditions for a common cause, or may even be a common cause. Thus we have multiples of events constituting a coincidence (ordinarily a *mere* or *casual* coincidence) that nevertheless loses its "coincidentiality" once we discover a single (common) cause.[10] Of course, we can see that the "cause" here is multi-factorial, but it is nevertheless *common* to, or *concurrent* with the events in question.

Effects brought about by a common cause do seem to be quite frequent (as evidenced in Browne's [2017, p. 43] examples above), and it turns out that they are more probable than chance coincidences, as proven by Reichenbach (1956). Of course, while common cause can explain much, there may be more to consider. For example, it was *at the very same time* that Darwin had been anguishing over whether to publish his evolutionary ideas that he received the fateful correspondence from Wallace.[11] Even though there were two separate causal chains leading to a single evolutionary theory with clear socio-cultural antecedents, the coincidence of Darwin's personal ordeal with the timely arrival of Wallace's letter (specifically its *contents* that served to crack Darwin's indecisiveness and inertia) is very much synchronistic (like Swedenborg's vision of a fire coupled with an actual fire in Stockholm or, even better, Jung's scarab case in its dénouement).

Another example of chance grouping suggesting synchronicity is the phenomenon pointed out by Jung (1952/1969) known as the "compulsion of the name" (para. 828, n12)—the coincidence or correlation of a person's name with certain peculiarities or profession. Jung gives some examples:

> Herr Gross (Mr. Grand) suffers from delusions of grandeur, Herr Kleiner (Mr. Small) has an inferiority complex … Herr Feist (Mr. Stout) is the Food Minister, … Herr Freud (joy) champions the pleasure principle, Herr Adler (eagle) the will-to-power, Herr Jung (young) the idea of rebirth, and so on.
>
> (para. 828, n12)

Not surprisingly, all these examples of so-called "aptronyms" are German names (*Synchronicity* was originally written in German), but examples abound in all languages. For example (and apropos to this book), the initials J. B. of botanist and parapsychologist, J. B. Rhine, stand for Joseph Banks; Rhine's namesake happens to have been Joseph Banks, the botanist who travelled with Captain James Cook aboard the HMS Endeavour to seek evidence of the postulated Terra Australis Incognita ("unknown southern land"), later to become known as Australia. One is compelled to ask, Did Rhine's parents know he would become a botanist, or did Rhine feel compelled to become one? Jung (1952/1969) asks if such coincidences are the "whimsicalities of chance [i.e., meaningless chance groupings], or the suggestive effects of the name, … or are they meaningful coincidences?" (para. 828, n12). It could be any of these: chance is a logical first-choice; self-fulfilling prophecy due to the persuasive force of the name may be a likely explanation in some instances (this is the "egotism" argument), and there may be the rare case where synchronicity cannot be ruled out. Before we could be sure synchronicity is a likely explanation, we must find the full complement of synchronistic elements (how this is done is described in a later section).

There could, however, be a genetic element at play in *compulsion of the name* (also called "nominative determinism")—perhaps sometimes a person can inherit a trait from an ancestor who was given an appropriate name. This inherited factor has been demonstrated in two studies (see Voracek et al., 2015). While they found no difference in actual physique between random samples of people with the names Smith and Tailor, the Smiths tended to have higher ratings for "strength-related activities (professions, sports, hobbies)" compared to the Tailors, who rated higher than Smiths on "aptitude for dexterity-related activities" (2015, p. 1). These findings suggest that the name can sometimes define a vocation across time, leading Voracek et al. to suggest that the genetic-social explanation is superior to the "egotism" argument. Of course, one can never be "blind" to the effects of one's own name (which would be a fundamental control criterion in any true experiment of this kind), so we cannot rule out self-fulfilling prophecy entirely.

We should also dismiss as contrived or constructed those coincidences (false synchronicities) derived from deliberate priming or 'front-loading' of the conscious mind with themes or symbols which then brew in the unconscious waiting to be discovered as environmental patterns with apparent meaning (see also Coleman et al., 2009, for a similar observation). Browne (2017) describes these correspondences as "essentially meaningless" (p. 130). He gives examples of "equivalence without meaning" (p.130), courtesy of author and synchronicity pundit, Kirby Surprise (his real name), who had this front-loading tendency (see Surprise, 2012). In one case, Surprise was thinking about NASA's space-shuttle launch delay, when a co-worker in his office just happened to mention how the shuttle would be late. Surprise's colleague, however, was talking about the office shuttle bus which had been held up due to a freeway accident.

Although the appearance of the same word in two different contexts is not necessarily synchronistic, a form of meaningful coincidence (i.e., word matching) has been tested by William Braud (1983) with significant results (see the review in Appendix B). Also, while such coincidences may not seem to be strikingly meaningful (if at all), the quaint delay motif in the shuttle example given by Surprise (2012) is replicated; an oddity in itself. Consequently, a synchronistic argument could be made concerning the delay problem, but that would require further details which Surprise does not supply because his focus is altogether elsewhere. Surprise does, however, report more impressive personal experiences of synchronicity, and Browne does not dismiss these out of hand.

There are two important issues here: First, priming for synchronicity is not necessarily the same thing as "volitional" or "intentional" synchronicity, which works best if the individual is emotionally engaged (and probably so because there is some kind of "archetypal depth" to his/her aims) from which we can expect the experience to be meaningful (discussed further in Chapters 2 and 3). Otherwise, we must remain noncommittal in cases where we cannot discern whether coincidence proneness could be chance, or associative thinking, or anything of that nature. Second, the interpretation of a meaningless chance grouping as synchronicity can arise when one's sensitivity to such groupings is not matched by one's capacity to discriminate. Very often, this means an incapacity to move out of the pure sensation of the experience, or even a resistance to do so because basking in the soporific warmth or mystique of a pseudo-numinous experience can be so beguiling.[12]

Of course, the same caveat applies in regard to numinous experiences. Those individuals inclined to be overly religious or overly spiritual tend to be of such a persuasion, though psychosis-related symptoms may be contributing factors (see also Beitman, 2011, p. 568; and Browne, 2017, p. 129, for similar comments). I necessarily do not include individuals experiencing so-called "spiritual emergency" where psychic opening is often reported, but there is no evidence of psychopathological factors such as depression, anxiety, and stress (see Storm & Goretzki, 2020, 2021). Overly religious/spiritual tendencies can give rise to the "projection of meaning"—especially in a "coincidence not really present" (Browne, p. 129)—where the individual sees more than is there. Jungian scholar, Marie-Louise Von Franz (1997) writes very cogently on this issue of projection, first spoken of by Freud (for a basic outline, see J. A. C. Brown, 1971), and developed further by Jung (1959/1968). She also writes in a cautionary manner, warning us that psychic energy can flow regressively, enlivening a content (a subjective image), but reflection is blocked so the individual projects false meaning onto that content (in such an instance, there either was no synchronicity in the first place, or there was, but the energy did not flow towards a "creative discovery"; p. 198). When there is no projection, progression to a deeper self-analysis of the experience may be possible through insight and realization, which could carry the individual forward psychologically speaking.

Some Synchronistic Terms

Apropos to the points just made, explanations of some of the terms used to describe the factors underpinning the synchronistic process may be helpful, and these are now presented.

Archetypes

Jung (1952/1969, para. 841, 847) described archetypes as nodal points or structural components of the collective unconscious (deep in the mind) that govern or influence our "patterns of behaviour" (para. 841). In other words, archetypes play a pivotal role in how we think, feel and act (for neuropsychological parallels and justification for the construct, see also Haule, 2011a). They are innate and inherited. It may help to conceive of them in a similar way instincts are understood.[13] However, rather than applying them strictly to actions (*modes of behaviour*), archetypes align more with *modes of apprehension*, in that they govern how we get a grasp on a situation—how we understand, perceive, or interpret our environment and experience, including synchronistic experience. Thus, for the most part, the purpose of the archetype is to aid the individual in establishing order and meaning to life processes and experiences. Jung (1987) postulates the existence of archetypes because they give

> co-ordinating and coherent meaning both to sensuous and to inner perceptions, which at first appear without order or connection, and in this way frees psychic energy from its bondage to sheer uncomprehended perception. At the same time, it links the energies released by the perception of stimuli to a definite meaning, which then guides action along paths corresponding to this meaning. It releases unavailable, dammed-up energy by leading the mind back to nature and canalising sheer instinct into mental forms.
>
> (p. 116)[14]

We see how prediction and even precognition become possible as archetypal courses of action are effectively pre-defined in accordance with the archetype. Going further, Jung (1952/1969) sees archetypes as providing a "foundation" or "a direct connection" to synchronistic experience (para. 845, 912).

From an evolutionary or hereditary point of view, archetypes have become so distinct and well-defined as human factors that govern whole ways of being, they can be depicted and observed as motifs or idealized characters (*though these are only ever representations*) in various myths, folklore, and fairytales, ancient and modern, as well as movies and literature, but they can also be represented in consciousness as religious symbols, geometrical forms and shapes, and lower forms of species such as flowers, trees, insects, and animals. At the human level, examples of archetypes include Hero/Heroine, Wise Old Man/Woman, Child, and contra-sexual components of the hero and heroine (i.e., *anima* and *animus*, respectively). Other psychological constructs include the persona (one's social mask or public image), the ego, and the "central archetype" or Self (Jung also spells it as "self"), which is sometimes referred to as "higher self" to avoid confusion.

Archetypes can also manifest more broadly as themes or storylines that play out in typical ways—these are represented as the basis themes and plots of myths, folklore, fairytales, and sacred texts (for examples of how these themes and plots play out, see the epic work by Booker, 2004). These various factors (motifs, characterizations, themes, and plots) can also give structure to our dreams and fantasies, and embed them with meaning for they actually represent psychological principles, dispositions, and complexes.

Most people have learned to spot archetypal representations (motifs) in novels and movies because they are used over and over again in predictable ways. Even children come across them in tales based on the writings of the Brothers Grimm, Hans Christian Andersen, etc., and they very soon, and very easily, comprehend the basic plot lines—these are archetypal. For example, most people are familiar with *Snow White and the Seven Dwarfs*, or *The Lord of the Rings*, and the aims and objectives of the key characters in these dramas. These motifs ultimately serve as learning tools to show us how we behave, or indeed how we should or should not behave; they show us the consequences of our actions; they therefore function as cautionary tales.

Often at the centre of these encounters is the hero who saves the day by rescuing someone in danger, or recovering something of great value that has been stolen; these being essential steps to continuation or progress of the individual, community, society, or nation. A Wise Old Man ("magician") or Woman ("old woman of days") may feature—his or her knowledge, wisdom, and experience, are essential in providing guidance to the hero who is always over-confident (even foolish), and not necessarily prudent, or discriminating, or aware of the nuances and subtleties that underpin even the most innocuous situations. We may also find the contra-sexual embodiment of the hero, which may take the form of a woman in danger (the classic damsel in distress of medieval folklore); the same applies to the heroine and her contra-sexual embodiment. Thus, archetypes permeate the arts and media; they form central themes and bind key characters together in quests, journeys, victories, tragedies, and ordeals. Most novels, television programs, movies, musicals, and so on, could not be written to completion without appeal to archetypes.[15]

While themes and plot-lines are readily identified when they appear in art and fiction, their appearances can also be expected in real life. To illustrate this point, in September 2017, a middle-aged man, Earl Melchert, from Alexandria, Minnesota, USA, rescued a kidnapped girl, 15-year-old Jasmine Block, who had disappeared almost a month earlier.[16] Melchert, who was supposed to be at work managing a fertilizer plant, raced home to pick up a diesel-fuel can which he wanted to refill so he could mow the grass later that day. From his window, he thought he saw a deer until he realized it was a girl, only learning later that it was Jasmine. She had just escaped from an abandoned house where she had been physically and sexually assaulted. This horrific treatment had gone on for 29 days in a series of houses before the three abductees finally moved Jasmine to a house across the lake from Melchert's property. When the abductees stepped out to buy food, Jasmine escaped and swam across the lake to reach Melchert's house. Melchert called the police, the men were arrested, and a reward of $7000 was presented to Melchert, who gave it to Jasmine. Mr. Melchert said: "It's the best thing I've ever done."

Apart from the frightening aspects of this real-life horror story, one of the surprising features of this case is the archetypal aspects: Jasmine's encounter recalls the maiden of any number of fairytales and myths who is held hostage and treated badly by a wicked person or persons: She marshals her own resources to effect an escape (as did Rapunzel in Disney's 2010 adaptation of the eponymously named fairytale by the Brothers Grimm), but she ultimately needs the assistance of a kind-hearted fellow (e.g., the prince in Hans Christian Andersen's *The Little Mermaid*), who is able to offer compensation for her ordeal. Melchert, however, has a deeper psychological experience—he is taken out of his humdrum existence through an encounter with his *anima*, which first takes the form of a creature of nature before it transforms and takes on a human aspect (a common theme in myths and fairytales). Here we can see archetypal motifs actually manifesting in real-life situations for that is their natural domain.

Static archetypal images *and* dynamic archetypal scenarios can define the synchronistic experience. Evident in the example just given, archetypal experiences tend to carry a theme (a narrative) which is not a characteristic of two-dimensional archetypal objects or figures, but even these are not devoid of context, action, and purpose, and therefore numinosity (e.g., in special cases, mandala images are evoked; see Jung, 1959/1968). The archetype forms the substructure of a synchronicity, giving it its common theme, and acting as a defining quality throughout the experience, thereby, intensifying the meaningfulness (Jung, 1952/1969, para. 912). As pointed out in the quote above, archetypes help us navigate and negotiate a world of unknowns with a degree of confidence, rather than the bluster and false certainty characteristic of the archetypal hero. I refer to this process as *archetypal facilitation* and it stands above those cues we get from mere learning. This term "archetypal facilitation" was first used by Bradshaw and Storm (2013), where it was found that the recall rate of the meaning words associated with archetypal symbols was above and beyond the rate reasonably attributable to "descriptive similarity" that underpins conventional memory tasks (p. 170). (For details, see the subsection "On Model Building" in Storm, 2025.)

A final but important point about archetypes is that they can go beyond the collective unconscious. In this sense, they exist as primordial, eternal elements in a "supracelestial place" (Jacobi, 1974, p. 50) similar to Platonic Ideas (Forms) that are transcendent, beyond consciousness, and "psychoid" (see *Psychoid Factor* below). For example, Jung (1952/1969) has defined number as "an *archetype of order*" (para. 870): Numbers can manifest in the physical environment, but they have reality in the human psyche and physical body. Therefore, the division between the psyche and the world of things (e.g., number representations or manifestations) is relative and not absolute.

Causality and Acausality

The notion of causality has always been a contentious issue for laypersons and scholars alike, including parapsychologists and philosophers. German philosopher Immanuel Kant (1781) argued for the Axiom of Causality whereby all events must have causes preceding them, this reasoning being self-evident and needing no proof. The only problem with that axiom, apart from the fact that it does not allow for an acausal world, is that it implies infinite regress, meaning there can be no beginning, unless metaphysical appeals are made as in the Aristotelian sense of a "first cause", an "unmoved mover whose necessary existence underpins the ceaseless activity of the world of motion" (Shields, 2007, p. 196). A point to note is that synchronicity does not violate this axiom because the two (or more) elements or aspects of a given synchronicity can have their own causal chains, while the connection between the event streams can be through meaning alone. Synchronicity, therefore, contrasts with "causal absolute coincidence" (Melas, 2013) in which a connection is traced but not through meaning. The 'absolute coincidence' is merely "the effect of the intersection of independent causal processes" (p. 108) with nothing assumed or implied beyond the intersection, whereas synchronicity does imply something more. This view—that meaning and cause both serve binding functions—is unsatisfying to some philosophers (see also "Meaningfulness" below).

English philosopher David Hume (1738/2007) stated that there is no absolute way of empirically demonstrating how an event may have a causal connection to some other event, yet it may still be considered causal. Given Jung's theory concerning the archetypal 'connection' found within synchronistic events, it might therefore be assumed that an archetypal substructure provides the causal thread that links or determines these events. This was the opinion of Arthur Koestler (1974), journalist, author, and benefactor of the Koestler Parapsychology Unit in Edinburgh, Scotland. But that kind of causality only applies if we embrace the 'magic' of so-called 'scientific causality' (which only needs to follow the '*if* A, *then* B rule'), as opposed to *mechanistic causality*, which shows physical connection in the classical sense of a relationship between (say) two or more material objects (e.g., in collision), or a material object and a field (e.g., magnetic attraction and repulsion), and so on. However, as Jung (1952/1969) describes synchronicity, we must not fall back on rational (causal) thinking to explain its phenomenology; especially in relation to the role of archetypes in the synchronistic mix:

> As soon as [one] perceives the archetypal background [one] is tempted to trace the mutual assimilation of independent psychic and physical processes back to a (causal) effect of the archetype, and thus to overlook the fact that they are merely contingent.
>
> (para. 965)

Thereby, Jung sees cause and contingence as two different things, whereas others, following the scientific precedent, suggest contingence implies a cause (e.g., Palmer, 2008). This resolution comes from the fact that science has reached that stage where *efficient causes* have been replaced by relationships for, as Bertrand Russell (1917/1953) has argued, scientific laws need only be *functional* to serve their purpose, which we may refer to as *functional causation*. Of course, in some instances, this view can give acausality the patina of causality (more to be said on that issue later). Mackie (1980) argues further that *functional causation* is a limiting case, and a refinement and extension of the conventional understanding of cause.

Though philosopher Antony Flew (1953) is critical of some aspects of synchronicity, he is helpful in noting that archetypes do not have causal aspects, as that assertion would strip coincidences of their acausality and they would no longer be coincidences; he believes archetypes may have an important part to play in psychological enquiry:

> [...] it is essential to remember that however regularly he [Jung] uses causal words of archetypes—speaking of their *activities* in *constellating* and *arranging* and so on—he definitely does not want us to think of them as the *causes* of non-causal synchronicity. But rather as what provides a context and helps to give point and meaning to them. Indeed it seems that the function of the archetypes is not causally to explain coincidences. ... But rather to show why certain concurrences are found striking, pointed, meaningful, even numinous; and subsumed under the concept of coincidence, while others are not.
>
> (p. 201)

On a similar thread, these words from Ira Progoff (1973) amplify the concepts quite well:

> [...] the archetypal element in a situation cannot be encompassed in any of the usual definitions of causality. It is not causal, but rather recrystallizing and restructuring. It reconstitutes a situation across time without respect to the causal connections within it, without respect to boundaries of space, and without respect to any directive factor of the conscious mind. It moves across causality, and its effects are beyond causality.
>
> (p. 162)

Jung (1952/1969) cuts to the chase, referring to such 'reconstituted situations across time' as "*creative acts*" or as "continuous creation" (para. 967), which parallels Gatlin's (1977) 'meaningful information creation' (see Storm, 2025).

When it comes to teasing apart the complex causality/acausality issue, Flew's and Progoff's statements are amongst the clearest (or at least not too dense) and most accurate in expressing in plain language Jung's conception of two *underlying* principles of synchronicity; namely, archetypes and acausality. Here I use the word 'underlying' in the same sense that Jung (1952/1969) uses it to refer to an "existing quality, an irreducible contingency which is 'Just-So'". (para. 965). The archetype can be seen as an acausal but common thread or contingence by which synchronistic events can be linked. The various elements that make up synchronicity may have their own causal pathways, but when these events cross paths, the causality ends, coincidence results, and synchronicity proper gains the ascendency provided its meaningfulness and other contingent factors are determinable.

Dual-Aspect Monism

The so-called Pauli-Jung Conjecture is a variant of dual-aspect monism (a.k.a. double-aspect monism or dual-aspect theory) and naturally is attributed to Jung and Pauli through their joint work, including their correspondence (see Atmanspacher & Fuchs, 2014; Meier, 2001). Dual-aspect theory is prefigured in works by philosophers Baruch Spinoza (1632–1677) and Arthur Schopenhauer (1788–1860), and physicist David Bohm (1917–1992). Jungian scholar Harald Atmanspacher defines the term thus:

> *dual-aspect monism* merges an ontic monism, reflected by a psychophysically neutral background reality, with an epistemic dualism of the mental and the physical as perspectival aspects of the underlying ontic reality.
>
> (Atmanspacher, 2014b, p. 181)

This dense philosophical expression simply means reality is *experienced* as being comprised of either physical phenomena *or* mental phenomena, but the actual or fundamental framework underlying the two is said to be unitary (monist). That is, the apparent dualism suggested by the aspects is *not* metaphysically ontological, but the monism *is* ontological. Dual-aspect monism does not diminish the general ontic status of dualism, but the "aspects" are not generally considered "properties" as in the case of property dualism (Benovsky, 2016; Skrbina, 2005).

Historically, the closest ontological parallels to dual-aspect monism may have been prefigured in psychophysical parallelism and Leibniz's "pre-established harmony", the former of which is endorsed somewhat by Jung (1952/1969, para. 949) insofar as it is considered possible that "meaningful orderedness" could explain some correspondences where causal orderedness could not. Pre-established harmony, however, is regarded by Benovsky as "frustratingly unconvincing" (p. 339). Indeed, Jung argues that under pre-established harmony the synchronistic principle would become "the absolute rule in all cases where an inner event occurs simultaneously with an outside one" (para. 938), which clearly cannot be the case—in fact, Jung even regarded synchronicities as "so exceptional that most people doubt their existence" (para. 938).

In dual-aspect monism, mind and matter are phenomenological (subjective) experiences only, which include objective (instrumental) measures because any modified perspective that results from the measures will merely be to accommodate expectations and suppositions for the sake of a version of "reality" that can be manipulated to advantage. Taken together, these experiences are at the core of our epistemology (theories, knowledge, beliefs, and opinions), and they are all we can gauge of indivisible reality as it really is, which Atmanspacher (2014a) refers to as "neutral reality" (pp. 252, 253; see also "*Unus Mundus*" below). Albeit a rather clumsy and misleading term, *neutral reality* (or better *ultimate reality*) is not free of those two aspects, mind (the 'head side' of the 'coin' of reality) and matter (the 'tail side'), for that would be definitive of neutral monism. And as Atmanspacher (2012) notes:

> For neutral monists both mind and matter reduce to an underlying, neutral domain, while for dual-aspect monists mind and matter are two basic and irreducible aspects of that underlying domain.
>
> (p. 1)

Also, the two aspects do not reduce one to the other—in that sense, each is fundamental.[17] Therefore, mind and matter are not emergent phenomena. As aspects of ultimate reality, mind and matter are bonded, so the conceptualization of "cross-realm causality" or the two "working together" (interacting) is redundant (see Benovsky, 2016, p. 349). And nor can each term, mind and matter, describe (say) both cognitive (thoughts/feelings) *and* neurological events according to context (that would also be *neutral monism*, which sees all things as neutral entities).

Pauli argued that dual-aspect theory is compatible with quantum theoretical constructs such as complementarity, nonlocality, and the observer effect. In regard to complementarity, mind has a mental source, and matter has a physical source—they mutually exclude each other, and neither a mental framework on its own, nor a physical framework on its own, describes reality completely (similar understandings apply to all complementarities). So only the two (mind and matter) taken together give a complete picture of reality.

Physicist Thomas Filk (2014) adds that Pauli regarded quantum entanglement (an acausal quantum correlation involving same-source particles whose states are dependent on each other regardless of distance) as "a model for the relationship between mind and matter in the framework of the dual-aspect monism" (p. 110). Some parapsychologists see entanglement and psi as phenomenologically similar in that they both appear to transcend the constraints of spacetime, and thus their effects are considered nonlocal (e.g., Dossey, 2013; Radin, 2006; Schwartz, 2018). However, while the one (entanglement) is purely a correlation, the other (psi) is thought to involve causal processes.

The best example of the two phenomenological variants, mind and matter, occurring together is synchronicity because we can see (get a sense of) these two complementary aspects in one (Atmanspacher & Fuchs, 2014). Synchronicity is an experience of corresponding events often complementary as in the typical situation of a mental event *and* a physical event; their relationship through meaning (that which unifies) implies the underlying reality.

Complementarities are examples of fundamental unities that are polarized in their manifestations, thus forcing on us two mutually exclusive experiences.

Just as we see complementarities at work in the synchronicity/causality dyad, we see them in quantum physics (wave–particle duality; position + momentum), dualism (mind + matter), electromagnetism (electricity + magnetism), spacetime (space + time), brain (hemisphericity), psyche (consciousness + unconscious),[18] psi (ESP + PK), bistable optical illusions (e.g., the rabbit–duck illusion),[19] and even common-place dualities as in the coin example just given (heads + tails), and so on. Thus, for example, in synchronicity, we experience two related events, but we cannot see the mental aspect in the physical component, and we cannot see the physical aspect in the mental component, just as we can never see tails while looking at heads, and *vice versa*. The more common everyday examples may seem frivolous because they are taken for granted when in fact they should stand as important reminders that illustrate complementarity and the problem of unification. Actually, their being taken for granted is proof that we have only learned to accept their novelty and live with that, but we have never really pondered their higher meaning, for if we had, they would stand as crucial symbols in our culture rather than mere curios.

Conventional parapsychological understandings of psi do not take these issues into consideration (see Chapter 1 in Storm [2025] where it will be seen that ESP and PK set up a complementarity). While the ultimate unification of ESP and PK as psi is mainly a conceptual or theoretical issue, perhaps drawing in speculative transcendent and metaphysical issues, their phenomenological experience is dual. Dual-aspect monism gives more status to mind/consciousness than Materialism, which classes mental experience as epiphenomenal or identical to brain processes, whereas Idealism tries to undermine material solutions when these generally work quite well (see also Benovsky, 2016; Stubenberg, 2016).

Individuation

The concept of "individuation"—the person becoming undivided, one, and whole—actually underpins nearly all of Jung's psychology. Generally, psychology is an attempt to understand the psyche or mind by modelling its functions. With the knowledge gained from its various enterprises, psychology's other aim is to help realize the full potential of the individual. Most people wish to reach their fullest potential, and they strive to that end, encountering a host of experiences along the way. Jung (1921/1971, 1952/1969) found that synchronicity can play into those experiences, and he felt that synchronicity provides the opportunity for transformation of personality in some way.

As the word individuation implies, it is a process; a movement towards an undivided state—"oneness" is therefore a key aim of individuation. The idea of oneness evokes images of totality (see Storm, 2008e). In the idea of totality (wholeness) can be seen the fundamental concept of unity, a monadic conception of reality that is taken as underpinning all reality, and this unifying aspect of existence appears to be a way of seeing the world as a direct result of an inner propensity to aspire to oneness, or develop in a direction of wholeness and completion that equates with the idea of oneness. In other words, there is a dynamic sensibility in us that enables us to project our oneness (unity) *and* introject it.

Thus, the idea or image of unity is built up from unitary images and concepts. Our experience of the world, then, is not simply the result of projection,[20] but the world itself is the source of our ideational, affective, and imaginal being as reflected in the unitary phenomena of the world. The ordering capacity of the Self is the instrument and mechanism of this structural process which constructs the psyche, culminating in a state of oneness that is dependent upon the world for its representations, but is capable of acting independently according to its capacity to construct, of itself, a representation or entity that has autonomy and being in the world.[21]

Seen this way, the individual and the world interact and are interdependent, so that the idea of the microcosm being a reflection of the macrocosm gains an empirical foothold in synchronicity. As Progoff (1973) puts it: "The individual microcosmic life is an aspect of the larger general pattern of the macrocosm" (p. 128). This statement implies "certain regularities and therefore constant factors" (Jung, 1960/1969, para. 965), and Progoff lists these as

> characteristics of the archetypes, their numinosity, the ways in which they are activated, their effect on upsetting the equilibrium of the psyche, and their constellative quality in drawing other psychic contents into complexes around them.
>
> (p. 129)

This macrocosmic/microcosmic mirroring is itself archetypal, and studies on archetypes themselves are now gaining evidential status (Gibson, 2010; Grof, 1985; see also the entry on *Archetypes* above). Indeed, studies like these help put paid to the idea that there is "no testable theory of archetypes" (Grattan-Guinness, 1983, p. 65).

The mounting evidence from the astrological findings suggests there are also influences on our consciousness, and the defining aspects of our being, that have sources extending beyond the parameters of our individual physicality (Currey, 2017, 2018; Ertel, 1988, 1992, 2003, 2007; Eysenck & Nias, 1982; Gauquelin, 1983; Tarnas, 2007; West, 1992). The exact nature of these sources is not entirely known, but they would not necessarily be exclusively material, but have metaphysical essence. That is, it may be that astrology is the art of working with, and relying on archetypal regularities (depicted macrocosmically as 'planets', 'constellations', etc.) which, in true synchronistic fashion, are reflected in those innate, microcosmic layers of the deeper psyche as pre-set by archetypes. Without thinking about it in quite those terms, astrologers would nevertheless take advantage of those 'constant factors' in their prognostications and predictions (for a theory on a physical mechanism underpinning astrology, see Douglas, 2020).

It is odd that the index of Jung's *Synchronicity* essay does not include the word individuation, but the work of individuation is implied in cases such as the scarab incident; Jung writes that his client's intellectualism gave way to another more cooperative attitude (1951/1969, para. 982). However, I do not feel that synchronicity is exclusively therapeutic *per se*—it is "not of existential significance", to use Mayer's (2019) words—and nor should it necessarily be taken so far, in the sense that some kind of "clinical" reward must be effected and drawn out from a meaningful coincidence by hook or by crook, or by gentle and persuasive means, just because it is thought (or hoped) to be in the client's best interests. It is, however, up to the individual to make the decision as to what deserves attention, however mundane or numinous, immanent or transcendent the experience. As will be seen next, meaningfulness is not altogether dismissible, no matter how innocuous the experience.

Meaningfulness

The concept of meaningfulness (necessarily disambiguated from its root word "meaning") was touched upon in the examples of synchronicity described above. In its simplest form, meaningfulness manifests as the end result of a process of recognition, interpretation, and acceptance of the synchronistic experience and its implications, entailing decisive reflection and integration of subjective and objective aspects that pertain to the synchronicity experient.

Based on statements made by Jung in the relevant literature, Aziz (1990) describes four levels of interrelated meaning involved in synchronistic experience and interpretation, each of these levels being steps towards a fuller or broader understanding of meaningfulness: The first level of meaning is the mere observation of a parallel between elements. Of course, level-one meaning (recognition of correspondence) can apply to any coincidence—not just synchronicity—although Aziz still feels it is only archetypal in the case of synchronicity, but I suggest it must be of a very broad (nonspecific) character. Then follows the second level of meaning which refers to the emotional or numinous overtones of the experience—this meaning is not based in reason or reflection. Aziz then moves to the third level of meaning which refers to subjective significance (how it figures in one's personal life). The fourth level of meaning refers to objective, archetypal, transcendent meaning.[22] All these levels overlap—that is, the parallel, the numinosity, the personal references, and the archetypal factors are all interrelated (Aziz, 1990, pp. 64–66). "Higher" levels may require deep personal introspection and reflection, and considerable effort, research, and insight to discern the objective meanings, as these are likely to have historical and mythological antecedents.

Braude (1979) asserts that events or things cannot have inherent (i.e., objective) meanings—the person merely imposes meanings, so that whatever is deemed meaningful is largely subjective. That is, events are "parsed" in a subjective way that can be meaningful or not, according to the interpreter: "Nature ... does not dictate how we individuate events" (p. 219). Palmer (2008) develops that argument by suggesting that "events differ in their capacity to evoke meaning in a person" (p. 175). These criticisms do not address all four levels, and we must recall Aziz's (1990) fourth-level meaning. Thus we can say that, to the degree we all tend to encounter the same types of experiences repeatedly, and tend to respond in the same ways (by which I mean we share a phylogenetic predisposition to perceive and cognise in the same ways, which psychologists call *basic processes*), very many reactions, cognitions, feelings, and meanings, will tend to be shared in a population. Jung (1961/1989) frames these points differently, and refers to the "method of the necessary statement" (p. 310). That is, for the purposes of interpretation, the arbitrary statement cannot be taken as a legitimate "meaning"; there is room to derive meaning using logical processes delimited by unassailable facts embedded in the content. Just as this reasoning applies to numbers with their "just-so" qualities, which give them unique meanings, dream content (images from the unconscious), mythological motifs, etc., are not devoid of specific and inherent meanings. Whenever we find unanimity, or even universal trends, we can speak of corresponding degrees of objectivity, especially when there are archetypal factors involved. Even the merest relativity subsides if the meaning is so human-wide, no one is left out; these are situations in which there is no comparable species that can disagree, tell us we are wrong, or are generalizing. Jung goes further, adding that transcendental, archetypal meaning is not incompatible with the individual's limited frame of reference—as Main (2014) puts it: "The meaning expresses itself through archetypal imagery inflected by the experiencers' circumstances" (p. 231).

Meaningfulness does not come automatically. In the typical synchronicity, meaningfulness may come after content in the psyche "coincides" with a physical event, whereby implied in the word "coincide" is that meaning, or equivalence, or contingence is recognised (Jung, 1952/1969, para. 858). At this point, we can speak of synchronicity in practical terms. These terms, "meaning", "equivalence", and "contingence", are Jung's (1952/1969, para. 963), and have different connotations, though I must admit it is unfortunate that Jung chose for technical and theoretical usage, words that also happen to be used colloquially. Many commentators (including Jung himself) use the terms interchangeably, and even combine them. For example, "meaning-equivalence" is an obvious conflation, with Jung (1952/1969) using a variation of it as "*equivalence of meaning*" (para. 865), and "meaningful equivalences" (para. 896; see also Browne, 2017, p. 117).[23] Of course, what might be understood by the casual use of the word "equivalence" in these instances is that the two aspects or components of the synchronicity are recognised as having something in common—that they are the same (equal), or similar (*equivalent*), or they *parallel* each other. Aziz (1990) would class that type of meaning as *first-level* meaning, but it may only be the first step towards an understanding of the synchronicity in terms of the meaningfulness (higher levels of meaning) the experient draws out of the experience.

The third of these three words, contingence, seems to be used less often, possibly due to a linguistic prejudice or preference for terms like meaning and equivalence and their conflations. In fact, Jung's model indicates that contingence holds equal but mutually exclusive status with meaning and equivalence (see Jung, 1952/1969, para. 963–965, 968). It should come as a surprise then that so much attention is given to discussions of meaning and equivalence, while the notion of contingence is side-lined (Aziz, 1990; Main, 2014). Also surprisingly, even physicist and Jungian scholar, Victor Mansfield (1995), a stickler for detail, undermines contingence when he says: "… *in synchronicity the meaning is primary while the objective and subjective events that correlate are secondary and contingent*" (p. 26). But to undermine contingence (as in archetypal contingence) is to undermine the very process of synchronicity, for the legitimacy of the meaningfulness is predicated on the contingent factor of the archetype. The upshot is that colloquial use of the word "contingent" (i.e., "fortuitous" or "subject to chance") to describe synchronistic coincidences renders them serendipitous (accidental) and subject to spurious meaning-making.

Theoretically, and according to Jung, "a synchronistic event remains a synchronistic event whether or not its meaningfulness is recognized" (Aziz, 1990, p. 76). Of course, that means that the experient at the time may not recognise (at least from a psychological perspective), or may be unconscious to, the deeper and fuller ramifications of a synchronicity experience until some time later, if ever (recall Swedenborg's vision; we do not know if Swedenborg saw its personal relevance, and it is probable that the numinosity of the experience drowned out the personal factor). Of course, Jung has said "there are synchronicities where, with the best will in the world, you can't figure out the meaning" (1960, as cited in Schellinger, Wittmann & Anton, 2019, p. 450).[24] And Browne (2017) argues that if the "*meaning-equivalence* … central to a synchronistic event" (p. 117) is not recognised by anyone involved (and let us assume for argument's sake it never will be), we may only have a "wonderful coincidence" and we might have to categorize it as something other than synchronicity (e.g., "chance"). Browne was thinking of the Buxton girls' case when he said this, and as I said of that case, there is something archetypal and profoundly meaningful missing from this account (the parallel events barely extend beyond Aziz's first level of meaning). Perhaps the doubt comes from the repetitive, unrelated series of matches that have the same effect as "queering the deal" in a business transaction. But social context offers a clue—two young English girls with so much in common mean (somewhat tautologically) we have to expect matches (i.e., commonalities). What we can say is that a disparate series of matches can over-complicate what we already expect may be a challenging task—namely, reading synchronicity for meaningfulness. A cluster of matches throws the whole exercise into disarray. Thus, due care is necessary: We neither want to fall into the trap of labelling each and every single "coincidence stack" as a synchronistic jewel, nor dismiss a slight but genuine synchronicity as "just-one-of-those-things".

Numinosity

Some dictionaries do not define the noun "numinosity", but they do take the adjective "numinous" to mean "mysterious",[25] or define it as "having a strong religious and spiritual quality".[26] These sources also refer to the "presence of divinity", which is in keeping with Jung's usage of the term numinosity to mean the power or presence or realisation of a divinity. For example, Jung (1952/1969) notes how "numinosity and mystery" can be extended to numbers, the numbers 1 to 9 being considered "sacred" by the ancients (para. 870). Given that certain geometrical, arithmetical, mathematical, and biological configurations of the natural numbers have "just-so" qualities that are clearly not circumstantial or ephemeral, but are inherent, definitive and eternal in their alignment with intrinsic physical laws, the ancients who thought deeply about such phenomena, realized that the numinosity in and of "particular" things may logically extend to a more general natural order, which the Greeks called *cosmos* (the universe governed by physical laws).[27]

Jung expanded on the concept of *cosmos* by including a domain he labelled General Acausal Orderedness (GAO)—a cosmic order of knowledge, or "absolute knowledge" that Jaffé (1967) likened to a "universal metaphysical background" (p. 272). In line with certain philosophical views, which hold that the objective (noumenal) world is usually described in subjective (phenomenal) terms, I suggest this "metaphysical" aspect refers to archetypes and the archetypal underpinnings of physical reality. In fact, rather than using the word "metaphysical", which refers to conceptual entities in the philosophical realm, it may have been better if Jaffé used the term "transcendent", meaning "beyond consciousness" and so includes phenomena within our spacetime realm and could be perceivable (see Jacobi, 1974, p. 50).

Giving weight to these ideas, Marialuisa Donati (2008) traces the term numinous to the Latin *nuere*: "to show signs" (p. 44), through the action of fate or of a divinity. For want of a better word that does not needlessly imply supernatural agency (recall Colman's, 2011, "non-human intentionality"), one may almost imagine something "divine" going on in synchronicity, just as there may be in the cosmos or GAO, but we must note that numinosity also applies to experiences or objects that affect the higher emotions, or give us an aesthetic sense. As Hefner and Arnold (2018) claim, without numinosity

> things and other persons remain mere images to the individual because there is no psychic energy exchanged; that is, the individual feels no emotional attachment.

One way of reading this statement suggests numinosity is an inherent factor outside the individual (as in the GAO), but the quote could also be taken to mean projection may be an operative factor in numinosity. Critically then, an issue of concern for us is whether numinosity is *inherent* in living beings, inanimate matter (material things), and things in the GAO (such as natural numbers, geometrical forms, quantum events, etc.). And we may wonder if this *inherence* (innateness) is identifiable as such, *and unmistakably so*, or can numinosity spring from projection onto anything that presents a suitable hook, thus evoking subjective, aesthetic, and emotional responses? For example, Jung (1952/1969) suggested the possibility of "projection" in divination (para. 866). It becomes self-evident that physical characteristics are one thing; numinosity, quite another. Thus we might say that *numinosity* explains how things in themselves (e.g., the elements of synchronicity) have an effect on the individual, who is drawn into the experience through whatever psychological/parapsychological processes prevail at a given time, but *projection* can have equal explanatory power.

So, while numinosity is the *sine qua non* of synchronicity, and it is brought to the fore more and more as the synchronistic components accumulate, it may be that a complex set of factors (i.e., projection, coupled with our propensity for meaning-making, pattern seeking, and pattern recognition) gives some coincidences their numinosity (their "charge", or "dynamism", or "emotional power"). To put it another way, while numinosity may be the element that gives coincidences their "wow" factor (as Browne notes), we must note cases where the "numinosity of a series of chance happenings grows in proportion to the number of its terms" (Jung, 1952/1969, para. 827, n.10). How can one be sure the "wow" factor is not indicating "pseudo-numinosity"? Some very intense analyses of coincidences have been published by well-meaning authors (e.g., Inglis, 1990; Rawlette, 2019a; Vaughan, 1979), who may speak of chance, and try to assess its influence, but they ultimately concede there is no foolproof method of deciding which coincidences are meaningful and which are meaningless—that is left to the experient. Jaffé (1967) believes an "inkling" of the above-mentioned universal metaphysical background "explains the feeling of awe-inspiring numinosity that usually accompanies the experience of synchronistic phenomena" (p. 272). But again, projection can evoke the same responses and feelings, and the contents themselves can be numinous without the added element of the universal metaphysical background, which for some people does not even enter into it—the inherent meaning may be numinous enough.

Taking a stance that provisionally leads to a solution, Schwartz (2018) gives us one way of looking at the problem, assuring us numinosity grows with frequent attention—the kind of attention that leads to the assumption, for example, that Chartres Cathedral has more numinosity than a warehouse, so that the former has a better chance of being remote viewed (like clairvoyance) than the latter: "Numinous constructs excite a stronger psychophysical response than mundane objects, and as such they can be unconsciously discriminated from less-numinous objects" (p. 403). Schwartz notes that the remote-viewing (RV) literature suggests this is so. RV is thus made that much easier and is more productive so long as numinosity prevails as an inherent factor in targets. Of course, an unmentioned factor key here is the archetype since numinosity and archetypes go together.

To go further, and by giving examples, Schwartz's (2018) review suggests numinosity is an embedded factor. We see that in traditional alphabetical and phonetic systems (e.g., Hebrew, Persian, Chinese, Japanese, and Cyrillic), words in sacred texts, and even Morse Code. Characters, word forms, and Morse signals derived from these sources are preferred and more readily remembered and recalled than bogus controls. I regard this kind of numinosity as direct evidence of archetypal dimensions embedded in our gene code. The work by Bradshaw and Storm (2013), and Sotirova-Kohli et al. (2011), also suggests that archetypes run deep in the fabric of our being.

Conveniently then, as long as targets are (or can be) intrinsically numinous (or have been loaded with numinosity over time spans), they should also prove to be archetypal, and *vice versa*, so we might not expect projection because the material stands on its own, and we can even reach a consensus about numinosity (see Krippner et al., 2019). At first blush, we would assume that targets in a parapsychological study that do not fit the bill (they are low in numinosity) are not likely to be hits (except by chance), and they are not likely to encourage projection, nor the false sense that a target is numinous. However, misses may still be the result of projection (due to the personal relevance of a decoy; i.e., non-target)—and the same goes for chance hits.

The distinction Schwartz (2018) describes may be ideal for proof-oriented (lab-based) research, and I would argue it proves the case for archetypes, but operationally (e.g., in the field), "boring" targets (low in numinosity that do not evoke anything archetypal in the remote viewer; a.k.a. "RVer") pose a problem for investigators—the RVer simply will not be interested, and will probably make poor guesses, or bow out of the task, giving spurious reasons and even excuses for doing so (for an example, see Stillman, 1975). If, however, a projection-making factor in the RVer may evoke a range of deeply felt emotional responses, the situation is just as bad because the wrong (non-target relevant) archetype(s) may be evoked. Then only by chance may the information be valid. Investigators might be better able to deal with projection if they have intimate and comprehensive biographical and psychological profiles of their RVers.[28] We immediately see how emotional factors play a part in triggering archetypes (not always the desired ones)—the personal component is usually embedded in synchronicity, and that will not necessarily help prove "the case for psi" in the Rhinean sense, which goes some way towards explaining the failures in psi testing.[29]

Taking all these points into consideration, we are not sufficiently advanced in our research and understanding to state categorically when apparent numinosity is actual numinosity or is only pseudo-numinosity wrought by projection. Numinosity is a marker for synchronicity, but pseudo-numinosity has spurious origins either in a meaningless chance grouping, or as an embellishment derived from projection.[30] But we can say that archetypal content is numinous and that may delimit projection. At the risk of being overly schematic, until the one is distinguishable from the other in a fool-proof way, we have to be on our guard that the emotional factor does not overwhelm us every time something synchronicity-like comes our way. The same *caveat* applies to psi research generally. Our best approach has always been to look for archetypal configurations in assumed synchronistic encounters. These configurations, as representations in one form or another, appear to be readily detected without special skills or training, and their numinosity also seems assured. We can at least endeavour to discover the meaningfulness of the experience, and consider Aziz's levels of meaning. Failing that, it is best not to dwell on the experience, but wait for insight or a confirmatory event. And as von Franz (1997) says, whether it is synchronicity (or not, in the case of projection), the psychic energy must flow towards a "creative discovery" (p. 198). (In sections to follow in this chapter, these issues are considered in more detail.)

Psychoid Factor

When Jung spoke of the *psychoid factor*, he was partly referring to archetypes as contents of that part of the psyche that are *incapable of consciousness* (the unconscious archetypes); so that they are "quasi-psychic" in the same vein as reflex-processes (Jung, 1947/1954, para. 368). Archetypes *per se* cannot be brought under conscious observation for evaluation or assessment, although their representations can be (from which we infer archetypes). In that sense, archetypes are like instincts (see footnote 13). Our best evidence for archetypes are their manifestations in consciousness as modes of apprehension, just as modes of behaviour can indicate the instincts. Since unconscious archetypes *per se* are "irrepresentable" (para. 840; see also Jung, 1960/1969, para. 417), Jung (1952/1969, para. 912) uses the word *psychoid* (psyche-like) to characterize archetypes as factors neither exclusively psychological ("psychic"), nor physical ("vitalistic"). The *psychoid factor* binds, or underpins the link between psyche and body.

Going further, Jung then gives the material world a psychological (psychoid) dimension, just as the brain has a psychological dimension as "mind". This understanding provides a crucial insight into the workings of synchronistic phenomena because the psychoid factor is the "activating" principle of the archetype, said to "arrange" inner/outer connections that can go beyond normal (local) parameters:

> You can never say with certainty whether what appears to be going on in the collective unconscious of a single individual is not also happening in other individuals or organisms or things or situations.
>
> (Jung, 1952/1969, para. 912)

These 'goings-on' (these psychoid activations) might be interpreted as paranormal, but one needs to keep in mind that even the broad domain of the collective unconscious is essentially private (primarily of concern to the individual) unless and until something archetypal springs into action. Then the outer world may be drawn in. Hence, Cambray (2009) sees the psychoid factor as a "capacity or propensity for organization …" (p. 108), not only applying within the organism, but extending beyond the physiological framework. That is the sense in which the psychoid level can be seen structurally as a level beyond the collective unconscious, more generally extending to Nature (Haule, 2011a). However, insofar as the psychoid factor is evident when psyche and matter merge on the evident basis of archetypal contingence, Haule (2011b) goes on to assume that the process is partly causal in the Rhinean sense so that the two aligned human psyches (Jung's and his patient's in the scarab case described above) psychokinetically "exert a draw upon the psyche of the rose chafer" (p. 209). That would very much not be synchronistic, making Haule's assumption incorrect.

Lorenz (2006) sees it differently. She notes a parallel between the psychoid factor and the more recent conception of "self-organizing systems" in "complexity theory". For example, she spoke of "unexpected and acausal orderings that could develop out of the connectivity of numbers", which she sees as *a priori*, archetypal, and "at the heart of life, world, and consciousness" (p. 6). We could acknowledge two frameworks or "dimensions of order" from which a broader science could develop: One causal and the other acausal—a schema which Jung promoted in his Synchronicity essay (Jung, 1952/1969, para. 947–968). Our already evident *causal* world would then be coupled with a host of acausal phenomena—a "general acausal orderedness" (GAO)—but I suggest that not all the phenomena in the GAO are synchronistic (see "The Reach of Synchronicity" in Chapter 2).

Synchronicity ultimately becomes "a highly abstract and 'irrepresentable' quantity" (Jung, 1952/1969, para. 947), insofar as the usual or normal range of synchronistic experience *seems* able to extend to apparent paranormal realms purely because this psychoid factor underpins it—the "moving body" (i.e., the living being) has "a certain psychoid property which, like space, time, and causality, forms a criterion of its behavior" (par. 947). And in this instance, Jung means the psychoid factor embodies meaningful ("intelligent") behaviour and equivalence. This rationale allows Jung to draw a distinction between meaningless chance groupings and meaningful coincidences, the difference being that the latter rest on an archetypal foundation which clues us in to the meaning—that is, meaningful coincidences are based in the "activation of the psychoid archetype" (para. 846, n41).

Along with archetypes, the *psychoid factor* is an ambiguous Jungian concept that "lacks explication or definitional precision" (Mills, 2013, p. 33); a "mythic invention.... [having] no logical or rational justification at its foundation" (Mills, 2014, p. 236). Indeed, Mills (2013) is critical of the idea that anything can be psychoid without an "agentic function". Perhaps overreaching, he supposes that Jung meant that archetypes, because they are psychoid, can impose their will, make choices, are "arrangers", and even have supernatural aspects. I believe these assertions go beyond Jung's intent, in spite of what people may infer from the Jungian literature. Jung is very clear about the archetype functioning (metaphorically) like a dry river-bed that needs a flow of water for its potential to be realized, or a blueprint that is not evident in the sky-scraper itself but must be presumed to exist. Seen this way, archetypes are like DNA. Such metaphors should help avoid the assertion of an agenda on Jung's part to anthropomorphize, or even "supernaturalize" (make "agentic") concepts like archetypes and their psychoid aspects.

With the particular expression *psychoid*, Jung points to the psychophysical nature of the archetype and the unitary reality consisting of both *psyche* and *physis* that he refers to as *transcendental*, because it underlies the whole of our phenomenal world. These concepts are clearly related to Kant's (1781/1952) philosophy, as Jung himself attests in many passages (e.g., Jung, 1959/1968, para. 148–198). On the surface, it is not difficult to see Jung's archetype *per se* as a kind of Kantian *noumenon*, where the *noumenon* is the unknowable reality underlying its associated *phenomenon*; the archetypal representation then would be interpreted as a phenomenon that can be grasped by cognitive means. Despite any apparent connection with Kant's philosophy, however, it is necessary to disambiguate the Jungian archetype *as such* and the Kantian *noumenon* because the archetype is dynamic and non-rational,[31] whereas the *noumenon* is unchangeable and rational.[32] It is possible, therefore, to place Jung near Kant only to the extent that they both postulate the existence of a psychoid reality that is placed beyond the phenomenal world and is in itself unknowable.[33]

Main (2004) sees a problem with the above—Jung's (1952/1969, para. 960) claim that synchronicity theory is based in the empirical observations (phenomenology) of meaningful coincidence is *undermined* by this psychoid factor. The noumenal aspect of the archetype *per se* can only be assumed, making synchronicity not merely an empirically derived concept, but one that depends on philosophical or metaphysical premises. Perhaps "depends" is too strong a word and "draws" is preferred. Jung explains how the concept arose; he necessarily starts with objective observations that give synchronicity an empirical grounding, but he also states that synchronicity cannot rest exclusively on either materialistic or metaphysical premises. That would allow Jung to say synchronicity "is not a philosophical view" (para. 960).

Synchronicity

Jung (1951/1969, para. 984) defines and describes synchronicity in the following ways:

1 The coincidence of a psychic state in the observer with a simultaneous, objective, external event that corresponds to the psychic state or content (e.g., the scarab), where there is no evidence of causal connection between the psychic state and the external event, and … such a connection is not even conceivable.
2 The coincidence of a psychic state with a corresponding (more or less simultaneous) external event taking place outside the observer's field of perception, i.e., at a distance, and only verifiable afterward (e.g., the Stockholm fire).
3 The coincidence of a psychic state with a corresponding, not yet existent future event that is distant in time and can likewise only be verified afterward.

Jung (1951/1969) adds:

> In groups 2 and 3 the coinciding events are not yet present in the observer's field of perception, but have been anticipated in time in so far as they can only be verified afterward. For this reason I call such events *synchronistic*, which is not to be confused with *synchronous.*
>
> (para. 985)

These definitions need clarification due particularly to the omission of key words such as "acausal" and "meaningful" (among others): According to Jung, two or more events constitute synchronicity when a *meaningful* connection—a meaningful association—can be made between the events, but I suggest it is only synchronicity *proper* once meaningfulness has been established (which may come sooner or later as synchronicity *proper* is the end product of a process that only starts with the synchronistic events). I say "synchronicity *proper*" to demarcate it from a *provisional* meaningless chance grouping whereby the former is proved not to be a case of the latter, and to do that we need meaningfulness beyond "shared meaning" (beyond a parallel).

In the case of (2) and (3) above, the "psychic state" (i.e., "psychological state" nothing to do with psi) can correspond with a psychic state *elsewhere* instead of an "external event" or "future event". An example comes from Jung of a father and son sharing dreams, the son having them for his father, and *vice versa* (Jung, 1975, p. 63). Jung states: "This peculiar phenomenon is at the base of Rhine's famous ESP experiments" (p. 63). But an external event can include a purely and exclusively (and supposedly mental) connection to another person (i.e., a parallel thought or cognition) because it is perceived as originating externally, in which case we may infer a psyche–psyche link, so that no physically external component is evident (other than a human brain as in certain psi experiences). Jung (1952/1969) implies this possibility by including "telepathy" as a form of "meaningful coincidence" (para. 974, 983). Also accepted as synchronicity is the case where there are *two* physical events and a corresponding psychic state—"a peculiar interdependence of objective events among themselves as well as with the subjective (psychic) states of the observer or observers" (Jung, 1989, p. *xxiv*). (See also Beitman's clarifications in the section "Forms of Synchronicity" in Chapter 2).

The other premise is that the connection between the events is *acausal* (true of all coincidences), so that synchronicity is established *not* through demonstrated *causal* connections, but only through "meaning", "equivalence", or "contingence" (not true of all coincidences; Jung, 1952/1969, para. 849–850). In the synchronistic context, these three words are meant to indicate *acausal* relations. Thereby synchronicity has been used interchangeably with the terms: "*meaningful coincidence*", "acausal connection" (para. 827); "*equivalence of meaning*" (para. 865); "Inconstant Connection through Contingence" (para. 963); and an "acausal connecting principle" (the last of these is the subtitle of Jung's, 1952/1969, major essay *Synchronicity*).

Apart from *meaningfulness* and *acausality*, there are other distinguishing factors that define synchronicity. These include *archetypes, numinosity*, and the *psychoid factor* (defined and discussed above), as well as the *unus mundus* (discussed next).

Unus Mundus (Psychophysical Reality)

In essence, the *Unus Mundus* (= "One World")—also written in lower case: *unus mundus*—refers to an all-encompassing unity back to which psyche and matter can be traced. Jung (1968b) states that psyche and matter "may be identical somewhere beyond our present experience" (para. 765), or similarly: "it is not only possible but fairly probable, even, that psyche and matter are two different aspects of one and the same thing" (Jung, 1960/1969, para. 418). Here, Jung hints at *dual-aspect monism* (defined above). The "psychophysical neutral background reality" (or simply, *psychophysical reality*) is Pauli's preferred term for the *unus mundus*. Physical and mental aspects derive from this single reality.

Borrowing the term *unus mundus* from medieval alchemist, Gerhard Dorn, Jung describes it as a "hidden unity of the inner and outer worlds" (Mansfield, 1995, p. 7). As Harald Walach (2020) so succinctly puts it, the *unus mundus* is "a kind of transcendent, ultimate reality that we humans do not have access to" (p. 8). This unity is not identifiable in concrete terms; we can only be privy to the two polar aspects or expressions of the *unus mundus*—namely, psyche and matter.

The *unus mundus*, therefore, is not mental, and it is not physical, but their common ground suggests the phenomenology of synchronicity—indeed, the synchronicity experience allows us to see "the complementary realms of psyche and matter as *one* reality" (von Franz, 1992, p. 40). That is, we can be privileged with an experience or effect of the *unus mundus* through synchronicity. Von Franz adds: "synchronistic phenomena provide *empirical* evidence for the existence of such an *unus mundus*" (p. 41), which Donati (2008) calls "a transcendental realm that pervades the universe as a whole" (p. 48). This extension beyond the psyche is an important distinction for it not only invites parapsychological discourse, but also has ramifications for science (as will be seen in later chapters).

Physicist and Jungian scholar Harald Atmanspacher elaborates on how experience of both opposites may bring us closer to that "neutral reality", that oneness, that is the *unus mundus*:

> From the mental, the neutral reality is approached via Jung's collective unconscious; from the physical it is approached by quantum nonlocality.
> (Atmanspacher, 2014a, p. 253)

Again, these ideas are encapsulated in dual-aspect monism. The collective unconscious can be experienced in a variety of ways, mainly involving non-ordinary states of consciousness such as dreams and fantasies, and some anomalous experiences. Of course, non-ordinary states of consciousness include those altered states of consciousness that can be induced meditatively and pharmacologically, though the term "altered" is blunt—the only real change is the mental environment out of which emerges one's subjective experience. These experiences immerse or put one in close proximity to the *unus mundus*.

The collective unconscious is Jung's conception, and it refers to that deeper domain of the unconscious that is human-wide—its contents, the archetypes, are shared across our species, and across all cultures. The collective unconscious, as the domain of psychic activity of a universal nature characterized by the archetypes, is distinct from Jung's other postulate, the personal unconscious, which contains our own individual histories of experiences and memories, either forgotten or remembered. The contents of the personal unconscious are usually recognized and owned, since they were, for the most part, in consciousness at one time or another. But the collective unconscious contains the archetypes which, in the form of "analogous representational structures" in consciousness, can have ambiguous effects. They are often characterized by their numinosity; they arise spontaneously, and have a symbolic aspect.

Quantum nonlocality takes the form of a range of physical manifestations such as entanglement (see Orzel, 2014). Atmanspacher (2014a) refers to quantum nonlocality as "*quantum holism*", which he parallels with "Jung's conception of a basic reality that does not consist of parts but is one unfragmented whole—the *unus mundus*" (p. 252). Such effects take place at the microphysical level, although quantum mechanics (QM) governs the behaviour of all physical systems, irrespective of size. Quantum nonlocality is uncanny and ultimately inexplicable, and although it defies classical understanding, it has been adequately modelled and demonstrated.[34] (A treatment of quantum phenomena in terms of parapsychological and synchronistic effects is given in Storm, 2025.)

Remo F. Roth (2002) says this of the *unus mundus*:

> … there has to be a world in which inner and outer world, psyche and matter are connected in an undifferentiated unity … Carl G. Jung and Wolfgang Pauli looked for this world and called it the *unified psychophysical reality* ("die psychophysische Einheitswirklichkeit") beyond the split in matter and psyche. One must consider this a potential world out of which causeless new creations can occur. Synchronistic events show the moment that this potential world will incarnate into the concrete.

Browne (2017) notes this creative aspect, and he also points out the undividedness of mind and matter in the *unus mundus.* He emphasizes the importance of the *unus mundus* as it pertains to an overall understanding of Jung's theoretical position:

> Jung considered the creativity displayed in synchronistic events to be evidence of the ancient idea of a continuous creation, or *creatio continua.* In this view, creation is not a one-off event but rather an ongoing activity which underlies our existence at each moment. In Jung's articulation of this process, the *creatio continua* is born out of the original undifferentiated unity of all existence, the *unus mundus.*
>
> (p. 14)

Jung (1963/1970) parsimoniously referred to the *unus mundus* as an "idea" and a "postulate", albeit founded on an "assumption … of an underlying unity" (para. 767). Conceptually, the *unus mundus,* with its paradoxical and metaphysical connotations, is a challenge to the intellect. Critically, the *unus mundus* could be seen as a construct derived from a burgeoning need to bind certain causally unrelated, meaningfully connected phenomena into a consistent whole that has universal extension to "one and the same world" rather than a multiplicity of worlds existing "side by side" or "mingled with one another" (para. 767). Once again, we can take that to mean that Jung is advocating dual-aspect monism—ontologically, there is one reality, but dualities are only manifestations in our subjective experience and must be seen as approximations or epistemological variants of that reality. As von Franz (1992) states, synchronicity may be taken as empirical evidence for the mind/matter link in the *unus mundus,* but it may be debatable whether such empirical evidence can really confirm such a view, or it must remain an intuition or inspired idea. What can also be said is that the construct is not only a thought-provoking archetypal motif, but (being archetypal) is more than impossible to resist, and is in fact a necessary postulate.

An *unus-mundus* mechanism is not yet discernable to the sciences, though QM might be a step in the right direction. Also, scientists cannot seem to make a going concern of the "meaning" concept; more so, they cannot make a going concern of the concept of an archetypal sub-structure to reality. Beitman et al. (2010) make a good point in this regard when they note that the quantum connection "lacks the meaningful quality that defines synchronicity" (p. 453). However, they are open to the ideas implied in QM: "Theorizing by analogy can be a first step toward better understanding. As with archetypal reasoning, we can state with confidence that two events *correspond* with each other—particle with particle, loved one with loved one" (p. 453).

What *is* accessible to the intellect is an appreciation of an implied unity manifesting in those synchronistic moments when the psyche and the world seem to bind in those correspondences of mental and physical events. A more important consequence, more psychological than scientific, is growth in (expansion of) human consciousness not achievable through wilfulness or the blunt force of other causal factors. Those new life possibilities also stand as creative moments we can infer in "the ancient idea of a continuous creation, or *creatio continua*" (Browne, 2017, p. 14).

Synchronicity vs. Meaningless Chance Groupings: Some Diagnostic Tools

This section describes approaches (diagnostic tools) that help differentiate synchronicity from meaningless chance groupings. A symbolic approach to coincidences may be helpful since synchronicity depends on material that creatively tends to emerge from the psyche, whereas meaningless chance groupings occur naturally but with only superficial inner parallels. Aside from the archetypal factor, and the meaningfulness of the experience, synchronicity should be critically evaluated in terms of social context and numinosity. The four steps provided at the end of this section may help in that evaluation.

A Symbolic Approach

In writing this section, I am reminded of a quote from Jung's *Synchronicity* essay:

> Synchronicity … consists of two factors: a) An unconscious image comes into consciousness either directly (i.e., literally) or indirectly (symbolized or suggested) in the form of a dream, idea, or premonition. b) An objective situation coincides with this content.
>
> (Jung, 1952/1969; para. 858)

The keywords here are "literally", "symbolized", and "suggested". There is a 12th-century religio-philosophical text, *The Guide for the Perplexed*, that is one of the major works by Rabbi Moshe ben Maimon, better known as Maimonides (1135–1204), to whom the Maimonides Medical Center in Brooklyn, New York, owes its name (the now-defunct Maimonides Dream Laboratory was located there). Briefly, the *Guide* sought reconciliation between Aristotelian philosophy and the theology of the Hebrew Bible. Apart from his "enlightenment" objective (centuries in advance of the Age of Enlightenment movement might I add), Maimonides (1904/1956) aimed to show how obscure biblical motifs should be interpreted, *not* in a literal sense but in a "figurative" sense (p. 2). He proposed that "informed persons ... are entirely relieved of their perplexity" (p. 2) once these motifs are stripped of their literal dimensions—hence the title *Guide for the Perplexed*. What does Maimonides mean by "figurative", and what does that have to do with synchronicity?

For the sake of deeper clarity and insight, Maimonides avoids the reductive literal-mindedness that later became the driving force of "materialistic scientism", and that is where his work is most important. He gives many examples, but I can only give readers a taste. Terms such as the "hand of God", or God as "loving" or "wrathful", have given people an illusory image of God as a corporeal being, often depicted in our own image (for an example, see Michelangelo's renowned *The Creation of Adam* of 1512).

Maimonides also discusses issues to do with the Creation and Prophecy, and he references key figures who have mythological dimensions, in the sense that they are ideal types, such as Ezekiel, whose experience of the Chariot (the wheels, the beasts, the man above the beasts) is described as more than a theophany. In that example, Maimonides, in a broad-minded and holistic (macrocosmic) way, connects the cosmological or "heavenly" realms to our inner struggle and the vicissitudes of corporeal existence. Historically, other authors have had similar aims to those of Maimonides (for a discussion, see von Franz, 1997). Jung (1958/1969) sees such visions as representations of the Self (a.k.a. the "central archetype" reflective of one's inner divinity, higher functions, and even one's highest potential).

What might be helpful to the inquirer is an approach to synchronicity that can somehow minimize the phenomenological perplexity of synchronicity. Maimonides' approach may be useful as it resembles the approach adopted later by Jung (for examples, see Jung, 1952/1969, para. 845, which I cover in this section and elsewhere). To take such an approach with synchronicity may be seen as letting categorical criteria guide the process of interpretation and understanding.[35] That, however, is a mere starting point for Jung was also aware of a "content problem" in synchronicity, and pointed out how the meaningful connection is "obvious enough" when there is "approximate identity" (giving us a reason to be literal), but it is not so obvious when the synchronistic elements are "incommensurable" (para. 845). It is at that point that Jung launches into practices he applies in the analytical setting.

Of course, attempts at categorization (often a misleading approach), interpretation, and explanation, must not do damage to the material, or the more crucial or essential aspects of synchronicity, which can open the experient to a transpersonal dimension of mind that is enmeshed with the ebb and flow of the material world. That is why, since the psyche is so entrenched in this process, synchronistic images, ideas, and thoughts, are first noticed as likenesses or *simulacra* that also happen to manifest symbolically or metaphorically—in a word, "figuratively". We can expect no less when the imagination is at play. Taken this way, a fuller, more holistic understanding may result. An example from a precognitive dream may help here. Barker (2021, p. 38) describes a dream by English psychic Christopher Robinson: On the night of September 6, 2019, Robinson dreamt that a bottle of *Corona* brand beer was being shaken by his grandmother, and when she removed the bottle top, the beer sprayed everywhere. In the dream, Robinson's grandmother told him that Corona was going to spread across the world killing millions. Three months later (December 8), the "first COVID-19 case was reported" (Yu et al., 2021, p. 4). (Note that COVID-19 = COrona VIrus Disease 2019.) Clearly, a purely literal interpretation makes no sense, but the symbolic image of the beer spray suggests just one obvious mechanism (i.e., sneezing) for the spread of the virus (as "foretold" by Robinson's grandmother, the death toll was in the millions).[36]

If we return to our example from Maimonides, but fast-forward to the 20th century, we see how literal-mindedness turns the Biblical configuration of Ezekiel's entity-girdled chariot suspended in mid-air into a flying saucer, courtesy of Erich von Däniken (1969) with his particular bent on materialistic scientism (see also Fowler, 1974/2001). But it does not end there—following the very same precepts of materialistic scientism, the psychiatric profession would not necessarily fair much better because it tends to reduce transpersonal or anomalous experiences to abnormalities of brain function or mental illness. Thus, modern mainstream interpretations, which conflict with any kind of holistic aim, would have it that either "Ezekiel saw a UFO", or "Ezekiel was delusional". But what would Ezekiel have gained with those diagnoses? Both demonstrate the very conclusions Maimonides sought to avoid.

A superb modern-day example is Travis Walton's (1979/1996) *Fire In The Sky*, which describes Walton's UFO abduction experience, made all the more convincingly "real" by the corroborated multiple-witness accounts given by Walton's co-workers of the "physical" phenomenon. This approach is a form of explanation that reaches for an understanding in purely physical terms, but it results in truncated pigeon-holing of experiences (hence, my hesitance in the use of the word 'categorization'). As Walton makes clear in his autobiography, he was never able to accept a transpersonal (anomalous) explanation because his experience was too real for him to go down the path of 'dismissing' it as 'all in the mind'. But he should not be expected to see his experience as merely 'all in the mind' (a simplistic delusion with no substance). The trouble is, no plausible and well-accepted, sound and reasonable, option is readily available to him; an option that does not question his sanity. Conventional leanings cheapen numinous experiences of the "Self" (as Jung calls it). Far from dismissing anything so profound, the experience might have alerted Walton to another side of his being or psyche, or Self; the very same Self (as central archetype) to which authorship of dreams, visions and fantasies are attributable, and which has a hand in synchronicity.

One can go further, and we will see in later chapters that some pundits in the science of parapsychology, in acting categorically, 'reduce' synchronicity to psi, but in ways that accord with the parapsychological rules, so that (say) a telepathic experience is dissected and interpreted thus:

- Person A dreamed about event X happening to Person B the following day;
- Person B experienced event X;
- Person A is psychic (i.e., information was transferred paranormally).

The parapsychologist has little or no concern with the elements of event X other than it being the target of interest (the proof), and there is no real interest in the psychodynamics of the persons involved. The failure of this approach is in the lack of inquiry into whether (i) something archetypal was prevalent that might explain an ordinarily unpredictable experience; and (ii) the experience was meaningful to one or both parties.

Literal-mindedness can distort the essence of the experience and detract from the message; it focuses on the envelope rather than the letter inside, and leads to statements like 'psi is an ability that people have' rather than 'synchronicity is a snap-shot of how people and events inter-connect meaningfully'. Note that my critique on literal-mindedness is not meant to denigrate the informational and applicational aspects of synchronicity (what some might naively call 'psi aspects'). My aim is to arrive at a holistic conception of psi by seeing it in a synchronistic light, so as to appreciate the numinosity of the experience in terms of the importance and relevance of the event to the experient.

As far as synchronicity is concerned, one might compare the 'merger' of the inner and outer to an altered state of consciousness similar to a vision, fantasy, or dream, or, what is essentially true of these, the play of the imagination—only, when one has a synchronicity, it is like the imagination has come to life and the usual rules do not apply. Viewed this way, we are better placed to understand a "simultaneous occurrence of a psychic state with a physical process as *an equivalence of meaning*" made all the more so on symbolic grounds (Jung, 1952/1969, para. 865).

On the Relevance of Numinosity and Meaningfulness

In referring back to a previous section, it is interesting to note that Wilmer's (1987) pipe-smokers scenario, Jung's (1952/1969) fish series, and the Buxtons case—none of them synchronistic—are similar in a number of ways, each case pointing to the under-riding phenomenology of chance. They are amusing, novel, and quaint, and we note how the experients are often left musing over the events (even for quite some time as with the Buxton girls) but, if we probe for something more, we tend to get a sense that there is missing from these accounts something archetypal and profoundly meaningful. That is, we cannot advance beyond Aziz's first level of meaning. On the face of it, the seemingly impossible odds gives these cases numinosity, but it is a pseudo-numinosity, and one must be wary that it does not hinder the differentiation of the "genuinely meaningful coincidences from 'wow' factor ones" of which the latter are spurious in this context (L. Browne, personal communication, October 3, 2017).

It would be easy to dwell on the sensationalism of these cases, tag them as synchronicity, and not commit them to further scrutiny. However, as mentioned, an important determinant of meaningless chance groupings, *social context*, rears its ugly head. In our pipe-smokers example, we have two men living near a park (i.e., the same neighbourhood) who both smoke a pipe—they too have much in common socially, although their story is fictional so we need not speculate on the whys and wherefores of such a scenario. Instead, we have Jung's fish series, which I have dealt with in its social context as a series of events strewn together by the sociological circumstances of Jung's profession (as well as the time of year). And, as I pointed out above, the Buxton girls have so much in common *because* they are young girls living in the UK.

Getting emotionally swept up in synchronicity is no way to keep a clear head, but certainly, as a starting point, we need that factor which so closely evokes affect, feeling and emotional charge—that is, numinosity. We also need evidence of an archetype, but archetypes are not easily identifiable beyond inference (and more research does need to be conducted in that area). It is far easier to take the path of least resistance and pounce on what is the most obvious to us—namely, numinosity—because, by definition, it is a force unto itself. Unfortunately, it is a force that can mislead—it can give the illusion of something archetypal under-riding it when in fact an archetype may not have been constellated.

As a case in point, I give the following example of ostensible synchronicity, primarily based on its objective (non-personal) numinosity and the mere hint of an archetype, as put forward by Roderick Main in his book *Revelations of Chance*. In 1973, while on holiday in Cambridge, England, school-teacher Stephen Jenkins saw "four horses: red, black, dapple, and white" (Main, 2007, p. 12). Jenkins photographed the horses as proof of what he had seen due to the fact that he had been studying apocalyptic literature, including Zechariah's vision of four riders astride four coloured horses (red, black, dapple [i.e., pale], and white), famously referred to as to the Four Horsemen of the Apocalypse in the biblical books *Zechariah* and *Revelation*. Nearly a year later, Jenkins was taking photos of a rock formation in Devon, when he happened to see a group of four Dartmoor ponies also coloured "red, black, dapple, and white", on Okehampton Common (Main, 2007, p. 12).

I must point out that this case is reminiscent of Jung's fish series, perhaps varying only in degree of numinosity. The numinosity inherent in the four-horse motif is unquestionable—after all, the imagery *does* appear twice, and on both occasions, we get four horses of the right colour—but it falls short. For one thing, we have horses, but we do not have horsemen. And Browne (2017) notes that the "chariots" pulling "in different directions" (p. 126) in *Zechariah* are missing in Jenkins's account (in fact, there are no chariots, and it is worth pointing out that Jenkins was also studying the visions of Ezekiel, the most famous of which involved a chariot, but not in Jenkins' direct experience).

It cannot be understated that the archetypal values inherent in the 'quaternity' motif (in both *Zechariah* and *Revelation*) have profound psychological, socio-cultural, and religious consequences and connotations, symbolically pertaining to, for example, bloodshed (red), woe (black), sickness (dappled/pale), and peace (white). For the meaning of these colours in quaternity symbolism, see Laughlin (2015; see also Jung, 1937/1968). But are we to understand that Jenkins had, beyond the typical researcher's interest, such a profound psychology and/or personal myth that it measured up to the scale of the imagery before him? If so, Main does not discuss it. While we cannot be sure that the same archetype was constellated, there may be a case for it. But we surely need something more than Jenkins's interest and study in apocalypses, which is on par with Jung's scholarly interest in fish symbolism, yet Jung dismissed his experience as categorically *not* synchronicity. Of course, if there was overt *psychological* evidence that archetypes had constellated in these two examples (Jung's and Jenkins's), both Jung and Jenkins may have been privy to synchronicity, and certainly Jung would have said as much.

By definition Main refers to the Jenkins event as a coincidence—Jenkins himself called it a "significant coincidence" (p. 13)—and Main notes there are no causal links, and numinosity seems apparent, and even something clearly archetypal, but we must also have meaningfulness for the event to be synchronicity. After some in-depth analysis of the details, Main does eventually decide to call it a "meaningful or significant coincidence" and a "synchronicity" (p. 14). But the meaningfulness seems lost here, or it is not apparent. That is, the equivalence has a certain *correlational* meaning and emotional tone (Aziz's first- and second-level meanings)—it is "parallel in content" (Main, p. 22), and Main further regards it as having meaningfulness, but only because of its "significance" (p. 22). I suggest there is some meaning but I cannot be sure of its meaningfulness which, guided by numinosity, seems to be a privilege exclusive to Jenkins. To assuage our apprehensions, we might argue for the kind of meaning referred to by Flew (1953), who argues that *all* coincidences (not just synchronicity) are meaningful (he actually uses the word "meaningful"; pp. 198–199), but Mansfield (1995) demands more, whereas there is simply too little for us to go on in the Jenkins case. If there was a sufficiently *personal* history and purpose behind the events, we are not privy to it, so we never get a sense that compensation and individuation ensued for Jenkins; there is no dénouement.

In a later section in this chapter, I again suggest that meaning is not quite meaningfulness *per se.* [37] Main (2007) makes a similar point, but then he leaves it to the experient to decide. At the very least, a comprehensive investigation of all the circumstances (in particular, the psychological parameters governing Jenkins's life on both occasions of his sightings) is necessary to make any firm conclusion, for who knows what lurked in the depths of Jenkins's mind?[38] The scale of these sorts of cases do stir our interest, but we must do more than speculate on their coincidentiality. It is hoped that this next subsection will be of some help in that regard.

Four Steps to Synchronicity

We can draw from Jungian psychology a serviceable procedure that can help differentiate meaningful and meaningless coincidences.[39] When we witness Jung evaluating synchronicities and meaningless chance groupings, it is as if he follows a series of four steps, based on the embodiment into a single heuristic of the essential aspects of the four-function typology featured in his book *Psychological Types* (Jung, 1921/1971)—namely, Sensation, Thinking, Feeling, and Intuition. Each of these can be applied in that order. Jung (1977) describes four functions by which the ego perceives and interprets reality: "Sensation tells you that there *is* something. Thinking … tells you *what* it is. Feeling tells you whether it is agreeable or not, to be accepted or rejected. And Intuition … is a perception via the unconscious" (pp. 306–307). Aziz's (1990) four levels of meaning suggest Jung's schema, though the order may differ (see "Meaningfulness" above).[40] Applying this heuristic is a mental operation, a cognitive process, involving not only conscious but much semiconscious processing that happens so fleetingly, it is easy to miss a step or two, and not even notice if all four steps were taken.[41]

First, the experience manifests through our Sensation function (a purely irrational process). The experient can be captivated by the experience, noticing an immediate parallel of inner and outer elements. As we have seen, in dealing with synchronicity or a meaningless chance grouping, the experient cannot be blamed for calling the experience profound or numinous given the scale of the experience, or the urgency of the moment, or its seeming rarity—how it stands out from the mundane—which can be mistaken for acausality leading to the interpretation that it must be synchronicity. To avoid fixating on the problem, the experient must not dwell in the sensation of the moment.

Second, the experient must make a mental reckoning of the various phenomena that comprise the experience—this 'reckoning' involves the rational function of Thinking, and requires one to draw upon their experiences in memory, and/or attempt to hypothesize normal causes. As described above, the experient must weigh up the likelihood of the experience in terms of chance factors and social context. In truth, context is not easy to assess—thinking, being rational, is learned; reason does not come naturally.[42] One has to ask, or learn how to ask the right questions, and then answer, or learn how to answer them. This 'Q&A' process is made easier by considering the 'circumstantiality' of the experience (i.e., the prevailing social situation, the environment, the human activity, which may generate the events out of that particular moment). The analyses of the three cases above show how this reckoning was done.[43]

There are two more steps to take before we can be certain the coincidence may be elevated to the status of synchronicity proper—the experient must push through the final two barriers of Feeling and Intuition. Once these waters have been navigated, the experient is in a better position to rule on his or her experience.

In this third step, Feeling requires a rational evaluation of the episode (how it 'feels'): Is it agreeable? Does it highlight a relevant issue and get to the crux of the matter? Does it touch a raw nerve, or does it give solace? And why? Much of this process will depend on the personal understanding of the value system of the experient, but the process is further complicated by how the experient has prioritized those values. Are personal idiosyncrasies pitting the various values against each other? The ability to answer this question, and the others, will stem from the honesty of the experient and his/her level of intuition, which is the second of the two irrational functions (the other being Sensation).

Fourth and final, the experient must use Intuition to pool the various elements together and draw a conclusion based on what has been happening in his or her life. When dealing with a true synchronicity, the experient must be able to draw out the potential, the purposes, and the possibilities, of the experience.[44] This last step rounds out the analysis by giving the third of three ingredients in the "synchronicity occurrence that distinguishes it from chance coincidence"—the so-called "*flash of total insight*", as described by Browne (2017, p. 105). These three ingredients are: "*equivalence of meaning* …, feeling of *numinosity* …, and a *flash of total insight*" (p. 105), though I put numinosity before equivalence of meaning.

The process may not stop there—there may be good cause to redeploy one of the functions for the sake of clarification (something may not seem right; some feature may have escaped assessment). Johansen and Osman (2015) refer to a similar "recursive" process of repeatedly going through one's memory to revise and replace a causal hypothesis if an earlier version does not satisfactorily explain a coincidence. Also, the order may be different from the sequence proposed above (e.g., Feeling may precede Thinking). It is, however, preferable (indeed, logically imperative) that the process starts with Sensation because it is by that function that the internal (mental) and external (physical) perceptions are first encountered. Similarly, it is very likely that the process will conclude with Intuition.

Once all these steps are taken, and something crystallizes out of the process, there may be an awakening or expansion of consciousness, a realization, and even a transformation. Jungian psychotherapist Dr Suzanne Gieser (2005) puts it quite well: Synchronicity is often marked by "a transition from an unstable state of consciousness into a new stable state, when consciousness has expanded and an equilibrium with the unconscious has been established" (p. 284). And, we can go deeper still into the psychology of synchronicity—the experient

> is either drawn into the event so as to learn from it, or one denies it out of ignorance. But seldom does one get the chance to be impartial, for the nature and power of the *numinosum* compels a reaction; a *search for some explanation ....*
>
> (Storm, 2008d, p. 250)

Alternatively, if all this work leads nowhere, and no helpful, or useful, or meaningful solution, or conclusion can be reached, it is best to regard the entire event as a meaningless chance grouping, and not dwell on what might have been. Of course, the above heuristic may produce results that are strictly personal (subjective) when we would aim to be objective (as does Mansfield, 1995), but a degree of objectivity can be achieved through consultation with others; especially those more experienced in their own synchronicity experiences (for a discussion on this issue, see Storm, 2008d).

Alternative Explanations of Synchronicity: I. Chance

There are those critics of psi who seem to have a "watery" character; they follow the path of least resistance, and avoid dealing with the mind-boggling complexities that psi research throws up by simply arguing from their own belief system that chance factors explain psi phenomena, as the following quote suggests: "*chance co-occurrence of two non-related events is probably responsible for more belief in paranormal powers than is any other single thing*" (Alcock, 1981, p. 96).[45] I will broaden the category of "psi phenomena" to include synchronicity, especially since I have already argued for its parallel with ESP/PK (Storm, 2025). That aside, my main concern is the concept of chance *per se*, and what it implies, for it is a little more complex than is ordinarily understood—as Jung (1952/1969) has said:

> Chance, we say, must obviously be susceptible of some causal explanation and is only called "chance" or "coincidence" because its causality has not yet been discovered.
>
> (para. 823)

Mansfield (1995) agrees: "implicit in the usual use of the word *chance* is a deep commitment to causality" (p. 80). They seem to be saying that chance itself is comprised of causes. It is likely Alcock does not understand chance in this way, but there is a logic to these two statements that is hard to resist: Any so-called chance outcome must of necessity be seen as having been driven by multiple forces, effectively unobservable and undetectable (assumed to be minor), all of them jostling with each other, so that *exact replication of a chance occurrence as a process in itself* is operationally impossible *technically speaking*. But it never need be, for in science, chance is well-behaved—it is consistent, and the scientist regards chance factors as *generally* inconsequential and even random. That is why privilege is granted to the notions of randomicity and randomness; these concepts underpin hypothesis testing. In other words, whatever chance is, it is our baseline against which we can measure an effect, so under the null hypothesis (that there truly is 'no effect'), any effect that might happen to emerge could conservatively (but tentatively) be regarded as random until it is shown to be otherwise. This standard applies equally to a series of events (e.g., a 'run' consisting of some number of single events or trials in a psi experiment).

Of course, this whole argument would not bother Alcock, who would feel especially vindicated each time a subset of 'hits' in a run is exactly what chance would deliver, irrespective of the unobservable, undetectable multiple forces, and all their jostling. However, taking Jung's and Mansfield's words into consideration, it is possible that a *deep commitment to causality* intuitively drives parapsychologists to think twice about so-called chance outcomes; data may need further scrutiny, and by so doing, there may be found a variable or two that is not so inconsequential but, in fact, introduces into the data a bias of interest. Indeed, parapsychologists often plan for that. Perhaps, for example, ESP performances in a series of runs might fluctuate between the two extremes of psi *hitting* and psi *missing*, [46] which can average out to chance as an aggregate even though run comparisons might indicate non-chance deviations (a.k.a. *run-score variance*; for examples, see Carpenter, 1991; Rogers, 1966; Schmeidler, 1964; Stanford & Stanford, 1969; Storm & Thalbourne, 2005a). Any significant performance differences would be extraordinary and raise curiosity.

Similarly, data suggesting overall chance performance for a sample of participants may hide a *sheep-goat effect*, which has been demonstrated in many datasets (e.g., Storm & Tressoldi, 2017).[47] Outcomes like these have been familiar to parapsychologists for many decades—for example, Schmeidler (1964) noted "there are detailed, meaningful, and self-consistent patterns within ESP data" (p. 15). Thus, without the appropriate analyses, it is impossible to show how not all trial matches (the 'hits') are "chance co-occurrences" of "non-related events". The opportunity would then be lost of uncovering a circumstance that does not reduce to those multiples of causes that make up chance, but is instead statistically determinable.

Whenever chance explanations of data are invoked, the examples just given show that those explanations can be premature; even fallacious. Of course, the kinds of analysis that expose the superficiality of the chance assumption most easily apply to runs of trials, or bouts of behaviour, whereas the isolated (unique) spontaneous cases (psi or synchronicity) are very much a different kettle of fish. These spontaneous cases are often more compelling as anomalies, but they are the least susceptible to statistical analysis, if at all. As is true for single cases of ESP and PK, Jung ultimately decided that the statistical approach was inappropriate for testing single cases of synchronicity given their sporadic nature (1951/1969, para. 986; 1952/1969, para. 912, 958).

Interest in statistically proving rare (ostensibly paranormal) phenomena may not be chance outcomes is rare in itself: Three decades after Diaconis and Mosteller (1989) made their major contribution to coincidence explanations (more on them later),[48] Rawlette (2019a) weighed in on the psi vs. coincidence (chance) debate in her attempt to "compute the probabilities" (Diaconis & Mosteller, 1989, p. 860). Note too that she recognise psi and synchronicity as similar phenomena, though she mistakenly includes synchronicity "under the umbrella of psychic causation" (p. 11). Rawlette argues that multiple endpoints (all the other possible outcomes that could have happened besides the actual one) should be factored into the probability-determining process, so that the seeming rareness of an event may or may not reduce to mean chance expectation (MCE) depending on the number of endpoints. Too detailed and complex to go into here, Rawlette describes a step-by-step statistical method for calculating a chance baseline ("baseline correspondence potential"; p. 11) so that a quantitative evaluation of the " 'misses' a person could encounter can be used to offset the 'hit' in question.[49] For the most part, Rawlette's statistical method is effective; she states:

> It *can* tell us how often we should expect by chance to encounter correspondences at or above a particular level of improbability … it allows us to show that certain correspondences … are *so* improbable that it is extremely unlikely on chance that we would ever encounter them in an entire lifetime, or even in 3 million lifetimes or more.
>
> (p. 36)

Unfortunately, by this method, coincidences (and synchronicity, and psi) are legitimized (or not) on the basis of a calculated probability, thus making *conditional* the content and the message synchronicity offers the experient. That may be neither here nor there for those parapsychologists who are satisfied with a co-occurrence being validated statistically, but synchronicity pundits are more discriminating and wish to test each case of coincidence against the definition of synchronicity, its underlying factors, and life situation. To put it another way, Rawlette (2019a) is arguing that *statistical significance* (discussed shortly) justifies belief in a coincidence being something other than chance, whereas the "synchronist" (as journalist, Brian Inglis, 1990, uses the term) has more interest in a meaningful outcome—the last thing they want to see is a meaningless chance grouping pass a statistical test; for what should that furnish but a contradiction? The point made here is not to denigrate significance testing, which can be of practical use, for example, in identifying correlates and performance differences in psi studies.

Ironically, the vast majority of coincidence cases in Rawlette's (2019b) massive book are never subjected to Rawlette's statistical method; instead, Rawlette draws meaningful insights from them *on face value* when these may have failed her own test. Nevertheless, Rawlette is to be commended for taking a rational approach to coincidences, as does Jung himself:[50]

> Meaningful coincidences are thinkable as pure chance. But the more they multiply and the greater and more exact the correspondence is, the more their probability sinks and their unthinkability increases, until they can no longer be regarded as pure chance but, for lack of a causal explanation, have to be thought of as meaningful arrangements.
>
> (Jung, 1952/1969, para. 967)

Jung also notes that it is "generally assumed that all coincidences are lucky hits and do not require an acausal interpretation", even if we have ruled out a causal chain, but when their "incidence exceeds the limits of probability", we have a "proof" of "non-causal combinations of events", and we look for a "meaningful cross-connection" (Jung, 1952/1969, para. 827). However, Beitman (2017b) points out: "Every coincidence has at least theoretically a probability …. So, that's a quality of a coincidence to have a probability [but] it's not necessarily an explanation", by which he means we should not *solely* resort to statistics to make decisions about coincidences, including meaningful coincidences (which is what Diaconis and Mosteller do).[51] To emphasize Beitman's point, Rawlette's (2019a) method "does *not* show that correspondences occurring at or even below the baseline rate [of improbability] … can't be evidence for a psychic link" (p. 36). Skeptics would consider this 'drawback' inconsequential (as would many a parapsychologist) because they argue that kind of correspondence automatically reduces to chance if it falls within the realms of the probable.

In conversation with Beitman, Browne makes a further clarification:

> […] if something has a low probability of happening, it can still be chance and not synchronicity; and a 'synchronicity' can have a much higher chance of happening and can be synchronistic, and its synchronistic quality is far more significant than its chance factor.
>
> (Browne, as cited in Beitman, 2017b)

Inglis (1990) makes the same point: "the improbability does not make it meaningful … a coincidence which ordinarily would be readily attributed to chance can become meaningful" (p. 196).

While not talking about synchronicity specifically, British philosopher John Stuart Mill (1806–1873) effectively pre-empted Beitman's, Browne's, and Inglis's statements when he said: "The question is not whether the coincidence occurs often or seldom, in the ordinary sense of those terms …" (p. 314). But then Mill goes on to say that the question is "… whether it [the coincidence] occurs *more* often than chance will account for …" (1846, p. 314). Here is where Mill aligns with the statistician. For Mill, a greater-than-chance expectancy allows one to infer causality. I note that Mill does not discuss acausality (not a major concern in the 19th century), but he would have to argue that mere occurrence does not prove synchronicity either, and he might be interested to know whether synchronicity occurs *more often than chance will account for* (to use Mill's own words). Like Beitman and Browne and Inglis, Mill does not regard rarity as indicating anything special on its own, but Mill does wish to dispense with chance and then proceed to establish a cause, to some extent *reasonably* warranted by the fact that a higher-than-expected relative frequency is tantamount to a "low probability" of occurring by chance (much as Jung and Rawlette are saying).

Since the scientific way is to think statistically, it is perhaps not surprising that Jung, the self-confessed empiricist, puts weight on frequency of detail (low probability of chance) as a determinant of synchronicity such that multiplicity (the piling up of evidence) slowly but surely trumps chance—that is, if it seems improbable that chance is at work because there is too much detail (too much happening inter-connectively), chance probably does not explain it. Main (2007) emphasizes the same point in saying synchronicity needs to not only be *rare*, but also be sufficiently *detailed*, so as to be notable. This argument really only holds for the single case, but even then, only up to a point. While Jung and Main and others seem to be offering a protocol that allows one to zero-in on synchronicity with confidence, there are problems. How much detail is *enough* detail for a synchronicity to be likely? This dilemma raises a key issue for the experimenter: Unless the factor of meaningfulness is addressed on an individual basis in studies that run multiple trials, there seems to be little on offer in the way of reliably identifying all those coincidences (hits) that should pass as synchronicity while safely discounting the chance hits.

Fortunately, we can go a little further with Jung's (1952/1969, para. 967) statement for he has not only linked chance, acausality, and "meaningful arrangements" with *probability*, but also with *unthinkability*. The two are concomitant so that *probability* must be considered alongside *unthinkability* in the sense Jung means where chance *and* causality come into question. I see Jung as implying a conflation of two distinct conceptualizations of probability so that a double-edged argument emerges: one part is *statistical* (concerned with stochastic processes and chance) and the other is *epistemic* (concerned with reasonable degrees of expectation or belief; see Hacking, 1975). Collins (2009) shows that there is strong justification for making a distinction between statistical probability and epistemic probability, but he stresses the importance of both.[52] The former is grounded in the testing of data (concerned with stochastic laws or chance processes); the latter is used in scientific confirmation of proposed theories (e.g., evolution, atomic theories, and even QM). In his own way, Jung sidelined chance and causality by placing as much importance on the *empirical adequacy* of the synchronicity concept (its "likelihood" or "probable truth"; Collins, p. 226) as he does on the statistical justification of the concept. And he logically prepared for the dénouement of his main essay, as embodied in the above quote (i.e., para. 967), by saying earlier:

> [...] we have an inveterate conviction of the absolute validity of causal law .... But if the causal principle is only relatively valid, then it follows that even though in the vast majority of cases an apparently chance series can be causally explained, there must still remain a number of cases which do not show any causal connection.
>
> (para. 823)

Given the soundness of this logic, and provided chance explanations have been abandoned (e.g., for statistical reasons), *and* given that the search for causes has failed, synchronicity can be classed as acausal (nominally or provisionally). Similar concessions have long been made by physicists in the field of QM. Koestler (1974) certainly did not miss the point when he stated, "the unthinkable phenomena of ESP appear somewhat less preposterous in the light of the unthinkable propositions of physics" (pp. 11–12). Although synchronicity may also be unthinkable, there is no justification in seeing it as preposterous if it is *epistemically probable.*

These ideas have not helped change current thinking. Note, however, that Johansen and Osman (2015) have at least criticized the standard two approaches to coincidences: Either the coincidence is induced in some special way due to occult or paranormal causes operating in the world (these causes even justify paranormal belief), or the coincidence is a misinterpreted chance occurrence due to cognitive biases such as poor probabilistic reasoning and/or unwarranted paranormal beliefs. To their credit, Johansen and Osman try to move things along—they propose a third, "rationalist" definition of coincidence by building on descriptions of coincidences that take into account low probabilities, connected mental states, causal phenomena, and pattern repetitions:

> [...] *coincidences are surprising pattern repetitions that are observed to be unlikely by chance but are nonetheless ascribed to chance since the search for causal mechanisms has not produced anything more plausible than mere chance* [italics in original].
>
> (Johansen & Osman, 2015, p. 36)

So, chance is an "unlikely" explanation of coincidence, but if we fail to find a cause, we should default to chance anyway because it is the most "plausible" explanation! This baffling definition concedes that the search for causes of coincidences may fail, but in no way is it meant to diminish the legitimacy and purpose of certain coincidences (they are "meaningful", and have "direct personal relevance"; p. 34), though others are only "interesting but trivial and have little meaning for the individual experiencing them" (p. 38). The authors recognise coincidences as being acausal events, but the crux of the paper is that coincidences are "*psychologically experienced*" (p. 34), and do not have the objective reality (ontological status) that Jung (1952/1969, para. 967) claims for synchronicity. The authors actually say synchronicity ignores "the possibility that coincidences are a psychological phenomenon" (p. 38), and the idea of "actual but hidden structures in the world" (p. 38) is anathema to them. Later, I will show how this distinction is to be found wanting (for example, see the subsection *The Two Agentive Forms of Synchronicity* in Chapter 2), but for now the above (italicized) definition does little to shift entrenched thinking.

In the light of these points, we come back to the issue of frequency which was raised earlier, but it bears revisiting one last time for another reason, as suggested by Beloff (2008), who speaks more speculatively about the statistical issue of frequency in relation to synchronicity:

> The idea of synchronicity, of an "acausal connecting principle" is not, despite what critics have said, incoherent or devoid of meaning. Given the appropriate world view it would make good sense. ... we may well have to settle for a universe which exhibited meaningful and yet acausal connections. In any case, there could be no *a priori* reason why the world should not be so constituted that coincidences occur to a greater extent than they should do given the accepted laws of probability, however fantastic this may seem.
>
> (p. 106)

Here is one of the few times Beloff made an argument for synchronicity (he even concedes a place for acausality), but he also raised the principle of relative frequency—he needs "coincidences" (synchronicity) to occur more frequently than chance can explain, as does Flew (1953), who suggested that synchronistic phenomena occur more "commonly and less arbitrarily than they should 'by the law of averages'" (p. 199). While Flew only hints that there may be a 'functional law' (x varies with y) underlying synchronicity, various other statements by Jung (1952/1969, para. 938, 965) suggest Jung is otherwise relieved in only having to impart *contingence* to archetypes, not *lawfulness* as that implies causality. Yet common sense would suggest that some number of archetypes, provided they constellate (say, in an experimental situation) more often than chance can explain, might be demonstrated in some formulaic way, so that

Flew's justification for his proposition (and Beloff's)—that a higher-than-chance frequency is necessary to prove synchronicity—could be supported on evidential (statistical) grounds.

Jung accepted the fact that repeated observation that graduates to a replicable effect is the researcher's best defense against self-deception: "They [synchronicities] certainly occur much more frequently in reality than one thinks or can prove", but he goes on to say: "we still do not know whether they occur so frequently and so regularly in any field of experience that we could speak of them as conforming to law" (1952/1969, para. 938). Jung still thinks in terms of the unique case, and seems to be referring to the *absolute* frequency of these, and wonders how to establish *relative* frequency. But Jung does not go so far as Mill (1846), who said *relative* frequency allows the scientist to *infer a law or a cause* after all else fails, such as when no law can be deduced, or the various methodologies are unsuccessful.

Fortunately, not all methodologies are unsuccessful as shown by Rhine (as cited in Jung, 1952/1969, para. 833). Rhine's success in the laboratory even gave rise to a somewhat contradictory statement from Jung: "The results of the ESP and PK experiments have provided a *statistical basis* [emphasis added] for evaluating the phenomenon of synchronicity, …" (para. 863). Indeed, Jung was quite sure, right up to the end of his essay, that ESP and PK were synchronicity, though he clearly meant ESP and PK were exceptions that could be subjected to statistical assessment (see Jung, 1951/1969, para. 981, 995; 1952/1969, para. 965), whereas the single-case of synchronicity was too sporadic and unpredictable by nature to be statistically evaluated (1951/1969, para. 986; 1952/1969, para. 912, 958). This latter set (single cases) posed for Jung the problem he had with determining relative frequencies, and his position is understandable, but the dichotomy—and it applies to spontaneous psi phenomena as well—is granted some degree of resolution given the argument from epistemic probability. If the idea of a phenomenon having a cause is "unthinkable in intellectual terms" (Jung, 1952/1969, para. 967), then the phenomenon may have to be classed as acausal in its own right, but it still makes sense to accept the phenomenon, such that (in the case of synchronicity) the meaningful connection has its own degree of validity, and indeed is a self-defining factor (which is how the coincidence drew attention in the first place).

No doubt, there are (or will be) problems understanding certain kinds of coincidence in this way, and these will have profound *ontological* and *epistemological* ramifications on the viability of psi,[53] and more generally synchronicity and its place in a scientific framework for which Jung wished to make a case. Nevertheless, from the above discussion, the following statement suggests itself: *The unique and detailed, ostensibly synchronistic experience draws serious attention from the experient, but only a large (frequent) number of them gains scientific interest*. In the latter case, it helps if the phenomena are objectively observable. In the end, we make of the phenomenon what we will: The experient thinks *epistemically*; the empiricist thinks *statistically*.

This whole section on chance sees the various points raised above converge on a key issue already considered: Mill's "often or seldom" remark, which is mirrored in the great variability of effect sizes demonstrated in psi research. A mountain of published literature has accrued since the 1930s, and I would argue that this body of work could lead researchers to make appeals not only on behalf of psi but also synchronicity, given the parallel made by Jung (1952/1969, para. 965).[54] At the apex of this mountain are the meta-analyses. In its most basic form, meta-analysis is "the statistical analysis of the summary findings of many empirical studies" (Glass, McGaw, & Smith, 1981, p. 21). By combining the data from a number of studies featuring the same (or similar) experimental design, meta-analysis produces an increased dataset that may be analysed to yield a more powerful result. It is a form of data reduction—investigators overwhelmed by the mass of published evidence for and against any given effect want to be able to reduce that volume to a manageable yet comprehensive list of studies that can be reduced further to a statistic, or a handful of statistics, that tells us what that mountain of publications means.

Before I go into more detail on the meta-analyses in relation to the chance factor, I must say that if chance were a beast, rather than a "little god", as Camille Flammarion called it (1900, as cited in Inglis, 1990, p. 1), it would make a low-maintenance pet (albeit an undisciplined one) because its very existence is dependent upon null results; paradoxically, it thrives on "nothing"; the zero effect. Continuing the metaphor, the only problem with this animal is that it cannot swallow a statistical result of "substance"; one that deviates too far from zero (where zero means "no effect"). It has some tolerance, and can make dismissive remarks about sufficiently small effects but, at the end of the day, chance (and the closed-minded psi skeptic) cannot digest significant effects if they are overly challenging. For all practical purposes, "significance" (a term used in statistics) means "not likely to be explained by chance".

What irks psi skeptics most is that the chance factor in most parapsychological meta-analyses is usually eliminated, based on a commonly used statistical rule that supports the likelihood of an effect if an inferential statistic derived from a given dataset has a corresponding chance probability of occurrence up to 5% (the "level of significance") under the condition that the null ("no-effect") hypothesis is true.[55] If the probability is greater than 5%, the observed result is not considered statistically significant (not enough evidence to conclude that the effect observed is real); it could reasonably occur by chance alone. However, there is up to a 5% risk that we may mistakenly conclude an effect exists when, in fact, there is no actual effect present. From this point on, I shall refer to this protocol as "the 5% rule" (not to be confused with the "Rule of Five").[56]

Over the decades, through the use of *statistical significance testing* (e.g., by using the 5% rule), the meta-analyses have repeatedly eliminated the chance factor in tests of paranormal effects. A full range of significant effects covering the meta-analyses of nine experimental psi domains have been tabled by

Storm and Thalbourne (2000). Magnitude of effect size can range from the very weak ("seldom") in Random Number Generator (RNG), dice-throwing, and "forced-choice" studies,[57] to moderate-to-strong ("often") in the case of ganzfeld,[58] and psi tests on living (biological) systems (a.k.a. DMILS = "direct [or distant] mental influence on living systems"; Braud & Schlitz, 1991, p. 3). Later reviews on the various meta-analyses saw very little change in the statistics, though as of late dream-ESP, remote viewing, and presentiment (a.k.a. predictive physiological anticipation) have taken the lead (see Cardeña, 2018b). So effects range from *seldom* to *often*, but more importantly they all occur *more often than can be explained by chance*. And there is more: Beyond card-guessing, picture-guessing, sheep-goat studies, and mental influence on physical systems, there are a number of significant relationships, including extraversion/ESP,[59] religiosity/ESP,[60] hypnosis/ESP,[61] perceptual-defensiveness/ESP.[62] Thus, skeptics who claim that chance explains psi have a bigger burden on their shoulders than merely attempting to dismiss psi-hitting; they must convincingly explain away all those significant relationships.

It is important to note, however, that synchronicity (with its key factors such as archetypes and meaningfulness) is not proven by these studies, and I stress that *only by inference* do the meta-analyses provide statistical support for synchronicity. However, there is *some* direct support for synchronicity (specifically as divination; one of the best ways of demonstrating synchronicity) for some studies on divination have positively contributed (as far as effects are concerned) to the meta-analytic databases (i.e., Storm & Tressoldi, 2017; Storm, Tressoldi, & Di Risio, 2012). The most voluminous, and also the most consistent evidence of a synchronistic effect, are the studies on the *I Ching*. I have spear-headed research in this area (Storm, 2001, 2002, 2006a, 2008a; Storm & Rock, 2014a, 2014b; Thalbourne & Storm, 2014—for details, see also the subsection *The Two Spatial Forms of Synchronicity* in Chapter 2, and Appendix B for examples), but some pioneering *I Ching* studies have been designed and conducted by others in the field, including Christopher Roe (Roe, Martin, & Drennan, 2014), and the two-man team James Houran and Rense Lange (Houran & Lange, 2012; Lange & Houran, 2013). These studies are not always conclusive, and there is an insufficient number of them to be making overtures about laboratory synchronicity.

If, however, we include psi research as evidence for synchronicity (as Jung would opine), the story changes, for psi meta-analyses stand as positive testimony that anomalous effects beyond chance exist and are therefore in need of explanation. On the facts, since the parapsychological literature is replete with reports of above-chance outcomes or effects (albeit nominally referred to as "psi", and rarely as synchronicity or meaningful coincidence), I suggest the frequency issue is (or can be) demonstrably resolved, and the argument from chance dissolved. All very fine, but my earlier points have shown there is more to synchronicity and psi than "statistical realism". It also seems to me Flew and Beloff both missed the opportunity to make the case for psi *as a synchronistic effect*, even if the role of archetypes and meaningfulness in psi tends to be poorly demonstrated. As I will argue later, this missed opportunity is more than an oversight as it would never occur to most parapsychologists to equate psi and synchronicity given the completely different theoretical premises thought to underlie the two. What I do also add to the debate is the suggestion that weak effects may indicate that there can be difficulty in constellating archetypes, but strong effects might indicate the occasional ease at which archetypes can be constellated (or let us say, testing synchronicity is not impossible) given that correspondences or 'hits' do seem to depend on archetypes being constellated (see Jung, 1952/1969, para. 841).

In closing, there are a number of ways of addressing problems associated with the chance factor, but the options can seem paradoxical. Taking a statistical approach, it has been argued that the truth in data can be concealed, and that probability, improbability, and frequency are concepts that need close scrutiny. Events, common or rare, "often" or "seldom" (Mill), can be chance occurrences, or actually mean something other than chance. We have found ways around this dichotomy, but we do not have the whole picture. Like other disciplines (biology, physics), conventional parapsychological thinking has to include issues other than appeals to a large, statistically supportive body of literature. It must also reckon with the *unthinkability* of acausal phenomena: *Epistemic probability* allows us to conceptualize the meaningful cross-connection (as but one example) that can stand as a rational proposition even when pitted against chance and causal factors. I give the last word on these points to a long-time colleague, the late Peter Delin:

> One might have thought that to the scientist, striving to obtain an objective view of the universe, a piece of evidence for a proposition would have a status independent of his previous opinions, but this is not so .... [H]e attaches a certain probability to the phenomenon or theory, and demands stronger or weaker evidence in accordance with this a priori probability.
>
> (1972/2002, p. 248)

This statement also applies to anyone 'doing stats' on psi and synchronicity, and I include all those mentioned in this section. And yet Delin's statement of many decades ago anticipated the now-common and popular statistical technique known as Bayesian inference. This procedure arrives at estimates of probability from likelihood ratios that are drawn from prior research findings or, for want of a better word, guesstimation, which is often based on opinion and belief, as Delin points out. However, as American statistician Andrew Gelman (2008) contends, "as scientists we should be concerned with objective knowledge rather than subjective belief" (p. 2). Unfortunately, when scientists work with opinion and subjective belief, they are "... working more or less in the dark", to quote British statistician Tony O'Hagan (as cited in Gelman, 2011). In this section, I not only raised questions about chance and statistical inference, I also put forward the claim that epistemic probability was a way around problems like subjective belief, much as other disciplines have shown (e.g., biology, physics).

Alternative Explanations of Synchronicity: II. The Law of Truly Large Numbers

Another ostensible explanation for synchronicity (and, in fact, psi phenomena) depends on an appeal to the Law of Truly Large Numbers, the explication of which may be seen as a continuation of the previous section on chance, except that the Law works with the absolute precision of a surgical knife, whereas the 5% rule is rather blunt.[63] Unfortunately for this Law, 'precise' does not mean 'accurate'.[64] This Law, as defined by John Allen Paulos (1991), is effected when the "difference between the probability of some event and the relative frequency with which it occurs necessarily approaches zero" (p. 39). If that sounds pretentious, that's because it is—buried in statistical verbiage, it simply means "any outrageous thing is likely to happen" provided one has a "large enough sample" (Diaconis & Mosteller, 1989, p. 859).

Telling is the fact that Paulos does not seem obligated to explain how one is supposed to get around the problem inherent in situations/events where probabilities and relative frequencies cannot be calculated. Furthermore, as Sober (2012) points out, "it isn't true … that any outrageous thing is likely to happen with enough trials" (p. 371). And getting a "large enough sample" is almost tantamount to saying 'seek and ye shall find' or 'if at first you don't succeed, try, try again'. Perhaps that is why the Church has a patron saint for lost causes; namely, Saint Jude!

Yet Cambridge logician and mathematician John Venn (1866), in his book *The Logic of Chance*, argued: "There can be no doubt that, however unlikely an event may be, … if … we keep on trying hard enough, we shall meet with such an event at last" (p. 274). Similarly, there are multiple opportunities for any piece of random or imagined information to be true of someone when psychics read for a large audience (Barker, 2022). Note that John Venn also argued that any given work by Milton or Shakespeare could be composed by chance merely by a single man drawing out letters of the alphabet from a bag—given sufficient time!—or, the modern variant, a monkey on a typewriter. Philosopher Herbert Spencer put his own unique twist on the Law by claiming: "If meaningless coincidences are thus frequent, there must occasionally occur coincidences that have meaning" (as cited in Duncan, 1908/1911, p. 372). In other words, Spencer suggests we must expect meaningful coincidences to filter out of the dross purely by chance, so we ought not make too much of them.

Having defined the Law rather cryptically, Paulos (1991) then argues it is reasonable and appropriate to represent whole domains of psi phenomena (in fact, parapsychology in its entirety) by a single psi phenomenon, so that debunking the one, debunks them all—that single psi phenomenon is precognition in the guise of premonitory dreams (which I feature here since we learned above that paranormal dreams can be classed as synchronicity). Indulging Paulos for the moment, he notes (rather stoically) that coincidences of people's premonitory dreams of natural disasters with the actual real-life disasters are "unimpressive" and to be expected. Speaking of the US population in the 1990s, he stated: "[g]iven the half billion hours of dreaming each night in this country—2 hours a night for 200 million people—we should expect as much" (p. 187). His argument sounds remarkably similar to the argument in the section above about chance groupings, whether that be for birthdays, the two pipe-smokers, or the Buxton girls. Statistically, a vast number of topics, themes and scenarios in people's dreams would be covered in the time available—especially with so many people (that's the "large enough sample") with different backgrounds, different problems, and real-life issues on their minds. Any match with real-world events is inevitable and inconsequential—neither paranormal causation, nor for that matter "inconstant connection", meaningful coincidence, or synchronicity, need be postulated to explain these alleged anomalous matches.

Ultimately, the principle underlying the Law of Truly Large Numbers carries with it the implication that now more than ever, with over seven billion people on the planet, there are more *meaningless* coincidences than ever before being passed off as meaningful. A similar argument is run by mathematician J. E. Littlewood (1953), who claims that "miraculous" (surprising) events with odds of one in a million are quite regular and occur for each of us once every 35 days. But what makes them "miraculous" or "surprising", to use Littlewood's words? Mathematician Warren Weaver (1963) reminds us that "an event is *surprising* only providing its probability is very small as compared with the probabilities of the other accessible alternatives" (pp. 293–294). For example, a coin landing on its side is surprising. Otherwise, an event may be *rare*, but not *surprising*. Thus, a winning hand of cards dealt first time is not surprising because it is only one of many that are equally likely, but we may consider it rare. But in synchronicity, there can be other (non-statistical) reasons for rarity (e.g., archetypes do not constellate easily or on demand).

Weaver (1963) adds that a *rare* event is only *interesting* if the experient thinks so. It is tacit in Weaver's remarks that the experient's interest is governed by circumstance and contingency. More broadly, then, the Law embodies the clear assumption that paranormal outcomes (psi, synchronicity), no matter what impression they make on the individual, are meaningless (or may as well be thought of as meaningless) on probabilistic grounds because they can arise from time to time. Therefore, as far as the critic of synchronicity is concerned, what makes an event *interesting* (i.e., meaningful) is nothing other than the interest it holds for the individual, which is generated from within the individual's life situation, thus making the meaning *a posteriori* at best, or more likely *ad hoc*. However, as we are given to understand Jung's

(1952/1969, para. 942) position on synchronicity, the meaning in synchronicity is *a priori* based on its archetypal substructure. The statistician cannot speak to that issue.

It is ironic that Flew (1953) effectively undermines the Law when he argues that *all* coincidences "are necessarily both 'non-causal' and 'meaningful'" (p. 198). For Flew, labelling synchronicity as *meaningful* coincidence is "to utter a tautology" (p. 199), for every coincidence is a "pair or set of occurrences, ... [for which] there is something remarkable about their coming together" (p. 198). We seem to be at an impasse here, for the Law tells us the exact opposite: there are events (coincidences) that happen together by chance (i.e., they are merely probable), but they are all meaningless *for the very reason that they happen by chance.* Perhaps Flew means something 'notable' happens in a coincidence, and he would probably say that the meaning is in the implication one can draw from the irony of the situation, the oddity of the moment, the ease at which a conclusion can be reached based on the *contiguity* or *falling together* of events, all of which can give the experience some kind of meaning. Then Flew could be correct if we can speak of those factors as the binding and defining element of *all* coincidences. In that sense, though, this interpretation would not be satisfactory to Jung because that meaning would not be *meaningful* as defined synchronistically. Rather than indiscriminately using the word meaningful to describe *all* coincidences, Flew would probably have fared better if he accepted the very concession he makes that archetypes "are to be built in as *part of the meaning of* synchronicity" (p. 199).

My previous points can be extended even further to the absolutism of the Law whereby it is possible to dispense with considerations of meaning or meaningfulness *in any outcome.* The cracks in the Law begin to show for its absolutism precludes the possibility of other explanations that may be deemed preferable for various phenomena or findings. Paulos (1991), and Diaconis and Mosteller (1989), imply that the Law is the tool of choice for identifying those events that are *a priori* meaningless because they claim these occur by chance in a long-enough run. Venn, and Spencer (both cited above), are of a similar mindset. However, it is possible to apply the Law more generally (not just to claims of psi and synchronicity) so that the scientific method becomes devalued. By such a statistical law one can say that if enough trials are run, if enough samples are taken, if an experiment is repeated often enough, the result one wants is not only probable, but highly likely.[65] By this reasoning, one is even free to believe that a first observation, a first trial, a first run, or a first experiment, may yield a result that should be considered a *mere* (casual or chance) coincidence—especially if the result challenges our causal worldview, or in fact, even if it is believable and well within normal experience and our expectations. And it does not matter how meticulous the experimenter is, or how good the experimenter thinks the tested theory is, or how well designed the study is, or that the test apparatus is fault-free. Of course, repeated experimentation (and replication) is supposed to determine whether or not these 'coincidences' are to be taken as new facts about the world, but that is not so easily achieved. For example, a team of almost 200 psychologists tried to replicate the findings of 28 published psychological experiments, but their best efforts only yielded a 50% success rate (Yong, 2018). But the replication problem in other disciplines (e.g., economics, medicine) is also of considerable concern (Bohannon, 2016; Ioannidis, 2005). Parapsychology is not alone in this problem (Utts, 1999).

Since the Law's weakness is that it can be broadly misapplied, one ultimately has to apply a *determination of meaning* to an outcome in order to be rid of the problem of the Law. This point about *meaning* supports Jung's view on synchronicity; meaning is the fourth element missing in the "triad" of science (see Jung, 1952/1969, para. 960–964). In fact, scientists *do* appeal to the meaning of a finding more often than they may care to admit, but evidently not to the degree that they feel it needs to be incorporated into science as a fundamental principle (as Jung intended), antithetical to, and independent of, causality.[66]

To summarize, the Law of Truly Large Numbers only speaks to *frequency* (what is possible given many *hypothesized* events), not *order* (what might be expected on a *given* occasion). While the statistically-minded should thus be at a loss if only a single event is available for scrutiny, precognitive dreamers can make their own judgements based on how the dream events unfold in time. Appealing to the Law can be a strategy by which the sceptical statistician deals with an inconvenience. In some instances, we must reserve judgement and await further evidence, and it would be to those instances that we may apply meaning. But there may also be times when investigators (and dreamers) *can* draw conclusions about their findings, simply because they can answer the question, What has been found that actually *means* something? Indeed, something that can be put to good use, thus requiring that they ignore the Law altogether.

Alternative Explanations of Synchronicity: III. False Memory Syndrome and Other Inanities

In this section, I will give some attention to the arguments from false memory syndrome, lying (a.k.a. fraud), and issues of that ilk. Skeptics resorting to these explanations often do so in a dismissive manner, without acknowledging that the burden of proof is on them. By inane, I do not mean these alternative explanations do not carry *any* weight under *any* circumstances; in some psychological situations, they make sense, but logic tells us that not all synchronicity experients are fabricating or reconstructing their memories unwittingly; nor are they all liars, fraudsters, daydreamers, or incompetents. Nevertheless, these arguments should be scrutinized for their feasibility.

Synchronicities tend to come in such diverse forms, it may be a stretch to propose that a complex series of events could be misremembered, but it is possible. Therefore, as far-fetched as the hypothesis of false memory syndrome may be in this instance (i.e., as an explanation for synchronicity), it is possible that a person claiming synchronicity might be 'remembering' a series of events that never really happened, even though they firmly believe it did, or they erringly collate a disparate set of similar events and misremember them as being related—even philosopher and premonitory dreamer, J. W. Dunne (1927) made the latter concession, albeit unconvincingly.

The term false memory syndrome (FMS) proposes that false memories can result from a diverse range of therapeutic techniques (e.g., hypnosis, guided imagery, sedatives, etc.) that actually encourage confabulations (Olio, 2004). We might imagine it possible to concoct an ideal synchronicity in the ways just described, but we face a few problems: First, while FMS usually concerns recovered memories during intense forms of therapy, accounts of synchronicity are never presented as if they were *recovered* this way, or by any other technique. They may be described by psychiatrists or analysts as material that has emerged in session (as in the scarab case), but the accounts are freely given, and not as by-products of the therapeutic process as is similarly the case with abreaction or those 'breakthrough' moments sought by clinicians. Indeed, Coleman and Beitman (2009) found that their sample of high-frequency synchronicity experients "did not reflect a level of schizotypal thinking characteristic of individuals in a clinical sample" (p. 278). Also, most accounts of synchronicity are described in locales as remote from the clinical setting as one can get, and not under the guidance of a clinician (as in Swedenborg describing the Stockholm fire to dinner party guests).

Second, we often find that recovered memories are trauma-related, but few accounts of synchronicity contain references to trauma. Affect is usually an element of synchronicity (as, for example, with the Evans's fiancé case), but synchronistic emotional responses invariably result from numinosity, or concern for others who are in danger, but not from recovery of long-forgotten trauma. While we might still allow for the remote possibility that FMS could explain rare instances of synchronicity, I suggest only the most ardent skeptic would appeal to it to explain synchronicity.

Proponents of the argument from lying/fraud imply, if they do not outrightly state, that synchronicity experients simply make up their stories to get attention, or to promote a New Age agenda, or to make money and/or to achieve notoriety. That argument is not easily disproved. This situation recalls the many cases from the Victorian-era parapsychological literature (and occasionally today), such as cold-, warm-, and hot-reading,[67] and séance shenanigans, which are often debunked, or looked at askance for good reason. Fraudulent synchronicity may be harder to debunk, except that there are numerous cases where the focus person (e.g., Swedenborg) had multiple witnesses, so it is very difficult to run the argument from lying or fraud in such cases (in relation to this issue, see Toksvig [1948] whose analysis is both detailed and convincing).

To this section can be added a few more alternative explanations for synchronicity that, for the strong cases of synchronicity, miss the mark and detract from the more important message that synchronicity is a class of experience in its own right. These alternative explanations include *apophenia*, the *availability heuristic*, and the *representativeness heuristic*. These explanations are not confined to fantasy-prone daydreamers or delusional types.

Apophenia was brought to prominence by German psychiatrist Klaus Conrad (1905–1961). It concerns the misinterpretation of innocuous phenomena as having inherent meaning merely because normal perceptual processes create connections that are not there (Conrad, 1959). In extreme cases, it has been taken as a sign of paranoid schizophrenia (Shiel, 2020). Apophenia embraces *pareidolia* (which focuses on visual phenomena), and generally refers to unwarranted assertions of meaning in meaningless data, or misperceived pattern detection such as seeing faces in random stimuli such as clouds, smoke, or burnt toast (Sagan, 1997). These connections or relations are purely accidental, but nonetheless are typical responses derived from fundamental cognitive functions. Apophenia can explain outlandish hidden meanings, and "overfitting" (i.e., statistical modelling that fits the noise of a limited dataset, but misses the signal that actually exists in the population from which the data is drawn).

At a clinical level, particularly salient examples of apophenia are evident where psychosis or paranoia prevail, and these experiences can be disturbing, even terrifying. Mishlove and Engen (2007) concur that the problem of apophenia does exist, but they "remain unpersuaded that the phenomenon of apophenia can adequately account for all ostensibly paranormal experiences" (p. 237). In truth, any parapsychologist can see the sense in that statement. Mishlove and Engen extend their argument especially to synchronicity, and make the intriguing point that blunt and sweeping declarations to do with errors in judgement may eliminate effects that are genuinely there in the environment and have legitimate parallels in human experience. Critically, however, apophenia is a very poor excuse for synchronicity because 'apophenics' are not playing by the rules of synchronicity where they are expected to carry an *a priori* inner image in consciousness that will resonate with a real-world event. It may be the limited reality testing skills of the apophenia-prone observer that helps facilitate a spuriously meaningful interpretation of an otherwise meaningless phenomenon, but the meaning is derived from an *a posteriori* image of convenience that pops into the head of the apophenic—by definition, the encounter simply does not qualify as synchronicity, and so, *in phenomenological terms,* apophenia cannot be used as an explanation for it.

It is likewise the case with the *availability heuristic* and the *representativeness heuristic*, which can also be over-applied (Tversky & Kahneman, 1974). To deploy the availability heuristic is to estimate the frequency of an event in terms of recency, familiarity, and vividness of the experience. Whatever most easily comes to mind, because it is recent, or familiar, or vivid, becomes the reference point for making a judgement. In such an instance, a person might (falsely) think they can predict that a certain friend is calling on the phone when it rings, but the successful prediction is only due to that friend being a frequent caller. While that can happen, studies that have controlled for that heuristic have still yielded significant psi effects (e.g., Sheldrake & Smart, 2003a; Sheldrake, Godwin, & Rockell, 2004), although the effect has not always been replicated (Schmidt, Müller, & Walach, 2004).

That other 'rule of thumb', the representativeness heuristic, is adopted when we fail to realize that extreme outcomes can easily and randomly arise in small samples—for example, it might be a mistake to think that five hits in five trials has special psychic or synchronistic significance if further testing over a very long run sees the hit rate return to MCE as statistical law would dictate. This heuristic accounts for the so-called gambler's fallacy (i.e., the erroneous belief that a particular event that has occurred more frequently than is perceived to be normal must give way to other possible events within that system).[68] The problem with appealing to this heuristic is that real-world events are sometimes limited to a single 'trial' (e.g., the typical synchronicity), or only a few 'trials', with no absolute means of proving that we are *only* dealing with random fluctuations in the flow of events.

Given these points, it remains generally true that 'error theories' are not able to make necessary exceptions to those genuine scientific anomalies that could prove to be of the greatest importance to our understanding. The broad applicability of the Law of Truly Large Numbers works in exactly the same absolutist way in that the advocate may end up 'throwing the baby out with the bath-water', as explained in previous paragraphs.

Main (2004) sees these two *heuristics* as being amongst the more salient of alternative theoretical explanations of synchronicity, and he adds cryptomnesia to the list. Cryptomnesia is recall of a forgotten memory, with one proviso—the memory is not thought to be one's own, and is therefore thought to have a source outside one's being. Naturally, the notion of a paranormal experience (telepathy, clairvoyance, etc.) may then be unnecessarily invoked. When cryptomnesia occurs, however, it is usually identified as such by friends, or family, or the clinician, notwithstanding the fact that the mistake may dawn on the individual at a later date. More to the point, experiments like those of Sheldrake and Smart (2003a), and Sheldrake et al. (2004), control for cryptomnesia.

It may be worthwhile giving a brief mention to the so-called *illusion of control*. Some individuals may feel they can rig an outcome outside their sphere of influence that extends well beyond the parameters of parapsychological expectation (given that typical psi effects are notoriously weak). The illusion of control might be proposed as an explanation for intentional synchronicity (discussed in Chapter 2, "Types of Synchronicity"), where the individual believes he or she can have such a psychokinetic influence that the ever-present random forces that usually prevail are subverted. This practice surely still occurs in gambling situations where the dice-thrower believes blowing on the dice, or throwing them a certain way, can have a favourable effect. Such practices may prevail on the casino floor, and even in games of chance, but most people would consider it superstitious behaviour for good reason. Also, there is a unique ethical consideration in synchronistic *praxis* (as in *I Ching* usage) whereby attempts to subvert the process completely miss the point of trying to bring into effect an authentic meaningful coincidence (for further discussions on the limits of intention, see Chapter 2).

While Main (2004, pp. 27–35) has put forward a range of alternative explanations for synchronicity (the major ones having just been covered here), he also claims that synchronicity is a genuine phenomenon for three reasons, which he calls "principal qualities": Synchronicity is (i) "grounded in empirical considerations"; (ii) "experienced as meaningful"; and (iii) "transpersonal" or "spiritual" in nature (p. 34). Main argues that the alternative explanations do not account for all three principle qualities. The prevalence of archetypal factors in the context of these qualities is not overt, but it will be seen later that synchronicity theory, insofar as it is grounded in paranormal and holistic considerations, depends on archetypal factors to firm up that ground (for a particular example, see Chapter 4).

Last but not least, we must consider the psychological defense mechanism of projection and the role it might play in generating experiences that have only the patina of synchronicity. I feel it is relevant to discuss this mechanism here although, for some reason, Main (2004) does not present it as an alternative explanation (although see Main, 2007, on "projection of meaning"; p. 76). As I said earlier, Jung described projection as a *regressive* flow of psychic energy (ego to Self) that enlivens an unconscious content (an inner image), whereas synchronicity is a *progressive* flow of psychic energy (Self to ego) towards consciousness and the external world. Without being aware of this difference, something synchronicity-like might seem to manifest if the 'strangeness' or alien nature of an unconscious content is immediately disowned and regarded as 'other', and a suitable hook is therefore sought, or happens to present itself by chance. As a consequence, there can be a resonance between the internal image and external image (the hook) due to the similarity. As I suggested earlier, it is in this sense that pseudo-numinosity can be an offspring of the delusional state. Of course, any correspondence or parallel that results from the projection-making factor is arbitrary.

How do we know a supposedly genuine experience of synchronicity is not a delusional state? Ordinarily, any confusion should be preventable in the sense that synchronicity is its own safety-net:

> [... synchronicity has a way of undermining, though not necessarily eliminating, projection because the inner (psychological) state is made known to us, or how else could we experience it as synchronicity in the first place? With projection, on the one hand, we have to go to great

> efforts to catch ourselves out doing it, whereas synchronicity, on the other hand, somehow relinquishes us of that responsibility (though the responsibility then becomes an issue of deciding what to do with the experience).
>
> (Storm, 2008e, p. 251)

Though true under ideal circumstances, *deciding what to do with the experience* involves reflection and realization (if not, wise counsel), and the safety-net of synchronicity can fail if these resources do not kick in, or are unavailable to such types as those who are naïve, paranoid, or psychotic. Von Franz points out that people like that, even when they do experience true synchronicity, may be projection-prone so their synchronicity might be interpreted incorrectly for meaning as a direct result of their pathological condition (for an example, see von Franz, 1997, pp. 196–197). In those instances, the individual cannot see through the delusion brought on by (say) morbid fantasies or wishful thinking. In the case of a non-synchronistic experience thought to be synchronicity, projection may be evident in the same way described above in the case of apophenia, where the inner content appears *a posteriori* purely out of convenience to fit, say, a curious environmental stimulus—that is not how synchronicity works by definition. Generally, the implausibility of projection as an explanation for synchronicity becomes clear when we realize that vast numbers of synchronicities are not experienced by individuals nursing various psychopathologies (for some statistics, see the next section), including projection-proneness (I made a similar claim at the beginning of this section in regard to FMS).

It needs stating that the onus is on the serious investigator to deliver judgements about ostensible synchronicity on a case-by-case basis, but not to make sweeping or dismissive generalizations, or jump too quickly to whatever heuristic seems to fit the bill. Even in well-meaning common-sense deliberations, when none of the above explanations seem to fit, we may witness the deployment (even by mental health professionals) of counter-measures such as the 'near-miss' heuristic ('not even close'), the normalization heuristic ('narrative adjustment' or tweaking the account), the parsimony heuristic ('finding a logical explanation'), and so on, all aimed at managing (i.e., dismissing, debunking, devaluing) anything remotely anomalous. (For further comments on these sorts of explanations, see Beitman, 2022.)

On the Problem of Credulous Belief

I will now deal with another concern that could be raised whenever claims of synchronicity are made: Belief-based credulity, referring in this instance to *beliefs in synchronistic phenomena* based on social and/or psychological disposition or predisposition, such that the beliefs may be unfounded, there being no generally accepted proof or overwhelming evidence underpinning those beliefs (to take a skeptical position). I must note that credulous belief is not simply about false beliefs; a belief may be justified after having been verified, but the credulous believer is one who prematurely believes in such a belief *prior to gaining good evidence for it*. That is a problem in its own right, but I will not deal with it here, having touched on the issue of verification in the section above on diagnostic tools. In this section, I will play devil's advocate, and not generally take synchronicity for granted, but will assume as a possibility that a *report* of synchronicity (the actual *claim*) is questionable—this is *alleged* experience not necessarily covered by any of the alternative explanations above—or a belief is held but no direct experience accounts for it. This section, therefore, offers explanations as to why it is *thought*, or why it is *believed* synchronicity did or can take place. Given the aims of this book, I will regard *belief* in (meaningful) coincidences as a particular instance of a more general *belief* in paranormal phenomena, given that the two are often tested together (Blackmore, 1997; Bressan, 2002; Henry, 1993).

There is next to no research on belief in synchronicity or, by its other name, meaningful coincidence (the few exceptions include Coleman et al., 2009; Moore, Thalbourne, & Storm, 2010; Storm & Thalbourne, 2018). But it is fair to say that we can make inferences about that particular kind of belief from the general findings about *belief in, and experience of paranormal phenomena*, which I will call 'paranormal belief' for convenience. Irwin (2009) has described four hypotheses that have been developed by various researchers over the years to help explain how paranormal beliefs are formed: (1) the 'social marginality' hypothesis, which was formulated primarily by sociologists (e.g., Bainbridge, 1978; Wuthnow, 1976); (2) the 'worldview' hypothesis which has historical, even ancient antecedents (see Zusne & Jones, 1982, 1989); (3) the 'cognitive deficits' hypothesis (see Alcock, 1981); and (4) the 'psychodynamic functions' hypothesis (see Katz, 1960; Taylor, 1983).

1 *The social marginality hypothesis*: Believers are seen as "isolated" in some way (e.g., by age, gender, socioeconomic status, ethnicity, or culture, etc.) so that belief acts as a buffer to the vicissitudes of a life so often associated with marginal status. After an extensive literature review, Irwin and Watt (2007, pp. 225–227) report that this hypothesis has not been supported.
2 *The worldview hypothesis*: Believers hold paranormal belief as only one subjective and esoteric aspect of a much broader picture of life, humanity, and the world in general, where mental and metaphysical religious beliefs and practices are incorporated into that worldview. According to Irwin and Watt (2007, pp. 227–229), there is partial support for this hypothesis.
3 *The cognitive deficits hypothesis*: Believers are said to have uncritical, naïve, and irrational thought processes based on deficits in education, lower average levels of intelligence and poor reasoning skills. Evidence for this aspect of the hypothesis is inconclusive at this stage (Irwin & Watt, 2007, pp. 229–231). Believers may also have overly creative imaginations,

and there is some support for this aspect of the hypothesis (Irwin & Watt, 2007, pp. 231–232).

4 *The psychodynamic functions hypothesis*: Believers are seen as being in some way psychologically disadvantaged or maladapted, or socially deviant in respect of their personality characteristics so that paranormal belief is seen as fulfilling a psychodynamic need. There is "general support" for this hypothesis, but Irwin and Watt (2007) propose that a "specific version of the hypothesis that posits more precisely the nature of the psychodynamics involved" is required (pp. 232–234).

Overall, there is some evidence supporting the last three hypotheses (see also Thalbourne, 2010), with particularly strong support from the correlational studies testing the psychodynamic functions hypothesis. In that respect, claiming to be a paranormal experient may tend to be the result of inadvertent distortions of actual events based on certain mental dysfunctions. Generally, however, when any of the four hypotheses do garner support, the relationships between paranormal belief/experience and their numerous correlates tend to be weak-to-moderate in strength, which means the *variance* (i.e., the scoring range) in paranormal belief is only partly explained by those correlates, and not to a very large degree, even when these correlates work in tandem as predictors (see Billows & Storm, 2016).

There may be some justification to consider belief/experience in synchronicity in a similar light as paranormal belief/experience, for those who reported a high number of synchronistic experiences "ranked themselves as [significantly] more religious and more spiritual than low scorers" (Beitman, Celebi, & Coleman, 2010, p. 468), which aligns with the worldview hypothesis. Indeed, most examples of synchronicity in the literature do not appear to come from psychologically disturbed or cognitively compromised individuals. For example, one study in particular, with a very large sample (N = 750) comprised of students, faculty, and staff of the University of Missouri, showed that a very high 85.5% reported having a meaningful coincidence, albeit to varying degrees ranging from "seldom" to "very frequently" (Beitman et al., 2010; Coleman et al., 2009). Given such a large majority, we would hardly expect widespread maladjustment. Such high proportions are way in excess of figures for paranormal belief/experience: For instance, less than half as many participants (42%) in a study at a British university experienced *at least* one paranormal occurrence (Dagnall et al., 2016), and findings are comparable elsewhere (e.g., Germany, United States, Latin America; see Drinkwater et al., 2021).

Beitman et al. (2010) found a majority of participants (63% and 74%) in two surveys (Ns = 330+) reported that their meaningful coincidences helped them "grow spiritually" (see also Roxburgh, Ridgway, & Roe, 2015). That response suggests the experience itself was beneficial, though the paper does not state whether (or how many) experients sought professional guidance.

After all, some experients do obtain immediate therapeutic gain, or seek psychotherapeutic assistance, with analyses of the coincidences being a usual part of the therapy (Beitman et al., 2010; Jung, 1952/1969; Schwartz, 2008). If we can make inferences from the data, such findings suggest that a not-so-novel therapeutic approach of some import might justifiably be incorporated into mainstream mental health practice (as argued by Beitman et al.). My previous remark about knee-jerk debunking by mental health professionals becomes particularly pertinent. Of course, many other experients are quite capable of reaching their own unaided understanding outside the therapeutic domain. Beitman (2022) lists a number of benefits that can emerge from meaningful coincidence, including aids to decision-making, decision reformation, and need-serving. In closing, the worldview hypothesis does not fully explain synchronistic belief due to the complexity and potential validity of synchronistic experience.

***

To summarize the major points of this chapter, synchronicity is the "simultaneous occurrence of a certain psychic state with one or more external events which appear as meaningful parallels to the momentary subjective state—and, in certain cases, vice versa" (Jung, 1952/1969, para. 850). These events are *acausally* connected; not causally linked—i.e., there is no demonstrable cause-and-effect relationship.

There is a characteristic numinosity to the synchronistic experience that is concomitant with affect (feeling or emotion), which tends to resonate with the experient at a deeply personal level, resulting in a shift in outlook. In such cases, synchronicity comes at just the right time for the person who may have reached a hiatus or crisis in his or her life—synchronicity can provide the impetus for change or action.

Synchronicity may not be easily differentiated from meaningless chance groupings, so tools are needed to discern the difference between the two: Jung's four psychological functions can be employed to draw out important distinctions.

It may be argued that determinations of meaning are subjective. Relatively speaking, this claim is inadequate as it does not speak to all the data. We can envisage a spectrum of meanings ranging from the subjective to the objective as meaning becomes less personal and more archetypal.

Explanations of synchronicity based on the laws of chance and truly large numbers, or fraud, or aberrant memory and/or compromised mental functions, are not entirely persuasive. The synchronicity experience is characteristically unique for the individual, whereas statistical rules and averaging techniques tend to swallow up that uniqueness. Perhaps as a consequence, many critics of synchronicity are not interested in arguing that belief in synchronicity and claimed experiences of such indicate misjudgements, mental aberrations, misinterpretations, and so on. Instead, they try to debunk synchronicity at the grass-roots (theoretical) level. In the next chapter and subsequent chapters, the analysis of synchronicity will continue along those lines, and in other ways, in order to achieve greater clarity of the synchronicity concept.

Notes

1 Generally, Jung uses the term "psychic" to mean "of the psyche"; not "paranormally gifted". However, Jung's usage of the term is context-bound. In particular, his *Synchronicity* essay shows considerable ambiguity, to the degree that the reader could think Jung is talking about one thing or another (psyche *or* psi), or both simultaneously.

2 A fire case was described by Icelandic researcher Erlendur Haraldsson, who noted the similarities with the Swedenborg case. Haraldsson (2011) reports on Icelandic physical medium Indridi Indridason, who channeled a once-living man named "Emil Jensen". In November 1905, Jensen claimed, through Indridason (in Reykjavik), that a lamp factory fire was burning in Copenhagen at that very moment, which was later verified. Jensen had lived near the site of the Copenhagen fire, but had died in 1898.

3 I use the term "fuzziness" in the same way as Croft and Cruse (2004), and May et al. (1990).

4 See also B. D. Beitman's descriptions in "Forms of Synchronicity" (Chapter 2).

5 Mansfield (1995) identifies three misconceptions about synchronicity: it is not "solely subjective" (p. 35); it is not "magic" (pp. 35–36); and it is not a "product of the ego" (p. 36). While these *do* define what synchronicity is not, Mansfield is not here demarcating the key differences between the two types of coincidence (the "meaningful" ones and the "meaningless" ones).

6 The above case of the pipe-smokers is completely fabricated for illustrative purposes, so testing the odds of a match on so many details is ultimately impossible because we lack much vital information. For example, we do not know the first name they share, and the chance of a match on first names is entirely dependent on how common the first name is.

7 Surprisingly, in a sample of 4470 different kinds of coincidences, shared birthdays are the most common, constituting 11% of the sample.

8 Browne (2017) does not mean one inventor mysteriously influenced (caused) all the other inventors to "simultaneously" invent the same invention (the effect).

9 I note as a casual coincidence that I cite here two authors by the surname "Browne".

10 The term "coincidentiality" is defined as "the underlying principle, or state or condition indicating a concurrence of events or circumstances with no apparent causal connection" (Storm & Thalbourne, 2018, p. 64). I note the use of the word "coincidentiality" in the study by Johansen and Osman (2015, p. 41), where it is undefined but appears to be used in the same sense. Storm and Thalbourne independently coined the term to describe a single factor resulting from factor analysis. This definition is a catch-all (neutral) term for coincidences that fall into two categories: (i) meaningful coincidences—i.e., synchronicity (Jung, 1952/1969, para. 850), implied in the words "underlying principle"; and (ii) "meaningless chance groupings" (para. 846), which are covered by the terms 'state or condition'. Beitman (2022) would expand on (i) above to include serendipity, seriality, and simulpathity, as these are meaningful coincidences.

11 I am grateful to Laurence Browne for pointing out this Darwin/Wallace synchronicity.

12 I use the term "pseudo-numinous" to mean the experience (especially of meaningless chance groupings), despite first impressions, may or will ultimately lack the emotional power and intrigue that gives it an extra-mundane quality. (See also "Numinosity" in this chapter.)

13 Many other alternative terms for instincts are used these days, including "innate priming mechanisms", "innate releasing mechanisms", "fixed action patterns", and "modal action patterns".

14 For more in-depth discussion about archetypes, see the chapter "The Archetype of Number" (Storm, 2008e, pp. 19–31), which also addresses some of the usual criticisms made against Jung's theory of archetypes.
15 For most of the 19th century, the optimistic works of Charles Dickens compensated for the one-sidedness of his era as captured so well by Emily Brontë in *Wuthering Heights.* However, in the late-19th century, "literary realism" emerged, epitomized in the works of Henry James and Thomas Hardy, much to the chagrin of many, including author and literary critic Christopher Booker (2004). Today still, the ideal of a satisfactory resolution through archetypal processes is often absent in the modern novel. Plots invariably have a broken narrative structure; all hope is lost, and the reader is forced to deal with the consequences. Ironically, von Franz (1995) points out that many fairytales do not always end happily either, but that does not mean the situations are not archetypal.
16 I am grateful to Laurence Browne for bringing this story to my attention. The account gained widespread coverage, which included *The New York Times* in 2017.
17 For other ways in which dual-aspect monism differs from neutral monism, and the complications inherent in the latter, see https://plato.stanford.edu/entries/neutral-monism/
18 Danish physicist Niels Bohr actually regarded consciousness and the unconscious as a complementarity (see von Franz, 1992, p. 294). Jung (1960/1969) says as much: "As soon as a psychic content crosses the threshold of consciousness, the synchronistic marginal phenomena disappear, time and space resume their accustomed sway, and consciousness is once more isolated in its subjectivity. We have here one of those instances which can best be understood in terms of the physicist's idea of 'complementarity'" (para. 440).
19 When trying to illustrate the principle of complementarity underpinning dual-aspect monism, one should avoid using analogues such as the so-called Klein Bottle (Stillwell, 1993), the Möbius Strip (Pickover, 2005), and many of M. C. Escher's artworks (Ernst, 1978). Close inspection of these and other 'paradoxical objects' shows they fail to exhibit two fundamental aspects that confirm the complementarity; they are fundamentally unitary despite appearances.
20 In the original Freudian sense, projection is an ego defense mechanism aimed at ridding oneself of one's faults by seeing them in another person or object (Freud, 1988). Projection can be extended to apply in any instance where an unconscious content (e.g., one's own inner divinity or numinosity) is attributed to something "other" than oneself, but not seen in oneself—it is "the expulsion of a subjective content into an object" (Jung, 1921/1971, para. 783).
21 For Jung, Self = consciousness + the unconscious, and "designates the whole range of psychic phenomena in man [*sic*]" (1921/1971, para. 789).
22 Not all scholars are in agreement on the archetypal and transcendental aspects of synchronicity (e.g., Colman, 2011, 2012; Giegerich, 2012). While Colman and Giegerich are aligned in refuting this ultimate (fourth) level of meaning, they disagree with each other on the other levels of meaning and precisely where meaning is generated.
23 Jung's synchronicity quaternity refers to "Inconstant Connection [i.e., Synchronicity] through Contingence, Equivalence, or 'Meaning' " (para. 963). Jung is clearly flexible in his terminology so that "meaning-equivalence", "equivalence of meaning", and "meaningful equivalences" all have the same interpretation, albeit limited to the identification of similarity through correspondence of the "inner" and "outer" synchronistic elements. However, "meaningfulness" and "meaningful coincidence" are operative terms of prime importance, meant to convey an elevated notion of meaning (see also Mansfield, 1995).

24 "… also Synchronizitäten gibt, wo man also mit dem besten Willen in der Welt keinen Sinn herausfinden kann" (Schellinger, Wittmann & Anton, 2019, p. 450).
25 See "numinous" in Collins online dictionary (https://www.collinsdictionary.com/dictionary/english/numinous).
26 See "numinous" in OxfordDictionaries.com https://www.oxfordlearnersdictionaries.com/definition/american_english/numinous.
27 The "just-so" (archetypal) qualities of numbers extends to the structural units and laws of nature: Pauli sought a way forward in developing his Exclusion Principle by resorting to the "quaternity" symbol: "My way to the Exclusion Principle had to do with the difficult transition from three to four, namely with the necessity to ascribe to the electron a fourth degree of freedom (soon explained as spin) beyond the three translational ones" (Gieser, 2005, p. 191). On the problem of three and four, see the chapter 'From Three to Four' in Storm (2008e).
28 I discuss this problem further in Chapter 5 in the section "Remote Viewing and the Rashomon Effect".
29 For more on numinosity, see my review of Krippner et al. (2019) in the section "Towards a Synchronistic Understanding of Psi" in Storm (2025).
30 The problem of projection has not gone unnoticed by Mishlove and Engen (2007). See the section "Dark Psi and Dark Synchronicity" in Chapter 5.
31 By the expression "non-rational" is meant the formulation of the archetype concept transcends the sphere of a purely rational definition and includes emotional aspects. For our purposes, "non-rational" is preferred rather than "irrational" in order to avoid the opposition between rational and irrational, which could be misleading in this context.
32 Brooks's (2011) argument faulting Jung's use of Kantian ideas does not take this distinction into consideration.
33 For a better understanding of what Kant means by the terms *phenomenon* and *noumenon*, see Kant (1781/1952, pp. 96–99).
34 As a well-grounded science far removed from mere theoretical and speculative notions, quantum mechanics has revolutionized the electronics industry, making possible modern computers, smart phones, lasers, and atomic clocks (see Orzel, 2015).
35 Chapter 2 assesses Jung's 'wider' conception of synchronicity, and introduces 'forms' as synchronistic categories.
36 https://ourworldindata.org/explorers/coronavirus-data-explorer
37 See the section below, "Alternative Explanations of Synchronicity: II. The Law of Truly Large Numbers".
38 Browne (2017) plays Devil's advocate with the Jenkins case, making slight changes to the scenario for illustrative purposes. He does note that the *Revelation* and *Zechariah* visions differ quite substantially from each other, and from Jenkins's sightings, raising the issue of "fuzzy relations" to be raised in later chapters (see footnote 5 in Chapter 2; see also Chapter 3).
39 Though Jung never expressly refers to an interpretational procedure in any schematic or formal sense, the clues are evident.
40 Beitman (2016) also describes four steps of a "formal coincidence analysis" (pp. 225–226), but these steps (also in a different order) borrow from Main (2014) who in turn describes Aziz's 'levels of meaning'.
41 Main (2004) looks at the relationship between synchronicity and the Jungian functions and orientations, but only to "type" the experient on the basis of the synchronistic contents (pp. 16–17). My deployment of Jung's typology is aimed at helping to decide whether synchronicity did transpire in the first place.
42 Browne (2017) offers the insight that one's reasoning is helped by "*pre-rational* [associative, immature] and *post-rational* [transcendent] modes of cognition",

which he describes as "non-rational" though they are "not in themselves deviations of rationality" (p. 132). In this sense, the *pre-rational* and *post-rational* modes are closer to Jung's (1921/1971) Sensation and Intuition functions, respectively, which I treat separately.

43 The Thinking stage of the heuristic also hangs on making a decision as to whether the ostensible synchronicity is acausal or not. Acausality is not addressed too deeply in the synchronicity literature (see Storm, 2008d, for a consideration of the problem). The reader can find a treatment of the acausality issue in "The Trick of the Cause in Parapsychology" in Storm (2025).

44 In the same sense described here, intuition as a decision-making process has been tested successfully under laboratory conditions (see Lufityanto, Donkin, & Pearson, 2016).

45 While Alcock (1981) does raise the issue of belief here, I will refrain from looking at paranormal belief in the context of synchronicity until a later section in this chapter to avoid confusion.

46 Psi hitting and psi missing are, respectively, correctly and incorrectly guessing unknown targets more frequently than mean chance expectation.

47 The terms "sheep" and "goat" (applied to psi-believers and psi-skeptics, respectively) were adopted by Schmeidler from a New Testament simile that describes how a shepherd "separates the sheep from the goats" (Matthew 25:31–33). It is claimed that sheep tend to score significantly above mean chance expectation (MCE) on psi tasks, whereas goats tend to score at or below MCE. A sheep-goat effect is evident if there is a significant scoring difference between sheep and goats.

48 Watt (1990–1991) also gave a very thorough review of normal coincidence explanations, mostly drawing from two major sources (i.e., Diaconis & Mosteller, 1989; Tversky & Kahneman, 1974).

49 It is important to note that there are three ways to assign probability to an event; (i) the "classical" approach (where the probability of an outcome is $1/n$, as in 1/6 for any given dice roll); (ii) the "relative-frequency" approach (where a ratio is determined for the event of interest in the overall count); and (iii) the "subjective" approach (where a belief-based judgement is made about usually unrepeatable events). Rawlette's (2019a) method is subjective as it depends on a considerable amount of guesstimation.

50 For a practical development of this idea, see "False Positives and False Negatives" in Storm (2025).

51 Earlier, Beitman (2016) had shown interest in calculating coincidence probabilities, and gives an example that might be a "low-probability event" (p. 228). These days, he seems less interested in this approach.

52 Escolà-Gascón et al. (2023) touch upon this point when they refer to "anomalous cognition" and "statistical anomalies" (specifically their own significant findings and "similar observations" of others)—the latter are not evidence of the former. They state: "Such findings do not equate to explanations, so they do not establish the ontological reality of putative psi" (p. 17). They do not raise the important issue of epistemic probability, but only refer to the need for an "*adequate scientific explanation*" (p. 17).

53 Ontology refers to the verifiable nature of reality, being, causes, etc., and functions from either a realist or relativist framework; epistemology refers to knowledge, knowledge claims, theories, interpretations, beliefs, and opinions, and adopts either a subjective (emic) or an objective (entic) methodology.

54 I hope to make a stronger case for the psi/synchronicity parallels in later chapters.

55 If we wish to be more conservative, we can set the level of significance to 1% (or even smaller). Significance levels are always set prior to testing the data.

56 The "Rule of Five" gives a surprisingly high 93.75% certainty that an estimated median (mid-point) value of a population parameter is between the lowest value and the highest value of five cases taken at random (Hubbard, 2010).
57 A "forced-choice" test is a test of ESP where the target-guess is "one of a limited range of possibilities which are known in advance" (Thalbourne, 2003, p. 44).
58 The ganzfeld is a "special type of environment (or the technique for producing it) consisting of homogenous, unpatterned sensory stimulation" to the eyes and ears of the participant, who is usually in "a state of bodily comfort" (Thalbourne, 2003, p. 45).
59 Extraversion/ESP refers to the relationship between ESP performance and the personality variable extraversion, which is significantly positive (Eysenck, 1967). See also Honorton, Ferrari, and Bem (1998).
60 Religiosity is a construct measuring religion in a behavioural context (i.e., religious involvement; see Haraldsson, 1981). Religiosity/ESP refers to the relationship between religiosity and ESP, which is significantly positive (Haraldsson, 1993).
61 Hypnosis/ESP refers to the relationship between hypnosis induction and ESP performance, which is significantly positive (Stanford & Stein, 1994).
62 Perceptual defensiveness is a mental response to a subliminal threat that causes anxiety (Haraldsson, 1993). Perceptual-defensiveness/ESP refers to the relationship between perceptual defensiveness and ESP, which is significantly positive (Haraldsson & Houtkooper, 1995).
63 There is also the lesser Law of Large Numbers, concerned with testing the probabilities of theoretically determined outcomes. This Law comes in a "weak" and "strong" form, with the latter *more confidently* expressing the same principle as the former using different mathematical proofs; the principle being that a sample average will converge to an expected value.
64 Note that other limitations to the Law have been pointed out by mathematicians (see Dekking, 2005).
65 This argument has been run previously (Moore, Thalbourne, & Storm, 2010; Storm, 1999, 2008d). See also Sober (2012). Rawlette (2019a) runs with the same argument, illustrating it with two rather quaint examples (pp. 28, 40).
66 It is perhaps a step in the right direction that Nobel-Prize laureate and physicist Brian Josephson (Brian Josephson, 2018) recognises the lack of meaning in science, and he advocates an array of approaches whereby meaning can be incorporated into fundamental physics. Even so, he never mentions synchronicity.
67 Cold reading is basically guess-work on the part of the psychic, helped by direct and indirect cues and clues from the unsuspecting client, and thus appears as ESP (i.e., telepathy between cold-reading psychic and discarnate entity). Some psychics also practice warm reading, which relies on broad statements true of most people. And then there is hot reading (information collected before the sitting through prior research and even clandestine interactions with persons known to the sitter).
68 The gambler's fallacy is not entirely wrong thinking provided the gambler *confines his/her assertion to very long runs.* All possible outcomes have to make their statistically expected appearance at some time in the run for the relative frequencies to emerge. A world that happened to be otherwise would make the statistician's job impossible. In other words, in the long run, trends *do* have to end despite the independence of events.

Chapter 2

Types of Synchronicity

> "Chance and synchronicity will look the same in their display of an event but they are worlds apart .... Chance happens to us, synchronicity happens in us"
>
> David Richo (2007, p. 102)

When we put a name to an experience (i.e., categorize it), we feel we have uncovered a hidden truth. In this chapter, I discuss the processes of categorization in the context of meaningful coincidence, and coincidences in general. How far can we go in that process? Is the entire acausal world synchronistic? Do we need to (or can we even) extend synchronicity to a universal principle? Synchronicity takes various forms in terms of temporal, spatial, and personal factors. These forms are discussed using examples.

The Perils of Categorization

Putting a name to a problem is a form of categorization, and a pattern of behaviour well-represented as a central motif in myths and fairytales where the hero or heroine must find an answer to a question, or guess a name. There is a kind of liberation for the key figure who has broken the hold and found a direction, and so can complete the journey to recovery, freedom, or greater wisdom and understanding about self, others, and the world.

However, for all the good it can do, categorization can prove to be too arbitrary in its execution, or can be viewed as 'heroically' forcing restrictive or reductive explanations and interpretations on phenomena—a process which is a slippery slope. And since the literature often shows that heroes and heroines invariably fail the first time they attempt anything, we can assume that failure sometimes stems from getting the labelling wrong. We see this problem of questionable labelling in Delin's (2003) breakdown of coincidences as seen in three different senses A, B, and C:

> *coincidence in sense A*, is coincidence as a description of a situation or set of events, prior to any question of whether this outcome has arisen by chance, or through some as yet unidentified causal agency. ... *coincidence*

DOI: 10.4324/9781003561330-3

> *in sense B*, is the one we invoke when we say such things as "it's only a coincidence," or "it was purely coincidental." … *coincidence in sense C* is the sense of "coincidence" we are usually using when we say things like "It's a very remarkable coincidence," or "What an extraordinary coincidence!"
>
> (p. 94)

A coincidence in sense B *never* has a cause. A coincidence in sense C "requires explanation in some causal or quasi-causal way" (p. 94)—it is "*not* a coincidence in sense B" (p. 94). Delin starts his paper with an example of a coincidence in sense A: "Kennedy's secretary was called Lincoln, while Lincoln's secretary was called Kennedy" (p. 94). In fact, this coincidence has been debunked,[1] but we see Delin's point. For argument's sake, if the claim *was* true, and assuming (for argument's sake) we could find a cause, it would be elevated to coincidence in sense C by Delin's definition. However, Delin never draws attention to the fact that coincidences in sense C can no longer be coincidences because *technically* causes explain them. Therefore "coincidence in sense C", as a category, cannot be of any further use to us.

Another problem here is that Delin uses the term "coincidence" just as it is used in common parlance (everyday speech), and he does it to a fault: Why does a coincidence have to have a cause just because it is "remarkable" or "extraordinary"? And are people really so dismissive of coincidences in sense B (see the above quote)? In fact, I suggest the only true coincidence is in sense B. Regardless of whether Delin is right about how poorly people think (e.g., how they decide what is probable or improbable), our only concern, in fact, is that we should disambiguate that category, sense-B coincidences, for they could be synchronicities *or* they could be meaningless chance groupings. Both are acausal, but the latter are self-explanatory and we *can* dismiss them, whereas the former are meaningful as Jung intended, and they are therefore special cases warranting more than careless dismissal. In the context of synchronicity, just a casual inspection is enough to reveal that ultimately coincidences in sense B *as a category* are not sufficiently discriminatory of the material to hand to be of any use to us.

Thus, the major reason categorization can be a slippery slope is succinctly given by Browne: "As far as categories go, there is a hell of a lot of crossover" (L. Browne, personal communication, October 3, 2017). The more there is crossover, the less there is distinction. Thus are we instinctively *onto* the conscientious academic who suggests that categorization can be final, or is always necessary. James (1909/1997) even warned us about the "*viciously privative employment of abstract characters and class names*" (p. 246), and Fuchs (2014) suggests that the "world is constructed of every particular there is and every way of carving up every particular there is" (p. 85). However, looking back over Chapter 1, I would say the aim there was an important and necessary effort (following Jung) at differentiating synchronicity (meaningful coincidences) from meaningless chance groupings (meaningless coincidences) as a first step towards resolving the psi/synchronicity dichotomy—every Jungian knows a coincidence is not always synchronicity, just as every parapsychologist knows a 'hit' is not always psi.

The *caveat* duly noted, it is for the sake of further understanding that it be considered necessary to re-examine the various coincidences a little later in this chapter to see if they are of a single type, or whether there is the possibility of further differentiation. Also, now that we have synchronicity sufficiently defined for our purposes, it might be worth considering whether it is possible to push for further categorization of meaningful coincidence. If, for example, we focused only on match-accuracy (i.e., literal correlatedness) of coincidence content, we might call the 'Stockholm fire' type of synchronicity, Type A—the 'perfect-match' kind—and we might call the 'scarab' type of synchronicity, Type B—the 'close-enough' kind. Empirically, Type A seems to pass muster with our senses and sensibilities—the synchronistic elements (the mental 'fire' and the actual fire) seem to go beyond similarity or equivalence to identity (they appear to be the same or, more accurately, each *corresponds* to the other, or one is a copy of the other); we get a sense that there has been a direct transfer of precise (referential) information—as suggested by the term 'clairvoyance' in the parapsychological sense.

Type B, however, seems almost to give us the slip as far as matching is concerned—if we are critically honest, the synchronistic elements correspond only somewhat; any likeness is only apparent, and we get a sense of fuzziness in the response. Using our scarab example, Jung admits to only an "approximate identity" (para. 845) of the Egyptian Scarabeid Beetle (*Scarabaeus sacer*) with the common European rose-chafer (*Cetonia aurata*) that crawled across his window-pane. Furthermore, there is another conceptual shift, for the scarab was represented as a piece of jewellery in the dream of Jung's client. As an aside, it is important to note that the explanations in parapsychology for these kinds of 'fuzzy relations' reduce to three main factors: (i) poor perception (due to the limited ability of the individual and/or the poverty of the so-called 'psi signal'), (ii) target obscurity or complexity (the target is either unexpected or carries too much detail), and (iii) lack of prior experience with the target (the memory cannot provide a suitable match).[2] Working on their own, or in tandem, these factors can lead to incorrect assumptions, lapses, misjudgements, and inappropriate decisions and inferences.

Synchronistically, however, the *representations* (analogues or manifestations) of the archetypes that reach consciousness are *always and only* drawn from the experient's memory, while the archetypes *per se* form the bedrock of the collective unconscious and are universal, so the image is invariably 'the truth' *per se* at that given moment. But it is not the kind of truth that might lead to a match in a psi task for it has deeper significance (a point of departure for 'psi purpose' and 'synchronistic purpose' as formally understood). In both cases, the real challenge is in the interpretation, and there are two ways to go about it depending on whether one adopts a parapsychological view or a synchronistic view: either (a) the psi function is reliable to the extent it furnishes accurate (verifiable) information, and if it does not, the individual, or the target, or the signal is at fault, or (b) synchronicity is *always* reliable, fuzzy or not, because an archetype is *always* being represented in synchronicity; not externally-sourced information that can occasionally be distorted/misread.

In this section, I contrast (a) and (b), but first I will weigh up the apparent differences between Type A and Type B synchronicities. I suggest the two types only superficially appear to be poles apart—the one with a somewhat literal dimension; the other with a figurative or emblematic/symbolic dimension—because we are able to *equate* the two elements of the Type-A kind via an *identity* criterion, whereas we have to *parallel* the two elements of the Type-B kind via an *approximation* or *similarity* criterion. However, there is only the suggestion that Type A and Type B might be two workable categories of synchronicity, as these 'types' have never been put to the test a sufficient number of times—arguably just as well, for dichotomizing coincidences (i.e., differentiating the literal from the figurative) on the basis of subjective criteria may be too arbitrary, like judging works of art, and may therefore be misleading and unproductive.[3]

If we view the elements of any given synchronicity as primarily figurative (and dependent upon, for example, metaphor, analogy, or symbol), we can break the hold that literal-mindedness has, and thus move away from all manner of distinctions that may mislead (I covered this point above in "A Symbolic Approach" in Chapter 1). And while Jung (1952/1969) repeatedly used the word "correspondence", more commonly in reference to "meaningful coincidences" (para. 967), he also used the word in the context of "acausal combinations of events" (para. 833), specifically referring to 'hits' (i.e., matching) as in Rhine's work (para. 833, 834, 838, 857), *as well as* connections between human happenings and astrological signs (para. 869) or astronomical events (para. 875). Jung did not appear to use the word *correspondence* to mean 'one-to-one correspondence' (e.g., one bead *corresponds* with one sheep), but nor did he necessarily mean 'direct correspondence' (e.g., the simulation is in *direct correspondence* with the observation). Certainly, the notion of literal correspondence (matching) applies in psi research, evident in free-response tasks where the psi factor is invoked purely on the strength of subjective judgements and best-fit criteria.[4] Gatlin (2008) made this observation when she noted that meaningful coincidence is determined by "some simple identity or similarity criterion which attracts our attention" (p. 196). She referred to a single "criterion", but one can draw a distinction between 'identity' and 'similarity' (identity = 'the same'; whereas similarity = 'resemblance'), which is why Jung's term "approximate identity" (of the chief objects) is preferable because it meets the dichotomy half-way for the reasons just given. In other words, these two types, 'perfect-match' (Type A) and 'close-enough' (Type B), only differ if we judge them a certain way.

To clarify, we normally *equate* an internal image, something like an inner *simulacrum*, with an existing original in the real world, and this pairing results in a legitimate (literal) correspondence (as, for example, a perception in psychology). The term 'correspondence', as used here, means 'mapping' (which Gatlin, 2008, takes to mean 'corresponding') between two elements that can stand for or represent each other. The mature development of the ability to make or see correspondences extends to making connections between a mental form (an image, idea, or sound) and its physical counterpart in the world, even as a picture or word. Therefore, correspondence can apply, for example, to a direct (literal) correlation or matching of the mental image one holds of one's face with one's actual face, or one's mirror reflection, or one's passport photo, or a sketch of oneself, or these days a computer-generated 'avatar'.

In parapsychological research, we must question the point of origin of a correspondence. The ironic message in Magritte's painting *The Treachery of Images* (1928–1929) highlights the point about correspondences or mappings being representations only. That painting is replete with a textualised 'anti-analogue' in French: "*Ceci n'est pas une pipe*" (English: "This is not a pipe"; see Plate 2.1). Magritte's painting is often given as an example of differentiating the real thing (a physical pipe) from a mere representation of a pipe painted on canvas. Magritte is pointing out the fallacy of taking literally (buying into) the

Plate 2.1 *Ceci n'est pas une pipe*—graffiti in Bucharest. (*Source*: © 2008, bixentro/Wikimedia Commons; Creative Commons Licence)

representativeness inherent in correspondence, although the image in the canvas is still a "correspondence" as Jung (1952/1969, para. 967), and Gatlin (2008, p. 199), and I use the term. Semanticist Alfred Korzybski (1933/1941) tells us "A map *is not* the territory it represents, but, if correct, it has a *similar structure* to the territory, which accounts for its usefulness" (p. 58). It seems these ideas are not so difficult to grasp, but the message here is easily obfuscated when the notion of correspondence in psi research is powered by the ideology of information transmission. This bias probably derives from the term 'extra-sensory perception', understood to mean an advanced form of *perceiving*—from that perspective, all correct correspondences (hits) are easily regarded as target *identification*, which is as reasonable a term as any other, except that controversy arises if and when there is dispute over the image being a perception directly derived from 'incoming' information from an external source. That is why I said above: In parapsychological research, we must question the point of origin of a correspondence.

But the above foray into the nature of correspondence does not end here: Going beyond representation, our tolerance for deviation permits a certain degree of flexibility in interpretation so that the more fluid concept of fuzzy relations can be drawn on for explanatory power, though evidence from psychological and parapsychological studies indicates that fuzziness has its limits (as, for example, when a participant or judge overlooks or misconstrues the fuzziness of a target because their modes of interpretation and understanding lean more towards the concrete than the abstract). Thus there are instances where the elements go beyond the figurative, making it difficult to draw even a parallel, let alone an approximate identity. Jung (1952/1969) drew attention to these kinds of elements in synchronicity, and noted their archetypal overtones at a deeper, more challenging level (para. 845). Here, we enter the realm of the symbolic. We have, for example, the archetypally loose birds motif *symbolizing* death in the following case: A woman reported a gathering of birds at the time of her grandmother's death, and then later, her mother's death (para. 844). When a flock of birds appeared outside her house a third time, the woman had an anxiety attack for she 'knew' intuitively that her husband's life was in danger, as she was to discover later when he was brought home dying from a heart attack. Jung notes that "the flock of birds evoked the corresponding memory-images and consequently her fear" (para. 857), but "the death and the flock of birds seem to be incommensurable with one another" (para. 845). Nevertheless, Jung points out the archetypal references; basically, the dead are identified with birds (there are historical antecedents for that association). Some cases of synchronicity can be difficult to decipher when the main elements are abstract or symbolic; their fuzziness takes us away from so-called 'crisp' interpretations.[5]

While fuzziness of targets could be a problem in parapsychological testing, it seems that crispness could be a problem too. Furthermore, if synchronicity is not just *a key component* in ESP testing, but ESP *is* synchronicity, and it is being overlooked in free-response studies, then participant mentation may not be as transparent as we may think, even when crispness seems certain. It is even evident that this combination of factors can complicate judging. Work that has come close to revealing this problem was done by Westerlund et al. (2006). Using film clips from a ganzfeld study, they found that mentations can correspond remarkably well to targets *and* decoys, which puts a question mark over the parapsychological enterprise. The authors wondered if the correspondences were due to "some form of anomalous information transfer" or "a cognitive illusion" (p. 23), and they suggest this problem may be generally true of ganzfeld studies.

Ordinarily, synchronicity theory suggests a single archetype constellates in a free-response trial that tends to correspond to target content, but occasion may arise where a different archetype constellates and matches not with the *target* content but with content in at least one of the *decoys*. I suggest psi-skeptics (those who do not believe in a psychic function; a.k.a. 'goats')[6] are more likely to be driven by an experimentally noncompliant intention that aligns with their skepticism and/or disbelief, but under the strict principle of synchronicity, they are not unconsciously identifying the target and *avoiding it* as the typical parapsychologist argues—rather, the goat is unconsciously stirring up one or any number of ill-fitting archetypes the content of which is more likely to correspond with content in the decoys (they even have a threefold advantage in a typical ganzfeld four-choice trial).[7] Such opportunity is highly probable since free-response decoys are just as rich in content as the target. The issue here is that Westerlund et al. (2006) think the "remarkable correspondences" may not be "paranormal", but could be explained by "chance alone" (p. 45). I suggest these effects are not necessarily chance, but are perhaps chance-like, revealing a synchronistic process at work.

Most parapsychologists would insist psi is at work in ganzfeld studies, and Westerlund et al. (2006) do not entirely doubt it, but they add that the problem lies in "distinguishing between correspondences that are due to psi and those that are not" (p. 45). Parapsychologists may say that those 'problem mentations' are excessively generic and thus too open to interpretation. Here, the authors would disagree for their study is about mentations that were deliberately chosen for their 'crispness' (to use my word). Others may say individual differences in the participants, and/or their limitations in psi perception and information processing account for the complications. But those explanations beg the question—if (through psi) a specific target image (or parts of that image) resonate with a participant, then the cognitions that lead to selection must be bound by the specific stimuli that matter while others are ignored or do not register. And under the psi hypothesis, since participants are especially asked to *identify the target*, then *in the long-run*, by way of intention and the special filtering through of pertinent psi information (i.e., signal), they should be drawn to the correct target and not be lured by deceptive decoys. All this should be evident in the hit rates and the mentations, but since the evidence says otherwise, as Westerlund et al. show, the workings of the process *as psi* are sketchy at best, and probably misunderstood.

If, however, the process is synchronistic, and archetypes may constellate, those archetypes carry pivotal and no doubt stronger impetus, even if they happen to be represented in decoys, so that target identification is deprioritized—participants (I suggest mainly goats in all probability) may tend to describe decoys instead of targets in their mentations, and therefore select and pick those decoys accordingly as if they were the targets.[8] Even given the well-accepted import of intention, the archetype rules, so it is no surprise that we see constant failures ('missing') in ESP studies. For example, while the ganzfeld domain delivers an impressive effect (Storm & Tressoldi, 2020; Storm, Tressoldi & Di Risio, 2010), it could be stronger if meaningfulness and its pertinence to the participant was made a priority.[9]

We do not know how frequent this problem is, but Westerlund et al. (2006) have indicated that it may be more frequent than we care to admit. Unfortunately, they do not see the problem they describe as having anything to do with synchronicity. I suggest that what matters, and what is missed in free-response studies, is the archetypal aspect. Ideally, the archetype behind the 'outer' component (the target as potential hit) in the synchronistic event (or in a psi trial) is the same archetype behind the 'inner' component that is represented by a pertinent image in the participant's mind. The spanner in the works, that makes ESP testing what it is, is the possible and actual constellation of an archetype that happens not to be represented in the target but is represented elsewhere (e.g., decoys), and when that happens, all bets are off—the free-response methodology is compromised and outcome efficacy suffers accordingly. Mentation proves the source; it suggests the process behind it is more synchronistic than psychic.

From all of the above, the many instances of synchronicity and psi tell us that crisp relations are rare (not the norm), and even when they are crisp, there may be difficulties. Nevertheless, we must make an important distinction—the argument in psi research for information transmission or energy exchange is not tenable in synchronicity theory on the principle that any kind of transmission or exchange creates a causal link so that the assumption of coincidence *per se* no longer applies. There is no good argument that correspondences (the 'coin of the realm' in parapsychology) are literal representations of reality, be that as *simulacra* or in any other sense suggesting they are causally tied to the reality of the target; they represent only the archetypes that happened to be constellated at the time of testing.

Phenomenologically, synchronistic elements and their relations can be situated across a spectrum of fuzziness, and we could speak of *degrees of relation*, which are given voice in such terms as 'association', 'correlation', and 'relationship', whereas terms like 'match', 'identity', and 'correspondence' suggest *parity*, sameness, equality (type and value), or equivalence (value only). But, as already indicated, even these latter terms (match, identity, and so on) do not refer to sharpness or crispness in a relative sense—certainly, usage of the terms in the social sciences is often loose, and does not completely eliminate vagueness, ambiguity, or inconsistency. The situation is no different in fields that use statistics where reference is made to correlational 'strength' which implies fuzzy relations (i.e., 'weak', 'moderate', or even 'strong'). I suggest there is a double-standard at work when parapsychology is taken to task on issues of fuzziness, but not the sciences, which leads to my next point.

Perhaps not surprisingly, Diaconis and Mosteller (1989) imply a 'problem' in fuzziness when they argue that many seemingly special coincidences result merely from "counting of close or nearly alike events as if they were identical" (1989, p. 853). Of course, Diaconis and Mosteller are not altogether certain and concede that their "inexperience with and lack of empirical information about the kinds of problems coincidences present do make for *many surprises* [emphasis added]" (p. 860). Did they mean that perhaps not all 'hits' in the parapsychological sense are necessarily mere coincidences due to chance? I do question both the dismissive attitude Diaconis and Mosteller have towards the 'close-or-nearly-alike' rule, *and* their lack of consideration of analytical approaches that acknowledge symbolic elements (which is a general failing of statistical approaches). But both parapsychology and Jung's analytical psychology (and other schools) depend on it. A multifactorial standpoint seems the best way to avoid damage to the synchronicity assumption, for I make a virtue of the meaning-making that may ensue, and I do so at least to the same extent that Diaconis and Mosteller allow for "many surprises".

We can regard the representations (the elements or objects) that comprise synchronicity as non-literal—they are symbols, emblems, similes, metaphors, analogues (whichever word suits on a case-by-case basis); they have fuzzy characteristics. No matter how familiar they are to us in real life, or how much bearing they have on real-world situations, we should look for more than their literal value, even when there is good cause to glean them for their informational value. This idea of *abandoning* the 'assumption of identity' (or at least not depending on it exclusively) relates to the so-called *concretistic fallacy*, and is not a new idea (e.g., see Edinger, 1986). When the more incisive analyst considers the material in dreams and fantasies, the focus is usually on meaning and meaningfulness, and the material is to be interpreted at the so-called 'subject level', as Jung (1953/1966) calls it (i.e., the endopsychic meaning to the individual); *not* necessarily or merely the 'object level' (i.e., *not* the contents themselves as superficially understood, which can be misleading).

As indicated in the previous chapter, synchronicity holds the promise of individuation in its contents. It is important to remember that those contents, those psychological elements or motifs—as vague as they may be; generated in an inner world notorious for its obscurity—are nevertheless the keys to understanding one's inner nature and presence in the world. Even a test trial in a free-response study is an opportunity to gain more than a hit. As the critics have demonstrated, the potential value of coincidences is easily undermined and made superfluous, by means not only of reductive statistical arguments, but also (and critically) parapsychological information models which generally also have reductive aims (I expand on these ideas in Chapter 3).

The categorizations that follow later in this chapter—particularly the 'forms of synchronistic manifestation' (or 'forms' for short)—do no harm to these points. That is because the forms do not refer to the synchronistic essence of the contents (i.e., their meaningfulness, numinosity, and archetypal dimensions). These forms are presented not merely for the purpose of classification, but also to aid understanding. Before I come to that, I will need to consider Jung's more speculative notion on how far the synchronicity concept can be extended.

The Reach of Synchronicity

The problem of synchronistic categorization does not end with representations. Jung (1952/1969) asked whether the "definition of synchronicity" is "capable of expansion, or requires expansion" (para. 965). For Jung, the reach of synchronicity could extend from a *narrow* conception to a *wider* or *broader* conception. The *narrow* conception has synchronicity as "only a particular instance of general acausal orderedness—that, namely, of the equivalence of psychic and physical processes ..." (para. 965). The "wider conception" has synchronicity as a *philosophical principle* that embraces a host of *acausal* phenomena, including coincidences between independent nonpsychic events. The narrow conception refers only to limited human experience which Donati (2008) notes is "clearly distinguished from the microphysical phenomena in which there is neither the direct participation of the observer's psyche nor the relevant presence of 'meaning' ..." (p. 52). Donati hails this wider conception as a way of reconciling science with its

> archetypal origins and with the ancient holistic knowledge of nature symbolized by synchronicity .... [W]e have to grant privilege to a unitary worldview in which both science and philosophy (including metaphysics) together should help to create a fertile ground for the emergence of scientific theories.
>
> (p. 60)

Some scientists seem to have benefited from this "fertile ground"—examples range from Gottfried Wilhelm Leibniz (*I Ching* 'yin'/'yang' ⊠ 'zero'/'one' in binary code; Ryan, 1996),[10] to Freidrich August Kekulé (*ouroboros* ⊠ benzene ring; Coudert, 1980).[11] However, most scientists would regard discoveries like these as mere coincidences (in the plain non-synchronistic sense) and argue from simplistic explanatory constructs such as the imagination running wild, serendipity, good fortune, or guesswork. This myopic viewpoint may well be what Donati wishes to supplant, for Jung and Pauli endeavoured to foster the greater understanding that inquiring minds (like Leibniz and Kekulé) only get as far as they can with their ideas because physical (material), metaphysical (philosophical), and psychological (psychoid) aspects of reality converge *for good reason* into a 'oneness' underpinned by archetypal factors—Pauli (1948) makes similar comments about intuition (as cited in Meier, 2001, p. 203). Zwart (2019) goes into more detail about the process. This oneness may imply a fundamental and universal 'unity', suggesting the *unus mundus*, in much the same way as 'part' (microcosm) reflects the 'whole' (macrocosm).

However, correspondences like those found by Leibniz and Kekulé are uniquely synchronistic *because* of the human factors that pertain (e.g., the ability to create or identify appropriate symbols, or draw analogies), outside of which it is difficult to contemplate what synchronicity is supposed to be like. That is, it seems more the case that the only synchronicity that can be identified and drawn into science is that 'narrow' kind that involves *direct participation of the observer's psyche* and the *relevant presence of "meaning"*.[12] That simple ruling avoids category errors,[13] whereas the expansion may prove to be a case of over-reaching and/or create ambiguity. Given the aims of this chapter, it will be necessary, from a *categorical* perspective,[14] to critique those elements that are to be re-defined or conceptually reshaped to fit a wider synchronistic agenda, and to see if those concepts are viable.

General Acausal Orderedness

The philosophically wider synchronistic principle traces back to the Jung/Pauli correspondence (see Meier, 2001), out of which synchronicity and microphysical phenomena were seen as part of the "general acausal orderedness" (GAO; para. 965)—not a problem in itself; that viewpoint has come to be well-accepted, at least in Jungian circles (for examples, see Mansfield, 1995, pp. 33–35; von Franz, 1992, pp. 267*ff*). Specifically, we find the following provisionally sitting alongside each other in the GAO:

- narrow (i.e., psychic and half-psychic) synchronicity;
- ESP and PK (psi);
- astrological effects;
- microphysical phenomena (e.g., quantum discontinuities of modern physics);
- the ordering principles of the natural numbers;
- the constants of nature (e.g., speed of light).

In time, other acausal phenomena may be discovered and added to the list.

At first, Jung limited the role of synchronicity to a person-centred phenomenon. However, given those acausal phenomena just listed, he advanced a "wider" (broader) conception of synchronicity, and then stated "synchronicity in the narrow sense is only a particular instance of general acausal orderedness" (para. 965). To get slightly ahead of my aims, consider the Jung/Pauli quaternio (Figure 2.1) taken from Jung (1952/1969, para. 963), which suggests as a *fait*

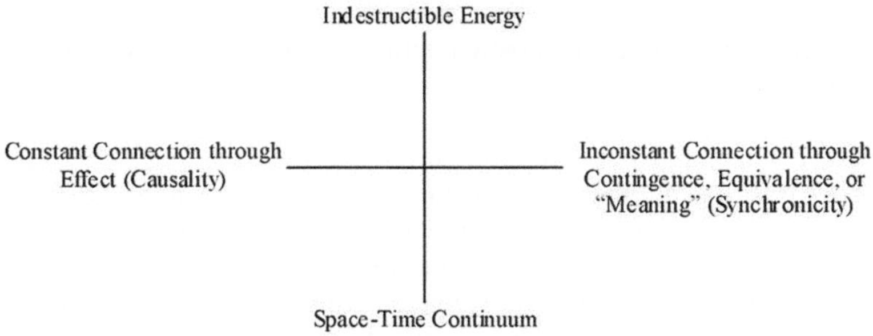

Figure 2.1 The Synchronicity Quaternio (Version II)—Jung and Pauli. (*Source*: © 2024, L. Storm, based on Jung's [1952/1969, p. 98] original figure)

accompli a schema whereby *all* acausal phenomena are synchronistic (i.e., they demonstrate "inconstant connection"). Some may see this schema as puzzling. The quaternio actually has "*Synchronicity*" instead of "*Acausality*" as the counter-pole to "*Causality*". Here Jung was thinking more broadly of synchronicity in the "wider" sense, and Pauli fell into agreement with Jung's idea, and even encouraged it.

In a letter to Pauli, Jung then created two synchronistic sub-categories, as he explains:

> I am inclined to subsume any instance of causally nonconceivable states of being *into the category of synchronicity* [emphasis added]. The psychic and half-psychic cases of synchronicity would be the one subcategory, the nonpsychic ones the other.
>
> (Jung, 1950, as cited in Meier, 2001, p. 60)

Thus, "causally nonconceivable states" (i.e., provisionally *acausal* states) would refer to anything in the GAO ("any instance"), and these would all be synchronicity more broadly defined. At this early stage, we may wonder how a single event is "coincidental" in that it does not coincide with anything and does not satisfy the criterion of "simultaneity". Even in casual parlance, we can barely call such an event a "coincidence" *per se* in that it does not 'fall together' ('partner up') with a corresponding other. There is more than a semantic problem afoot if the words synchronicity and acausality can be used interchangeably (I will return to this issue later).

To ascertain the validity of this wider principle, we must first consider how it might be represented. Narrowly-defined contents can form a subset within a more broadly-defined or superordinate set known as a *superset*, but the superset will naturally accommodate other subsets whose defining properties differentiate them from other subsets. This understanding can be illustrated with the principles underlying Venn diagram construction as used in Set

Theory where,[15] for example, the superset of Integers comprises zero, all the negative numbers, and all the positive numbers, but the positives on their own (thus excluding zero) form a *narrow* subset called Natural Numbers (see Figure 2.2). Thus, for example, natural numbers are integers, as are negative numbers, but negative numbers are *not* natural numbers.

Just as positive numbers and negative numbers are not like each other but they are all integers, Jung would have it that the psychic/half-psychic (narrow) synchronicities and the nonpsychic synchronicities (e.g., QM phenomena[16]) are not like each other, but they are all synchronicity under a "wider conception of synchronicity" because the phenomena demonstrate "acausal orderedness" (para. 965). As a first attempt to schematize, we may see Figure 2.3 as parsing the synchronistic realm fairly closely to Jung's liking. Narrow synchronicity can be divided into subsets of "psychic" and "half-psychic", while "nonpsychic" synchronicities fall outside that subset. But the figure is contradictory in a way that Figure 2.2 is not. First, the nonpsychic phenomena may be too heterogeneous a mix and may need scrutiny on a case-by-case basis. This problem is already evident with Rhine's ESP and PK findings (psi phenomena). Table 2.1 indicates this discrepancy and others, and generally follows Jung's assumptions (those I can determine), but basically it shows that narrow synchronicities have properties that tend *not* to be evident in the wider (less sharply

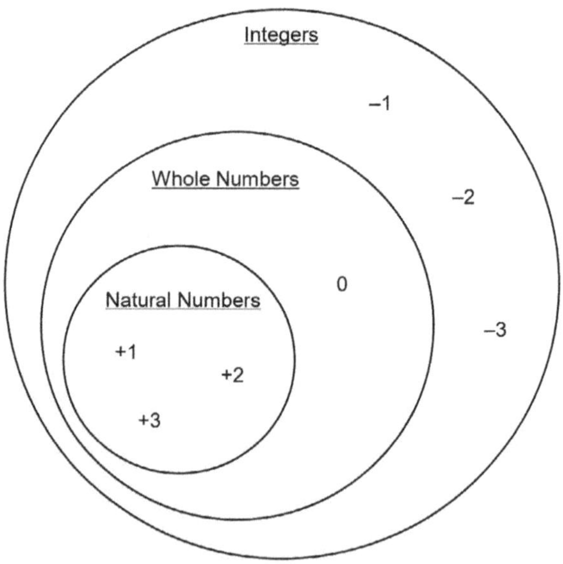

Figure 2.2 The set of Integers are those numbers with no fractional parts and are positive (i.e., "Natural"), or negative, or 0 (zero). (*Source*: © 2024, L. Storm)

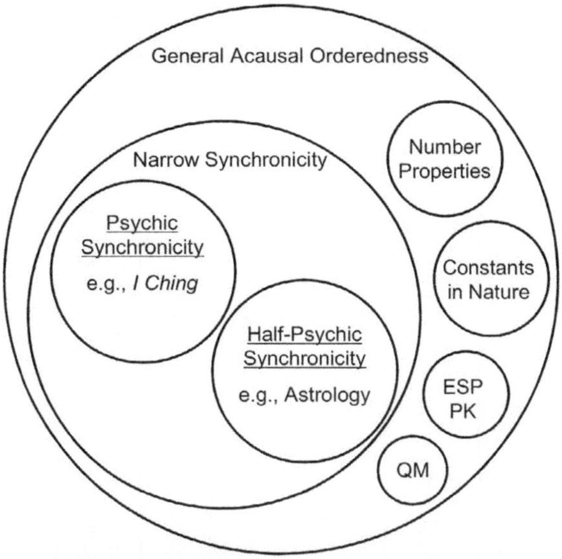

Figure 2.3 Jung's General Acausal Orderedness embraces all forms of synchronicity: psychic, half-psychic, and non-psychic (e.g., microphysical [QM phenomena). (*Source*: © 2024, L. Storm)

defined) synchronicities, and *vice versa* (these discrepancies lead to five categorical problems that I discuss in subsequent subsections).

Of particular note is Pauli's concern that a "broader" definition of synchronicity could mean "too much might get lost that is specific to psychic and half-psychic synchronicity" (Pauli, 1950, as cited in Meier, 2001, p. 63). To resolve that problem, Jung made a conceptual distinction between psychic/half-psychic synchronicity and nonpsychic synchronicity by proffering a two-fold rationale: First, by dropping "meaning" *per se* in favour of "similarity" in the case of the nonpsychic synchronicities, his final choice of words being "equivalence" and "conformity". These terms have been applied equally to psychic (narrow) synchronicities in that characteristically 'fluid' Jungian way to suit the situation. Second, Jung expanded the interpretation of the term "archetype" by making it analogous to "probability". Both steps are problematic, but there are three additional problems. We need to consider the categorical viability of the 'psychic'/'nonpsychic' distinction in a synchronistic context, and we need to assess the statistical aspects of synchronistic phenomena. Finally, an evaluation of the distinction between causal and acausal phenomena may give us a worthwhile perspective on synchronicity in its narrow form and Jung's proposed wider view. My analyses of these five problems will reveal a

Table 2.1 Jung's View on Synchronistic Classifications (the "*Narrow*" and the "*Wider*" Conceptions)

Conception	*Phenomenon*	*Presence of Meaning*	*Presence of an Archetype*	*Participation of Observer's Psyche*	*Statistically Testable*[a]	*Constant and Experimentally Reproducible*[b]
'*Narrow*'	1. Synchronicity	✓	✓	✓	×	×
	2. Astrology	✓	✓	✓	×	×
'*Wider*'	3. Psi (ESP/PK)	✓	✓ ('Affect')	✓	✓	✓
	4. QM Events, etc.[c,d]	?	✓ ('Probability')	×	✓	✓
	5. Constants in Nature[d]	?	?	×	✓	✓
	6. Number Properties[d]	?	✓	×	?	?

✓ = Yes; × = No; ? = Uncertain (Jung is not clear); [a] Effects not attributable to chance; [b] Repeatable, replicable, predictable; [c] Microphysical phenomena ("discontinuities of modern physics", "orderedness of energy quanta", radioactivity, entanglement, etc.); [d] Axiomatic ("Just-So"; they have "existed from eternity and occur regularly"; Jung, 1952/1969, para. 965).

range of categorical incongruities which are now discussed (the reader may note that some of these incongruities are speculative).

Categorical Problems: I. Psychic vs. Nonpsychic

There are physical processes (e.g., the formation of elements), and microphysical processes (e.g., nuclear decay), both of which have (effectively) "existed from eternity and occur regularly" (Jung, 1952/1969, para. 965). The physical processes are cosmological and causal (or at least causal at some defined level); they take place in the nuclear furnaces of stars, supernovae, or cosmic ray fission. The microphysical processes, particularly in the nonclassical realm of quantum mechanics, are accepted as natural, but appear to be acausal or nondeterministic (unpredictable at the level of the individual event).[17] In the following subsections, our interest is confined to those acausal phenomena conjectured to be part of a wider category of synchronistic phenomena.

Jung's claim for wider synchronicities (unlike narrow synchronicities) is that they embrace the proposed 'nonpsychic synchronicities' (e.g., QM phenomena)—synchronicity could even be "between nonpsychic events" (Jung, 1950, as cited in Meier, 2001, p. 60). This wider set is a 'world' of acausal things (i.e., the GAO), within which are the narrow synchronicities constituting their own set because of their "psychical character that reveals itself to be connected with a physical event" (Donati (2008, p. 52). As quoted above, Donati also says "microphysical phenomena" (e.g., "the discontinuities of microphysics"; p. 52) do not have "the direct participation of the observer's psyche" (p. 52). Her two statements go hand in hand, and reflect Jung's general points.

We can assume the nonpsychic synchronicities exist independently of the conscious observer who generally takes no part in their function. Having no psychic element of their own, we can also understand these phenomena to be soulless and not conscious. As far as Jung is concerned, microphysical events are nonpsychic *and* synchronistic because those events suggest an "*ordering system*" where "similar" things coincide without any identifiable "cause" (1950, as cited in Meier, 2001, p. 60). For example, Jung would view a random stream of subatomic particles being emitted from the same source (as in nuclear decay) as synchronistic because the particles are 'uniform' and are all bound by the same quantum principle that also happens to account for their acausality (see the next subsection for examples).

Jung regarded regularity and repeatability as characteristic of the wider synchronicities as long as they are nonpsychic. So where do ESP and PK (psi phenomena) belong in the schema? Jung (1952/1969) would not have them as a "narrow" form of synchronicity. He was disturbed by the fact that psi phenomena are not sporadic and unpredictable like synchronicity. He noted that psi is "experimentally reproducible", and shows "certain regularities" and "constant factors" (i.e., they are statistically testable), whereas individual cases of synchronicity differ too much and "cannot be repeated experimentally" (para. 965). However, only "some repeatability" has been demonstrated for psi, and it is only "statistical in nature" (Palmer, 2008, p. 180). Therefore, the stated regularity and repeatability of psi may be an overly optimistic presumption that does not square with the facts, so there may be no strong reason to relegate psi to the nonpsychic subset based on Jung's criterion.

Pauli had also pointed out to Jung earlier that neither ESP nor PK involve "archetypal contents becoming conscious" (Pauli, 1949, as cited in Meier, 2001, p. 36), but Jung (1952/1969) explained that the archetype in psi becomes conscious in the expectation or hope of effects that carry with them "affectivity … [which] rests to a large extent on the instincts, whose formal aspect is the archetype" (para. 846). Beloff (2008) regarded Jung's rationale as "lame" and "a piece of rather special pleading" (p. 103). Mansfield (1995) did not buy into the idea either, but he felt that psi was not even synchronistic. Criticisms like these are mere opinions, and what we do know is that the 'presentiment' literature indicates a strong role for emotions (i.e., physiological arousal) in psi events as indicated by correlated changes in skin conductance, heart rate, electroencephalographic (EEG) and functional magnetic resonance imaging (fMRI) responses prior to the presentation of arousing stimuli (Mossbridge & Radin, 2018b; Mossbridge, Tressoldi, & Utts, 2012). This is to say that synchronicity and psi are both linked to affectivity (emotion). Implied in these findings is not only that psi involves an observing or participating psyche (e.g., a test subject), but also there is a link to meaning and even meaningfulness in psi outcomes. Jung even states that "Rhine's experiments confront us with the fact that there are events which are related to one another experimentally, and in this case meaningfully …" (para. 840). Strangely, even his own words did not give Jung sufficient cause to move psi closer to a narrow type of synchronicity, and he merely called for its "expansion" (para. 965). So there is again a case for psi phenomena to be in the narrow set; indeed, the psychic subset (not where Jung would put them, as shown in Figure 2.3 and Table 2.1). All told, psi phenomena are *not* nonpsychic. In contrast, synchronicity's sporadic nature has only ever been referenced to spontaneous real-world cases, but it has never been adequately tested in the laboratory despite Jung's (para. 965) protestations that such control is not possible for narrow synchronicity. There is reason to dispute that claim. What has also not been shown yet is the link between affectivity and archetypes. Nevertheless, Jung seems to be on fairly safe ground in theorizing that the emotional system links psi with archetypes, but the importance of that link did not override his concern with the statistical factors associated with psi.

We may also wonder where astrology fits in. From the point of view of any general system that offers interpretation, including analytical psychology, Progoff (1973) thought astrology might be limited in scope and lose its "validity" (p. 65) if its symbols (archetypes?) were interpreted in a too rigid and fixed manner, but aside from that we cannot ignore the fact that human *and* cosmic factors are combined in astrological correlations. Therefore the connection Jung made between astrology and synchronicity is understandable and a matter of record—indeed, Jung's research in that area constitutes a large portion of Jung's (1952/1969) major essay. Even the staunch Rhinean parapsychologist, John Beloff (1920–2006), described synchronicity as never more clearly demonstrated than in astrology.[18] He states: "The logic of astrology requires the existence of a synchronicity relationship between the disposition of the celestial bodies and *individual human destinies* [emphasis added]" (2008, p. 102). Clearly, astrological effects indicate *half-psychic* synchronicity. However, while astrology may be seen as a narrow form of synchronicity, there are complications and the fit may only be provisional (see the subsection *Categorical Problems: V. Causality vs. Acausality*).

There are further issues: Jung's argument for a wider synchronicity embraces not only microphysical processes, but also conceptual entities that include the *properties of natural numbers* that dictate material forms (e.g., as crystalline structures that have mathematical regularity), and the *constants* in physics, engineering, astronomy, and so on (e.g., the gravitational constant G; the velocity of light c; Planck's constant h; the Hubble constant H_0). I suggest conceptual entities cannot be synchronistic; synchronicities are events, or happenings, or processes. The same problem arises in a later subsection in regard to probability (see *Categorical Problems: III. Archetype vs. Probability*). Jung had to be referring to the direct and actual *manifestations* of numbers and constants as seen throughout the universe, and it is from those manifestations that principles of nature might be derived, although any kind of causal factor underpinning them was "unthinkable" (a word used by both Jung and Koestler). As unthinkable (acausal) manifestations, they are therefore part of the GAO.

Apart from the fact that we can witness their constancy and reliability, Jung never made it clear how microphysical events *and* these two conceptual entities (numbers and constants) constitute a homogeneous set, but we can try to evaluate his broader reasoning: When Jung (1964/1970) deliberated over numbers, he saw them as "real" in the sense that "they are encountered in the realm of experience as *quantities* and thus form the bridge between the tangible, physical world and the imaginary" (para. 776). So numbers are "an aspect of the physically real as well as of the psychically imaginary" (para. 777). And earlier Jung (1952/1969) had defined "number psychologically as an *archetype of order* which has become conscious" (para. 870). No other archetype has this objective reality, and Jung even makes a special case of the number archetype referring to it and synchronicity as "incommensurable things":

> I cannot refrain from pointing out that not only were they [number and synchronicity] always brought into connection with one another, but that both possess numinosity and mystery as their common characteristics.
>
> (para. 870; see also Jung, 1955/1987, as cited in Meier, 2001, p. 132)

In being "brought into connection with one another", numbers can underpin synchronicity, and have "Just-So" qualities (Jung, 1952/1969, para. 965), but numbers and synchronicity are expressly different. The number archetype can be (a) identified in representational forms in the physical world (Jung, 1964/1970), but (b) as an "aspect of … the psychically imaginary" (para. 777), we can have an entirely endopsychic interface with the number archetype (ego with the numinosum) as in a vision. However, neither (a) nor (b) is a synchronistic experience; both 'merely' express archetypal realities. Since numbers and constants come in *conceptual* form and *manifest* form, they would be better regarded as archetypes *per se* in their *conceptual* form, but as parts of the GAO in *manifest* form. Either way, the number archetype, like any other archetype, can only be a *contingent* factor in synchronicity.

There is a further consideration, for we must consider the context in which the term 'nonpsychic' is used: Jung's schema satisfies an ideological need, but in certain respects it makes little practical sense. In the case of the psychic vs. the nonpsychic, physicists do not need to describe their microphysical phenomena as 'nonpsychic' for they have no need for the relative term 'psychic', which (the reader will recall) means 'of the psyche' or 'psychological' in the Jungian lexicon. The physicist's subject matter *is* matter; not psyche. For a physicist to say that their subject matter is 'nonpsychic' would merely be a round-about (redundant) way of saying they study matter. Some physicists like Pauli might be interested in archetypes up to a point, but they are intangibles as archetypes *per se*. And what is it about the nonpsychic that might be important to the psychologist? Indeed, the model may even drive a wedge between the two disciplines—the very outcome that Pauli and Jung would have wished to avoid for, in the Pauli/Jung quaternio (see Figure 2.1), Jung hoped to satisfy "the postulates of modern physics, and … those of psychology" (para. 963). This sentiment is not generally held in the disciplines. While Donati (2008) did note that Pauli and Jung developed an appreciation for each other's fields, she also mentions the fact that Pauli thought Jungian psychology should move towards a philosophical system, partly because he did not care for the "psychotherapeutic aspects of synchronicity and of archetypes" (p. 55). Alternatively, both Jung and von Franz thought psychology had to go beyond science which had no room for myth, meaning, and feelings. One might have thought the "archetypal ground" shared by the psychic and the nonpsychic worlds would bind the disciplines (Donati hoped so), but even the progenitors of this unification saw natural limits (more on the archetypal ground shortly).

Categorical Problems: II. Meaning vs. Conformity

Given the preceding comments, I will indulge Jung his nonpsychic synchronicity category for the time being merely to show how he argued his case. To extend the reach of synchronicity (i.e., to give it broader applicability in the sciences), Jung dropped 'meaning' *per se* in favour of "similarity" (Jung, 1951, as cited in Meier, 2001, p. 60) in the case of the nonpsychic synchronicities, with the "half-life period" given as an example.[19] But Jung (1952/1969) necessarily expanded the lexicon by including the terms "equivalence" and "conformity" (para. 942, n71) to characterize nonpsychic synchronicity, though the word "Meaning" still maintains a place for psychic/half-psychic synchronicity (para. 963). To illustrate 'similarity' (or better, 'conformity') in the case of the "half-life period" (Jung, 1951, as cited in Meier, 2001, p. 60), Jung would no doubt have argued (or I shall argue for him) that, probabilistically, two separate samples of the same radioactive isotope would demonstrate 'similarity' (though he does not use that term in his essay) or 'conformity' (i.e., as in conforming to some kind of law) in having *approximately* the same half-life because they are the same isotope, and calculations would show their rates of decay would effectively match (so there would be conformity).

Furthermore, those elements of the periodic table that have corresponding radioactive isotopes have half-lives, which differ in length of time (ranging from fractions of a second to billions of years) since they are different isotopes, but *conformity* or *similarity of property* (i.e., the half-life) is indicated because the same probabilistic law operates (i.e., all half-lives are calculated the same way). (The conformity principle can also be applied to entanglement properties of particles such as photons and electrons.) In Jung's view, then, the half-life would be an "instance of acausal orderedness" (Jung, 1952/1969, para. 959), because it says something consistent (ordered) and acausal about isotopes, so for Jung isotopic behaviour would pass as synchronicity under the wider (nonpsychic) conception.

The examples just described show how the word 'meaning' must be replaced, as it makes no sense to apply it if we are to speak of nonpsychic acausal phenomena. Jung argued that we can determine some forms of *order* as acausal conformities in nature, while others are causal. Being readily identifiable by a pattern-seeking species, these conformities could be *given* (could be *ascribed*) certain meanings (e.g., they can lead to scientific understanding where, say, prediction models become possible), but it is moot whether there is any absolutely objective reality to those meanings that may even suggest they exist at some transcendental level. At first, Jung (1952/1969) steered clear of such an assertion by saying:

> In view of the possibility that synchronicity is not only a psychophysical phenomenon but might also occur without the participation of the human psyche, I should like to point out that in this case we should have to speak not of meaning but of equivalence or conformity.
>
> (para. 942, n71)

In fact, the word "conformity" is used only once in Jung's (1952/1969) major essay, and only once in Jung's (1951/1969) earlier synchronicity paper. Jung's focus seems to be on "equivalence", but that word seems best applied to *coincidences* where meaningful parallels can be seen; not lawful conformities such as those just described. Yet Jung clearly wants the term "equivalence" applied contextually to cases of nonpsychic synchronicity, but since it does often appear amalgamated with the words 'meaning' and 'meaningful', it also applies contextually to psychic synchronicity (for more on this point, see the subsection "Meaningfulness" in Chapter 1).

Also, as I see it, this important footnote is in the wrong place, serving as an afterthought to an argument needing emphasis in the main text. I suggest it is almost hidden so as not to put too fine a point on an unfortunate complication to do with types of meaning. In the paragraph to which the footnote above refers, Jung has said: "Synchronicity postulates a meaning which is *a priori* in relation to human consciousness and apparently exists outside man [*sic*]" (para. 942). Only a few paragraphs later (albeit in his Conclusion), Jung launches into an overlapping argument from "meaningful orderedness" in a "psychophysical" context, by saying:

> ... "absolute knowledge" which is characteristic of synchronistic phenomena, a knowledge not mediated by the sense organs, supports the hypothesis of a self-subsistent meaning, or even expresses its existence. Such a form of existence can only be transcendental, since, as the knowledge of future or spatially distant events shows, it is contained in a psychically relative space and time, that is to say in an irrepresentable space-time continuum.
>
> (para. 948)

Here Jung entertains the possibility of self-subsistent, *transcendental* meaning that supports the idea of "absolute knowledge". As this statement is made in the context of the "body-soul problem", Jung would apparently be speaking in terms of *narrow* synchronicity; not the wider synchronicities of which there are no self-subsistent meanings—only similarities, conformities, and equivalences. That should be what Jung intends, but he is not hard-and-fast on the issue for (as I also said) his argument concerns "meaningful orderedness" *extrapolated* beyond psyche so as to embrace "psychophysical" realities. Thus there is room for disagreement, for while that which exists *outside* the psyche would not possess *a priori* meaning (Jung said so in the footnote), some might go so far as to suggest that self-subsistent meaning does exist *outside* the psyche, and Jung has said that too!

But if meaning cannot have independent existence, how can there be a form of it that is self-subsistent? Perhaps meaning might suddenly spring into reality *sui generis* the moment the psyche is involved with matter or external events. Self-subsistent (pre-existent?) meaning could then come into perceivable reality—a manifestation in consciousness of a certain meaning governed by archetypes which *are* transcendent and psychoid, and thus they bridge the gap between psyche and matter. Surely Jung meant that, but Main (2004) points out that synchronicity suggests that there "may be a dimension of objective meaning accessible to but not created by humans" (p. 2). I suggest those meanings, first and foremost, derive from archetypes. As we can see, Jung created for us a conundrum that constantly drags psyche and meaning back into the foray (for examples, see Jung, 1952/1969, para. 947–957), even when we try to confine ourselves to those cases of *wider* synchronicity that are supposed to be *nonpsychic* and *free of meaning*. We might be less confused if we simply viewed *as facts* those 'meanings' that are observable and measurable, and do appear to be objective (at least by consensus), and that is how we should characterize self-subsistent meanings—that is, as facts and not call them meanings.

Consider the following: we see that Jung is sympathetic to the inbuilt desire in us to maintain, as a "truth" rather than a "superstition", the idea that meaning can be "self-subsistent" (para. 944). Throughout Jung's essay there are evident examples from ancient and medieval sources such as "Tao, microcosm and macrocosm, sympathy, correspondence, and pre-established harmony [and] dreams" (Main, 2004, p. 38). To that list we may add ideas and practices that persist in modern times, including divination (e.g., *I Ching*, astrology), and number symbolism. I would like to think Jung knew well enough to limit his claim to the primordial (i.e., archetypal) factors that merely *suggest* self-subsistent meanings exist in what are cultural products that have evolved along with their *ascribed* meanings over the millennia in human societies. For example, Tao and *I Ching* principles are grounded in nature and natural occurrences (e.g., changes in the season, laws of balance, etc.; see Wilhelm, 1987); astrology is underpinned by primordial (celestial) factors that appear to have consistent influence across the eons of human history (Tarnas, 2007); numbers have fixed 'just-so' qualities, the principles of which can extend to the human sphere (Storm, 2008e). Confusion only arises if we do not see that the meanings *ascribed* to those systems are *derived* from the *so-called* self-subsistent 'meanings' thought to be embedded in those systems. The more important point, however, is that it would be more accurate to refer to these apparently embedded or self-subsistent 'meanings' as *empirical facts about archetypes.*

The problem here is not simply that meaning is ultimately a subjective, "anthropomorphic interpretation", as Jung states (1952/1969, para. 916): He allows for the possibility of "objective meaning", but he doubts it can be proved (para. 915). We can only make concessions for meanings that are archetypally and dimensionally humanwide, which are therefore "objective", phylogenetically speaking. The bigger concern, however, is with the claim that self-subsistent meanings are embedded in nonpsychic synchronicities (even in those acausal, purely physical events that occur throughout the cosmos). The claim is simply not called for in a world of fundamental activities (physical, geophysical, cosmological, and biological) as all these function independently of human involvement. And surely Jung meant to say as much by offering alternative terms like similarity and equivalence and conformity to avoid cornering himself, for he tells us he only included "meaning" in his synchronicity schema to satisfy "the postulates of … psychology" (para. 964). Yet Jung's persistent references to "*a priori*" meaning, "transcendental" meaning, "self-subsistent" meaning (meaning outside "man" and the "psyche"), and "absolute knowledge" always seem to go beyond psychology, and indeed beyond *psychic* synchronicity.

Some may think it reasonable to infer the presence of those kinds of meaning in the context of Jung's "wider [non-narrow] conception of synchronicity" (para. 965), but Jung himself holding out a hope for it puzzles me. But some may not be puzzled; Main (2004) suggests the idea of "objective meaning [is] not inherently absurd" (p. 178), and he makes no distinction between psychic and nonpsychic synchronicities when he says it. However, I suggest we must fall back on the quote above from Jung (1952/1969, para. 942, n71), and Donati's (2008) quote that opened this section, where both Jung and Donati referred to the *absence* or *lack* of meaning in phenomena that occur without the participation of the human psyche (i.e., the world of fundamental activity just mentioned). To do otherwise, is to blur the distinction even Jung himself tried to make.

In the human sphere, we might acknowledge archetypal meaning, where there may be some degree of universal (human-wide) objective meaning (i.e., archetypal meaning is *generally* meaningful). And we can accept those other terms (equivalence, conformity), even when they are akin to Aziz's (1990) first-level 'meaning'—the mere observation of a parallel between (say) external elements; the kind of conformity or consistency in nature that would draw a scientist's attention. However, 'meaning' in science (which is asserted, assigned, ascribed) is not in the same league as the breadth of meaning (in terms of the upper 'levels' Aziz describes) that elevates to full-blown meaningfulness in a psychic synchronicity. Jung's speculation about meaning, and its marginalization in favour of equivalence or conformity to firm up the wider synchronistic ground, is confused and confusing if self-subsistent meaning is to be coupled with nonpsychic synchronicity; it only shows up the wider conception for its discrepancies, leading to a clear category error.

Categorical Problems: III. Archetype vs. Probability

We now come to another of Jung's semantic defenses of his distinction between psychic (narrow) synchronicities and nonpsychic synchronicities (i.e., the remaining wider or non-narrow synchronicities). This time we consider a nonpsychic analogue of the archetype.

At the outset, we must note that Jung (1952/1969) says "archetypes are not found exclusively in the psychic sphere, but can occur just as much in circumstances that are not psychic" (para. 964). Then we should expect to come across archetypes in the world of matter—even microphysical processes. This point is arguable to some extent, but it does not seem to warrant refuting too extensively (consider the ordering properties of the archetype of number in nature). Pauli suggested a parallel between *psychic* and *nonpsychic* synchronicities, with an "ordering factor (archetype)" fundamental to the former; and a "law of probability" fundamental to the latter (1950, as cited in Meier, 2001, p. 64). He also says: "the *archetypal element* [emphasis added] in quantum physics is to be found in the (mathematical) concept of probability" (p. 64). Pauli very basically implied that probability works like an archetype because an "ordering factor" is inherent in its operations. Cued by Pauli, Jung gives the archetype a new dimension "via the analogy archetype–probability".

> In physical terms, probability corresponds to the so-called law of nature; psychically, it [probability] corresponds to the archetype.
>
> (Jung, 1951, as cited in Meier, 2001, p. 70)

We get a sense of what is sought here, but the proposition is flawed for a number of reasons, the first being that analogies do not serve the purpose of conceptually uniting fundamentally different processes or phenomena in nature; they are merely illustrations that serve a didactic purpose. Consider, for example, the solar-system analogy made about the atom: Although the principle of concentrically orbiting bodies around a central mass is common to both (hence the viability of the analogy), the two central masses are fundamentally different, as are their respective orbiting bodies, as are the forces and laws that apply. For an analogy to work properly, the two phenomena must have something in common, or be similar in some way, which is not the case with Jung's "archetype–probability" analogy. For a start, there is a major incongruity: Archetypes are thought to be ontologically real, as argued by Jung (1961/1989) and by others (Gibson, 2010; Goodwyn, 2022; Grof, 1985; Mills, 2023), whereas probability (even a "law of probability") serves an epistemological purpose only, being subjectively derived from, and dependent upon, limited knowledge of the given system under investigation (especially quantum systems). Ultimately, probability is a function of ignorance; it is an epistemological tool, but it cannot be *ontologically* analogous to the archetype.

We could modify the analogy if we are free to take Jung (and Pauli) to mean the *behaviour* of the archetype (when it constellates in the psyche) is similar to microphysical "behaviour" (e.g., radioactive decay) because both behaviours are bound by *laws of nature*, although there may be differences in the degrees to which the respective laws allow us to make predictions. Jung (1952/1969) even said the "archetype represents psychic probability", adding that it (the archetype) is "a special psychic instance of probability in general" (para. 964). Rather clumsy wording (or translation), but we can work with it.

This reworking of the analogy reads somewhat better, but two types of probabilistic behaviour that are theoretically comparable means we can go beyond analogy to a model: Especially since Jung has told us that archetypes may appear in the nonpsychic sphere (i.e., the microphysical world). But the whole dynamic changes—if archetypes can appear in the nonpsychic sphere, then the microphysical behaviour or function is not merely *similar* to the way psychic archetypes behave or function, but is the very example of an "archetypal ordering factor". Pauli seemed to have already accepted this view by opining that an "archetypal element" is found in "probability" (1950, as cited in Meier, 2001, p. 60), or better, probabilistic behaviour. Going further, we may be free to take these statements to mean acausal microphysical events are governed by the equivalent of archetypes that express themselves (or an archetype that expresses itself) probabilistically, just as in the psychic sphere. The upshot is Jung never needed to make an analogy; he only needed to propose that something 'archetypal' (or a range of these 'things') may constellate in the microphysical world in various ways, the difference being that they may be regular and reliable *within* their category, whereas psychic archetypes are not. I see the problem here centering mainly on the complexity of human behaviour which does not seem to be quite the same problem with matter.

A probabilistic model or schema implies *for both types of archetypes* that we (a) are ignorant of the underlying rules that govern their behaviours, but (b) can quantitatively determine the *probability* of their occurrence. However, while there may be a law of probability that accurately describes and predicts nonpsychic archetypal (microphysical) events *en masse* because those events are 'uniform' (Bohm, 1957), we know of no law or function that governs or predicts what psychic archetypes will do *en masse* in, for example, samples of people (i.e., whether or not any archetypes will constellate, and if any do, which ones, and how many). These are the qualitative aspects of the archetypes in *psychic* synchronicity that were a lasting problem for Jung, but it would appear not to be a problem for him when it came to nonpsychic synchronicity. The question then is, Should the word 'archetype' be used to describe microphysical 'behaviour'? Maybe 'archetype' is not the right word.

As will be seen in the next subsection, I suggest we can observe and statistically model generic outcomes in a synchronicity experiment (formally, a multi-participant psi test under the Rhinean paradigm) because much can be assumed—in particular, *some* number of archetypes would *probably* constellate (*probably* most of these would differ given the heterogeneity of the sample),[20] but in fact it is also *probable* that none will constellate. With the psychic archetypes, we can only *expect* them to constellate, and even when they do, we can only attempt identification *after* constellation. Jung (1968a) spoke to this issue: "synchronicity abolishes the assumption of [a continuum of] uniform objects and so ruins the statistical method" (para. 1198). I suggest Jung means *psychic* synchronicity here. As I have just said, I do not feel the statistical method is 'ruined' for psychic synchronicity, but Jung is nevertheless correct about the uniformity problem. Physicists do not have this problem with 'nonpsychic archetypes', though of course they do not use that term—microphysical events are of a kind (i.e., uniform). And, therefore, with established microphysical behaviours, physicists can reliably demonstrate effects (even guarantee them), which is to say subatomic particles do not 'hold-out' on the experimenter!

While the single microphysical event can still be elusive, the point is physicists are satisfied with their prediction models because they are proven to be extremely reliable, whereas little is understood about the elusiveness of psychic archetypes (i.e., how they constellate), and prediction is primarily or essentially hit-or-miss, literally. And yet, unlike the randomicity of the isolated microphysical event, the psychic archetype as an "ordering factor" is *not intrinsically* random—that would be contradictory. It matters not that psychic archetypes are not entirely predictable *to us*, but *in a given synchronistic event* we are permitted to infer the constellation of an archetype, and even hazard a guess as to its 'type' (though that may be claiming too much in some instances).

Thus, when it comes to the probabilistic functioning of the nonpsychic (microphysical) 'archetype' and the psychic archetypes, we see the two are contradistinctive to a marked degree. Archetypes or archetypal processes seem to apply in both cases, but they are of a different order, which is to be expected. Little that applies to one applies to the other. The only thing they have in common is that statistical analyses can be applied to their data (see the next subsection). But we cannot ignore the fact that statistical approaches have general applicability across disciplines for any number of behaviours and functions (in fact, hosts of them), no matter how random (including subatomic particles) or fickle (especially psychic archetypes and their unreliable presence as in hit-or-miss demonstrations of psi/synchronicity).

In further consideration of these crucial points, it is not a problem that the two types of archetypes are (or might be) somewhat different—we expect that to be so—but perhaps too great a difference *is* a problem. Then one might not even be an archetype. That notwithstanding, we have to consider whether their only commonality (i.e., probabilistic behaviour) is enough to support the model, but we see that the physicist's equivalent of an archetype (the probabilistic aspects of matter) does only one thing, and does it reliably (we might say 'mathematically'); the psychic archetypes (apart from being numerous and complex) are largely unpredictable. Like the meaning/conformity parallel, we have a chalk-and-cheese pairing which, from a disciplinary perspective, is unwieldy and even alienating. As I said previously, the aim in Jung's model was to serve an ideological need to unite two polarized disciplines that have little in common other than their acausal phenomena that are proposed to be synchronistic. Seen as a way of uniting psyche and matter by pointing out their hypothesized synchronistic commonalities, there is actually very little from a categorical perspective that unites them *archetypally*.

Categorical Problems: IV. The Individual Case vs. the Statistical Framework

Statistics was a hitch for Jung. What seems to have stumped him was his indecision over how to treat astrology and psi from a statistical standpoint—

in fact, I would argue that Jung never really settled the issue in his own mind, and it seems more likely that he was hedging his bets; others may argue that he was merely confused (Fordham, 1973, 1993; Mansfield, 1995).

In the case of astrology, Jung (1952/1969) at first attempted to prove *statistically* that astrology (specifically, "the marriage connection between two persons"; para. 868) was fundamentally *synchronistic* in nature.[21] Jung notes: "I decided to investigate the *empirical basis of astrology* [emphasis added], using a large number of horoscopes of married pairs just to see what kind of figures would turn up" (para. 877). But later (in 1954), in a private letter to a mathematician (Markus Fierz), he claims his intention all along was "to present a case of synchronicity, even though it proves nothing about astrology, which was never my intention anyway" (Jung, 1968a, para. 1207). He also acknowledges "significant figures" would help "prove the rightness of astrological expectations" (Jung, para. 1200). These statements read like Jung contradicted himself, which seems likely to some extent, but he might be covered *if* his correct understanding of the meaning of a "significant" statistic is *not* that it is a 'proof' *per se*, but that it *supports* a given hypothesis. I do not wish to make excuses for Jung if there is a good chance it is not warranted; besides which, an excuse like that would not entirely suffice in this instance—Jung's "case of synchronicity" was unquestionably treated by Jung as a case *for* synchronicity, which was to very much hang on what the astrological figures 'turned up'. To think otherwise would mean there was never any point running the study in the first place. It is also unfortunate and naïve of Jung that he was rather flippant about the significance *per se* of the astrological results, but only wanted a "statistical distribution" to show that synchronistic events "lie between mere chance events and caused events" (Main, 2004, pp. 60, 61).

Actually, Jung had the right idea to test *statistically* for a synchronistic effect in astrology—he actually investigated the effect in terms of a 'large-scale statistical framework', which I will focus on shortly. However, despite the correct approach, Jung switched his argument, having decided (prematurely in my opinion) that his attempts had failed,[22] and ultimately put a positive spin on findings he viewed as "inconclusive" (1951/1969, para. 989). He claimed that a case was not made for synchronicity by *statistically* testing astrology for significance (1952/1969, para. 901; 1968a, para. 1203), but any kind of non-significant deviation in itself might be useful, and so he maintained his belief that astrology was synchronistic—indeed *a narrow form* of synchronicity because it had the two key elements: an observing psyche and meaning (see Table 2.1). For Jung, that was the right decision—the *single case* was more important than a *significant statistic*.

Then we come to Rhine's parapsychological phenomena, ESP and PK (psi). Oddly, Jung (1952/1969) not only defended Rhine's statistical approach; he implied much more: "The results of the ESP and PK experiments have provided a statistical basis for evaluating the phenomenon of synchronicity …" (para. 863). Arguably, the only way to read this quote is that statistical testing and modelling, being a way of evaluating the truth status of psi, is therefore a way of evaluating synchronicity (or one form of it). Jung now endorses the statistical approach. But for Jung, making that exception for psi means the definition of synchronicity must change. And thus his reasoning flipped—now the *significant statistic* is at least as important as the *single case.* I suggest that Jung's way out of the dilemma, by expanding the definition of synchronicity, is a dead-end. As I have mentioned previously, psi is a narrow form of synchronicity because, like astrology, it too involves an observing psyche and meaning.

If Jung had fully grasped the point that even Pauli missed, the problem would have been resolved. In a letter to Jung, Pauli drew a distinction between a "discontinuum of individual cases" and a "continuum that can only be realized (approximately) in a large-scale statistical framework" (Pauli, 1950, as cited in Meier, 2001, p. 55). Jung acknowledged the difference, but both Jung and Pauli failed to see the possibility of testing synchronicity experimentally because of their unreasonable concern with the nonrepeatability of the individual case (see Appendix B for examples). Statistical frame-working *is* the key, for the parallels are obvious between an astrological effect (e.g., a marriage pair), spontaneous non-recurrent psi, the single quantum event, and the unique case of synchronicity. And just as physicists overcame the problem of the single event in QM, the statistical solutions devised by parapsychologists and astrologists to surmount the problem of the individual case should be applicable to the 'problem' of the unique case of synchronicity. In other words, in a properly designed study, we can look for trends and patterns in *collections of data*, and leave the single case to those interested in personal evaluation.

This argument does not apply to the properties (ordering capacities) of natural numbers and the constants of nature. Numbers do not need to be modelled statistically to prove their phenomenal aspects—their "Just-So" properties (Jung, 1952/1969, para. 965) are well accepted and require no elaborate analytic proofs *per se*—unequivocal and unfailing demonstration suffices (see Storm, 2008e). Numbers, as axiomatic representations in nature, constantly affirm and reaffirm the part they play in the cosmic order. As Jung (1952/1969) has stated of number properties, they are immutable and based "on the quality of being themselves, on a "so-ness" that cannot be expressed by an intellectual concept" (para. 871).[23] A similar argument applies to the constants, even if we must concede that only close approximations to their actual values have ever been determined (Sheldrake, 1994),[24] though it is demonstrably the case that these approximations suffice, even on a cosmic scale. Given their reliability, the constants function in the same way as numbers.

As far as astrological events and psi are concerned, the two are versions of synchronicity in the narrow sense and any apparent complications and contradictions are easily surmounted. Jung (1968a) seems overly concerned with losing synchronistic phenomena (both "narrow" and "wider" types) *absolutely* to the 'causality' category, which destroys his bigger aim for a synchronicity/causality *complementarity*:

> It seems … that a *complementarity relationship* exists between synchronicity and causality. Rhine's statistics have proved the existence of synchronicity *in spite of unsuitable methods*. This aroused false hopes in me as regards astrology.
>
> (para. 1198)

Jung's concern was later echoed in a statement made by Fordham (1993) who argued that a statistically significant astrological finding "would make a *cause* [emphasis added] for the data more likely" (p. 105). By conventional rules, Fordham's (1993) argument might apply equally to psi (see Fordham, 1973), but in truth, a statistically significant finding does not necessarily imply a cause *per se* accounts for the observed effect. These issues are discussed next.

Categorical Problems: V. Causality vs. Acausality

The conflicting statistical issues just outlined constitute a fourth categorical problem, but they tie in with a fifth categorical problem to do with causality and acausality already hinted at. Being mindful of the fact that Jung sees synchronicity and psi as equivalent processes, he regarded psi as acausal (synchronistic) and belonging to the GAO. As physicist Victor Mansfield later explained: "Paranormal phenomena are acausal in that no energy or information exchange can be responsible for the correlations measured" (1995, p. 32). Experimentation failed to demonstrate causality in psi, but apparently psi's probabilistic character in being "constant and experimentally reproducible" offsets that concern, giving it a certain regular or causal character (see Jung, 1952/1969, para. 965). So why did Jung nominate psi for membership in the GAO; an exclusive club for *acausal* members only? The reason appears to stem from his observation that psi is not *mechanically* causal, and that is in line with Rhine's position on psi.[25]

One might excuse Jung for his naïve argument from mechanical (historical) causality—even Victor Mansfield revised his position on psi, subsequently taking psi to be *scientifically causal*, whereas synchronicity was deemed *scientifically acausal* (see Mansfield et al., 1998). Figure 2.4 shows that Mansfield et al. envisioned a very slight intersection of psi and synchronicity

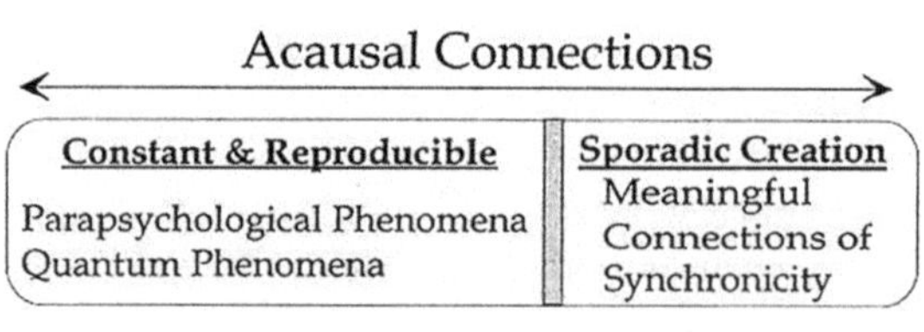

Figure 2.4 "Jung's categories of acausal connections" (*Source*: Mansfield, Rhine-Feather & Hall, 1998, p. 18; 2008, p. 145; Used with permission.)

because the "distinction … may not always be precise" (p. 30).[26] But generally they make a strong distinction. Justifying their stance, they state:

> Although they [parapsychological phenomena] are clearly acausal (in the Jungian sense of historical causality), they also exhibit scientific causality in being repeatable and controllable phenomena. In this sense, parapsychological phenomena are acausal expressions of natural laws—but not, as in the case of true synchronicity experiences, acausal expressions of the archetype of meaning, the self, guiding the process of individuation.
>
> (p. 16)

However, Palmer (2008) takes issue with this quote (thus also disagreeing with Jung), justifiably claiming that "we are not very good at predicting when it [psi] will occur and when it will not: In other words, there is no 'repeatability on demand' in parapsychology" (pp. 180–181). Psi has merely gained the patina of a reliable and reproducible phenomenon based on a decades-long and ongoing research agenda that has nevertheless yielded results that *at the very least* have confirmed psi to be an "anomaly that needs explanation" (Utts, 1991, p. 389). Synchronicity lacks that history, partly because of its novelty, but mainly because there is a cultivated mystique surrounding it that has discouraged rigorous experimental investigation. Therefore, until we know more about synchronicity and psi, the distinctions are vague and uncertain.

Mansfield et al. (1998) go further by running a questionable argument based on a non sequitur—*vis-à-vis*, parapsychological (psi) phenomena are not "synchronicity experiences" *because* psi is "repeatable and controllable" (p. 16), as well as "Constant and Reproducible" (see Figure 2.4)! As we have seen, those latter assumptions about psi are debatable, but that aside, the authors are saying "synchronicity experiences" cannot be repeated or controlled. That may only be true at the individual level, as I have argued in the previous subsection. Alternatively, Mansfield et al. regard "quantum phenomena" as "constant and reproducible" (see Figure 2.4). However, the individual QM event is not "constant and reproducible" (i.e., not causal), but (recalling Pauli's words above) a large-scale statistical framework yields a probabilistic (repeatable and controllable) phenomenon that can be regarded as scientifically causal.

Physicist Roger G. Newton (1967, 1970) runs a different (correlational) argument: "the only foolproof method of scientifically testing a *causal connection* between *A* and *B* is "wiggling" one of them and watching the response of the other" (p. 1571). He also noted:

> The notion of cause and effect is defined by invariant (or statistical) correlation of the latter with the former …. The temporal order of the two is an *observational* fact. We may not believe that new experiments will ever

> find effects that precede their causes, but if they do causality itself is not thereby endangered.
>
> (Newton, 1967, p. 1274)

Newton even admits precognition into the foray as retro-causality (effect before the cause). It needs stating that this viewpoint is claiming that the proven correlation *indicates* causality, but that is not so; at best, it may only *imply* causality, and ideally a search should be made for same. But physicists see 'acausality' as a relative concept, and they overcome the problem on the strength of correlational findings (recall my comments on functional causation in Chapter 1, *Causality and Acausality*). QM effects, for example, are repeatable and can be modelled, but that gets us no nearer to the *cause* of the single event. To a similar extent, phenomena like psi and synchronicity are also circumstantially causal or acausal, being acausal at one level but not another. We can observe the phenomena on an individual basis, where the effects are acausal, or test the phenomena *en masse* (by sampling) where patterns emerge, so the effects are considered causal (predictable, deterministic). Whether nominally determining the causality of a phenomenon by those methods is legitimate or not, the approaches are widely accepted. By adopting the methodological practices and theoretical approaches of physicists and statisticians, virtually all Jung's synchronistic phenomena listed in Table 2.1 (those that apply) could nominally be classed as 'causal', albeit based on a very simple criterion—nevertheless, we have a categorical problem. We have seen how these methods have been justified and applied to nonpsychic phenomena, but psychic (narrow) synchronicity is not excluded.

So saying, the very term "general acausal orderedness" may have limited applicability given certain conditions. A prime example is astrology. Since Jung's day, we have learned that there is some statistical evidence of the efficacy of astrology (Currey, 2017, 2018; Ertel, 1988, 1992, 2003, 2007; Eysenck & Nias, 1982; Gauquelin, 1983; Tarnas, 2007; West, 1992). The massive tome by Tarnas (2007) goes to great lengths detailing the many personal and cultural effects of key aspects of the outer planets on individuals, societies, and countries over the millennia. While Tarnas considers these relationships 'correlational', and describes them as "archetypally patterned" (p. 461), he actually offers no causal explanations. But Jung (1952/1969) entertained the possibility that there might be a "causal connection between the planetary aspects and the psycho-physiological disposition" (para. 876), which if shown to be so would certainly exclude astrology as a narrow form of synchronicity. Recent research suggests astrological causality is based at the solar/geomagnetic level with each of the planets warping our Sun's field, thus giving a unique, constantly changing character to Solar activity. In turn, these characteristics have unique influences on the foetus (Douglas, 2020). These alignments (i.e., the planetary aspects) may explain natal charts. Although astrology might currently be classed as a narrow form of synchronicity, we may one day see astrology shift to the "Causality" pole of Jung's 'quaternio' (see Figure 2.1).

Summing Up

These five major problems (i.e., the psychic/nonpsychic differentiation, the semantic issues over meaning and archetypes, the statistical evaluation of synchronicity, and the causality/acausality dichotomy) bubble away below the surface of a wider re-conceptualization of synchronicity. To clarify what is being tested in this section, I started with Jung's argument that any phenomenon that falls under the rubric of the GAO is definably synchronistic. One point of contention is whether a subclass of synchronicity is nonpsychic just because a few loosely re-defined criteria are met (assuming that nonpsychic synchronicity is not a contradiction in terms). For the more pragmatic person, a psychic product of primarily personal relevance (necessarily involving meaning and observer participation) is the crucial starting point in seeking a synchronistic spin on events, but the loss of that twofold contingency suggests the nonpsychic synchronicities on their own (outside human experience) are not synchronistic in any *substantive* sense, in spite of their being nominally acausal, which only justifies a position for them in the GAO.

One might tentatively advise that the acausal phenomena Jung and Pauli regarded as 'nonpsychic' be treated in the same way these phenomena are (or would be) treated in the conventional sciences; for example, microphysical phenomena (many of which are acausal) were ultimately accepted, and they revolutionized physics and our technological world. Apart from the controversy over 'fundamentals' in the field of quantum physics (e.g., the measurement problem, decoherence; see Becker, 2019), such moves do not seem to have a crippling effect on scientific progress; besides which, as I said above, a unitary worldview is not so far removed from how scientific discoveries are made through inner personal experience. Consider the earlier examples of Leibniz and Kekulé, whose discoveries seemed inspired by archetypal realities. However, while their discoveries are synchronistic, these are only in the narrow sense.

Many decades ago, Progoff (1973) argued Jung's case by stating that "Jung became increasingly interested in establishing Synchronicity as a general principle of knowledge relevant for all the sciences and not limited to the study of man [*sic*]" (p. 141). But Progoff also told us no progress had been made to achieve Jung's "very large vision" (p. 142). In the new century, nothing has changed. Jung hoped to convince scientists of a synchronistic underpinning to reality, or more correctly, the fundamentally acausal side of reality, but his expanded model leaves much to mull over, with a number of aspects clearly lacking plausibility. These aspects are not confined to human factors. The key points are these:

1 *The observing psyche*: It seemed wise at the time for Jung and Pauli to differentiate narrow (psychic) synchronicity from those wider synchronicities that exist independently of psyche, but that distinction did not help unite physics and psychology (or other disciplines), and may even have helped firm up the division.[27] For a few physicists working in the field of

parapsychology, psi is seen as a psychic (i.e., psychological) phenomenon and, given the parallels, they may even regard synchronistic phenomena as necessarily psychic. It is moot whether those same physicists have use for the term 'nonpsychic' when describing matter.

2 *Meaning*: Jung's proposed category of wider (nonpsychic) synchronicities, that includes microphysical phenomena, makes no room for 'meaning' *per se*, by which we should mean those phenomena are not meaningful—i.e., not "a living experience that touches the heart just as much as the mind" (von Franz, 1992, p. 257). Jung suggested words like 'equivalence' and 'conformity' serve as suitable replacements for the word 'meaning' so that these terms would maintain the semblance of synchronicity. But Jung's toying with the idea that those synchronicities may carry a "self-subsistent meaning" (1952/1969, para. 912) and his reference to "absolute knowledge" (para. 948), undermines his original aim. While the key to inspired and innovative discoveries may depend on identifying kinds of 'meaning' in nature, those meanings are ascribed and would even be regarded as observable 'facts'—this approach is not alien to science.

3 *Archetypes*: Jung proferred a "new interpretation of the term archetype" (Jung, 1951, as cited in Meier, 2001, p. 70) to cater for an expanded definition of synchronicity. But paralleling archetypes with analogues like probability (or a law of probability) is a conceptual shift of questionable validity. The "archetype represents psychic probability" (Jung, 1952/1969, para. 964), and it is "the introspectively recognizable form of *a priori* psychic orderedness" (para. 965). It may not achieve very much to describe *both* acausal microphysical *and* acausal psychic behaviours in terms of archetypes. We see both are ordered and predictable within probable limits, but the former is effectively 'mechanistic' (consistent, uniform), whereas the latter can only be *inferred* (e.g., as images or ideas) on a case-by-case basis as befits the complex nature of the psyche and psychic archetypes. The proposed nonpsychic 'archetype' cannot be much more than an ideological convenience borne of a spurious appeal to orderedness (albeit governed by statistical factors) in the acausal world of matter.

4 *Statistics*: One of the cornerstones of science is statistics, yet Jung paradoxically frowned upon its use in the context of supporting evidence for psychic/half-psychic synchronicity, as in the case of narrow synchronicity and astrology, but not in the case of psi (which involves the psyche), or the various microphysical phenomena (which do not involve the psyche). Such inconsistency shows how a wider definition only dichotomizes synchronicity further, and encourages statements such as "mathematical analysis" is an "entirely wrong" method for "understanding synchronistic phenomena" (Mansfield, 1995, p. 34). This argument may be partly true in the context of analytically discerning the meaning of an experience, but then much qualitative information can be gleaned from synchronistic data that is collected using quantitative methods as has been shown with

studies of psi and astrology. In the case of microphysical phenomena, worthwhile large-scale statistical frameworks still principally and practically yield findings that are *de facto* (i.e., we have to accept them regardless of what logic or formal laws say). While these frameworks are a way around our limited knowledge, meant to curb our ignorance, they do marginalize the individual event.

5 *Acausality*: The argument that any phenomenon, not just synchronicity, can be acausal in nature cannot be settled without making certain allowances that entail learning to think differently about so-called 'causes'—that is, deciding what causality and acausality are going to mean, and determining the extent to which those terms can be applied, and to which phenomena.[28] Some events observed to be causal at one level (i.e., they demonstrate *constant connections through effect*) can be acausal at another (this point is borne out in QM phenomena), just as some events observed to be acausal at one level are causal at another (see Gatlin, 2008; Tart, 2008). Psi and synchronicity may demonstrate scientifically acausal attributes, but certain kinds of predictability or determinism or functionalism are evident as patterns in multiple observations (note how these may only be correlational yet are deemed causal). Without wishing to make a semantic issue of it, causality and acausality are relative constructs. As a result, *acausality* (like causality) enjoys a certain paradoxicality, so that its contribution to the debate is minimal in the context of finding justification to *expand* the definition of synchronicity so as to embrace the microphysical phenomena.

Perhaps, if the connotations in the agreement between the two (Jung and Pauli) had been felt more deeply—that nonpsychic synchronicity, on the one hand, and psychic/half-psychic synchronicity on the other, are "*phenomena or effects on different levels*" (Pauli, 1950, as cited in Meier, 2001, p. 56)—they might have seen that their unifying agenda was going to riddle the categorization agenda with nothing but contradictions. Given the speculative nature of much that has been presented above, one could argue that Jung and Pauli were on the right track, but at this stage it does look like they pushed very hard, and possibly too hard. For all these reasons, I suggest a re-design of Figure 2.3 that was merely presented as my understanding of Jung's earlier ideas. The main changes evident in Figure 2.5 show that (i) synchronicity is part of the GAO but not all contents of the GAO are synchronicity; (ii) 'ESP' and 'PK' ('psi') phenomena and *I Ching* effects are psychic synchronicities (but I use the terms 'ESP' and 'PK' only in a nominal sense); (iii) the old term 'narrow synchronicity' is redundant; (iv) the acausal properties of *numbers* and *constants* are not synchronistic, but when represented and demonstrated in manifest (physical or otherwise observable) form, they are examples of acausal orderedness only; because (v) there are no 'nonpsychic synchronicities'.

Admittedly, in spite of the aims of this section, points about synchronistic categorization can easily be lost, but as I have been arguing thus far (see the

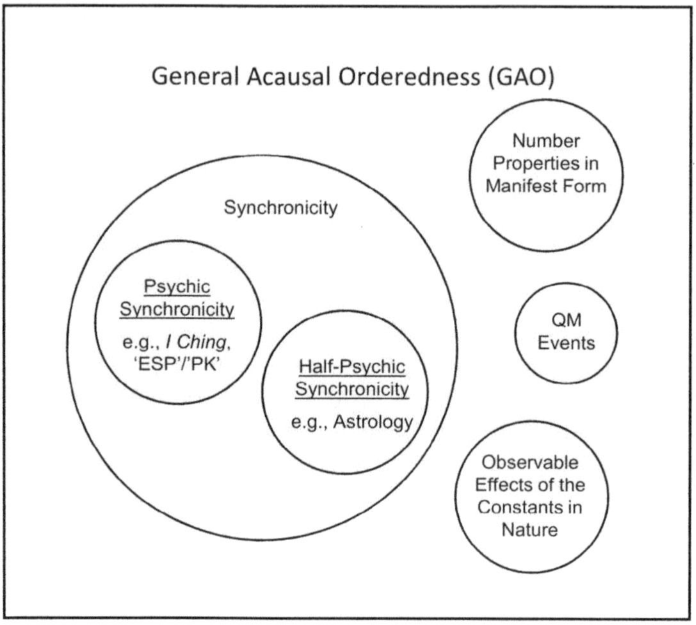

Figure 2.5 A revised version of Figure 2.3 (*mutatis mutandis*), includes the set of psychic/half-psychic (formerly 'narrow') synchronicities and its complement (formerly, Jung's 'nonpsychic' synchronicity). (*Source*: © 2024, L. Storm)

section "Alternative Explanations of Synchronicity: I. Chance" in Chapter 1), and will continue to argue in later chapters, all phenomena can be modelled statistically, even those that are part of the GAO—outcomes can be predicted on a statistical basis, and the phenomena can be adequately and satisfactorily fitted to stochastic models if deterministic models are beyond our reach. Even Mansfield (1995) agreed that the "scientific procedure is appropriate for the study of general acausal orderedness" (p. 34).

On this same point, however—and it is a crucial one—I close this section with a quote from von Franz (1980), who appears to have had the same naïve understanding as Jung:

> [...] there was much discussion as to whether one could not still discover a law under which synchronistic events would have a certain regularity, or would follow certain laws and therefore become predictable so that one could say now, in that situation, a synchronistic event *must* happen. This it has not been possible to find and Jung, after long reflection and discussion, came to the conclusion that we have to admit, much as it annoys our rational minds, that synchronistic events are just-so stories.
>
> (p. 100)

The trouble here is that von Franz (1992), throughout her book *Psyche and Matter*—a collection of her essays published across many decades—continually equates psi processes with synchronicity without seeing her contradictions, just as I have outlined in this section (for further comments, see Chapter 5). The lengthy quote just featured undermines quantitative (statistical) testing and general observations of a qualitative nature from which inferences and models can be made. Von Franz speaks of an *orderedness* in the GAO that gives our world a constancy and invariability ("no individual deviations"; p. 100). That should have been a clue to von Franz that even the 'probable' behaviour of any given archetype (which underpins synchronicity) has some degree of predictability, but she was more focused on individual synchronistic manifestations as being 'just-so', as if to imply they are incontrovertibly unpredictable. And in von Franz saying "we", one assumes other Jungians (and even Jung himself) were on the same page as von Franz, yet anyone reading Jung (1989) would surely see that he believed synchronicity took place in his *I Ching* experience when he "made use of the coin method" (p. *xxvi*).[29] One has to ask, 'Did he assume the *I Ching* works *synchronistically* first time, every time?' Perhaps, but I wish to go further: *If* multiple *I Ching* users are tested (see Storm, 2016), or even a single user in multiple trials (e.g., Thalbourne, 1994),[30] *then* certain kinds (and a certain number) of synchronistic effects are determinable from the data in the same way astrological effects have been shown statistically (Jung, 1952/1969, para. 905; see also West, 1992), despite doubts from Jung himself about experimentation with the *I Ching* (Jung, 1951/1969, para. 986), and astrology (Jung, 1952/1969, para. 901). Parapsychologists collect data, and run tests on that data; so do physicists. The situation today for synchronicity might be very different, and favourably so, had Jung, with or without Pauli's aid, and later with von Franz's able assistance, given more thought to this fact, and made just that one concession about synchronicity and astrology, as they had done for ESP and PK—that all are 'statistically testable and constant' and 'experimentally reproducible' under appropriate conditions, as is to be expected of phenomena that demonstrate a *general orderedness* (irrespective of *acausality*).

Although the other mentioned categorical anomalies still necessarily remain under the spotlight, what is also brought to light in the above analyses is the fact that making too many categorical assumptions about seemingly diverse and disparate phenomena can have dire consequences. With that in mind, I now discuss Browne's sobering approach to categories of explanation that serve to keep synchronicity separate from other categories of coincidence.

Browne's Categories of Coincidence

Australian researcher Laurence Browne has gone to considerable effort to categorize the various coincidences and explain them in order to draw out their phenomenological differences. Browne gives particular attention to the fact that synchronicity is exceptional; in fact, Browne's Ph.D. dissertation focused primarily on this aim. As such, the book based on his dissertation, *The Many Faces of Coincidence* (Browne, 2017), is superior to most in the same genre for his broader approach, his depth of analysis, and his capacity to explain with ease very dense synchronistic and related concepts. Browne argues for four distinct categories of coincidence explanations, and while they initially address all manner of coincidences, Browne emphasizes that the categories, and therefore the explanations, are not mutually exclusive. The categories are:

- Random chance explanations;
- Conventional causal explanations;
- Paranormal causal explanations;
- Synchronicity explanations.

Regarding the first of these, we must recall the previous comments by Jung and by Mansfield about chance and the possibility of hidden causes (see the section "Alternative Explanations of Synchronicity: I. Chance" in Chapter 1). However, Browne's (2017) use of the word "random" is meant to stress the fact that something that happens by chance can be truly random, as in the "absolute randomness that lies at the heart of quantum physics" (p. 178). Other forms of randomness (classical and chaotic) are dubious. As for the second and third of these "explanations", any "coincidences" that ultimately prove to be "causal" (conventional or paranormal) are immediately eliminated as coincidences *per se* since, by definition, coincidences are not supposed to have causes explaining the *connections* between the parts, although those parts taken independently can demonstrate causal chains. Quite serendipitously, I came across an article by Alice Johnson (1860–1940)[31]—an early researcher and one-time secretary of the Society for Psychical Research (UK)—and found that two, possibly three, or even all four, of Browne's coincidence explanations can be worked into Johnson's three 'provisional classifications':

> (A) Coincidences suggestive of "Causation" [e.g., common cause]; (B) Coincidences suggestive of "Design" [e.g., they are fortuitous, fateful, 'karmic']; (C) Coincidences due to "Chance" [i.e., random, probabilistic].
> (Johnson, 1899, p. 165)

Going back well over a century, Johnson's (1899) book-length article is little-known today, which is unfortunate since she went to painstaking efforts to get to the heart of the various coincidence problems. She gave very detailed attention to coincidences set up by chance, such as the occasion of two British men in Paris who shake hands and introduce themselves, each to the other, as "Rev. Charles Bingham" (p. 195). This coincidence recalls the Buxtons' case in Chapter 1, and two golfers called Kevin O'Brien whose golf balls happened to collide (see Browne, 2017). It is worth noting too that while Johnson proposed that telepathy, albeit "supernormal", is the type of coincidence that has causal ('subliminal') determinants (Browne's "paranormal causal"?), a somewhat different argument is evinced when a supposedly wound-down "musical box *commenced playing*" at precisely the moment the two Binghams expressed interest in the whereabouts of their recently deceased "old friend Professor Cope" (p. 233). One must wonder if Professor Cope was a music lover. Although Johnson often tries to uncover the natural (e.g., probabilistic) mechanisms underlying 'Professor Cope'-type coincidences, as if to test the waters, she ultimately calls them 'coincidences by design', for she has in mind that they (like premonitions) are not explained causally to a satisfactory degree (if at all), but are nevertheless somehow "of real moment", or are "due to a special intervention" (p. 205). These we might now call synchronicity, but we have at that particular time in history (the *fin de siècle*), the barest hint of a rudimentary 'meaningful coincidence' concept in its developmental stage, and of course, Jung was still a youth with his full-blown synchronicity concept still decades away. It is not known whether Jung knew of Johnson's work, but she is not cited in his essay.

Browne's (2017) explanations are helpful to our understanding, but in the following I mean to put his categories to the test by mere illustration: We should expect that the meaningful coincidences described in the previous chapter would be covered by "synchronicity explanations", but it would be necessary for meaningless chance groupings (or aspects thereof) to fall under one or more of the other three categories. A convenient example is Jung's fish series as I find it works at many levels; we see "random chance" at work when a series of events happen to occur during the window of opportunity of that April Fool's weekend—perhaps, for example, that opportune moment when Jung came across a fish-themed inscription. Also, a "conventional causal" explanation can be invoked when another friend spoke of making an April Fool of someone as is to be expected on the first day of April.

Out of interest we might ask if Jung's fish series features occurrences that require a "paranormal causal" explanation. While Jung (1952/1969) classes the whole series of incidents as a meaningless chance grouping (para. 826–827), that does not mean we have to assume there were no paranormal occurrences. Spontaneous paranormal cases can be difficult to spot, let alone prove, so we can only hypothesize instances of psi, but it is reasonable to propose, for example, that the fish dream of Jung's patient may have been initiated telepathically by Jung (otherwise we can settle with it being a random event, or causally related to the therapeutic process the patient was undergoing).

Browne (2017) later adjusted his categories to help "cater for the ultimate cosmological questions" (p. 80), thus:

- Random chance explanations;
- Natural causal explanations;
- Supernatural causal explanations;
- Synchronicity explanations.

We see that "conventional" in the prototypical set of categories is replaced with "natural", and "paranormal" is replaced with "supernatural". As it happens, supernatural causation is anathema to some parapsychologists who have enough trouble with the seeming irregularity of the psi process without having to deal with possible meddling from uninvited and unruly (albeit hypothetical) supernatural entities such as angels, or demons, or uber-intelligences, so the switch from "paranormal" to "supernatural" will not be appreciated. As Palmer (2008) states: "We resent it very much when psi is labelled as 'supernatural' or 'miracles'". (p. 182). Nevertheless, while parapsychologists are interested in post-mortem survival that centres around discarnate entities, researchers do not yet have methodologies that conclusively differentiate discarnate agency from supernatural agency (but see Rock & Storm, 2015, for a suggestion); indeed, the unresolved debate over post-mortem survival vs. living-agent psi is far from settled. Therefore, the problem for parapsychologists, like it or not, is that the term "supernatural" is viable in some circumstances until they know better.

Browne (2017) says "supernatural causation" is proposed to cover "creative intelligence" because the "apparent fine-tuning for life of the universal parameters or constants of nature is *so* precise …" (p. 80), something or some 'thing' must have had a 'hand' in it. Supernatural causation is proposed as a counter to the causal and/or statistical arguments put forward to explain our unique presence and place in this particular epoch, in this particular galaxy and universe, living as we do in a 'Goldilocks zone' where the physical parameters just happen to make the universe tick in a 'just-so' life-sustaining fashion. Browne is arguing for a more extensive form of coincidence in that we are privileged to experience a spectacular array of cosmic phenomena that would not otherwise be available to us in any other eon. In other words, "supernatural causation" is an answer to the question, Why are we here now, rather than earlier or later?[32] It does not seem possible that random chance explains this instance, but I cannot see why it could not be "natural" (i.e., in accordance with Nature) rather than "supernatural".

Of course, *if* the universe is 'fine-tuned' for life *supernaturally*, then it would be 'designed' (the word Alice Johnson would use) or planned, so it can no longer be explained as a coincidence. But it could also be argued that life *naturally* is a relatively smaller, extended event enfolded in and *causally* related to (not separate from) a much greater, singular event that we might call the universe in flux or motion—everything has its time and certain physical parameters must prevail (e.g., ideal temperatures, breathable atmosphere), so that the many species, rather than being here coincidentally or supernaturally, necessarily emerge out of contingence rather than necessity; they would have *natural causes.* For similar arguments against 'anthropic coincidences' and 'fine-tuning', see Bottoms and Davis (1999), who note, for example, possible alternatives to carbon-based species, and *ad hoc* factors in the way solar systems form. Such a notion as 'natural cause' even suggests a role to be played by Reichenbach's (1956) 'common cause' (see "Examples of Meaningless Chance Groupings" in Chapter 1)—once life processes are set in motion, certain evolutionary laws generally apply, with many biological entities tracing back to common causes. Even prior to the origins of life, the physical laws still pertain.

Even if a causal or statistical argument has a certain soundness (i.e., "life-permitting" universes are naturally occurring; not just possible, but probable), Browne (2017) suggests that such arguments cannot explain the ultimate origin of the universe—that is, the very first 'kick-start' of our universe, which may be one of many in sequence, or any number of multiverses though these are thought to be unprovable. That aside, White (2000) argues that the multiple universe hypothesis does not make the fine-tuning of our universe any less improbable. However, there are alternatives—Kaufman's (2001) 'serendipitous creativity' speaks to 'creativity' rather than 'creator'—an acausal force that is not an anthropomorphic form of God *per se*, or any other form of 'personal being', but is a perpetual acausal unfolding of creation, conveniently 'serendipitous' (beneficial) for *Homo sapiens* as part of a "cosmic evolutionary process" (p. 415). This conceptualization seems similar to the idea of a universe in flux (as just mentioned) from which the more complex forms naturally evolve from simpler forms (e.g., atoms, molecules, enzymes, and so on up to the species), but whether all those processes in combination point to some overarching teleology is an open question. In that instance, like the concept of 'destiny', it would be as if some kind of 'attractor' in the so-called 'future' was pulling us inexorably towards it, so that causality would really be retrocausality. (This notion would probably have more metaphysical than physical appeal.) After all, what seems too convenient, let alone coincidental for the universe (and us), is how sub-atomic particles (e.g., electrons and protons) just happen to form atoms, which just happen to form elements, which just happen to form molecules, and so on, when no subsequent form seems anticipated by a prior form. That is as good an argument for a teleological universe as any (see Collins, 2009). We can perhaps understand why Kaufman referred to this creativity as "very close to being a synonym of the concept of mystery"; hence, a "metaphor" (p. 412).

It is worth noting that some related thought has gone into the cosmological idea of a self-perpetuating, infinite, and repeating ('conformal cyclic') universe that resurrects itself like the Phoenix bird (Laszlo, 2003; Penrose, 2010). Laszlo (2003) proposed that our universe is a culmination of a series of universes, each one ending and the next beginning, with each prior universe structurally contributing to the next one under the assumption that "traces of prior universes" survive (p. 85). A similar theory championed by cosmologist Roger Penrose might lead one to ask why the universe he proposes (the endlessly recycling one) came to be so in the first place. Browne frames the problem in a similar way: "… the question must eventually arise as to the nature of the origin, if indeed there is one, of the universe, multiverse, or whatever else is proposed" (p. 80). But Browne also wonders "if indeed there is [an origin]". When dealing with infinity the 'origin' question ('how it came to be so') may make no sense because infinity can imply no 'beginning' and therefore (it would seem) no cause. And, surprisingly, one does not need to ask about ultimate purpose either.

The argument from infinity seemingly short-circuits further speculation, but we might still be in a kind of ontological stalemate because a supernatural origin to the universe does not preclude the possibility that a 'created' universe or 'self-emergent' universe could be maintained (or maintains itself) infinitely from that point on. Whenever there is appeal to infinite factors we find them hard to wield in intellectual terms; hence, a mythological dimension tends to make its presence felt, made more unsettling when replete with especial images like the *ouroboros*. We are in the territory of the cosmologist and the metaphysician when we try to tackle these issues, and aside from all that, we would do better to keep our feet on the ground and see whether Jung's previously mentioned fish series accommodates Browne's two revised explanations. At least there may be some satisfaction in that.

As it happens, the element in the fish series described above as "conventional causal" easily accommodates a "natural causal" explanation, but (as already stated) the relabelling of "paranormal causal" as "supernatural causal" does raise issues. Recall, of course, that the fish dream of Jung's patient was proffered as only *possibly* telepathic in its origins (purely for illustrative purposes), but a "paranormal explanation" does demand fewer entities (no pun intended), whereas any of the events in the fish series could, on the face of it, involve a "supernatural explanation" at some level given the implied scope of the latter explanation (if one wanted to go that far). Browne (2017) sets logical limits on that kind of speculation. Furthermore, the definition of supernatural can be expanded beyond supernatural agency *per se*. As it happens, supernatural may mean:

- of, relating to, or being above or beyond what is natural; unexplainable by natural law or phenomena; abnormal;[33]
- (of a manifestation or event) attributed to some force beyond scientific understanding or the laws of nature.[34]

Indeed, it would be to prejudge Browne to ignore these definitions, for he states:

> According to the *Oxford English Dictionary*, the term 'supernatural' has a wide range of meanings and can therefore readily accommodate not only the postulation of a creator God but also the possible existence of all sorts of anomalous phenomena, including ESP and telepathy.
>
> (Browne, 2017, p. 72)

Thus, for any nominally supernatural phenomenon, a force beyond or transcendent of scientific understanding and/or nature may be attributable to human agency (formerly requiring a 'paranormal' explanation), or we find that human involvement is decisively absent (as in cosmological phenomena), or at best is provisionally so. The question then arises, How is it that humans, who are *not* beyond nature, can express, manifest, or wield a force that is *beyond* nature? But then again, 'paranormal' (psi) phenomena are 'beyond' normal. In fact, could we ever be sure in the case of psi that it does not have a 'cosmological' element, or at least requires an holistic interpretation, especially for those instances that look like miracles? (For a response, see Chapter 5.)

Speaking generally of his revisions, Browne thinks they are workable, and "without too much distortion of meaning" (p. 116), but there is another issue here: One of my major aims in this book is to merge psi with synchronicity, yet a categorical anomaly is immediately evoked because psi cannot be both supernatural *and* synchronistic under Browne's (2017) schema. My suggestion is that we merely shift all psi phenomena to the synchronicity category (with a question mark over those cases suggestive of supernatural agency), call them holistic, and recognise that the causality/acausality dichotomy is actually a pseudo-problem (see Summing Up in the previous section). In the meantime, I will now look at the various forms synchronicity may take.

Forms of Synchronicity

In this section I describe three forms of synchronicity: spatial, temporal, and agentive. Form refers mainly to the structure and operative *framework* of synchronicity, but not the *elements* or *contents*. To avoid an extremely complicated task, I do not take on the impossible task of describing the multitudinous range of synchronistic elements or contents, which would be akin to preparing a dream dictionary.

In describing the various forms meaningful coincidences may take (not necessarily synchronicity), Beitman (2017a) uses the same term 'form', by which he means 'mind' and 'thing' as the "basis for form", each 'base' in combination forming three possible pairs: "mind-thing (thought and object), mind-mind (subjective parallels), and thing-thing (a series of two or more observables)." Hence:

- *Mind-Thing*: the intersection of a mental event with an environmental event;
- *Mind-Mind*: the intersection of two mental events. Two (or more) people experience a similar thought and/or feeling at a distance usually around the same time (very common amongst closely-bonded people and twins; see Chapter 5);
- *Thing-Thing*: the appearance of two or more unexpected, similar, environmental events.

'Mind-thing' and 'mind-mind' are the two more common synchronistic forms experienced by an observing psyche that incorporates its own *mental* (meaningful) content, thus making it recognizable as synchronicity. The 'thing-thing' form ("a series of two or more observables"), although it involves an ostensibly objective, observing psyche in order to draw the parallel, would not necessarily incorporate that psyche's *mental* content, although it would appear it must for one cannot discount the privileged position of the observer (on synchronistic variance, see also Main, 2007). In other words, meaningfulness by definition would have to be embedded in 'thing-thing' synchronicity for it to be truly *synchronistic*, although Beitman (2022) refers to those kinds of purely objective experiences as serendipity. Recall Aziz's words from Chapter 1: "a synchronistic event remains a synchronistic event whether or not its meaningfulness is recognized" (Aziz, 1990, p. 76).

Beitman's (2017a) three pairs may fit Jung's main definition of synchronicity ("a coincidence in time of two or more causally unrelated events"; 1952/1969, para. 850), but the parallels with form as I use the term end there. Beitman's forms ultimately refer to the *contents* (mental or physical). Beitman (2022) later changed 'mind-thing' to "mind-object", and 'thing-thing' to "object-object" (pp. 22–23). In mind-object coincidences, these objects can be animals, inanimate things, physical places, media, machines, and even disease and future events (pp. 25–31). Object-object coincidences can be convergences, for example, of two or more ideas, numbers, or names. We may find that some of these could reduce to meaningless chance groupings not easily elevated to the level of synchronicity proper, but closer inspection suggests, as I said previously, that the privileged position of an observer may mean mental content is involved, with meaningfulness possibly (or even inevitably) emerging out of the observation.

By 'form' I mean the 'dimensional framework' in which the contents are situated; how the synchronicity manifests (temporally and spatially), and how it got that way (agentively). While the forms give structure, the unique characteristics of the contents are of personal interest to the experient, but the forms described here are not intrinsically relevant to the meaning beyond the inherent meaning that gives synchronicity its ontological significance.

Each of the three forms is dichotomized:

1 The *temporal form of synchronicity* refers to the phenomenological structure of synchronicity in terms of how its elements are temporally related. There are two temporal forms: *synchronous synchronicity* (e.g., Swedenborg's Stockholm fire), and *asynchronous synchronicity* (e.g., Jung's scarab case; i.e., the client's dream occurring *a day prior* to the rose chafer's appearance);
2 The *spatial form of synchronicity* refers to the phenomenological structure of synchronicity in terms of how its elements are spatially related. There are two spatial forms: *proximal synchronicity* (e.g., Jung's scarab case; i.e.,

the dreamer telling the dream and the rose chafer are both in Jung's office), and *distal synchronicity* (e.g., Swedenborg's Stockholm fire);

3 The *agentive form of synchronicity* refers to the motivating agency behind the synchronicity. There are two agentive forms: *intentional synchronicity*, which is deliberate and purposive, via conscious agency (e.g., *I Ching* usage—see also Palmer, 2008, on "*Volition*"; p. 181), and *nonintentional synchronicity*, which is adventitious and chance-like, but unconscious and *not* via conscious agency (e.g., all three examples of synchronicity given in Chapter 1).

Crucially, synchronicity is either intentional or nonintentional. Also, *within* and *between* combinations of the other two forms are possible—that is, a synchronicity may contain one or both temporal forms, and/or one or both spatial forms.

The temporal and spatial forms are to be understood as phenomenological variants of synchronistic experience that can occur *within* the spheres of our sensory modalities or *outside* those spheres, but those modalities do not work in tandem with synchronicity; they only 'position' the individual in the experience, which is to say they give a perspective. This understanding gives synchronicity a categorical foothold only, which may or may not be of interest or relevance to some. It does not mean synchronicity behaves differently outside those spheres compared to what might transpire within those spheres.

Having proposed these two forms, there is no intention to replace the corresponding psi modalities used in the Rhinean model even though the terms related to the latter are ambiguous (on the problem of parapsychological nomenclature, see Chapter 1 in Storm, 2025). These two forms are convenience terms that illustrate how synchronicity *seems to manifest paranormally*, which is to say it appears *as if* synchronicity/psi violate spacetime or relativise it; instead, contingent archetypes create the perceptual (phenomenological) illusion that synchronicity/psi violate spacetime (see *The Spacetime Factor and Archetypal Inevitability* in Chapter 4 of Storm, 2025).

Both agentive forms (intentional *and* nonintentional) accommodate the conventional understanding in parapsychological circles that the psi function can be initiated consciously or *seemingly* unconsciously, with the proviso that synchronicity is not the exclusive expression of a psi ability *per se*.

The three forms are now described in more detail.

The Two Temporal Forms of Synchronicity

Synchronicity can take two temporal (i.e., chronological) forms: synchronous and asynchronous. The first type, synchronous synchronicity, manifests as two (or a series of) acausally connected incidents that can be psychic and/or physical, and effectively occur simultaneously. There would be no time lapse (no delay) between the elements. An example is Swedenborg's vision of the

Stockholm fire because the fire occurred at the same time as the vision in Gothenberg 500 kilometres away (i.e., Swedenborg reported the fire *while* it was underway). The distal component adds emphasis to the ostensibly acausal nature of the vision, but synchronous synchronicity can still be acausal even if it involved *proximal* components, as in a typical case of mind-reading between (say) a sitter and a psychic giving the sitter a real-time reading *in the same room*, ostensibly described as telepathy (assuming the essential controls).

One of the major reasons most people are intrigued by synchronicity is that it often manifests asynchronously.[35] This temporal form manifests as a minimum of two acausally connected incidents displaced in our perception of time. In such cases, we find some substantive amount of time has elapsed between the two incidents (one being the normal event; the other being the critical event). Most parapsychologists probably think of asynchronous synchronicity as akin to precognition and retrocognition, although the latter is difficult to prove as a paranormal effect since earlier (prior) events often form part of a verifiable historical record, so it can therefore have a cause attributable to (say) cryptomnesia (but clairvoyance could not be ruled out). Of course, there are those cases where normal (or alternative psi) explanations for retrocognition stretch the imagination and/or do not seem parsimonious, though some think not (see Lamont, 2016; Stevenson, 1977).

An example of asynchronous synchronicity comes from my own collection involving my videocassette recorder (VCR) which stopped working, thus causing me some concern as I needed to use it that day. I thought I should take it to a repair shop, though I did not know of one in my area. That very night, I continued my regular viewing of pre-recorded episodes of *The Saint* series (Charteris et al., 1962), starring Roger Moore as crime-sleuth Simon Templar. Working my way chronologically through the series, the next episode in line ("The Careful Terrorist") concerned a corrupt union boss frustrated by Templar's meddling, who therefore strong-armed the owner of a radio-repair shop to make a remote-controlled bomb to kill Templar. The following day, I went to my usual petrol station to refuel my car, and while holding the dowser, I idly looked around to pass the time. For the first time over my many years frequenting that particular petrol station, I noticed an electrical repair shop ("Cheap TV Video Audio Repairs") across the main road—the signage was very old and fading, suggesting the shop had been there for decades (The Repair shop's website boasts "Over 30 years experience in TV, video and audio repairs").[36] The two main elements to this meaningful coincidence are chronologically separated—the repair shop featured in *The Saint* episode, and the later 'discovery' of an actual repair shop opposite the service station.

This discovery might be seen as serendipitous, but that ignores the backstory replete with other necessary elements (not just the faulty VCR, but the timing of the video viewing and its relevant content), making it synchronicity by definition, and thus something more than serendipity. An explanation in a paper by Caroline Watt (1990–1991) suggests that the later observation only gained my attention because of the earlier priming event (i.e., the first exposure to the radio shop in *The Saint* episode). Prior to that, the real-world repair shop only had a peripheral effect on me and basically never came to my attention due to its irrelevance. As with serendipity, this explanation ignores the complexity of the case involving a string of coincidences in a short space of time. Ordinarily, I might have noticed a repair shop in my neighbourhood *just because* the VCR provided the right trigger, and had the problem been that simple, I could agree with the explanation put forward in Watt's paper.

Parapsychologist Charles Tart's (2008) presentation of "being-specific synchronistic causality" (p. 119) gives us a parallel to the dynamics of synchronous and asynchronous synchronicity, although we will ignore the causal factor for the moment. In Figure 2.6, event S at a "synchronistic level" is a causal factor underpinning the meaningful link between the two events A and B that have "no connection" at the "physical space/time level" (p. 120). Figure 2.6 could effectively illustrate either *synchronous* synchronicity (where A and B are cotemporal), or *asynchronous* synchronicity (A occurs noticeably or measurably before *or* after B). The model serves equally well for both. As the model here is causal, Tart's line of thinking follows the "*if* A, *then* B rule", but instead of A being antecedent, and B consequent, the rule is "*if* S, *then* A and B".[37] Tart gives an example where "some event S" affected both A and B.

Tart (2008) explains that being-specific synchronistic causality "goes beyond the limits of our sensory and cognitive capacities, and the limits of our being (including whatever technological aids our minds produce)" (p. 119), but our intelligence might develop along evolutionary lines so that

> observations which were formerly being-specific synchronistic to us would seem intelligible, becoming reduced to well understood or presumed physical or psychological causality or paranormal causality.
>
> (p. 121)

The term "paranormal causality" could be regarded as a misnomer (if not, an oxymoron). Von Franz (1992) describes the "causal relations" of being-specific synchronistic causality as "definitively unknowable" (p. 233), but she is also

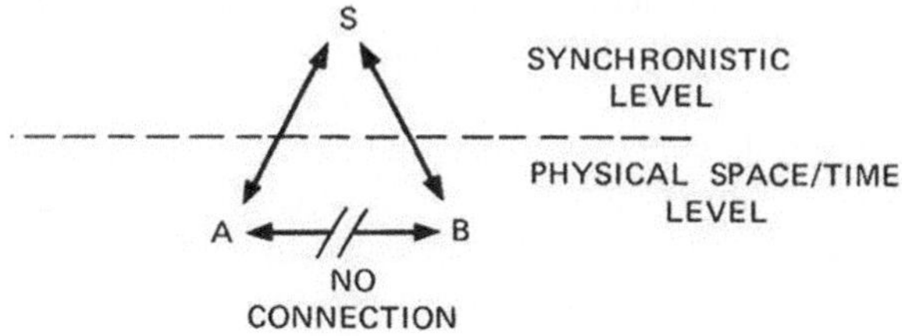

Figure 2.6 Tart's (2008) explanation of being-specific synchronistic causality. (*Source*: © Tart, 2008, p. 120; Used with permission.]

opposed to the connotation that a certain kind of synchronicity could have a cause *per se* (p. 320). Tart does admit that this type of causality is only promissory, and stems from an "anthropomorphic projection of our belief that everything is caused, even though we recognize that we will never be able to prove it" (p. 119). Ultimately, Tart says he is not sure how to "distinguish in practice absolute synchronicity from being-specific synchronistic causality" (p. 122), where absolute synchronicity is the relationship "between two or more events, but even though the events happen in a meaningful pattern, they are not caused at any level" (p. 121).

If anything, Tart (2008) is only being cautious here, but the model does raise issues to do with "space/time", and we can consider that issue further. Tart regards the 'synchronistic level' as being outside 'physical space/time'. In the context of effects demonstrated in Rhine's card-guessing experiments, Jung (1952/1969) reminded us that "the time factor seems to have been eliminated by a psychic function or psychic condition which is also capable of abolishing the spatial factor" (para. 836). For Jung, space and time are "elastic", and are "hypostatized concepts born of the discriminating activity of the conscious mind … created by the intellectual needs of the observer" (para. 840). Synchronicity is thus a "psychically conditioned relativity of space and time" (para. 840). We must be careful how we read Jung, for he might have left the door open to the Rhinean idea that synchronicity is a process independent of space and time, just as psi-power (i.e., psychic ability) is thought to be. It is worth noting that a complication in the psi theory put forward by physicist and parapsychologist Helmut Schmidt required him to abandon the "assumption of the space-time independence of psi" (Stokes, 1987, p. 144). At the very least, the *caveat* is to treat spacetime as *relative*, but *not* let subjective experience drive the opinion that spacetime is not *relevant* (I argue, under the principle that archetypal contingence is ubiquitous, that spacetime cannot be 'eliminated' or even transcended; not by psi, and not by synchronicity).

Though the parapsychological literature suggests many things, we cannot be sure that anything existing within spacetime (including consciousness) has the *causal* power (the omnipotence) necessary to (literally) transcend spacetime in order to furnish the desired psi effect. In an age of information, and given our advances in understanding the nature and application of energy, the paradigms of information acquisition and energy transmission have given rise to the notion of a psi signal, which in turn has helped perpetuate the idea that *psi is human consciousness acting independently of spacetime.* Hence statements such as the following arise:

> This [sheep-goat] effect has been replicated in meta-analyses (e.g., Storm & Tressoldi, 2017) and, of course, does not make any sense unless humans can somehow cognize stimuli temporally or spatially distant, otherwise there would not be any significant difference between the two groups.
>
> (Cardeña, 2018a, p. 6)

Properly understood, the synchronicity paradigm has no use for this idea. It is therefore somewhat surprising that Jung constantly makes reference to 'psychic relativity', and I find Jung's use of that and similar terms inappropriate. Not specifically Jung's fault, but such terms have been taken at face value, and have even been adopted by some parapsychologists who borrow from Einstein's relativity theory to support the naïve assumption that the paranormal process is some kind of unexplained spacetime-transcendent function. Jung places this process in the unconscious (1952/1969, para. 856–858). We may presume Jung means the collective unconscious because therein lie the archetypes, upon which synchronicity and psi are contingent. However, Jung tries to balance two disparate explanatory concepts that do not mesh, and could give rise to misunderstandings: First, there is the notion of a "factor in the psyche that is not subject to the laws of time and space" (Jung, 1975, p. 398), which is how he speaks of ESP and PK phenomena (i.e., psi). Similarly, as quoted in the previous paragraph, and in his earlier synchronicity paper, he is quite explicit in stating that synchronicity (like psi) involves the "psychic relativity of space and time" (1951/1969, para. 984):

> Though synchronistic phenomena occur in time and space they manifest a remarkable independence of both these indispensable determinants of physical existence and hence do not conform to the law of causality.
>
> (Jung, 1963/1970, para. 662)

These statements unequivocally suggest spacetime is malleable and can be subjected to psychic 'warping'. That is, Jung is most likely to be taken to mean a *future*, or *past*, or *distant* event beyond the senses, can be *perceived* in the here and now—hence, the relativity.

Fortunately, Jung (1975) makes a second point, which almost (but not quite) puts Jung on safer ground:[38] We learn that the archetypes can suppress "the laws of time and space … to a certain extent" (p. 398). I suggest not at all. By being "ubiquitous in space and time" (p. 398), archetypes are "one and the same inside and outside the psyche" (p. 399). That is how the psychic (psi) or synchronistic correspondences arise. The "eternity" (timelessness) and "ubiquity" (spacelessness) of the archetype (p. 398) gives psi and synchronicity the patina of paranormality in the sense that the effects of a constellated (excited, activated) archetype will maintain a continuity that gives only a *sense* of transcending spacetime, albeit a sense that has pragmatic value.

Jung was clear that archetypes underpin psychic and synchronistic processes, and even stated that he was "satisfied with the fact that there are indeed operative archetypes in many [parapsychological] cases" (p. 399). Experiences of archetypes can yield "flashes of insight" (von Franz, 1992, p. 295; see also pp. 296–297*ff*), intuitions and knowledge beyond that which is furnished via the normal senses, even certain forms of *déjà vu* and foreknowledge (ostensibly precognition). These experiences can manifest in all forms of synchronicity and are nuanced by the character of the given archetype. I suggest also that synchronicity and psi have (or should have) come down to us (thanks to Jung) as phenomenological equals, more similar than not (more on these issues in Chapters 3 and 5).

The Two Spatial Forms of Synchronicity

Synchronicity can take two spatial (i.e., chorological) forms: proximal and distal. The first type, proximal synchronicity, manifests as a pair or series of meaningfully related incidents, acausally connected, that can be both physical and/or psychic, that effectively occur at such a close range that all the relevant events are within the physical purview of the experient (i.e., within the functional distance or 'sphere' of at least one sensory modality). An example of proximal synchronicity is given in the second phase of Jung's scarab case (see Chapter 1). This crucial part of the synchronicity occurred during the analytical session with Jung, whose window pane became centre stage for the rose chafer, much to the consternation of Jung's patient who was giving an account of her dream to Jung at the time.

Distal synchronicity manifests as a pair or series of meaningfully related incidents, physical and/or psychic, acausally connected and separated at great distances from each other. The distance between any two of these incidents must be outside the range of the sensory modalities, which gives synchronicity its paranormal aspect. An example of distal synchronicity is the Evans case—home alone in her apartment, Linda Evans had an intuition that her fiancé was involved in a bridge accident (see Chapter 1). Evans's fiancé was many miles away when the accident occurred. The great distance renders unlikely any possibility of perception using the normal sensory modalities, thus removing the causal factor. The same theoretical points raised in the previous subsection about time and space apply here. Since Jung freely adopts Rhine's terms, he might readily compare distal synchronicity to clairvoyance, as in the Swedenborg case, or telepathy in the Evans case, though the mechanism underlying distal synchronicity is completely different and does not depend on the psi construct.

Due to the presence of normal physical interactions, the proximal form of synchronicity might superficially mask any proof of a paranormal (archetypal) effect, though the more impressive cases do suggest paranormality. For example, certain forms of divination are traditional ways of evoking proximal synchronicity because the outcome of the divining process occurs in the direct presence of the user—before the user's eyes, so to speak. (In that sense, appropriate forms of divination may also be referred to as *intentional synchronicity*—see next subsection). Jung, who had high hopes of experimentally testing synchronicity, discounted standard ESP tests because he believed they were "restricted to the fact of coincidence and only stress its psychic background without illuminating it any further" (para. 863). He needed a stronger ("illuminating") proof of a meaningful arrangement beyond mere coincidence so that he could claim a synchronistic effect. Thus was Jung led to the ancient Chinese divinatory system, the *I Ching*, it being an "intuitive technique for grasping the total situation" (para. 863).

In ancient times yarrow stalks were thrown to generate one of 64 so-called *I Ching* hexagrams, or six-line symbols, each with its own unique reading which can be taken as advice, or as a forecast, or an answer to an important (open-ended) question (details in Appendix C). In the modern era, one of many methods includes throwing three coins six times to generate the hexagram (see Hazel, 1990). Thus, the principle that the same living reality is ostensibly expressing itself archetypally in the psyche as in the world is tested each time the *I Ching* is consulted. The *I Ching* is thus "a method by which an inner state could be represented as an outer one and vice versa" (para. 865); thus a kind of paralleling of inner and outer events is sought.

Aziz (1990), and Main (2004), both argue that the 'paralleling' assumption may not always be true—oracular responses from the *I Ching* in the form of hexagrams and corresponding readings may only indicate compensation of a conscious attitude: "the relationship can be one not of paralleling at all but of compensation" (Main, 2004, p. 40). This problem is resolved by Main himself when he concedes that a reversed order of effects is permissible, as given in Jung's definition: Synchronicity is a "simultaneous occurrence of a certain psychic state with one or more external events which appear as meaningful parallels to the momentary subjective state—*and, in certain cases, vice versa* [emphasis added]" (Jung, 1952/1969, para. 850). We often see this reversed order of effects in the *I Ching* process:

> [...] it is conceivable that responses from the *I Ching* present outer contents that parallel already existent but unconscious images within the person asking the question. Users of the *I Ching* sometimes report that the textual image they obtain seems to correspond to their unconscious preoccupations, even if those preoccupations are not directly articulated in the question put to the oracle
>
> (Main, 2004, pp. 41–42)

Indeed, the very premise of my *I Ching* experiments starting in the late-1990s depended on the assumption that participants have such sufficient insights into their states of mind that the readings would resonate with them and reflect (parallel) those insights, as well as expand on them, which is to say compensate the conscious disposition (for a review, see Storm, 2008a; see also Roe, Martin, & Drennan, 2014).

One might ordinarily think that such effects could arise only as often as chance would dictate, complicated by the fact that people are quick to glean meaning from diverse sources; however, studies suggest otherwise (see Appendix B). Jung explains:

> These [*I Ching*] interpretations formulate the inner unconscious knowledge that corresponds to the state of consciousness at the moment, and this psychological situation coincides with the *chance results of the method* [emphasis added], that is, with the odd and even numbers resulting from the fall of the coins or the division of the yarrow stalks.
>
> (para. 865)

In this instance, Jung means "chance" in the sense of a statistically expected result in a single event that would come from the method.[39] The personal use of the *I Ching* as an activity that promises a meaningful outcome is not undermined by Jung's attribution of the coin-falls to chance (when he would mean *as if* by chance, or chance-like), for the correspondence between the meaning of the outcome *and* the psychic (psychological) condition is not thought of as a random product, but as the synchronistic aspect of interest. Yet Jung then came to believe that synchronicity cannot be demonstrated using statistical procedures, and so he thought the *I Ching* could not be investigated experimentally: the "procedures … do not provide any basis for a statistical evaluation" (Jung, 1952/1969, para. 867). However, if the experimenter is prepared to introduce some controls and modifications to the procedures, experimentation is possible (e.g., see Roe et al., 2014; Storm & Rock, 2014a; Storm & Thalbourne, 1998–1999).

Following the Rhinean paradigm, anyone who has ever used the *I Ching* will note that the *throwing* of stalks or coins (or even online use on the Internet) suggests PK might be the mechanism (e.g., an experienced user focuses on a particular outcome and 'steers' the falling coins to meet the desired end). However, PK effects are very weak, whereas the *I Ching* effect is comparable to ESP-type effects (see Storm & Tressoldi, 2017). Other users may suggest precognition explains the effect (e.g., there may be an intuition of the future outcome so the question is framed, most likely unknowingly, around that intuition), in which case, the physical component of the exercise is perfunctory. Combinations of PK and ESP might be proposed (for both experienced and inexperienced users); indeed, Rhine (1947) has suggested that "PK implies ESP, and ESP implies PK" (p. 129). But, despite the seeming evidence for ESP (mental) and/or PK (physical) effects, there also remains the possibility of a single synchronistic process with a corresponding single resultant effect that occurs via the "transgressivity" of the archetype when it constellates (archetypes "continually go beyond their frame of reference"; Jung, 1952/1969, para. 964).

The Two Agentive Forms of Synchronicity

Synchronicity can take two agentive (i.e., motivational) forms—intentional and nonintentional. Agentive form indicates agency, and refers to an instrumental source acting consciously or unconsciously. Nonintentional (spontaneous) synchronicity describes any synchronicity where there is no evidence of intention (i.e., no conscious design or planned outcome; it is unmotivated). Superficially, and without getting down to the nitty-gritty of unconscious forces or motivations that might suggest an intentional 'other' lurking in the darkest corners of the mind, the nonintentional variant would not ordinarily be seen as having a motivational aspect (i.e., agency) behind it, insofar as motivation or agency is ordinarily regarded as deliberate and therefore conscious. As has often been stated, intention does not imply cause—the individual might *intend* to bring about a synchronistic effect, but that only means he or she has a conscious wish or desire for it to occur. But a predisposed system might be driven by teleological (purposeful, goal-oriented, meaning-seeking) forces at some level in the synchronistic process. Jung assumes contingence rather than causality.

While synchronicity has effectively come down to us as always being nonintentional (not personally motivated)—something that happens to us because synchronicity is held to be a so-called 'principle of nature'—Jung (1952/1969) still allows for intention (or something akin to it) by stating, for example, that a person can "wish" for (para. 837), or "expect", or "hope" for a special outcome (para. 838, 848, 912), and he is speaking not just of psi as tested in Rhine's ESP and PK experiments, but of synchronicity. And Jung (1951/1969) definitely means it of his client at the centre of the scarab case. Thus, I do not make a distinction between psi and synchronicity when it comes to agency.

Gadway (2013) seems to have picked up on the same idea in his analysis of the scarab case where he implies intentionality on Jung's part, though there is nothing more in Jung's so-called 'intention' than a consciously held desire or hope that something might break his client's rationalism—a clear case of 'experimenter psi' for some parapsychologists (see Chapter 2 in Storm, 2025). The client too may have held a similar hope (or why undergo therapy), but it would not rate as conscious intention because the client has no particular goal or image in mind, so the rose chafer is as much a surprise to the client as it is to Jung.[40]

Surprisingly, the independent nature of unconscious forces such as complexes (as well as instincts, drives, reflexes,[41] presses, etc.) or diffuse unverbalised hopes and desires, suggest a form of intention (goal-orientation may be the preferred term) from endopsychic sources other than the 'empirical self' (i.e., ego; see Arminjon, 2011; Saunders & Skar, 2001; Shin et al., 2005). Instead of automatically assuming we only ever deal with nonintentional synchronicity (the default form of synchronicity), we should allow for the possibility of 'intention' from somewhere in the psycho-neurological system, even though we do not, may not, or may never, have ready access to people's unconscious processes to prove it (see also Hassin, Uleman, & Bargh, 2005). Indeed, some parapsychological theories speak to this issue (Carpenter, 2012; Stanford, 1974). This is not to say that the term 'nonintentional' is no longer relevant here—the term is relative so that it does apply if the conscious agent cannot profess intention, or be shown to hold conscious intention. The term 'nonintentional' will always be used in that context.

The intentional form of synchronicity is agentive because an incentivized individual can be recognized as an instigator or propagator of synchronicity, which again does not mean they cause it, or that it will even manifest. That is why the term contingence is preferable. We see that intentional synchronicity is demonstrated in the use of the *I Ching* (see previous subsection). Intentional synchronicity may relate to goals or outcomes that result from "learning to leverage experience" by using meaningful events to "inform our decisions" (Kutz, 2017, p. 74), or "seeking a window into one's psyche to focus a particular issue" using Tarot which is "essentially intentional synchronicity" (Vigorito, 2012, p. 215).

In a letter to British parapsychologist A. D. Cornell in 1960, Jung conceded the possibility of intentionally controlling synchronistic outcomes where he states that there are

> people who seemed to possess a supranormal faculty and were able to make use of it at will. But the apparently supranormal faculty consisted in their already being in, or voluntarily putting themselves into, a state corresponding to an archetypal constellation—a state of numinous possession in which synchronistic phenomena become possible and even, to some extent, probable.
>
> (Jung, 1975, p. 542)

Main (2004) gives this same citation, and although he does not use the term 'intentional', he does refer to "conscious and repeatable generation" of synchronicity (p. 49). He notes that intention is essentially behind the *I Ching* process because the "answers that can stand in a clear synchronistic relationship to the underlying conscious or unconscious preoccupations of the questioner are obtained not spontaneously by a prescribed process of consultation" (p. 49).

Seeds for the possibility of intentional synchronicity were also sown early on in this statement from Progoff (1973): "it does seem to me to be possible to develop in a person an increased sensitivity to synchronistic events, and especially a capacity to harmonize one's life with such occurrences" (p. 132). We can see that this kind of sensitivity could lead to mental and physical actions deliberately motivated by knowledge that one is immersed in a sea of ongoing synchronicities *in potentia*. Progoff makes the additional point that "atmospheres can be set up" by "deliberate purpose" (p. 163), but he also says: "no definite script can be written in advance, since causality is not involved in it" (p. 163).

But as long as archetypes *are* involved, some kind of script, however rudimentary, may be determinable. In that sense, and returning to Jung's point by emphasizing the pivotal role of archetypes, von Franz (1992) effectively adds to the debate over intention:

> [...] the most we can say is that something synchronistic might happen when an archetype is constellated; and if something does happen, then *it will have the same meaning as the archetype* [emphasis added]. But we cannot predict this with certainty—it might happen, it might not.
>
> (p. 27)

Breaking this down, von Franz means that synchronicity cannot be made to order, but she has indicated the means by which we can expect it, and she admits to a kind of 'script' (see the italicized text in the foregoing quote).[42] Mansfield et al. (1998) are somewhat more reserved:

> [...] ordinary mortals cannot "compel the gods," or control archetypal manifestations, [...]
>
> (pp. 22–23)

However, they do not completely dismiss the idea:

> [...] it would be very difficult to do scientifically controlled experiments on synchronicity ... [but] we have a chance of experimentally establishing synchronicity.
>
> (p. 24)

Depth psychologist, Angela Connolly (2015) argues that meaningful coincidence (with the accent on telepathy) may be induced in analytical practice if the personalities concerned situate themselves at the creative edge separating order from chaos. Gieser (2012, as cited in Laveman, 2014) feels that one "cannot manipulate synchronicity", though she concedes that one "might prepare conditions in a company or a group that could be fertile for inviting synchronicities" (p. 293). One would assume the same concession applies to the individual acting alone.

There does, however, seem to be the tacit understanding that synchronicity just happens; it cannot be planned or set up—synchronicity is out of our hands. Russell (2005) argues:

> We cannot control or manipulate the world in order to create synchronicities—their source is not of this world. Yet we can encourage their appearance; we can open ourselves to them.

Browne (personal communication, May 29, 2017) says this:

> [...] we can't really make synchronicities happen to order because if we could, they would never be a surprise and even if it's a small one, it's always a bit of a surprise. Perhaps by our openness we can encourage synchronicity to happen but if on the other hand we go looking for it or try to force it, then it loses its spontaneity and is no longer really synchronicity.

Russell's objection is born of the synchronistic necessity that the physical events must occur outside one's sphere of influence, and Browne is really referring to the absence of numinosity without which we only have a mere (casual) coincidence, or not 'real' synchronicity. However, in both quotes, there is reference to encouragement, and the other statements suggest a natural inclination or certain cultivation of one's mental functions can facilitate an effect.

For *experimentation* in synchronicity to be possible then, intention on the part of participants is mandatory, but that is not to assume that intention (and, for that matter, exposure to appropriate stimuli) will concurrently activate an archetype via the emotional system. Evidently, experimenters who recognise the importance of the emotional system in psi research have been successful in their studies primarily because they used targets that trigger that system (Mossbridge & Radin, 2018b; Mossbridge et al., 2012). Note, however, that the participants in those studies did not act with intention—they were caught unawares so as to ensure a genuine effect (i.e., by not creating physiological artifacts)—but the protocol could easily be 'intentionalized' with minor procedural changes.

Just as conscious intention is *not required* for an effect, I repeat again that intention will not guarantee an effect in a psi or synchronicity situation (for examples, see Palmer, 2016), but for participants to be consciously aware of what is meant by successful targeting, up-front intention is crucial, even unavoidable in some tasks. Thus, I maintain the parallel between synchronicity and psi because the essence or substance of intention in the former functions in the same way as in the latter, about which past research shows intention is prefigured in the term "*dirigibility*" (Pratt, Rhine, Smith, Stuart, & Greenwood, 1940/1966, p. 319). The participant has some degree of volition (control) over the paranormal effect and can guide and give the paranormal process "definite direction" (as noted, psi experimentation would be impossible without that). Insofar as the synchronistic situation is thought by some to be a 'principle of nature' in action to the exclusion of the personal quotient, even making experimentation impossible, I would argue that the individual psyche is part of nature and cannot be seen as an entirely autonomous and neutral (uninvolved) entity, but does have influence in accordance with mental states. Otherwise, the individual could not glean the personal relevance and meaningfulness inherent in a synchronicity experience.

Altogether, it would not be too difficult to concede the possibility that an experimenter could observe *en masse* individuals in synchronicity-like arrangements in a laboratory setting and note the general patterns of the intentional behaviour (of course, insofar as intentionality is of prime concern to the experimenter, ideal participants are those who comply with the experimenter's instructions). As an experimenter myself, I rarely have indication of when and where synchronicity (psi?) has taken place, or if indeed it did take place—rather, I primarily make inferences and assumptions based on statistical outcomes. And even Jung (1952/1969), despite his contradictory remarks in the previous subsection, *did* make the concession (albeit sweepingly) that the activity of the archetype can be "determined approximately" (para. 964).

As far as individual cases of intentional synchronicity are concerned, Mansfield et al. (1998) proposed the possibility of experiments with a single subject, but it "must be done with sufficient rigor that the larger scientific community would be satisfied with all aspects of the data taking, analysis of the data, and so forth" (p. 23). The previous subsection on the *I Ching* suggests the possibility of intentional synchronicity in individuals,[43] at least in principle. As far as broader evidence of an *I Ching* effect is concerned, readers may refer to Appendix B for a brief review of experimental research involving the controlled use of *I Ching* practices. The same appendix features two self-studies by Braud (1983), and my own self-study series: In 2013, 2014, 2015, and 2018, I conducted four gambling (horse-racing) exercises aimed at eliciting intentional synchronicity—three results were favourable; one was inconclusive. On Tarot, see Blackmore (1991), and *Towards a Synchronistic Understanding of Psi* in Storm (2025).

Most gamblers engage in a rudimentary form of intentional synchronicity (if they but knew it) when they make bets at racing events, or participate in games of chance. Ostensibly, these are seen as attempts at bringing about a wished-for event, or ostensibly seeing the future in order to bet gainfully. That is, intentional synchronicity might be seen as entailing either (a) the notion of shaping the future by having a pre-designated outcome in mind, or (b) the mere desire for knowledge of an inevitable outcome in advance of its occurrence without actually bringing it about. There is a very big difference between, in the case of (a), making one's horse win, or influencing the roll of dice (suggesting wilful influence or even interference) and, in the case of (b), wilfully attempting to gain future knowledge (suggesting percipience only). Or to combine the two, in a similar fashion to Shakespeare's *Macbeth*, who takes matters into his own hands in response to the three witches' forecast, the punter might have had a seeming precognitive dream of the winner, but thinks a good dose of mental spurring should be deployed to keep things on track! Indeed, how could any punter resist? Attempts to differentiate (a) from (b) have been inconclusive (see *The Psi Process and Parapsychological Nomenclature* in Storm, 2025).

But is such winning (when it is *not* a random effect) the result of self-fulfilling prophecy through real-time PK, or precognition on its own, or both, or neither? We could say psi mechanisms *per se* are not involved, and need not be implied, at all. In the real world, one might not be able to tease out the levels of involvement, so that any argument for a distinction between (a) and (b), or a combination thereof, remains theoretical, but involvement *per se* could mean being bound up in an archetypal contingency (a kind of resonance constellated under appropriate circumstances). In the laboratory, there have been many efforts at seeking support for the intervention hypothesis in precognition (for a review, see Chapter 5 in Irwin & Watt, 2007; for examples of specific studies, see Drewes, 2002). These authors make compelling claims, but neither they nor the studies make reference to *archetypal inevitability* (see *The Spacetime Factor and Archetypal Inevitability* in Storm, 2025). There are some typical (inevitable) situations in human affairs where archetypes will be constellated. In the cases just discussed, we not only can assume a synchronistic process has transpired if a match is found between a prior mental image and a subsequent physical outcome, but we may also be able to identify the situation as inevitably archetypal with a prefigured outcome (for an example, see *Archetypes* in the section "Some Synchronistic Terms" in Chapter 1).

The Forms in Action

In part, the nature of synchronicity is defined by its forms. To identify these forms, one need only determine whether the elements of synchronicity fall inside and/or outside the action spectrum of the individual, temporally and spatially (i.e., chronologically and chorologically). And as I have said, although synchronicity generally appears to be unintentional, synchronicity can be intentional (evident, for example, in some forms of divinatory practice). A primary aim in this section is to demonstrate that synchronicity cannot be explained or governed by hypothetical psi modalities as psychiatrist Jule Eisenbud (1980) would have it. Eisenbud believes synchronicity reduces to psi (ESP or PK), and the psi experience and its associated inner and outer elements are traceable to an individual as causal agent (for details, see "Rhine's Ideas under Scrutiny" in Storm, 2025). Given that one experiences synchronicity as if one's event timeline intersects or flows like a stream into another event timeline, each with its own causality and, in their merging, they combine acausally but meaningfully, one finds it difficult to imagine how an individual can orchestrate synchronicity in its scale and complexity, and to a satisfactory end. The following examples illustrate how the forms manifest, but they also show that psi is not likely to be the expression of ability through a special modality as is conventionally thought to be the case.

Lynley's faucet: This first example is from my personal files. One night, I watched a digitally pre-recorded episode from the television series *The Inspector Lynley Mysteries* (Block & Young, 2002).[44] The episode was not televised that night; I was working my way through the *Inspector Lynley* series at my own pace, and this particular episode just happened to be next in line on that night. Detective Inspector Thomas Lynley, 8th Earl of Asherton (played by Nathaniel Parker), who is assigned to Scotland Yard, and based in London, vainly tries to run a faucet in the bathroom of a private room in a college outside London. A murder has taken place on the college grounds, and Lynley is assigned to investigate. Thus, the image of a bathroom faucet was placed in my mind. The thought occurred to me to rush to my own bathroom to test the wash-basin faucet. Although water did flow from the faucet at that particular instance, the water supply *was* suddenly shut off seconds later. Only at that moment, on the main road in front of my house, did I hear the sound of machinery. Checking outside, I discovered council workers were setting up machinery and equipment in my street, and they had obviously just turned off the mains water supply. A leaflet left in my letterbox explained that they were there to conduct maintenance work on the mains-to-meter pipes. Lynley was not the only person experiencing interruptions to his water supply.

This example of synchronicity has an asynchronous element—that is, the Lynley scene was a cue to check my bathroom faucet under the expectation that something similar was *about to happen*. The skeptic might suggest that being cued by the video to check the faucet could be a normal response, but critically and formally my faucet's *imminent failure* (the asynchronous element) is the essential factor; accordingly, my response may not have been causally triggered, regardless of how it appears, even to me (upon reflection, my response seems unwarranted). In fact, I do not jump to action at the slightest provocation.

Under a conventional (Rhinean) model, precognition might suggest itself, since foreknowledge (anticipation) of a future event seems to be demonstrated. But given the video was playing at that critical time (not sooner, and not later), precognition in this sense does not explain the timeliness of the event (and why would I even need to have seen the video to have a precognition?).

Alternatively, precognition of the imminent fate of the faucet need not be involved if one appeals to telepathy only as an explanation (i.e., through telepathy, I may have become unconsciously aware of the council workers' aims), or clairvoyance (i.e., I 'saw' what the council workers were doing), or both. We may also consider clairvoyance of the leaflet in my letterbox, or retrocognition of an individual making letterbox drops earlier that day. None of these explanations account for the timing of the video unless I (as co-conspirator) unconsciously planned to watch the video at a specific time. These conventional parapsychological scenarios seem very unlikely. And although the arrival of council workers could have been purely circumstantial, that was still a coincidence and had a major part to play as events unfolded.

There is one other alternative solution (albeit far-fetched)—perhaps I used telepathy in a different way by 'instructing' a team leader to scramble a team of workers to my address *at a precise time* (no stalling). Supposing they would have complied with this tall order without question, this hypothetical telepathic connection would need to be made much earlier in the day to give the team time to assemble, and the telepathy itself would therefore have to be triggered by a different precognition; that of unconsciously 'knowing' that I would be watching that specific Lynley episode later that evening.

The major criterion in this synchronicity (i.e., the pivotal inner image of the faucet cued by the same video image) is not met in precognition, telepathy, clairvoyance, or retrocognition scenarios. On that point, not only the meaning-equivalence (the faucets), but also the meaningfulness *for myself as experient* is a cogent element—as it happens, I am ambivalent about water, perhaps traceable to childhood memories of my mostly-fruitless attempts at learning to swim, including a couple of close shaves.[45] Without this background—and let it be said that water is an age-old archetype (e.g., Jung, 1959/1968, para. 40, 246)—the faucet *as a source of water* would *mean* nothing and therefore evoke no action or reaction. The whole incident passes as non-intentional synchronicity with an asynchronous element. Thus, the incident is not satisfactorily (i.e., it is tortuously) explained under any Rhinean model. Only the synchronistic approach offers a full account (a side benefit is that it bypasses needless psi ponderings).

I also draw attention to the asynchronous form of synchronicity and its predictive element that makes it possible to glean synchronicity for premonitory cues. It is not always easy to spot these elements since one does not usually know that synchronicity is being played out *until* it plays out, but cautionary elements can often be spotted in advance. There are two examples illustrating the nature of their appearance, showing how one might respond to them; the one we have already seen in Lynley's faucet, and the other is Jung's birds case (Jung, 1952/1969, para. 844–845). To be brief, in the first example, Lynley's problem with his faucet became a cue for me to suspect a similar difficulty with my bathroom faucet; a cue upon which I acted. The next example is now described.

Jung's birds: The second example is Jung's birds case (described earlier in this chapter). The appearance of birds over the woman's house triggered the woman's anxiety, as she felt certain that her husband's life was in danger, which proved to be so. In this case, Jung explains that the woman had two ominous experiences with birds prior to her husband's fatal heart attack: the first related to her grandmother's death; the second related to her mother's death. In other words, the woman was not only conditioned to react in a certain way to flocks of birds, but she was also privy (had she but known it) to the workings of a particular archetypal process that we see underscored her emotional reactions. Jung (1952/1969) even gives some historical precedents for the bird motif and its association with death (para. 850–851).

There is a slight difference between these two cases, Lynley's faucet and Jung's birds: Faucets are mundane and can be taken as mainly literal elements, whereas the birds sighted by the distressed woman are symbolic of death (e.g., souls in flight) and therefore carry an extramundane quality. We see that it is sometimes possible to place synchronistic elements on a spectrum or scale of interpretation, ranging from the literal (real or representational) to the figurative (symbolic or abstract). They also range in importance or severity, but can even serve as a tool for prediction. In point of fact, the faucet case still has some symbolic depth in the form of the archetypal water motif, where the mains pipe is a carrier of water from the general (reservoir/

communal) to the specific (household/personal), and the faucet delivers that water, which has cleansing but also life-giving "vivifying" properties (Jung, 1959/1968, para. 246). We see then that the literal becomes symbolic—the faucet has a whole other meaning in the unconscious. This point about figurative elements leads to my final example of synchronistic forms in action. For this example, I also draw attention to intentionality and asynchronism.

Harary and Targ associative remote viewing: [46] In 1982, Keith Harary and Russell Targ conducted a so-called Associative Remote Viewing (ARV) exercise; ARV being a modification of the standard RV protocol to allow for "future seeing" (Harary & Targ, 1985). In ARV, future outcomes (e.g., stock market "price up" or "price down") can be represented by associated objects (considerably different to avoid confusion), and the object that is "remote viewed" determines how to predict. The company set up by Harary and Targ known as Delphi made nine correct consecutive forecasts of the silver futures price (whether it would go up or down by no more than 25 cents) five days in advance (said by one experienced commodities trader to be "impossible"), netting them $100,000, and more for the company's clients (for a more detailed account, see Edwards, 1983). The following year, however, Harary and Targ failed miserably, not once but twice.

In 1982, Harold Puthoff conducted a similar experiment on silver futures, netting him $25,000 after 21 out of 30 trades were profitable (Puthoff, 1984). At a later date, a team headed by Russell Targ used the ARV technique, once again with silver futures as the target (see Targ et al., 1995; for similar financial successes, see Carson, Laham, & Moddel, 2014; Kolodziejzyk, 2012; Smith, Laham, & Moddel, 2014). On this occasion there were no financial stakes, but six of seven trade predictions were correct.

As we have seen, the downside of ARV is that losses are possible. Indeed, Katz et al. (2021) reported that the Applied Precognition Project (APP) lost over $52,000 in a year-long study comprised of 177 predictions of foreign exchange (FOREX) executed trades. With a team of no less than 60 RVers, such a loss is heavy by any measure. Katz et al. argue that the data showed that many of the groups participating in the study had below chance hit-rates in similar financial predictions. It would seem that screening RVers on their prior success rates might be an important step when large sums are at stake. Nevertheless, ARV seems a reliable methodology—a collective assessment conducted by Bierman and Rabeyron (2013) reported a high 63% success rate based on the mean hit rate of 17 "known 'scientific' ARV-experiments" (p. 3). Their own study yielded a more conservative mean hit rate of 56% in a binary situation (betting on red or black on a computer-simulated roulette-wheel).

As stated, an essential factor underpinning ARV is that the so-called predictions are dependent on abstract correspondences (i.e., 'associated objects' such as photographs of garden scenes or cityscapes) that coincide with subsequent outcomes. In other words, synchronicity is possible without the need for literal elements (as already demonstrated in Jung's birds case), although the figurative elements lack symbolic worth since they are hand-picked for difference—they are chosen because they are thought to be neutral and thus avoid intellectual, emotional, and judging biases. In some cases, the future targets may be too similar and it is thought RVers may not be able to differentiate (say) a winning football team from a losing team. Certainly, there is some merit in using associated objects as RV in general is the most successful parapsychological paradigm to date, even surpassing the ganzfeld in terms of average effect sizes (Cardeña, 2018b).

We also have the two necessary components for synchronicity: the "normal, probable state (… causally explicable)", which is the discovery (becoming aware) of (say) the future price, preceded by a "critical experience", which is the ARV-induced image of the associated object that "can only be verified afterwards" and is thus taken as "extra-sensory perception" (Jung, 1952/1969, para. 855). Originally this quote from Jung describes how synchronicity manifested in two cases with which he was personally involved (the scarab case and the birds case), but he freely uses the term "extra-sensory perception" to describe the "critical experience" in both cases. Although Jung shows no aversion to mixing concepts (Rhinean and Jungian),[47] which I regard as an indiscretion on Jung's part, the quote nevertheless works well in describing the synchronistic process in the ARV experiments. Small wonder psi and synchronicity are often seen as similar.

The ARV example also brings to mind my intentional *Melbourne Cup* exercises, in which successful selections sprang from sufficient criteria (see Appendix B). A key difference in these examples is that the two cases cited by Jung give evidence of nonintentionality (also true of Lynley's faucet), whereas the ARV and the *Melbourne Cup* studies give evidence of intentionality. It also needs to be noted that the ARV and the *Melbourne Cup* studies differ slightly because images of future outcomes are not created in quite the same way—the protocol of the former requires predictions to be psychically created as responses to unrelated objects that are given a designation (this or that future outcome), whereas the protocol of the latter requires predictions to be derived from stimulus material that *are* related (i.e., they correspond) to the future outcome in some way (e.g., as salient colours or shapes in television images of horses and/or their jockeys indicating parallels with the future target). However, both protocols deliver a mental image, which is a defining principle of synchronicity.

Intentional vs. nonintentional synchronicity: Intentional synchronicity seems experimentally viable (even profitable), but it is known that there are seemingly random factors that foil successful outcomes (a point just made), suggesting synchronicity is as sporadic and unpredictable as psi (for examples of sporadic, unpredictable psi in the form of ARV, see Katz, Grgić, & Fendley, 2018). Apart from some practical issues that may pertain (see the description in Katz et al.), two major elements in intentional studies need special consideration: namely, archetypes and meaningfulness.[48] It may be that the systematic declines in correspondences (i.e., performance declines; a.k.a. effect-size declines) are due to a hiatus in the constellation of archetypes and therefore meaningfulness. This problem is most likely due to the fact that intentional synchronicity, being *intentional*, is devised and constructed within very limited parameters pertaining to personal gains, experimental goals, and other limited agendas (Schwartz, 2014, has similar views), whereas nonintentional synchronicity is not ego-driven, and involves the totality of the psyche as a more organised and structured system with a broader agenda not restricted to the demands of the ego. This difference also accounts for the relatively consistent finding of significant performance differences between intentional and nonintentional tasks, with the latter producing stronger effects (see Luke & Zychowicz, 2014).

In group efforts (as in ARV involving teams of researchers; again see Katz et al., 2018), the same criticism applies, but with variable inputs and influences from the members. Thus, when we see declines, we can expect them to be the direct result of declines in interest and motivation (perhaps due to satiated meaningfulness-seeking), though not just from participants, but from experimenters as well, and primarily *within* studies, especially when the runs are overly lengthy. If enthusiasm wanes, we cannot expect an archetype to constellate, and thus we see declines. However, we should not expect performance declines *between* studies across a diverse range of experimenters and laboratories (as is evident in the meta-analyses, and long-term programs such as STAR GATE; a remote viewing program; see May & Marwaha, 2018) because generally interest and motivation are usually optimal in those studies, implying that the presence of archetypes and the search for meaningfulness are consistent from study to study (I discuss these differences further in Chapter 2 in Storm, 2025). To make the point clearer, it was noted earlier (in Chapter 1), that affect (feeling and emotion) and purpose (meaningfulness) are fundamentals in synchronicity, and without them, we cannot expect synchronicity (and logically psi) to manifest.

***

Categorization of the various types of coincidences is not without its drawbacks, but it can be helpful in giving empiricists a focused approach to the analysis of otherwise conflated material. Given the forms synchronicity may take (temporal, spatial, and agentive), and various other points made above about archetypes and meaningfulness, a clearer picture of synchronicity, and even a more broadly defined study of paranormal phenomena, becomes possible.

Also evident is the fact that employing specifically Rhinean nomenclature (i.e., spotting the psi effects) can create category errors that confound interpretation. On the one hand, as in the case of Lynley's faucet, a Rhinean reading would have all the anomalous components of that event explained by *at least* one psi mechanism (possibly precognition), but we must attribute the scrambling of the council workers to chance (if we were to adopt an

Eisenbudian approach). Still assuming a psi process, if the council workers' presence *is* to be seen as a crucial (causal) element, telepathy and/or clairvoyance and/or retrocognition could all play a part (albeit each with their own spurious connotations), but we still need precognition (for I must have somehow 'known' when to start playing the video to get the faucet scene synchronized with external events). With psi, it is argued that any number of ecological factors may or may not have critical (causal) roles to play. Such renderings seem altogether needlessly complex and incomplete. The casual observer might suggest these complications never surface in 'simple' (lab) psi, but that does not mean they do not exist. On the other hand, all elements (even *distal* and *asynchronous*) will merely involve subjective (phenomenological) separations of events in space and time underpinned by archetypal factors, but not causes. We can then see that conditional or contingent factors are as crucial as so-called causal factors.

While making a theoretical distinction between the two *agentive* forms of synchronicity (i.e., intentional and nonintentional) could be a challenge psychologically, the practical difference largely centres on the presence or absence of volition, so that agency is very much tied in with psychological state. We see examples of nonintentional synchronicity in two of the cases presented (Lynley's faucet case and Jung's birds case), and we see intentional synchronicity demonstrated in the ARV tests of Harary and Targ (1985), and my *Melbourne Cup* exercises. Intentional synchronicity is otherwise seen in conventional parapsychology as conscious 'psychic ability'.

This chapter started with a discussion of the categorical problems associated with various types of coincidence. In the next chapter, the focus is on the imagination, which could be regarded as a category of experience, certainly *psychological* in essence. Synchronicity is as elusive as psi; unfathomable and broader in scope and experience than mere products of the imagination. Yet it may invariably be in the imagination—the 'deep' imagination—that synchronicity has its roots. Indeed, the imagination seems just the place for it. If we really want to explore that singular mystery that is synchronicity, we need to tap into the *imaginal realm*.

Notes

1 Kennedy's personal secretary was named Evelyn Lincoln, but Lincoln's secretaries were John George Nicolay and John M. Hay. There is no record of a Kennedy as personal secretary to Lincoln during his presidency (Link, 2020).

2 I note that allowance is *generally* not made for the imagination as contributing to the fuzziness (see footnote 5)—it is either overlooked, or the psi process is thought to be purely rational (see Chapter 3).

3 This is not to argue that an analytical approach towards synchronistic interpretation can be impeded by categorical distinctions for the evidence is not forthcoming (Schwartz, 2008, provides some good examples).

4 Free response is a term that "describes any test of ESP in which the range of possible targets is relatively unlimited and is unknown to the percipient [perceiver/receiver], thus permitting them to respond freely with whatever impressions come to mind" (Thalbourne, 2003, p. 44).
5 May et al. (1990) explain the terms "fuzzy" and "crisp" in terms of Set Theory: fuzzy refers to *degree* of membership (i.e., multiple memberships); crisp (i.e., sharp) refers to *kind*—i.e., specific (yes/no) membership. Parapsychologically, the ambiguities inherent in fuzzy relations make target identification (matching) problematic (the same applies to fixing the meaningfulness). A crisp relation is accurate and precise so that identification can proceed relatively unconstrained. See also Croft and Cruse (2004).
6 See footnote 47 in Chapter 1 for the definition of 'goat'.
7 We never really learn whether this 'decoy effect' *is* mainly coming from goats because Westerlund et al. (2006) did not report the paranormal belief (sheep-goat) scores of those participants responsible for the mentations.
8 For a further consideration of this issue, see "Is Laboratory Psi Research Eliciting Synchronicity?" in Storm (2025).
9 For one solution to this oversight, see "Towards a Synchronistic Understanding of Psi" in Storm (2025).
10 Ryan (1996) notes that the derivations of the *I Ching* system and Leibniz's binary system were both based on mathematical techniques, each inspired by metaphysical worldviews (see Appendix C).
11 Kekulé's eventual discovery of the structure of the benzene ring based on a dream of the ancient Gnostic symbol of the *ouroboros* (a snake seizing its own tail) was a leap from "mytho-poetic" reverie to science (Coudert, 1980).
12 Alongside Leibniz's and Kekulé's breakthroughs, I list the following as narrow synchronicity: (1) Mathematician Donald Newman sought a solution to a mathematical problem, but it was in a dream that Newman asked Nobel Prize laureate and mathematician John Nash for the answer. Newman's inner 'Nash' gave him the answer, but taking the encounter literally, Newman gave Nash credit (see Robb, 2018); (2) The 'inner' symbol that became an 'outer' symbol, the *caduceus* (the two intertwined snakes of ancient Greek medicine), can be seen as a precursor of the double-helix molecule deoxyribonucleic acid (DNA), the building block of life (Watson & Crick, 1953). The symbol was right under the noses of medical professionals for centuries, but its significance seems to have been overlooked until after the discovery was made. We cannot reject the possibility that the image had an unconscious influence that creatively steered the revelation.
13 A category error (a.k.a. category mistake, categorical mistake, or mistake of category) is "a semantic or ontological error in which things belonging to a particular category are presented as if they belong to a different category, or, alternatively, a property is ascribed to a thing that could not possibly have that property" (Blackburn, 1994, p. 58).
14 I note the use of the word 'categorial' (e.g., by Atmanspacher & Fach, 2016) to denote *dealing with*, or *involving a* category, but often in a non-exclusivist and even fictive sense. I prefer the more definitive term 'categorical'.
15 Venn diagrams were invented by the same John Venn who wrote *The Logic of Chance* (Venn, 1866), and introduced the idea of the Law of Truly Large Numbers outlined in Chapter 1.
16 Quantum mechanics (QM) describes sub-atomic phenomena at odds with the Newtonian cause-and-effect paradigm that currently and sufficiently explains the material world that we experience in everyday life. Examples of QM phenomena, include: (i) 'collapse of the wave-function'" (a sub-atomic particle reducing or

transforming from a wave-like state to a localized particle due to interaction with the external world); (ii) 'nonlocality' (entanglement between spatially separated systems); (iii) 'superposition' (the overlapping of two wave forms without interference); and (iv) 'quantum tunnelling' (a particle's motion through a barrier that it 'classically' could not penetrate).

17 Some microphysical processes are considered causal, or deterministic, or indicate cause-and-effect relationships. These include electromagnetic processes (involving charged particles and fields) and thermodynamic processes (entropy and conservation of energy). Jung's idea behind microphysical processes being *acausal* rests on a deeper consideration of what they are observed or thought to be *fundamentally* in terms of their "so-ness" (Jung, 1952/1969, para. 871), or "Just-So" qualities or properties (para. 965).

18 Beloff (2008) also includes alchemy and divination as prime examples of synchronicity in action. Beloff's depictions of the synchronistic principle in action do not, of course, make him a supporter of the synchronicity concept—he was never able to accept synchronicity, though he was sympathetic to the idea. It turns out that Beloff's chief grievance against synchronicity was born of his insistence that the causal factor could not be divorced from synchronicity.

19 A radioactive half-life is the average amount of time it takes for half of the mass of the original isotope to decay.

20 There are real-world examples of large-scale constellations of what is *probably* the same archetype (see footnote 6 in the Introduction). However, such cases are exceptions, and we still cannot predict which archetype or archetypes will constellate (if at all) in all human situations.

21 For details about Jung's astrological experiment, see "The Trickster in the Laboratory" in Storm (2025).

22 Mansfield (1995) even described Jung's astrology experiment as "fruitless" (p. 33), though I suggest that is not entirely true.

23 Of course, it is possible to apply statistical techniques to get a general (average) picture of how numbers may be represented in, say, a range of crystals, but that exercise can only proceed because number phenomenology in crystals is an *a priori* factor.

24 Sheldrake (1994) notes that the fundamental physical constants (e.g., the universal gravitational constant *G*; the velocity of light *c*) are supposed "to reflect an underlying constancy of nature" (p. 164), yet they are observed to be frequently changing. He suggests three possible explanations: (i) the constants are fixed and our methodologies are imprecise; (ii) the constants "vary in some smooth and regular manner with the age of the universe, or over astronomical distances" (pp. 187–188); or (iii) the constants "may fluctuate, within limits, around average values which themselves remain fairly constant" (p. 188).

25 For a reminder of the difference between mechanical causality and scientific causality, see *Causality and Acausality* in Chapter 1.

26 It is worth noting that Figure 2.4 is a final schematization, but Mansfield (1995) originally referred to "Acausal Connections" as "General Acausal Orderedness" in his Figure 9, with "Properties of Natural Numbers, Acausal Quantum Phenomena, etc." under "Paranormal Phenomena" (p. 33)—clearly a most unsatisfactory arrangement.

27 As an aside, the increase in interdisciplinary approaches these days comes mainly from a need for solutions to complex problems on a global scale that require multiple inputs.

28 See "The Trick of the Cause in Parapsychology" in Chapter 3 of Storm (2025).

29 Given the chance factor, casual use of the *I Ching* is not advised because an emotional (affective) commitment to the process seems to be tied in with archetypal

activation. Also, the *I Ching* process may involve some degree of projection, but that can be a helpful psychological tool that draws attention to exactly that which the user would otherwise fail to notice, and this confrontation, with a healthy dose of introspection, can lead to a solution.

30 In his longitudinal *I Ching* dataset, Thalbourne (1994) found a significant decrease in the number of changing lines with a subsequent increase in number of static hexagrams which, taken together, indicated a statistically discernible shifting focus in Thalbourne's life-perspective based on his motivations at the time.

31 At the time of writing (mid-2018), I first came across the reference to Johnson (1899) in Inglis (1990).

32 For arguments against probabilistic interpretations, see Collins (2009).

33 See "supernatural" in *Dictionary.com* (https://www.dictionary.com/browse/supernatural).

34 See "supernatural" in *OxfordDictionaries.com* (https://en.oxforddictionaries.com/definition/supernatural).

35 Jung (1952/1969) points out that prior knowledge of future events are "evidently not *synchronous* but are *synchronistic*" (para. 955). That is why I use the term "asynchronous" to describe synchronicity involving present and future, or present and past corresponding elements.

36 See www.cheaptvvideoaudiorepairs.com/index.html

37 I discussed *scientific causality* ("*if* A, *then* B") in Chapter 1 (see *Causality and Acausality*), albeit in terms of archetypes but the principle is the same.

38 I say 'not quite' because Jung still mixes up two conflicting ideas. Besides that, the role of archetypes as *seemingly* relativizing factors came late (in 1957), and had little impact because the explanation only appeared in a private letter to Stephen Abrams (see Jung, 1975, pp. 398*ff*). However, Jung still seems to suggest that archetypes can influence spacetime.

39 Jung also uses the word "chance" as a cover term for a cause or causes not yet determined (see the section "Alternative Explanations of Synchronicity: I. Chance" in Chapter 1). This apparent contradiction can lead to no end of confusion, which is why I prefer the term 'chance-like' when describing synchronicity in its haphazard or sporadic guise.

40 The problem I have with Gadway's (2013) conclusion about the sudden appearance of the rose chafer in the scarab case is that he makes a "horizontal causal connection between his [Jung's] "desire" and "hope" that something "unexpected and irrational" "*would turn up* and the subsequent fact that something unexpected and irrational did, indeed, turn up ..." (p. 12). This view could give the mistaken impression that synchronicity is causal.

41 An example of a reflex is given in the normal case of rolling over in one's sleep to minimize cramp and discomfort. Even though it is unconscious behavior and, therefore, not intentional, it is, at another level, never nonintentional. It is fully intended by the organism or, more precisely, by a self-system that is capable of perceiving and monitoring its environment to a degree far superior to that of the sleeping ego.

42 On this point, I have in mind Ted Owens whose alleged paranormal feats were not only intentional, but (as I argue) may be seen as synchronistic (see Chapter 1 in Storm, 2025).

43 Mayer (2018) would refer to intentional synchronicity as an "induced" effect (p. 206), which amounts to the same thing because 'to induce' an effect, one must first 'intend' it.

44 "Well Schooled in Murder" (2002, Series 1, Episode 2).

45 At the time of writing this section in April 2018, a months-long drought and water shortage in South Africa came to my attention quite by accident—see

www.mnn.com/earth-matters/climate-weather/blogs/cape-town-south-africa-second-largest-city-about-run-out-water

46 In Remote Viewing a percipient "attempts to describe the surroundings of a geographically distant agent [or location]" (Thalbourne, 2003, p. 107).

47 I have more to say on the interchangeable use of Rhinean and Jungian concepts and terms in Chapter 5.

48 I am ignoring, for the moment, the fact that intentional synchronicity appears to work best when we have access to the appropriate seed material, with no other requirements necessary (the examples in Appendix B draw attention to this advantage). Standard ESP/PK tasks, however, often require a panoply of conditions which must be met, and even then there is no guarantee of a successful outcome (i.e., the desired effect). This is not to say that intentional synchronicity conducted in the laboratory could not benefit from the theory-driven practices and protocols that account for the current parapsychological successes.

Chapter 3

The Map is Not the Territory

> "… the debt we owe to the play of imagination is incalculable"
> Carl Gustav Jung (1921/1971, para. 93)

Alfred Korzybski (1933/1941) tells us "A map *is not* the territory it represents" (p. 58). We do not fully understand the imagination, or how it might furnish us with a kind of map to human experience, the world, and beyond. Like quantum phenomena, psi, and synchronicity, the imagination boggles our minds. The artist and the psychic are both thought to be using their imagination when they visualize; they create vistas and perspectives that unfurl before their eyes and these creations are presented to us for judgement, but we must decide what is real and what is imaginary. Or are the two one and the same, sometimes and sometimes not? In this chapter, I present the idea of a synchronistic approach that sees the imagination as the principal source of paranormal material, but the 'mapping' of a mental image (the so-called response) to a nominated target (the so-called stimulus) is contingent upon the constellated archetype. Given its ubiquity, neither the transmission of information, nor an exchange of energy, need be proposed to explain the correspondence.

Imagination and the Unconscious

Some might be surprised if I claim *psi starts in the imagination*. Do I mean psi is daydreaming or fantasy? It is, if we can generalize from the words of artist, psychic, and renowned remote-viewer Ingo Swann (1933–2013), who said: "Remote viewing is not much different from day dreaming" (Rogo, 1988, p. 188). However, if one follows the line of argument put forward by Stevens (2002), there is a lot more to it. Not exactly revelatory, Stevens starts with the claim that ESP is "firmly seated within the continuum of human perceptual experience", and is "perturbed by a multitude of external forces" (p. 245)—points many parapsychologists would not challenge. I, however, do not regard ESP as a "perceptual experience" *per se*. Stevens also regards the imagination as a producer or creative centre of extra-sensory responses. I suggest this view

DOI: 10.4324/9781003561330-4

is essentially correct; I see the imagination as pivotal in ESP, although I do not see it as an information processing centre of extra-perceptual inputs.

Historically, imagination is associated with creativity, but rather than just being an 'internal force' (so to speak), Stevens (2002) also connects creativity to external reality. With those three (imagination, the external world, and creativity) now linked, Stevens goes on to propose that ESP is the "imagination that relates to the target" (p. 239), whereby the "target" *per se* is external, and somehow conveys information for the imagination to process. ESP is thus a creative process, and an aspect, or type, or sub-type of imagination that works paranormally. When the target and imagination (fixed symbols or verbal description—i.e., mentation) 'correlate' (Stevens also uses the word "correspond"), we have a case of ESP (assuming no normal explanation), but when they do not correlate/correspond, it is just everyday imagination since we cannot find a relevant external source.

Apart from the problem of source (no external sources are necessary), I have little difficulty with Stevens's idea that ESP is given birth in the imagination. Interestingly, Stevens sees no need for the organism to scan its environment, sift through, and select from a multitude of external stimuli—the organism processes all incoming stimuli on an ongoing basis, but only responds to that which is meaningful and relevant at the time; arguably a formidable task. For Stevens, the mind/brain complex is so sufficiently sophisticated that it is capable of a kind of discernment of events in the external environment, and attends to what it finds relevant, but can disregard all irrelevancies—this view aligns with evolutionary principles. I would suggest, however, that this process is conveniently reined in and limited to whatever archetypal circumstances happen to be constellated at that time, internally and externally. That limit in itself naturally explains psi as a hit-or-miss function that still works sufficiently better than chance as an explanation.

In consideration of the conclusions drawn by Storm (2025) concerning eight prominent psi theories, it would seem that most theorists do not like the idea of the imagination having such sway, since they never use the word, nor refer to the imagination *per se*, as an *operative factor* in the ESP process. In fact, their narrative might go something like this: *the imagination, since it's all about making up stuff, is going to deliver hit rates fluctuating at no better than chance levels.* Yet somehow ESP works behind the scenes just like the imagination in that mysterious 'black box' of the mind/brain complex, so what do we really know about ESP and the imagination, and how they relate? It is almost ironic that ESP is seen as some kind of cognitive process, albeit poorly understood, and mostly unconscious, yet it only deserves serious consideration if we avoid associating it with that word *imagination* (I will come back to this aversion later). As a consequence, what we see is the imagination (as a creative function) only occasionally being given a free hand as an ESP-related variable (e.g., Dalton, 1997; Holt, 2013), so that the conspicuous inattention to it must mask a deep suspicion, even in the parapsychological community.[1] The point I must make is that tests of ESP *are* tests of the imagination, but it is a special form of imagination; one which Stevens does not identify (nor has the parapsychological community).

My conjecture is that the imagination can *most often* be regarded as the *starting point* for both synchronicity and psi insofar as we can point to a mental product that would, in all probability, originate in the imagination. To be clear, there may be some cases of synchronicity and psi where evidence of the imagination at work might not seem obvious because the initiating archetypal influence that underpins the mental image has not reached consciousness. For example, Beitman's extra-ordinary "object-object" synchronicity indicates to the observer a *superficial* awareness that something meaningful is afoot, but its personal relevance is missed because the triggering image from the imagination has not reached consciousness (see the section "Forms of Synchronicity" in Chapter 2). The same may apply to some cases of recurrent spontaneous psychokinesis (RSPK). I also distance myself from the idea that a successfully 'imagined' target indicates information transmission *in any conventional psychological or parapsychological sense.*

At the outset, I also need to draw a distinction between 'imagination' as I use the term, and the "unconscious" as Jung uses the term in the following quote, previously given in Chapter 1, which states that synchronicity

> consists of two factors: a) An unconscious image comes into consciousness either directly (i.e., literally) or indirectly (symbolized or suggested) in the form of a dream, idea, or premonition. b) An objective situation coincides with this content.
>
> (Jung, 1952/1969, para. 858)

This "image" that "comes into consciousness" indeed comes from the so-called "unconscious" domain of the mind/brain complex but, *specifically* and *primarily*, I would argue that it comes via the imagination (especially since the image, when indirect, does not need to be literal, but can be "symbolized or suggested"); in fact, my preferred term is 'deep imagination' (interfacing with archetypal processes), which I distinguish from 'everyday imagination' often thought, for example, to be behind egoic daydreaming and fantasy. Stevens (2002) does not make that distinction. I suggest a great deal of the content in psychic readings results from the psychic's imagination at work even though the psychic believes otherwise; yet consider the fact that psychics invariably frame their responses in questions to the sitter, rather than outright statements directly from the alleged deceased (Barker, 2022). It is arguable whether the images are fuzzy because the imagination is poor, or the entity is a poor communicator.[2] However, those psychic images that constitute the essence of psi and synchronicity are not mere daydream or fantasy images that are *consciously* thought or willed into existence; but nor are they recalled, remembered, or transmitted (these points will become clearer later).

As a rather basic example of the deep imagination underpinning the psi process, one only has to think of the cognitive effort participants put themselves through in an ESP task where they try to *visualize* in their minds a concealed target that is to be revealed later—what more likely source of that *image* could we nominate other than the imagination? In fact, we see that the words 'image' and 'imagination' have the same stem (Latin: *imāgo*). Furthermore, in all likelihood, the participant (if they thought they were using their imagination) would not think the kind of imagination that was at work during the task was daydreaming or fantasy (even in the sense Swann may have meant); indeed, a compliant participant will probably say they tried very hard to imagine or picture the correct (target) image. So there is the intention to initiate some kind of process; something a little deeper than the run-of-the-mill imagination that produces daydreams and fantasies. Of course, they might also have hoped to be drawn to the target, or hoped to draw in the target from afar. As Storm (2025) has pointed out, some parapsychological theories propose such a mechanism, but again I suggest that participants are 'merely' deploying their imagination.

I do not, however, regard the imagination as a process that is consciously kick-started and fully performed and completed in consciousness in the way some artists might say they experience it: Creativity depends largely on how cooperative certain unconscious (e.g., psychological, neuropsychological, and psychophysiological) factors will be, with consciousness initiating and guiding, or at least responding to, those processes. That is to say, the path of the imagination might be altered (even thwarted) by the individual's conscious decisions, though some artists work automatically (semi-consciously with little to go on in the sense of a broad scheme or idea), as is best illustrated in the works of the abstract expressionist and 'drip-painter' Jackson Pollock (1912–1956), where "psychic automatism" literally represents the unconscious (Leja, 1990). But generally, the imagination may need a trigger, either from a content in consciousness (a thought or idea), or some element in the environment that draws the attention, or by some unknown factor—again we defer to the unconscious ("It happens like magic", said one artist).

All of the above needs unpacking, but to do that I must take a broader perspective on the deep imagination so as to embrace not just the paranormal, but also creativity and creative insight. This analysis is needed because simply deferring to the unconscious tells little about these processes, and it offers even less in the way of mechanisms for psi and synchronicity. I believe Jung (like Freud with his concept of the 'subconscious') has given the unconscious an incredible amount of credit (perhaps too much) as the 'go-to' concept for explaining a very broad range of psychological contents, stimuli, and responses that seem outside conscious control. Nonetheless, the idea of the unconscious provides good epistemological grounding, in that its functions reference the individual, and that effectively vanquishes projections of rejected personal causes and contents onto (say) supernatural entities or other externalizations (something that still goes on today). I start with American neuroscientist and neuropsychiatrist Nancy Andreasen (2011), since she gives an example from French mathematician, Henri Poincaré, that for her illustrates the unconscious at work (though I suggest it is the imagination) helping him discover Fuchsian functions (after the mathematician Lazarus Fuchs)—these functions are mathematical solutions to complex algebraic problems:

> One evening, contrary to my custom, I drank black coffee and could not sleep. Ideas rose in crowds; I felt them collide until pairs interlocked, so to speak, making a stable combination. By the next morning I had established the existence of a class of Fuchsian functions, those which come out from the hypergeometric series; I had only to write out the results, which took but a few hours.
>
> (Poincaré, 2001, as cited in Andreasen, 2011, p. 45)

As we read these words, and work our way through Andreasen's paper, we see that she depicts the creative process in terms of images arising from the unconscious; consciousness aids the process later, and even then has very little to do with the creative component. As Andreasen says: "we are led to the conclusion that the creative process arises from the unconscious rather than occurring as a conscious process" (p. 45). Andreasen's conclusions stem from a considerable amount of work in neuro-imaging using positron emission tomography (PET) and fMRI, and she and her team find considerable support for their findings. She goes on to describe Poincaré's reverie as the mind freely wandering: "thoughts and images float around without censorship" (p. 45). That is to say, the images are doing all the work, while Poincaré watches it happen, and then he gets to work formalizing everything later—this is why I say the conscious ego is not the creator of the images:

> At the neural level, it is as if the association cortices are working actively, throwing out feelers for possible connections between unrelated capacities—verbal and visual spatial associations, abstract and concrete associations, colors, images, concepts … a veritable primordial soup of thought.
>
> (p. 45)

We see the imagination in a primary role, but Andreasen never uses that word 'imagination' (not even once). I have given a similar example in Kekulé's experience that suggests his creative moment can be attributed to a deep level of the imagination, although Kekulé was fully unconscious (in a dream state), whereas Poincaré, though sleepless, appeared to be in some kind of hypnagogic reverie (see Chapter 2). (Leibniz worked a little differently, having been inspired by an archetypal 'binary' idea and worked on it in full consciousness, and perhaps that is *partly* why he never fully realized his objective; see Chapter 2 and Appendix C.) Interestingly, Andreasen contrasts the complementary but feverish fluidity of the unconscious against the subject's feeling of reverie and relaxation, as though these were two separate processes in opposition (like yin and yang) that nevertheless seem to function cooperatively. This feverish fluidity could be taken as the imagination 'revved up', as it were.

For Andreasen (2011), the creative process that starts in the unconscious is thought to move through stages: (1) *Preparation* ("basic information or skills are assembled"); (2) *Incubation* ("connections are unconsciously being made"); (3) *Inspiration* (a solution is reached); and finally (4) *Production* ("insights are put into a useful form"; p. 45). These stages are helpful, but the unconscious is still presented as if it is *knowingly* doing all the 'connecting', 'solving', and 'producing'—the brain "throwing out feelers"—and it strikes me as rather odd that Andreasen does not simply refer to this process as the imagination at work. Andreasen's model is mechanical, and she never firmly posits a centre that might have something to do with authorship *per se*. Her best guess is that the whole creative product is 'emergent'—a product of a self-organising system. Jung would say that process is guided by the Self, or that other side of the Self (i.e., outside the empirical self); outside conscious- or ego-awareness.

As indicated, Andreasen's (2011) paper depends heavily on brain modelling—it is 'as if' certain brain areas are doing all the creating. I note her use of the mental/conceptual term "unconscious" creates no schism with her theoretical approach, insofar as she is primarily referring to brain processes inaccessible to consciousness, but still her conclusion is that "unconscious processes play an important role in achieving creative insights" (p. 42). I believe that if Andreasen called that process 'the imagination', she would have refined her conclusion. As seems to be the case for Andreasen, Jung regarded the unconscious as a broad or general domain that houses mental contents (e.g., memories, nascent thoughts, etc.) that can, but do not always (and may never), reach consciousness. We may also include deep neuropsychological processes as 'contents' (or better, 'operations'), so that a psychological function like the imagination—given all that we know about it—should reasonably be considered a largely unconscious process. Going deeper, it is not enough to place just the archetypes—whatever one thinks of them—as *things* or *contents* in the unconscious (Jung's collective unconscious) without recognising that the *processes* that activate or constellate them are also unconscious (or largely so), even if a content in consciousness may act as a trigger.

These points culminate in a final point worth raising here: Research on the imagination *as a process* could be of benefit to parapsychological research and theory, especially in relation to psi, and we are at liberty to infer a correlated neurological substrate, given Andreasen's (2011) work. Contrary to that approach, Marwaha and May (2015), while acknowledging the neurological substrate as part of an unresolved issue in Phase II of their model, assign no role to the imagination in the psi process (see Storm 2025). The best they offer is some kind of unexplained cognition. Indeed, a specific instance of not going beyond the minimal (limited) role conventionally assigned to the imagination is evident in the context of their explaining entanglement as an "IΨ condition", whereas they say "imagining the target" is not 'informational psi' (IΨ) if it occurs "*within* the percipient, and not *between* the percipient and the target" (Marwaha & May, 2019, p. 96). Of course, that limited kind of 'imagining' is not psi in the sense Stevens (2002) means either—nor is it 'imagining' in the synchronistic sense I will propose shortly. Interestingly, if they were to concede that a percipient's 'imagining' could be "*between* the percipient and the target", then it could be said they see an *instrumental* role for the imagination, just as Stevens sees it, though still not as I see it for synchronicity, since I see the relationship as *coincidental* (or *correlational* at best, but not *causal*).

Returning to Jung's quote above, Jung mentions dreams, ideas, and premonitions that render the 'image', and to that list I add *unconsciously* generated (i.e., not exclusively consciously induced) visions and fantasies, and the products of altered states of consciousness (e.g., hypnagogia, hypnotic trance, and psychedelic states). And though all these products may result from very different processes *not necessarily governed by a single mechanism* (see the next paragraph), imagination can be seen as a uniting principle that binds them all. Thus, whatever we know or presume Jung to have thought, synchronistic processes and psi processes are not made clear if their inner manifestations (the images) are relegated to the unconscious, whereas attribution to the imagination aligns them with the creative capacity of the individual. In fairness to Jung, the following statements are about as close as we are going to get to an understanding and admission of a principal source, for Jung states that the unconscious has "everything that consciousness has, including perception, apperception, memory, imagination, …" (1960/1969, para. 362). So Jung concedes that the ego can imagine, but more to the point, Jung recognises the greater potential of a deeper level of imagination made possible by a 'linking in' to the collective unconscious. The true home of the imagination is the unconscious, but likewise in regard to paranormal processes, Jung also states that psi "is a product of pure imagination, of 'chance' ideas which reveal the structure of that which produces them, namely the unconscious" (1952/1969, para. 840). Apart from this quote, Jung's *Synchronicity* essay barely mentions 'imagination' (the word does not appear in the index; it only appears once in the main text—i.e., in the quote just given), and elsewhere in the essay we might only infer it.[3]

Another relevant literature source, yet one which does not mention the imagination (or a 'hard' parallel) in its brain modelling, but does parallel brain areas with the 'unconscious' and the 'unconscious mind', and indeed the 'collective unconscious', is the detailed paper on the entropic brain by psychologist and neuroscientist Robin Carhart-Harris and his colleagues (Carhart-Harris et al., 2014). The "entropic brain hypothesis" has it that there is a relationship between entropy and cognition, with so-called *primary* consciousness characterized by "high entropy, high disorder, flexible states" whereas *secondary* consciousness characterizes "low entropy, low disorder, rigid states" (p. 13). The "normal waking consciousness of healthy adult humans" is somewhere between these two levels, though slightly shifted towards the low entropy end. Primary consciousness is age-old (ancestral/prehistoric), whereas secondary consciousness is a relatively recent development in our phylogeny.

A highly-entropic brain experiences psychedelic states, sensory deprivation, REM sleep/dreaming and dreamy states, near-death experience, magical and creative thinking, and even psychosis. Low-entropy states include anaesthesia, sedation, deep sleep, seizure, rigid thinking, and even depression and obsessive compulsive disorder. Neither state (high entropy and low entropy) is ideal. However, the parapsychological literature tells us that many of these aforementioned conditions are associated not only with paranormal beliefs but also with psi experiences (Irwin, 2009; Luke, 2008; Storm, Drinkwater, & Jinks, 2017; Storm & Tressoldi, 2020). Carhart-Harris et al. (2014) never actually mention parapsychological phenomena *per se*; nor does Andreasen (2011). Their failure too to mention the imagination also speaks volumes—it is merely assumed that regular controls over psychological activity in certain regions of the brain can be subverted (e.g., via fatigue, or psychedelics, or too much coffee!) and what breaks free (irrupts) or is set loose into consciousness are random, meaningless images that can be infantile and fantastic, or even narcissistic and paranoiac. Carhart-Harris et al. do refer to "spontaneous personal insights" and "complex imagery" resulting from the "suspension of repression" (p. 13), and Andreasen goes a little further by acknowledging the unconscious as a creative source of "new concepts, ideas, inventions, objects or art" (p. 42). But direct reference to the imagination is completely ignored, and this productivity is never thought of as expressly compensatory as Jung would suggest, or helpful or serviceable in the shamanistic sense, or any sense other than therapeutic, and certainly not in a parapsychological sense.

It might be argued that the aims of both papers (Andreasen, 2011; Carhart-Harris et al., 2014) were never specifically psychoanalytic, but both texts reference exactly those effects—indeed, Andreasen is a psychiatrist by trade. Yet we have seen that the imagination can be tapped, and can produce contents that are rational (can make sense) and are directly related to the intentions of the experient. Fortunately, Andreasen (2011) does speak of this capability to some extent, but Carhart-Harris et al. (2014) almost valorise the self-organizing brain activity of the so-called "default mode network"' (DMN; the stabilizing centre of the brain), whereas it can on occasion (e.g., under psychedelics) slip into a collapsed state of formless, maximum entropy with the subsequent unfolding in consciousness of, for example, "archetypal themes shaped by human history" (p. 14). It is ironic that they acknowledge the therapeutic benefits of psychedelics, but only because these can restore (preferably with guidance) the DMN and re-align it with "ego integrity". All well and good but for the fact that this worthy viewpoint still overlooks the wealth of benefit inherent in the controlled imagination *and* the extensive limits of archetypes, both of which even seasoned parapsychologists barely mention.

Having made these statements, we wonder why Jung did not clarify his position in more detail; we never do get to the 'nut-and-bolts' of psi and synchronicity insofar as imagination might be at the crux of both phenomena. (I shall offer an explanation for Jung's omission in a later section.) I feel sure he thought the archetypes can be left to their own devices—they do not need our guiding hand—and if a particular archetypal situation is triggered, perhaps Jung would agree *the imagination might fire up.* It seems to me that is what Jung would have thought, though in the context of nonintentional synchronicity, whereas perhaps he would have it that psi is an altogether different (mostly ego-driven) intentional form of synchronicity in the *wider* context that I critiqued and found wanting in Chapter 2 (see "The Reach of Synchronicity").

To keep skeptics at bay, I am not talking about imagination expressed as "a matter of fancy" (Progoff, 1973, p. 104), but am referring to deeper, sophisticated inner (psychic/psychological) workings, whether individuals use their focussed (even trained) imagination intentionally and their intent draws on the cooperation of the necessary underlying unconscious processes (about which Jung seems so obscure; Andreasen, less so), or the process is entirely out of the hands of the conscious ego and largely governed by the narrative (story-telling) factor of the Self—that same structure that is able to mould inherently unconscious contents, day residues and the like, into coherent forms such as dreams. This latter variant of the imagination in action is particularly marked in the successful series of dream-ESP studies conducted at the Maimonides Research Institute in the 1960s and 1970s (Ullman, Krippner, & Vaughan, 1973).

To return to Jung, all is not lost—slowly, painstakingly, we get as near to a mechanism as we are likely to get when Jung (1952/1969) finally describes a process known as *abaissement du niveau mental* (para. 841), which refers to a lowering of the mental threshold (Progoff, 1973, also covers this phenomenon), defined as "a certain narrowing of consciousness and a corresponding strengthening of the unconscious" (para. 856). Enter our dreaming friends Poincaré and Kekulé, and we get some idea as to what they may have done. Then something like a dimming of consciousness (or a shifting of its sphere; an altered state of consciousness [ASC] of sorts), coupled with a simultaneous dipping into the unconscious occurs, and particular unconscious contents, in the guise of usually symbolic (archetypal) motifs may break through into consciousness with their concurrent affect (emotional or numinous charge). To their credit, Carhart-Harris et al. (2014) have modelled the process for us. Andreasen hints at it, though also in reference to (corresponding) brain processes. These experiences may even be *inspirational* resulting in personal, universal, or transcendental solutions (NB: *Inspiration* is that third stage mentioned by Andreasen, 2011). Poincaré describes it similarly, though not in so many words. Our two revellers were privy to the imagination at work, but they could do no more than watch images emerge while in a kind of semi-conscious but still lucid state. Many creative individuals would probably say that what Poincaré did is exactly what they may sometimes do when they create, but I raise the stakes and claim it for paranormal processes and how images are sourced, in just the same way that remote viewers like Swann might speak of their gift.

When it comes to archetypes though—how and why they do or do not constellate (especially when the will of the subject can have some influence)—we are left with a mystery. Clearly Jung implicates the individual in that mystery. From the point of view of Carhart-Harris et al. (2014), the process may lay in *primary consciousness*—the DMN (or more precisely its subversion) may be the key, not just in ASCs, but also in synchronistic and psi processes. Certainly, more research is needed. In the meantime, I suggest our deepest imaginative processes may be an aid to completeness (*production*) of our dimly formed ideas, and the constellating force that binds the parts like gravity is meaning. Seen this way, the imagination, so personally and intimately familiar to us in our everyday experience, does seem linked through meaning to the less familiar concept of archetypes. The next section will expand on that premise.

The Deep Imagination, Memory Theories, and Emotion

As we have seen, imagination is the complex cognitive process behind its many products (creativity, dreams, fantasies, etc.). Imagination may be called:

- "the faculty of imagining, or of forming mental images or concepts of what is not actually present to the senses";[4]
- "the ability of the mind to be creative or resourceful".[5]

It would not be going too far to say the first definition embraces ESP, and the second not only embraces ESP, but could also embrace PK. Outside the biological (reproductive) imperatives, the imagination is *sui generis* the ultimate creative aspect of the human being. The conventional understanding is that the typical outcomes that spring from the imagination include artistic products, novel ideas and concepts, and inventions, but previously I added to that list dreams and the 'deeper' forms of fantasy, and a host of other experiences produced during non-ordinary or altered states of consciousness, and the full range of paranormal experiences.

We have seen how Andreasen (2011) broke down the creative process into the four stages described above (*preparation, incubation, inspiration*, and *production*). She relegated a large part of the creative process to the unconscious, merely because those processes do not occur consciously. Paranormal processes can function in a somewhat similar manner. Psychics and mediums have ways of *preparing* themselves for the task at hand (even without priming information in the form of cues or prompts), but even the typical laboratory participant is thought to deliberate in the way Andreasen describes, and move through the subsequent stages. The unconscious, as much as it can tell us anything, is a preparatory ground in its own right (*incubation*). Carpenter (2012), in his First Sight Theory, makes much room for this necessary postulate, the unconscious, describing its "very great processing capacity"—how solutions involve "holistic weighting and averaging across large domains of material"—whereas consciousness is limited to a linear albeit precise problem-solving capacity (p. 51). All very well, but again I do not broadly assign the creative process to the unconscious; I attribute it precisely to the imagination. The unconscious is too conceptually nebulous to get us anywhere near to an explanation of the processes Carpenter describes. The unconscious is simply a place where processes (e.g., cognitions) take place, such as the four stages outlined previously. If any one stage takes priority, or bears the heaviest load, where all the work is done, it would be stage 2 (*incubation* where unconscious connections are made), and the hoped-for *inspiration* follows in consciousness, that may lead to insightful target selection.

In the case of spontaneous paranormal experiences however—particularly when they are psi/synchronicity of the nonintentional kind—the situation changes. No longer is it easy to identify Andreasen's stages, if at all. In these instances, the originating or generating sources of the experiences are particularly vague to researchers (purely by the correspondences they are ostensibly thought to be other minds, or other places, or other times). In later chapters, I give examples of cases where this point about the vagaries of paranormal sources seems to be true. Psychic individuals themselves (mediums, prophets, even ordinary people) are also confused as to the sources (see Chapter 4), or they have never really thought about sources as anomalies in their own right, but if they do, they make the same assumptions made by researchers (see Chapter 5 for analyses of this problem). In the next section, I consider the imagination and paranormal processes in terms of the contributing roles of memory and emotion.

Imagination, Intention, and Pro Attitude

Before I look at memory and emotion, I need to pursue another line of inquiry pertinent to the deep imagination and its role in psi/synchronicity. Instrumental in that process is Jung's collective unconscious, which (for convenience) is generally taken to be a *topos* or home ground of the archetypes. Unlike the generally broad notion of the unconscious, we know a considerable deal about the collective unconscious from its content, the archetypes

(Jung, 1959/1968). The deep imagination first utilizes archetypal elements, and then borrows from personal elements (memories, past experiences) to cloak the formless archetype *per se*, and thus give it expression. Jung suggests the archetypes play a major role in how the imagination works *synchronistically*, yielding what one could (inaccurately) call "externally-correlated imagination" (to borrow from Stevens, 2002, p. 243). We would wish to differentiate that process from normal or common-place practice involving recall of an image, or play of images, that comes as nothing more than freely remembering in order to serve some mundane or psychological purpose.

We must also avoid falling for the romantic notion that the imagination is an absolutely reliable source of the truth, and serves us with only veridical matches to events in the real world (by analogy, even our normal sensory modalities fail us on occasion). We have sufficient knowledge and understanding of the imagination to know when (and when not) to be unduly deceived by its products, but we find that there are standard ways of testing the imagination—validation, verification, reality testing, and so on (thus we witness the DMN in fine form), being crucial steps that help establish the truth status of psychological and parapsychological claims that originate in the imagination. Stevens offers a direct means of testing whether ESP did in fact transpire—namely, through verification to determine if the source is clearly more than a memory trace (i.e., one checks the response against the ESP-target).

Verification, however, does not rid us of the chance factor, and apart from testing the psi performances statistically, Stevens is not sure a psychic could ever really "distinguish between normal and paranormal sources of information" (p. 244), although some people are sure. For example, their premonitory dreams 'feel' different from ordinary dreams (Inglis, 1985, 1990; Krippner et al., 2002). Nevertheless, a number of parapsychology's sub-fields (e.g., remote viewing, psychic reading, mediumship) often produce material that is of dubious quality (e.g., irrelevant, indecipherable), and/or cannot be substantiated (for further comments, see Chapter 5). The limitations of intention then become clear insofar as the psychic's aim is most likely beyond his/her innate ability (I have dealt with the causes earlier; see Chapter 2). Worse still, one's intentions can be subverted by processes that are unclear, as in experiments that *have* produced significant psi effects, but these were categorically consciously unintended or unexpected. For example, the apparatus used by Carpenter et al. (2021) produced *increased* laser light intensity when decreased intensity was intended, and *vice versa*. Similarly, Storm (2022) found a sheep-goat effect that ran counter to expectation (i.e., the psi hit rate for goats was higher than for sheep in a free response task).

Attempts have been made to measure intention. Storm and Thalbourne (2000) conducted studies on 'pro attitude'. Pro attitude is essentially a form of intention—even expectation. As a critical element of Thalbourne's (2004) psychopraxia theory (reviewed in Storm, 2025), paranormal effects associated with pro attitude have been found (Storm, 2003a, 2006a, 2016; Storm & Thalbourne, 2005a; Thalbourne & Storm, 2014)—e.g., pro attitude correlated with psi hit rate—but these effects have not always been replicated (Storm, 2006a, 2008a; Thalbourne & Storm, 2014). But more than that, sometimes the conscious pro attitude was not associated with hitting in the conventional sense, but there was evidence of some other (unconscious) pro attitude at play (Storm & Thalbourne, 2005b).

Generally, then, intention plays a crucial role in psi processes and is far from unimportant, but it is still a relative factor so that conscious interaction with the imagination starts with intention, but psychic and synchronistic feats are possible without conscious intention as is suggested in RSPK, and as proposed in various psi theories (e.g., Carpenter's First Sight Theory, and Stanford's Psi-Mediated Instrumental Response (PMIR), both reviewed by Storm, 2025). Crucially, the capacity to express one's intention, or refrain from it, given either option, is a direct indication that one has a degree of free will, and outcomes are not entirely or always teleological as might seem to be the case in some instances of synchronicity.

I note too that Stevens's (2002) idea of the target source, because it *seems* external, also suggests specific information is transmitted, received, and worked into the imagination. I suggest the primary key to a resolution of sorts hangs on the archetypal evidence in conjunction with the other factors already associated with synchronicity including numinosity, affect (emotion), and meaningfulness (see Chapter 1 for details). Perhaps the most difficult hurdle to get over is the idea that an archetype is behind a specific and detailed response or reaction corresponding so well with a target, whether in a basic ESP test, a lab mentation, a remote viewing, a psychic's reading, or even a profoundly-felt intuition. It is no wonder that it is thought that psi information is somehow transmitted. This point has direct bearing on the role of the collective unconscious for if it is the *only* psi source, the responses can only be archetypal; not informational.

Resistance to this idea that an archetype is behind psi may subside when we realize that the range of archetypes is sufficiently vast that virtually all the 'bases' that underpin and lead to an accurate target description are covered adequately, even though remarkably accurate hits are rare, whereas the 'not-so-good' (or 'good-enough') fit is more probable. Contextually bound up in a process that is very telling, the 'not-so-good' (or 'good-enough') fit would be due to the occasional "inferior or primitive nature" of the archetypal images in spite of the wide palette that they constitute (Jung, 1952/1969, para. 841). And since the ubiquity of archetypes has given rise to the mistaken understanding that the spacetime factor can be transcended, the prevailing paranormal notion of psi as transmitted information from anywhere and anytime, becomes questionable (indeed irrelevant): ultimately "the psyche observes, not external bodies, but *itself*" (para. 840). As I read this important paragraph (para. 840; see also para. 841), I believe Jung almost, but not quite, closed the gap between psi and synchronicity (though he often equated the two), and instead continued to treat the two as having marked differences despite their similarities (more on this dichotomy in Chapter 5).

Memory Theories

My specific focus in this subsection is on the role of memory as a psi source rather than on so-called 'information processing models' of which memory function is but a part of that process. It is likely that the intuition of deep-seated archetypes has given birth to theories that suggest memory traces give ESP 'inputs' their substance (representations). Thus, like Stevens (2002), some theorists (e.g., Irwin, 1979; Roll, 1966; Shiah, 2011) refer to memory (implicit, long-term, etc.) as the source of psi images, or they at least imply a concordance. On this latter point, many have thought for some time that a relationship (*concordance*) is often evident between the "psi source (in the environment) and the psi input (in the memory system)" (Irwin, 1979, p. 106). But I also believe Irwin is correct in saying there is no justification in "interpreting ESP as paranormal reception" (p. 117).[6] ESP could just "happen" and the "concordance may stem from teleological [goal-oriented] rather than physical causes" (p. 117). While there is some degree of information processing, it is entirely 'internal' (within the mind/brain complex and is not triggered by external inputs), and functions unconsciously until the essential components reach consciousness.

Memory may seem a logical starting point as a psi source; studies show that ESP performance and memory capability correlate (for a review, see Palmer, 2006). Those who perform the best on tests of memory, tend to perform well in ESP tasks. So we may assume that participants with good memories also produce *qualitatively* better matches than those with poor memories because the former have richer, more sophisticated semantic networks. However, for those theorists who see ESP as involving target *perception*, Broughton (2006) notes that it is still a "mystery" how ESP "gets into the system" (p. 255).

This problem has not gone unnoticed, and by way of illustration, I give a recent example of how one theorist, Yung-Jong Shiah, explains ESP perception in terms of neurological modalities or processes (Shiah, 2011, 2012). Shiah (2011) proposed that cortical processes (mainly involving the visual cortex and frontal and temporal lobes) generate ESP images that start with perceptual cues from the target, which interact and are matched "with target-relevant memories" (pp. 129–130). ESP information penetrates human tissue where it triggers chemical reactions in "cryptochromes" (i.e., photoreceptors) in human cells (especially localized in "the inner retina and pineal gland"), whereupon a unified "meaningful synthesis" is created (Shiah, 2012, p. 150). The external carrier of the ESP information can come in the form of magnetic fields, electromagnetic radiation (e.g., ELF, ULF), photons, and other kinds of "weak energy force" (p. 148).

The general problem with *clockwise* (real-time psi) models like Shiah's is that they do not explain how the spacetime factor can be transcended for certain forms of psi (precognition, retrocognition, and even clairvoyance involving extremely distal targets),[7] unless these models dispense with such modalities so that all psi processes are effected in real-time (i.e., using only telepathy, clairvoyance, or PK), which is unlikely. The other problem is that conventional fields (e.g., EM radiation) are no longer thought to be credible media or carriers for ESP information since tests using Faraday cages to shield test subjects from the relevant fields still produce psi effects (Targ & Katra, 1998; Tart, 1988). Of course, that leaves Shiah with a few alternative forces that have been shown to penetrate a Faraday cage, while there is uncertainty about others. As we shall see next, there is a more pertinent, third problem to do with the sender's/agent's capacity to target (even unintentionally) a specific receiver/percipient (supposedly to the exclusion of all others), and indeed how (or whether) others are (or can be) excluded. This is a problem for most psi theories.

Taking a synchronistic stance, it is also important to point out that memories (which are acquired) and archetypes (which are innate) are not the same thing—memory images or traces are secondary, but they are not secondary to ESP (i.e., hypothesized psi signals); they are secondary to the archetype, which is primary. Of course, the percipient will see the triggered memory trace as primary—as, for example, a special telepathic message meant for them alone—and the percipient is not likely to see the broader connotations of its origins, or even recognise that others may intercept that message. Some theorists have come close to this idea of archetypal links behind ESP in the notion of a 'collective' or 'group mind' that enables the sharing of memories (for a review, see Irwin, 1979, pp. 76–82). Irwin notes that becoming "aware of the information in the collective unconscious" gives the "impression" that the information was "communicated" mind to mind as if by extrasensory means (p. 79). But again, this idea puts too much weight on memories *per se* (i.e., the memory traces), and again, it does not explain how individuals are selected or targeted for 'connection', or indeed how others may be excluded.

For such reasons, Stanford (2006) implies a limit to memory models given that a "sense of conviction [of having a psi experience] may derive from an inference that one's prior knowledge and experiences cannot possibly have elicited the [psi] experience" (p. 137). This conviction can be described as "just knowing" such as when a mother 'knows' that her child is in need or danger, which is later proved to be correct (Broughton, 2006, p. 263). In that instance, the image of the child in crisis is characteristic (a motif) of the Child archetype, discussed in detail by Jung (1959/1968; to get an idea of its manifestation, see para. 273–275; 286). The bond between mother and child can reach synchronistic proportions in those rare cases when the archetype is constellated in both (otherwise, no effect can be expected). This archetypal phenomenology aligns with inter-brain neural synchronization (IBNS) having an archetypal substrate underpinning its process (see Valencia & Froese, 2020). There is a notable connection between couples (friends, lovers), even groups, which contrasts with weaker connections between random couples (strangers). The synchronization is particularly pronounced in cooperative exercises as opposed to competitive ones (see also the next subsection *Emotion*). We may assume that the vast populace of mothers with infants is not likely to perceive a specific 'telepathic' instance when it is not pertinent to them. The memory trace of the specific child in the mother's memory (their unique bond) is *a priori* and, once it is archetypally activated, constitutes the representation that identifies *the* child as belonging to *that* mother. Still, the strangeness of the experience provides a sense of conviction (per Stanford) that the 'perception' is more than mere fantasy and should be taken seriously.

It is indeed worth noting that the conviction that one has had a psi experience actually gives away the fact that a memory alone cannot account for a psi experience; better to say, in a genuine psi experience, either a memory trace attaches to something 'other', or *vice versa*. But as we have just seen, it does not have to be the case that this foreign or alien (affect-laden) 'thing' must be information conveyed by extrasensory means for it to instil that conviction, and the same rationale applies to synchronicity. Warcollier (1938), for example, was one of the early researchers who alerted us to the problem of how a target image "gets into" the mind. His solution too was that the psychic images appearing in the percipient's mind (as dreams, hallucinations, etc.) spring from the memory, but he stresses that there is no "*carrying of the visual impression from the agent to the percipient*" (p. 133). William Barrett and Alan Gauld both made the same claims for telepathy.

- Barrett: "telepathy … should be thought of as transfusion, rather than transmission" (1924, as cited in Inglis, 1990, p. 180);
- Gauld: "We do not acquire the factual knowledge exhibited in so-called ESP by any quasi-perceptual or transmissive process …. The knowledge, so to speak, 'happens' " (1976, p. 36).

Warcollier thought the 'visual impression' was there with the percipient all along, suggestive of Jung's (1952/1969) "already existing, correct, but unconscious image" (para. 857), but in archetypal form. While this view could be read as synchronistic in very rudimentary terms, it is not likely Warcollier was thinking along those lines. However, he does seem convinced that his conception "gives the telepathic phenomenon a more objective bearing" (p. 133). Interestingly, Warcollier (1938) allows for the imagination, which "completes the material given incompletely by perception" (p. 166). It might appear that he is dallying with a transmission model (e.g., he refers to "perception"),[8] but there is a fine line between transmission and a term I used earlier, and prefer to use here; namely 'resonance'. Our addiction to the 'mental radio' analogy probably does not help when trying to draw a distinction,[9] but it is the difference between actual propagation of radio waves (or any energy form) as carriers of information between transmitter and receiver, on the one hand, and on the other hand, the conception that the archetype does not propagate *per se*, but 'resonates' like a set of tuning forks between separated systems made ready in the sense Warcollier means. Indeed, the parallels between Warcollier's and Jung's models are striking at a basic level.

Warcollier (1938) goes on to say that telepathy works analogously like vibrations that harmonize between the brains of agent and percipient, just as "striking a C" on a piano causes "the strings of neighboring pianos to begin to vibrate and to send forth this same note" (p. 189). Brains too can 'synchronize':

> [...] unknown vibratory movement ... having impinged upon a brain synchronously harmonized, will associate itself with the emotional vibration and will arouse in the percipient's brain the corresponding activity of the nerve cells; but the impression will remain subconscious.
>
> (p. 189)

The effect in the percipient's brain is the "telepathic vibratory movement", but in order for it to become conscious, "special attention by means of special preparation", or an "abnormal condition" is necessary (p. 189; see also Playfair, 2002), and the agent's emotion needs to be intense. While Warcollier has focussed on telepathy, the analogy extends to psi generally, just as it does to synchronicity. I take "vibratory movement" and "emotional vibration" as being synonymous with my preferred term 'resonance', which I use analogously, as it is not implied that some kind of physical wave or particle is the carrier or transmitting medium. In reference to emotional intensity just mentioned, some parapsychologists do refer to the emotional system as "unconsciously influencing the selection of the implicit memories that will make up the ESP response" (Roll et al., 2021, p. 127). The role of emotion is dealt with next.

Emotion

Emotional responses suggest the image is a 'psychic' one (deeply sourced), just as *numinosity* carries an emotional tone characteristic of synchronicity. However, we need to go further, for it not only seems clear how critical the emotional/archetypal link is to synchronicity *after* the fact, but theorists also find that emotion is psi-conducive *before* the fact. For example, Carpenter (1991) found that ESP effects were associated with physical/emotional experience, anxiety, and unhappy adjustment (see also Crandall, 1985; Schmeidler, 1988). In PK research, Lumsden-Cook (2005a, 2005b) showed that sadness, anger, and elation, mediate or influence outputs on random event generators

(REGs; a.k.a. RNGs). But again, the theorists certainly do not go so far as to say the process is holistic, so they cannot dispense with the need to bridge the spacetime divide between self and other; 'inner' and 'outer'. For them, the psi construct adequately accounts for it. Nevertheless, this dynamic between images and emotions, though incompletely understood, surely gets close to the crux of the synchronistic mechanism (Jung, 1952/1969, para. 846). By way of the emotional system, and akin to Warcollier's tuning fork analogy, the archetype is like a bell in resonance whereby prone individuals within earshot of the ringing bell cannot help but be aware of, and even be drawn into, the same vibratory (archetypal) experience.

In the case of the ESP variant of synchronicity, the resonance is better analogized as (say) two people unaware of each other's presence, each with a hand on the same very large bell, both feeling the same vibration and reporting comparable experiences. Interestingly, Warcollier's analogy parallels objectively determined inter-brain neural synchronization, which describes brains in resonance (see Valencia & Froese, 2020). Conventional research may even converge on a single overarching synchronistic conceptualization—cognitive scientist Tom Froese notes:

> [...] we [Froese, Iizuka, & Ikegami, 2014] did notice that participants could identify each other's emotional state based purely on the unfolding pattern of interaction, which perhaps suggests that there is some potential of discrimination while being 'blinded' to each other.
>
> (T. Froese, personal communication, November 26, 2021)

In the case of the PK variant of synchronicity, work with RNGs poorly represents psi research because the effects are very weak, but the RNG-PK effect is still characteristic of synchronicity (equally so for dice-throwing), but this time it involves a person and an apparatus. Whenever an outcome (a number or signal) is not exclusively random, the outcome may demonstrate archetypal resonance, albeit rare due to the limited range of meaningful choices (after all, choices are reduced to digits, or mere binary outcomes). Individual hits are not easily identifiable in any meaningful way,[10] and only tend to be evident statistically as significant deviations such as in the Global Consciousness Project (see Bancel & Nelson, 2008; Nelson & Bancel, 2011).

Similarly, the emotional quotient appears in a coincidence phenomenon concerning minds that are arguably in resonance, as reported by Wooffitt (2021)—so-called *poetic confluence*, which Wooffitt describes as "confluence of public talk and unarticulated conscious experience" (p. 14). Poetic confluence is characterised by speech errors or unusual words or phrases thought of (or verbally expressed) by a person in response to utterances of the interlocutor (for similar interactional encounters, see Marks-Tarlow & Shapiro, 2021). Two examples are given by Wooffitt: The first concerns person N, who spoke to person B about being sacked from his job, but B was preoccupied with thoughts of a disgusting rat he saw earlier that day. N then says the sacking "had really 'ratted' him", but he corrected his malapropism to "rattled", which "directly articulated the thoughts that B was having regarding the rat" (p. 14).

The second example concerns a gun-waving patient of Hungarian psychoanalyst, István Hollós, who was worried that his hot-headed patient might shoot someone. At the same time, a female patient spoke about her frantic mother who "shoots around in the flat", thus upsetting her. The woman's ungrammatical mix of Hungarian and German words stood out for Hollós, but his anxiety of a possible shooting is eerily captured in the expression "shoots around" (p. 14).

The scores of examples collected by Wooffitt (2021) tend to convey themes that are, in his words, "evocative" and "emotional" (p. 15), but I draw particular attention to the coincidentiality (however minor) of these and other examples he gives (see also Wooffitt, 2022). Wooffitt (2021) notes how poetic confluence is an "anomaly in the sense that we cannot yet identify the mechanisms by which it occurs" (p. 16), but I suggest we are possibly on track to at least one solution, as outlined by Valencia and Froese (2020). A common theme in all these ideas is the overarching synchronistic tone. We can also see in these examples, and the multitude of examples in the parapsychological literature, the likelihood that expressions of complex ideas (e.g., 'texts') can be shared in dyads and groups, which puts paid to the limited notion that archetypes are no more than blunt ideas, forms, and images that cannot be conceptually sophisticated.

On another theoretical point, I agree with Wooffitt that poetic confluence is not the result of "shared circumstances, the topic of the talk, intimate knowledge of one another, and so on" (p. 15). I also agree with Valencia and Froese (2020) that neural synchronization "is not a general effect of a shared environment" (p. 2). If Wooffitt, and Valencia and Froese, were wrong, we could attribute these phenomena to Reichenbach's (1956) "common cause" (see "Examples of Meaningless Chance Groupings" in Chapter 1). Also, I consider the loaded utterances not so much 'speech errors' but more as symbolic and meaningful but unconscious linguistic transformations charged (given their character) by the archetypal content constellated in each person's situation that culminated in the ensuing conversation, and to that degree they are not necessarily "infelicitous" (unfortunate, inappropriate), though they *are* "poetic" (Wooffitt, 2022, p. 91). It is appropriate to think of the resonance that results in a 'connection' as coincidental, but not in a mundane sense (Wooffitt agrees)—I suggest the meaningfulness of the coincidence is given in the archetypal facilitation. Therefore, the subtle yet still synchronistic tone should be readily apparent in these experiences, though some modern theoretical perspectives clearly fail to see the parallel (cf. Wooffitt, 2022). Moreover, the effects are steeped in emotion.

In conclusion, as we have seen, psi and synchronicity do not seem to be wholly explained as formal, step-by-step processes (e.g., via *preparation, incubation, inspiration*, and *production*) as is shown to be the case for creativity. But it does appear that imagination is key. When we try to opt for a brain model exclusively, in order to discover how psychic ideas and images might spring into consciousness, we see that parapsychological discourse ends up being couched in terms that break away from 'hard' modelling. For example, we see dyadic connections strengthened, honed, reined in, or brought to bear, through meaningful (archetypal) elements in relationships and conversations. Yet, we then witness recourse to psi processes being the inevitable explanation, though not necessarily the correct one. It is in part correct to speak of a memory (say, from life experience) that fulfils the role of a representation in consciousness of a psychic idea, but the psi theorist ends up invoking the causal factor of *transmission* simply because an external source seems to be involved. Alternatively, synchronicity indicates archetypal *resonance* as the principle connecting factor between the internal image and the external event; a process that is facilitated by the imagination. Psi is easily accommodated by this schema to the extent that psi may invariably be synchronicity.

In the next section, I will ponder Jung's tendency to avoid detailed theoretical dealings with the imagination as a source and mechanism behind psi and synchronicity. There appears to be a diplomatic reason for that, but that is not the only reason.

The Problem of the Imagination

Jung (1952/1969) has pointed out the role of the imagination in Rhine's ESP experiments, and though he specifically refers to the typical subject in a card-guessing experiment in the following quote, he is making a more general point:

> … the subject's answer is not the result of his observing the physical cards, it is a product of pure imagination, of "chance" ideas which reveal the structure of that which produces them, namely the unconscious.
>
> (para. 840)

Apart from this statement, Jung's *Synchronicity* essay is noticeably bereft of a detailed examination and discussion of the role of imagination in the synchronistic process. Yet it seems transparently obvious that synchronicity must involve the imagination—indeed, we see Jung has said enough to more than imply the need for the concept. So why did Jung fail to develop the idea further in his essay? Or at the very least, why did he *talk around* the topic?

Ironically, I suggest Jung did maintain the bigger aim of elevating imagination to a respectable status in science, but it is apparent he mainly did that within acceptable mainstream (non-parapsychological) parameters. Certainly, he is on record for stressing and upholding the importance of the imagination in two crucial areas of mental activity (see Jung, 1964): First, as a key process behind the creation of ideas from whence is built our entire cultural and scientific edifice—the crux of invention, and ultimate building block of civilization, the role of the imagination was perhaps too important to risk a strong association with an unproved and shaky parapsychological concept; and second, as a major factor in Jung's own therapeutic technique, so-called 'active imagination', which, by its design, is a procedure for resolving complexes—as the term suggests, the play of imagination is the *sine qua non* of active imagination, such that its role is pivotal in psychology and psychiatry.

One can see that if synchronicity is given a predominantly subjective tone by dint of the fact that it all came out of the experient's imagination, the psychopathological labels of hallucination, delusion, and "ideas of reference" are more easily invoked, which Jung repudiated (Jung, 1975, p. 409). Imagination has a certain place in the sciences—go beyond those respectable limits, and it is marginalized as pathological, although Roe (2020) notes that British classicist, philologist, and co-founder of the SPR, F. W. H. Myers, recognized "nonpathological hallucination" as early as the late 1800s. Roe describes "nonpathological hallucination" as a

> theoretical perspective within which veridical information received paranormally (such as by telepathy) could be brought to conscious awareness in an idiosyncratic, dramatized form. (p. 4)

All very well to make the paranormal link, but that does not interest the typical scientist.

Imagination can thus be seen as a two-edged sword in workplaces such as the experimenter's laboratory, or even the artist's studio—it can be fruitful or unproductive; its offerings can be uninterpretable and incoherent, or speculative and purposeful. How does the theorist get out of this bind? By being vague. I suggest Jung's proffering of the unconscious as the inner source of synchronicity allows him to be approximate in his claims, whereas if he singled out the imagination as *a key practical component of synchronicity*, his theory would have stood on shaky ground whenever the imagination failed as it often does, much like 'on-demand' demonstrations of psi (and I make that association with good reason). He would have no recourse to any other faculty. The upshot is the imagination would lose its status; so would synchronicity. Furthermore, and most importantly, if Jung ardently and didactically put imagination in the service of synchronicity, the so-called "already existing image"—whether from a dream, or a fantasy, or whatever—could be reduced to a work of art (again, Jung repudiated such assertions, especially those made about his own works as reproduced in *The Red Book*—see Shamdasani, 2009).

So Jung may have de-emphasized the role of the imagination because he saw his essay as a purely scientific (not psychological or artistic) treatise, and he wanted it to be taken seriously by scientists, especially physicists (see Jung,

1952/1969, para. 960, 963). Hence, for the purposes of developing and correcting the 'finer' aspects of synchronicity theory, he called upon Pauli to aid him in his venture (see Jung, 1952/1969, para. 963). Progoff (1973) made the same point, though he does not go into any detail about what was lost in the process:

> Jung spent his greatest personal efforts in attempting to persuade not the psychologists but the physicists. His main dialogue in his last years regarding Synchronicity was with physicists because he became increasingly interested in establishing Synchronicity as a general principle of knowledge relevant for all the sciences and not limited to the study of man. (p. 141)

But rather than give the conspicuously absent imagination a proper treatment, "the unconscious"—a very broad concept—is the dominant construct throughout *Synchronicity*, as it is throughout much of Jung's *oeuvre*. In its ubiquity, the unconscious (a reified, catch-all term) necessarily embraces all manner of psychological processes of which we are not aware, including the imagination, but it can extend to the psychoid realm and beyond when we introduce the collective unconscious. Thus, in Jung's work, we often do not get a clear idea what specific unconscious process Jung means in any given situation. Such is also the case with the many diverse forms in nature, animate and inanimate, that (for Jung) all come to represent the Self archetypally, often with little refinement by Jung in the way of their significance and specific meanings (Jung, 1936/1968). Thus, it must be said that Jung's (1960/1969) reference to "irruptions of unconscious contents into consciousness" (para. 430), which is his favoured and oft-used term for describing contents of the unconscious coming to our awareness, is often made without clarification.

I assert (and in doing that, I rely on the backing of modern cognitive psychology) that many an 'unconscious image' that comes into consciousness is the result of a largely unconscious process that can be specifically referred to as the deep imagination at work, including in the synchronistic context. In that and other contexts, Jung evokes in the reader's mind notions concerning the power of the imagination when he speaks of the unconscious as the source of our mythopoetic tendencies and propensities (Jung, 1936/1968, para. 186). This 'image' can come into consciousness in a variety of ways, with dreams, fantasies, intuition, and insight, tending to be the most common. The developed richness of the image or idea may even come into full consciousness merely at the vaguest suggestion from an external source, but even in that mundane way, it may set up a synchronicity down the track. That is, somewhat like a standard synchronicity, a context-relevant image or idea may be lurking in the shadows of the mind, not yet conscious, though we have the context (an ambience created, for example, by thoughtful engagement) that may trigger an archetypal representation which we may then meet in the environment. The following example illustrates this point:

At the time I started writing this chapter, and was looking for a meaningful nod of approval to these ideas (the context), I browsed the Internet searching for material on the relationship between synchronicity and imagination. I came across an entry on the Reddit website (TriumphantGeorge, 2015) that gives an example of how to generate synchronicity deliberately by focussing one's attention for "20 minutes" on a random image (the author of the web-page proffered "owls" as a topic). The author then explained that the reader would "spend the next week encountering lots of owls." Although I did not care to "spend 20 minutes … imagining owls", later that evening, I watched a Humphrey Bogart movie, *Dark Passage* (Warner & Daves, 1947), in which Bogart rides a San Francisco cable car that passes "*The Owl Drug Co.*". The next day, I needed clarification on the citing of websites in APA-Style, and one of the first Google entries to be listed was 'Purdue Online Writing Lab', which calls itself "Purdue OWL" for short (Purdue OWL, 1995–2017). In a meaningful way (inherent in the equivalences), the owl (a symbol of wisdom) may be taken to mean my explication on the role of the imagination in synchronicity is soundly expressed, even though I felt I had been struggling with the concept in this chapter.

Just this casual experience—I call it synchronicity (it is certainly more than serendipity)—is a hint that the synchronistic process (albeit not overtly obvious) is akin to the imagination at work (I suggest *preparation* and *incubation* are evident), and furthermore, theory would say an appropriate archetype was constellated. I do say I had been struggling because I was also trying to get into the mind of Jung. Interestingly, Jung asked the question, "How does the unconscious image arise, and how the coincidence?" (1952/1969, para. 858). From all the examples given thus far, we can see there are ways this can happen, but Jung only promises to answer that question "later", and after a very long exposition on the *I Ching* and his astrological studies, he attempts a redesign of the 'scientific causal triad' in his "Conclusion" section (para. 947–968). Jung's lengthy aside is somewhat constructive in offering a *place* in science for synchronicity, but it takes us no closer to an understanding, and it certainly fails to include a solid and grounded role for the imagination. In this context, Jung's quaternio is a distraction. The other 'expositions' are sketchy illustrations that describe but do not explain the 'mechanics' of the synchronistic process.

Before that, there is another problem. Jung (1952/1969) says: "there seems to be an *a priori*, causally inexplicable knowledge of a situation which at the time is unknowable" (para. 858; see also para. 931). Jung takes the scarab dream image as a "conscious representation … of the situation" that occurred the day after the dream, and he speaks in a similar way of his other examples. (Perhaps we might describe my experience with representations of the owl in the same way.) Fortunately, Jung says this "knowledge" only *seems* to be "*a priori*" and "causally inexplicable", but his statement is still misleading because he implies a knowing ("knowledge of a situation") at some level that suggests the presence of information not readily to hand that awaits only the cooperation of the unconscious to deliver it up for conscious use. Of course, the scarab dreamer had no more knowledge about the rose-chafer and how it might manifest than I did about the owl, but that is not Jung's point. While I might have suspected something, and I earlier pointed out how one's suspicions might be put to good use (see "The Forms in Action" in Chapter 2), Jung, whether he meant it or not, leads us to think we are not working with archetypal representations but are paranormally receiving and reproducing images.

The *a priori* image should not be classed as knowledge or information in the conventional sense on the mere premise that it later proved to be 'informative' or 'informational'—it should never be relegated to a status higher than an 'unconscious image'. I made this point earlier, but it bears repeating. As long as we have an unconscious image—a product of the imagination—we can never be sure that we are dealing with fact or fantasy. Verification is supposed to be the key that unlocks the truth, but that verification is merely the successful *matching* of an unconscious image with real-world content. Of course justifiably firm reliance on our sensory modalities puts us on safe ground, but we know *matching* only happens for the most part *approximately* in psi tasks and synchronicity, and only rarely is it ever done with conviction and confidence—after all, so-called 'hits' in psi tasks include many chance outcomes (false positives).

These points about perception have not gone unnoticed in philosophical circles: Main (2004) discusses the influence of Kant's philosophy on Jung who

> argued that things in themselves, whether material things or spiritual things, cannot be known other than as mediated to consciousness in the form of psychic images. Our primary reality, he [Jung] repeatedly stated, the only reality of which we can be immediately aware, is psychic reality. (p. 104)

That means we cannot really picture reality outside our psychological images of it, so that our entire experience is an interplay of inner activity resonating with reality in both its manifest forms and its underlying (hidden) forms or structure or 'architecture' that may reach consciousness via the unconscious by means of which we are not aware. We may speculate that imagination and intuition, and so on, come into play during these moments. We fantasize or dream our inner reality into existence—we only modify this version of reality if and when it constantly fails to square with the facts.

Not only do we interpret the real world this way, but it seems synchronicity emerges as a kind of exploitation of this process, and some scientific discoveries (e.g., those of Kekulé and Poincaré) would fit this scenario. They seem to be occasional occurrences, though we do not know how occasional. What we can say is we generally arrive at a correct (or an adequate) view of our mundane world but, going further, the psyche can sometimes provide helpful images that can be taken as symbolic representations of things otherwise external and beyond normal human experience—hence, synchronicity. In the latter case, it may be a moot point (especially for the skeptic) whether pure chance is at play, or we are really witnessing synchronistic contingence—that dichotomy itself forms the crux of the debate. Nevertheless, given the above, we get a helpful perspective on what the inner world of images should mean to us.

The above quote from Main (2004) is in the context of two of Jung's statements that did not specifically refer to the workings of the imagination (Jung's aim was more to describe how we perceive and interpret the world), and nor were they made in a synchronistic context. But *that* context is not my point; I only want to show that Jung's understanding of perception and the unconscious source of images is widely disseminated, but in the *Synchronicity* essay, Jung does not follow through on this understanding when it comes to meaningful *coincidence*, which he speaks of as if it were *extrasensory* perception. Thus, when Jung (1952/1969) *does* make pertinent statements, he still only hints at the workings of the imagination (para. 853, 931), but speaks more of images, adopting a conventional parapsychological interpretation that implies the images have an external source.

I feel the problem in a nutshell is that Jung could have made more detailed and crucial points about the role of the imagination in his essay, but much of his approach was obscured by a bigger aim. Jung wanted synchronicity to reach general acceptance (especially in the scientific community), and it seems he downplayed the role of the imagination to do that. When the opportunity came to illustrate the role of the imagination in synchronicity, Jung gave rudimentary explanations about images that include misleading notions about the informational content of those images as if they were of external origin. This is to undermine the very nature of coincidence and the role of archetypes.

Before I move on to developing the synchronistic model of the psi process, it would pay to look at the relevant experimental evidence to see just how much that research has concealed as much as revealed the very fact that the imagination is a key underpinning of paranormal processes.

Imagination and Psi—A Review

It can be argued that imagination is not only expressed in science in the form of experimental and technological design, but is also instrumental in the actual discovery and creation of new content (e.g., facts about the world). That is not only true in all the sciences (hard and soft), but applies equally in fringe areas such as parapsychology. Imagination in psi research has not been overlooked as a correlate or predictor of psi effects, but we can go further and regard it as the pivotal creative force that produces psi effects. In this section, I consider these claims.

Variables in Psi Research

Before I take a more considered approach to the imagination and its relationship with psi from a synchronistic perspective, I will make a few general comments about variables, which can have many qualifying names such as correlates, covariates, predictors, moderators, and modifiers. I will defer to the term correlate for convenience. First, a variable can be a correlate (i.e., it is associated with another variable). Correlates are sometimes loosely referred to as predictors if they have predictor capability, which is supposed to be shown through appropriate statistical analysis. A predictor is a variable that predicts an outcome variable (a.k.a. response or criterion variable in a non-experimental study). A causal relationship between variables is not implied just because the variables correlate, or one predicts the other. However, when a correlate is experimentally manipulated (rather than just measured), it is referred to as an independent variable, and the manipulation may then indicate a causal effect on the variable of interest (a.k.a. the dependent variable), provided the statistical test result proves significant. For our purposes, the variable of interest is a measure of performance on a so-called psi task (i.e., a psi effect, or anomalous or paranormal outcome). Variables that correlate with, or predict, psi are of most interest to parapsychologists in so-called process-oriented research because they help unlock the nature or 'processes' underlying psi. I would emphasize the fact that each time we learn something about psi, we learn something about synchronicity.

Second, correlates, when they are psychological, are better understood as short-hand terms describing human factors that are thought to ready the mind/brain complex for the task at hand so that the outcome is optimized; even in psi research. Correlates such as paranormal belief, relaxation, extraversion, etc., can fall under broader classifications indicating psychological, physiological, and personality factors, respectively, but correlates can also be neuropsychological (e.g., alpha waves, which are associated with a calm relaxed state), socio-cultural (e.g., religiosity), and biological (e.g., hyperthyroidism). There is no hard-and-fast rule that indicates which of the many variables are the strongest correlates of psi, but parapsychologists are confident about paranormal belief (Storm & Tressoldi, 2017), and relaxation as epitomized in the ganzfeld domain (Storm & Tressoldi, 2020).

Good cases can also be made for other presentiment-related variables (Mossbridge et al., 2012), and brain functions such as event-related potentials (ERPs), which typically occur "in response to direct sensory stimulation (such as when the skin is touched, a fingertip is pricked, or a bright light is flashed in one's eyes)" (Williams, 2015, pp. 29–30). ERPs may even be objective neurological markers of activated unconscious processes (e.g., in the deep imagination, in the collective unconscious, suggesting constellated archetypes). This idea may be drawn from work by Warren, McDonough, and Don (1992a, 1992b). They showed that ERP differed markedly when psychic

Malcolm Bessent looked at a future target compared to ERP when looking at decoys. However, only chance performances were elicited in the actual psi task (McDonough, Warren, & Don, 1990; Warren et al., 1992a). Williams reports similar ERP differences for non-psychics (Don, McDonough, & Warren, 1998; McDonough, Don, & Warren, 2002). Yet again, only chance performances were elicited in the psi tasks. Whatever was taking place unconsciously in the brain, no clue of that process reached consciousness to guide target selection. While Williams (2015) suggests "the effect reflects an unconscious precognitive 'response' to the outcome of a future event" (p. 58), the effect from a synchronistic perspective indicates the subtlety of deep (neurological) processes, which may simultaneously indicate archetypal processes. We begin to understand the importance of the link between consciousness and the unconscious because a strong link to the unconscious is a strong albeit indirect link to the world, which can be in the form of desired outcomes in psi research. Besides archetypes, other factors (some just mentioned) may prevail to establish that link, but without that link to the 'inner' (image), the 'outer' (target) remains undifferentiated.

Effectively, psi correlates and predictors can usually be seen as functioning in one simple way; they act like ON/OFF switches. When the switch is 'ON', a psi effect is likely; when the switch is 'OFF', a psi effect is not likely, and the rule may apply whether the sought-for effect is intended or unintended. For example, *belief in psi* = ON; *non-belief in psi* = OFF. Of course, the non-believer's 'psychic system' acts in reverse, but ironically it is thought the nonbeliever still has to detect a target in order to avoid it. This principle is captured in Palmer's (1972) "vindication" theory—namely, skeptics have only one agenda; target avoidance to disprove the psi hypothesis.

Research by Storm and Rock (2014b) has demonstrated similar reversals of effect attributable to 'reactance', whereby noncompliance (usually from skeptics) can lead to psi-missing as a so-called 'boomerang effect'. According to Reactance Theory (Brehm, 1966), an individual's freedom, if threatened, may result in reactance, which is "a motivational state aimed at restoring the threatened freedom" (Silvia, 2005, p. 277). Storm, Ertel, and Rock (2013) were the first to explore reactance effects in parapsychological studies. They found that the psi performance of reactance-treated nonbelievers was significantly worse than nonbelievers in the control (no reactance treatment) condition. Storm and Rock (2014b) replicated the effect, and similar effects have been reported (Storm, 2016, 2019a, 2019b). Emotional states (e.g., anxiety, tension, confusion) also work for or against psi effects like switches in response to the relevant conscious intention, or they inadvertently trigger an automatic response at an unconscious or conditioned level (Kruth, 2019; Storm, 2022; Storm et al., 2013).

Seen this way, the multi-factorial complexity set up by many potentially interlacing and interacting variables is ultimately an arrangement based on the presence or absence of psychological and emotional states that are difficult to control, which is why most psi experimenters at least try to get off on the right foot by recruiting proactive (cooperative and compliant) participants, although they might be willing to test reactant (uncooperative and noncompliant) participants if it suits their experimental aims. Ideally, a keen mind, in a state of readiness, is most likely to deploy the deep imagination, which parallels or is indeed related to processes in the collective unconscious, and that makes archetypes paramount in psi research and synchronicity; they too are like switches, or better, they are contingencies. Unfortunately, we simply do not know the degree to which archetypes have figured in mainstream psi research. Nevertheless, Jung (1952/1969) asks us to entertain the possibility that little in the way of psychic and synchronistic effects can be expected without them.

Imagination and Psi

For various reasons, imagination is praised quite highly by Jung, yet a number of important parapsychology textbooks over many decades have not even listed the word 'imagination' in their indices (e.g., Cardeña, Palmer, & Marcusson-Clavertz, 2015; Pratt et al., 1940/1966; Wolman, 1977). I wondered about this omission and I put it down to the arbitrary nature of the imagination, as well as the prejudice the word can conjure up in serious scientific circles (as Jung noted). No parapsychologist likes the idea that psi or synchronicity are not real effects, thought to be mere products of the imagination, will-o'-the-wisps, delusions. That is tantamount to saying the significant correlates and predictors of psi and synchronicity may be reduced to the occasional (sporadic) workings of chance, and parapsychologists have simply been very lucky whenever they find a significant psi effect or correlate of interest. Yet Jung has said: "the debt we owe to the play of imagination is incalculable" (1921/1971, para. 93), and the context in which he uttered those words concerned the "creative individual", whether that be a child, an adult, an artist, or a career professional, thus even extending contextually to the disciplinary worlds of the arts and the sciences (the pivotal ideas of Kekulé and Poincaré are but two examples from science).

Parapsychology cannot be precluded from these disciplines, and there is no good argument that can undermine the important role of the imagination in parapsychological studies. It might help critics if they yield a little and see the imagination as part and parcel of *imaginative thinking*, in the sense Zwart (2019) uses the term. He notes that "imaginative thinking is non-directed, spontaneous and free-floating" (p. 2), and when compared to rational thinking, it is older, and reflects "the spontaneous functioning of the human mind" (p. 3).

Imagination in psi research, however, has not been entirely overlooked, and some experimentation can be seen as focussing on the imagination as a direct source of psi responses. Surprisingly, even a well-known critic of the psi hypothesis, Susan Blackmore, writing with Nicholas Rose on psi and false memories (Blackmore & Rose, 1997), made the peculiar statement that psi responses might be misperceptions if they can be attributed to the imagination getting the better of prone individuals (psi experiencers and believers) so that recollections of psychic experiences are probably false memories. Alternatively, they concede that confusion between reality and the imagination is "psi-conducive" (p. 321). Both premises are easily tested, but I regard the latter as not saying enough about the psi process. What the Blackmore/Rose study does is inadvertently come very close to identifying the role of the imagination as the key mechanism underpinning paranormal process, and I mean that in a way supportive of the claims I have made thus far in this chapter. Instead, they identify the imagination as a source of mistaken psi, and argue that "the more effort it takes to conjure up an image, the more likely it is to come from the imagination; the easier it is, the more likely it is to be a real memory or external event" (p. 321). I suggest that in a parapsychological setting, imaginative effort can be intrinsic to a psi effect, and imagination is not necessarily a source of error.

Participants in the Blackmore and Rose (1997) study were shown slides of pictured objects with labels, and asked to imagine other objects (no pictures; labels only). A so-called false memory would be a memory of an object that was imagined, but never actually shown. (Note that a good deal of effort was made on the parts of Blackmore and Rose to help consolidate the false memories.) For the parapsychological part of the study, ESP targets consisted of half the imagined objects concealed in envelopes as the experimenters thought these would clairvoyantly firm up the false memories. When tested three weeks later, participants were required to report whether they had seen an object amongst the slides or imagined it, but a 'hit' was a false memory that corresponded with an ESP target picture concealed in the envelope, and a 'miss' was a false memory that corresponded with a non-target picture. The hits vs. misses difference was significant (12 to 6), with more false memories occurring for targets (12) than non-targets (6)—indeed, the effect was very strong and not typical of psi experiments.

Rose and Blackmore (2001) tried to replicate their findings in three experiments (although the second experiment failed due to "computer error"). In the first and third experiments, the hits vs. misses difference were not significant (10 to 9, and 73 to 75, respectively). Oddly, and without any compelling reason, Rose and Blackmore suggested the original experiment was a "chance effect" (p. 142). A quick tote of the combined hits and misses of the first two studies yields 22 and 15, respectively, which may be significantly different, but Rose and Blackmore did not test the combined data, and they did not table the new data as they did in their first study.

The reason I do not give much credence to the third experiment's data is because the experiment had some procedural changes, but more importantly it was explicitly presented to participants as a test of ESP. Participants were told of the "positive results found in the original experiment and were told that the purpose of the experiment was to measure ESP … [and they] were told that the envelopes stapled to the back of the imagination test contained ESP targets" (p. 139). This information makes the final experiment very different from the original design in that such instructions can easily elicit performance anxiety in believers and probably invoke reactance in nonbelievers. Furthermore, the single task (imagining an image) is changed to an exercise in multi-tasking that splits the participant's focus and intention. Advocates of Decision Augmentation Theory (DAT) and Psi-Mediated Instrumental Response (PMIR) would easily spot the flaws (for a review of these two theories, see Storm, 2025). Indeed, Blackmore and Rose (1997) described the original experiment as a "variant of … nonintentional psi tests" (p. 328), so there really was no need to break protocol.

Crucially, Rose and Blackmore (2001) did not find significant correlations between false memories and paranormal belief for their three separate sets of data, and the same nonsignificant result was found earlier (Blackmore & Rose, 1997). The four nonsignificant correlations suggest quite cogently that paranormal belief does not automatically make one prone to false memories (i.e., pseudo-psychic experiences). Importantly, the demonstrated effects are clearly attributable to the imagination, but the accent on the falsity of targets only serves to misdirect. To paraphrase Rose and Blackmore, one has to push the imagination really hard to conjure up an image, whereas true memories are easy to recall. That effectively confirms my earlier statement that ideal psi-test participants ardently set their imagination to work *because* they very much want to identify targets—they do not err just because they use their imagination. But thinking so is probably why some parapsychologists are suspicious of the imagination, and are wary of participants getting carried away with their imagination. One final point: If there is anything else amiss in these experiments, it is in the failure to test "true memories" (i.e., there was no test of the psi capacity to recall images actually shown to participants)—that would have given the experimenters a baseline.

Similar claims of the imagination at work in psi tasks can be made for creativity, which is relevant here if we may be free to assume a valid association between creativity and the imagination, with both related to psi and synchronicity (for examples clearly of a synchronistic tone, see Cardeña, Iribas, & Reijman, 2012). These relationships are described in a number of ways since creativity has many found and proposed correlates (e.g., openness and divergent thinking, respectively). Carpenter (2012) argues that creativity and its psychological correlates should predict psi outcomes because creative (e.g., artistic) people (i) tend to be motivated consciously and unconsciously to do well and therefore "construct allusions toward potential meaning at the psi level" (p. 177), and (ii) can suspend rational analysis, and draw on an "inner field of sensed preferences, impulses, and incipient understandings" (p. 177).

One of the most impressive examples of research that shows this relationship between creative/artistic people and their psi capacity is the study by Schlitz and Honorton (1992). They sampled students from the Juilliard

School, a performing arts conservatory in Manhattan, New York. Twenty undergraduates (a mix of music students, drama students, and dance students) served as "receivers" in a single ganzfeld session. The overall hit rate was a staggering 50% (MCE = 25%). Similar psi success rates for creative/artistic people were reported earlier by Schmeidler (1988), and more recently by Holt (2013), though there is dispute over how best to measure creativity (Holt, 2007, 2013).

Holt's (2013) participants had a mean hit rate of 43% (where MCE = 25%), but this figure applies to her heterogeneous sample of artists and non-artists. Unexpectedly, the artists hit rate was lower at 40% compared to the non-artists who scored at an impressive 47%. Holt suggests the difference was due to the "experience-sampling methodology" (ESM) working more favourably for non-artists than for artists. ESM participants self-reported their experiences at any time the impulse took them insofar as it pertained to the ESP-target. Holt did not report the specifics, but demands of the ESM protocol possibly conflicted with artists' lifestyles to a greater extent than they did for non-artists. However, Holt also reported that the two groups were not all that different from each other on a range of creativity measures. All these failings can be explained by the two sample sizes being too small (15 in each group), as statistics from small databases are very poor at reflecting the corresponding population parameters. More generally, however, Holt's review reports hit rates ranging from 30% to 50% across six ganzfeld studies, and Holt conservatively suggests "creativity itself" (p. 2) may be the reason for the higher hit rates.

Finally, we have a series of studies using Imagery Cultivation (IC), the theoretical principles of which were first outlined by Storm and Rock (2009a). The primary focus of IC (besides relaxation) is to guide the imagination of the participant in order to create a mental image of a concealed or future target. Essentially, IC is based on shamanic-like journeying practices, which often include repetitive drumming, and entails "voluntarily entering altered state of consciousness ..." (Walsh, 1989, p. 5). The link between shamanic-states and psi has been reported extensively in the literature, and the ASC appears to be tied in with that psychic experience (e.g., Krippner, 1984; Nelson et al., 1998; Radin & Nelson, 2003; Saklani, 1988). The IC treatment consists of guided imagery with constant drumming (both on a soundtrack delivered via headphones) while the participant is seated in a relaxed state (eyes closed).

Storm and Rock (2009b), and Rock, Storm, Harris, and Friedman (2012), have demonstrated the effectiveness of the shamanic-like principles underlying IC. Procedurally, after the IC treatment, participants tried to select a target image amid three decoy images (target sets used were those prepared by Thalbourne, 1981). As an aside, I hasten to add that these sets may be thought of as good for testing psi, but they are not so good for testing synchronicity because meaningfulness does not enter into the experimental foray (i.e., participants are not usually asked if their hit meant anything to them, which is why it is reasonable to assume that real-life psi is often more impressive than lab psi). An RNG was used to generate the array, and each image was ranked by the participant, with the expectation that ESP-targets were ranked #1 (1st choice = direct hit) more often than can be explained by chance.

Storm and Rock (2009b), and Rock et al. (2012), reported significant and near-significant psi effects in the two studies: 34.5% and 29.9%, respectively (where MCE = 25%). It is to be noted that the IC treatment is similar to the ganzfeld treatment, in that they both encourage image formation related to psi targets, and the two rates just reported are comparable to those found in the ganzfeld meta-analyses of around 30% to 31% (where MCE = 25%). Specifically, Storm et al. (2010) found a 30% hit-rate in 29 new ganzfeld studies (1992 to 2008) that were four-choice designs only (p. 475). In a later meta-analysis, a total of 117 four-choice ganzfeld studies (from 1974 to 2018) yielded "a 30.6% hit rate" (Storm & Tressoldi, 2020, p. 209).

Storm (2019a) then simplified the original IC procedure by (a) shortening the guided imagery component to a 9½-minute pre-recorded soundtrack (down from 19 minutes), (b) removing the drumming component from the soundtrack, (c) introducing background tonalities, (d) altering the wording of the guided imagery, and (e) using target sets prepared by May et al. (2012). These changes were not merely for the sake of expediency, but were aimed at testing the limits of the protocol. Also, the number of images (actual photographs) in the on-screen array was increased from four to five, thus changing MCE from 25% to 20%. As hypothesized, Storm found the direct-hit rate under a pure IC condition was *higher* (23.7%) than for the controls (15%) where MCE was now 20%. In a follow-up study using the same design, Storm and Goretzki (2021) reported a significant hit-rate of 25% for 200 participants who received the IC treatment. In a smaller study, Storm (2022) reported a hit-rate of 25.5% (albeit non-significant given N = 51) for IC participants compared to 20.4% for the control group (N = 49).

Thus far, the efficacy of IC is evident, though critics may dispute my argument that the relaxation has less to do with lowering the 'mental noise' in order to clear the way for the psi channel, and is more to do with preparation for an ASC. Besides which, the guided imagery and tonalities hardly instil quietude or clear the mind of noise *per se*. Of course, when persons close their eyes and go into a rested state, alpha waves increase in amplitude, and we know alpha is high when "a person is not deeply engaged in cognitive thought" (Williams, 2015, p. 29). In these states, the brain is still awake, and the mind is still conscious and capable of reverie, fantasy, and similar mental activity, but left alone, this activity is not given a direction and therefore has no specific purpose. We also find that alpha is positively associated with ESP (see Chapter 3 in Williams, 2015). So it is easy to see how alpha-conducive relaxation came to be associated with ESP (for details, see Storm & Rock, 2009a). However, while the evidence shows the ganzfeld state is psi-conducive, the ganzfeld treatment is solely a relaxation exercise, with no actual verbal instruction to guide the imagination and encourage the generation of images and impressions. In contrast, the ASC brought about by IC puts the experient in a more general state of openness to, and activation of, the imagination beyond the passivity of a relaxed mind, and beyond the limits of the ego and its needs. This process is thought to induce a creative connection to the collective unconscious that enables a possible archetypal experience.

The shamanic tradition speaks to an awareness, experience, and even exploitation of this higher state that touches the deeper levels of the imagination. But a specific aim is necessary (as in shamanism), and it is the guided imagery itself that verbally encourages and keeps the individual focussed and grounded in the task. Any 'connection' with the target image through visualization and imagination is theorized to actually be a particular representation of something more holistic but irrepresentable, and certainly beyond the thoughts and preoccupations of ego-bound consciousness. Out of convenience, the actual 'psi' task during IC has been pitched as if picture 'guessing' is required, but as a synchronistic effect, it can be conceptualized as an above-chance selection bias that manifests as identifying and matching the elements reported in the mentation (i.e., the reported image originally perceived in the mind) to corresponding elements in the target (and decoys), with each decoy presumed to produce fewer matches compared to the target. The task is facilitated by the resonance brought about by the archetypal theme(s) common to both the target and the mentation; not because the specific target elements were perceived by the participant. It also needs stressing that there can be no guarantee of an effect (outside chance) if no archetype is constellated. With these issues in mind, we can continue to the next stage of the journey into the nature of the deep imagination and its role in synchronicity.

Mapping the Psi Image as Synchronicity

To review my previous points, I have said that synchronicities happen more often than chance can explain simply because they are facilitated by archetypal factors whereas chance occurrences are effectively random. This is the usual way synchronicity manifests and is detected—an archetype constellates, a related dream content, or thought, or idea, or intuition, comes to mind (imagination), and immediately or at some reasonable time later, the world of objects/events acts like a palette from which a match to that imaginal representation may be drawn, and one finds oneself ideally placed in spacetime to witness an external parallel, a coincidence. This is a 'mapping' in the sense Gatlin (2008) means. She used the word "mapping" (p. 199), as in the sequence of letters c h a i r (chair) which "maps, or corresponds to, or means a simple piece of furniture with which we are all familiar" (p. 199).

However, as I have said above, I suggest as misleading the phrase which Jung (1952/1969) uses in the context of the scarab dream of which its content is said to be "… a conscious representation arising from an *already existing image of the situation* [my emphasis] that will occur on the following day …" (para. 857). Jung rightly connects this image to an archetype *per se* (i.e., not yet in representational form), but he confirms his belief that there is an "*a priori*, causally inexplicable knowledge of a situation which is unknowable at the time" (para. 858). This is to imply that innumerable outer-world objects and events come to be prefigured in the unconscious *acausally*. Though Jung's definitions of synchronicity have a degree of ambiguity, I hold that in instances like these, he has given his understanding of synchronicity a Rhinean spin that can be taken to mean synchronistic correspondence (mapping) is more than coincidental because *it appears as though* outer-world targets are communicated via ESP (i.e., they are paranormally 'perceived' or 'transmitted'). The question is, how did Jung slip up like this?

Better for Jung to have said synchronicity is based on 'archetypal paralleling' (we can call it the *equivalence hypothesis*, using the word 'equivalence' in its proper sense), and not entertain ideas of *transmission* of information (informational psi). We only have to think of examples given in Chapter 1 to prove the *equivalence hypothesis*: The piece of jewellery in the form of an Egyptian Scarabeid Beetle dreamt by Jung's client was *not* the rose-chafer that crawled across Jung's window-pane; Linda Evans's image of Senator Edward Kennedy was *not* an image of her fiancé, even though in both cases we do have correspondences, and more generally in parapsychology it should be understood that the typical match in a free-response study is also a correspondence.

We cannot let the persuasiveness of the play of imagination, in the form of impressive successes, cloud our judgement and deceive us into thinking that an "already existing image" in the unconscious is the real-world event or object somehow transmitted, or transmuted, or transmogrified—it (the image) merely "maps, or corresponds to" that event or object (Gatlin, 2008, p. 199). There is this idea, and it is pushed by commentators like Progoff (1973), that synchronicity should be taken as psi, or they imply it. Instead, and more likely, psi should be taken as synchronicity (i.e., psi = synchronicity). But fundamental psi principles (like energy exchange, information transmission, and causal relations) are not necessary in synchronicity theory. We should understand the parallels between targets and responses (it would be misleading to call them stimuli and perceptions) as "accidental" in the sense that Mansfield et al. (1998) mean when they say: "The archetypal meaning is the primary and essential aspect of a synchronicity experience, while the *psychological and physical correlates are contingent and accidental* [emphasis added]" (p. 21). To that extent, the whole synchronicity experience (and psi) becomes a matching (best-fit) process in its most mundane sense, and so we may call it symbolic because a particular image is conjured *with purpose*, which is the rule that precludes other (irrelevant) images. I understand the point raised by Mansfield et al., but I also recognise that the field of parapsychology (due to the mysteries it tries to uncover) has very much made the psi effect the pivotal point of interest (the *raison d'etre*), and without it, the enterprise becomes scientifically aimless. It would be wise to acknowledge the importance of both the therapeutic purpose of individuation *and* the objective effects that come with it—unlike psi (conventionally understood), synchronicity is a two-fold effect.

Must we see the 'accident' as symbolic, or *standing* for the target? And what does that mean for the equation, psi = synchronicity? If we adhere to that equation, what are we to make of 'exact' target guessing in laboratory psi experiments, even the impressive albeit low hit rate of complex alpha-numeric sequences ('five-character codes'; see Shen, Shen, & Li, 2020), or the successful 'prediction' of stock market fluctuations, and the like? I argue that it makes no difference—we can still use the coincidentiality of synchronicity for gain and purpose because the patterns have to be played out in real time, even into the future (i.e., predictably), according to the archetype. That is to say, the correspondence as an 'accident' is not a literal accident given the parallel derives from an under-riding archetypal form repeating itself, and is thereby a sufficient match, to the degree that an informed decision can be made—that is why synchronicity can look like precognition or other psi modalities.

I can illustrate these points another way—if I remember my phone number, the recalled phone number *equates* with the actual phone number, or if I recall the face of a family member, that image *equates* with that actual family member—these recollections *are* 'pre-existing' and are put there by life experience. These normal recollections are not taken as psi signals triggered by the external images. Though the scarab case and the Evans case are fundamentally different because they are deemed paranormal, the process is essentially the same—there are archetypes in the psyche, representations of which merely suggest 'pre-existing' images, and these are equated with those corresponding physical occurrences. While they are taken to be psi signals, that kind of thinking implies that the images in the minds of Jung's patient and Linda Evans were received transmissions or perceptions (much like Upton Sinclair's 1930/1962 'mental radio' analogy). That cannot be—in synchronicity, we can only speak of constellated archetypes uniting disparate events through their meaningful correspondences. In the scarab case, the relevance and the ubiquity of the archetype fortuitously triggered the deep imagination resulting in a *dream*. In other cases, the process is reversed—the deep imagination can be used fortuitously to help trigger relevant archetypal images as in the Evans case, via a *fantasy*.

Another example of a synchronistic correspondence or mapping comes from my personal files: One afternoon in 2017, I visited the YouTube website and was about to log-on to my own channel when I saw and watched a video of Karen Carpenter singing *Yesterday Once More* (TopPop, 2017)—an old hit from 1974. YouTube customarily offers random videos to gauge their viewers' preferences. That was the only video I watched, as I actually logged-on to check how many views my own videos were getting. Thus an image was planted in my mind from an external source in much the same way as I described in my 'owl' example earlier in this chapter. In the same afternoon, I went to a local supermarket to do some shopping. On the pavement just in front of the supermarket sat a busker with an acoustic guitar half-way through playing the same song, *Yesterday Once More.* Had I been delayed by a sufficient amount of time, even seconds, or parked my car elsewhere, I could easily have missed the performance.[11] Are the two performances of *Yesterday Once More* the same thing in essence? Not when one performance is by Karen Carpenter in a television studio in the United States in 1974, and the other is by a busker sitting outside a shopping centre in Adelaide, South Australia, in 2017. Hence, synchronistic correspondences are not to be taken as literal matches; they are mappings. It might seem that only the song and its title matters, so we might call it a 'psi hit' (telepathy, or clairvoyance, or precognition), but the devil truly is in the details. Though examples like these seem to prove psi can match or tie-in to real-world events, and with an impressive degree of accuracy, minimal scrutiny says otherwise. Psi interpretations unnecessarily complicate the basic synchronistic process.

As I said in Chapter 3, there are cases where the imagination does not seem to play a part. Beitman would describe these as "object-object" synchronicity because there appears to be no participating observer nursing an 'inner' image. *Yesterday Once More* is a case in point. But my initial exposure to the song *Yesterday Once More* on YouTube is an idea planted in my imagination. Likewise, in my 'owl' example, the word 'owl' was planted in my imagination, and Andreasen's (2011) *preparation* and *incubation* set the archetypal processes in motion. Archetypes in the deep imagination (in the collective unconscious) have a way of reaching beyond their bounds, which Jung describes as "transgressivity" because archetypes "continually go beyond their frame of reference" (para. 964), manifesting in psychophysical events. Von Franz's (1992) statement applies here: "… something synchronistic might happen when an archetype is constellated" (p. 27). Whatever archetype was constellated that afternoon in 2017, one can see how the image of recalling the past (*Yesterday Once More*) corresponds with deeply felt unconscious elements brewing in my imagination, and how, in its ubiquity, the archetype reaches beyond the psyche to the world and can even be described as a collating mechanism *par excellence.*

One final example of mapping (actually, the second of the three given in Chapter 1) is the classic case of Swedenborg's Stockholm fire. In his mind, Swedenborg held an image of a fire in Stockholm that he later equated with an actual fire in Stockholm. The story has come down to us that he 'saw' this actual Stockholm fire. But we can only say images came to light in his mind. Although his 'prediction' was proved correct, and it could be argued that he 'saw' the actual event in his mind's eye, synchronicity theory says we are not justified in assuming his experience was the same in principle as a televised image of a real-life event. When we discover a synchronicity (i.e., a psi event), we are most likely witnessing an archetypally triggered concordant mapping; the map is not the territory.

For some, it may seem unfortunate that the discovery of a synchronistic event only requires one to do no more than see parallels, patterns, and similarities—it is the same with psi. Until we understand the process better, we are almost forgiven for supposing it is paranormal or magical perception. It would be so much more convenient for scientific understanding, and it would satisfy our need for certainty no end, to believe that we are dealing with information transfer in psi and synchronicity; not some 'lesser' phenomenon that seems more like casual coincidence. But meaningful coincidence is not casual coincidence; nothing like that lesser phenomenon of meaningless chance grouping. Serious consideration should be given to the idea that psi is mapping or correlating one synchronistic element with another: Jung gives the effect objective bearing when he refers to synchronicity as "acausal parallelism" (Jung, 1961/1989, p. 374). This objectivity is not undermined just because we are subjectively involved in the process. That is why we can validly speak of "meaningful parallels" (Jung, 1952/1969, para. 850). Psi yields quite well to these assertions. Without closer scrutiny, these parallels do not seem to define the process beyond pattern detection—a psychological process. However, the initiating underpinnings or contingencies that embrace the full complement of synchronistic elements are archetypal, which for all intents and purposes, are grist for the mill of parapsychology.

***

There was a time, in certain parts of the world, when it was possible to find people who thought that a photograph of a person was virtually the same thing as that person in the flesh; or more correctly, that person's soul. Today, we all know the map is not the territory. We FAX a letter, but we know the FAX is a copy; not the original. With synchronicity, we are dealing with mental *simulacra* only, and we *parallel* these with real-world contents that come to our attention. But we must remember that the under-riding process is essentially archetypal.

Although I suggest synchronicity is firmly seated in the imagination (specifically, the *deep* imagination), nothing in this chapter is meant to align with the skeptical stance experts take when they try to explain away meaningful coincidence as mere chance (i.e., whimsical, mental meanderings); quite the contrary. I do not easily dismiss anything synchronistic in nature; rather I wish to get to the crux, the 'hows' and 'whys' of it. While the argument from paranormality (for want of a better term) may be sustained in such instances, I make the point that the meaningful parallels in synchronicity should not be seen as anomalous communication in the conventional parapsychological sense. We do need to re-envision the inaccurately defined and poorly understood 'paranormal' construct—something more holistic (archetypal) is afoot. For now, what I hope to have accomplished in this chapter is to have described a process that ties in the imagination to synchronistic and psychic functions, and by that very process, the 'inner' material cannot be taken *literally*; it must therefore be *figurative, symbolic*, or *metaphorical* in nature, no matter how close the parallel, for it always bears an *imaginative* (archetypal) quality. In the next chapter, we will see how such material can manifest in real-life accounts, and how crucial synchronicity is to our understanding of events in our lives.

Notes

1 There was a time when the importance of the imagination might have received a better reception than it does today (see Zollo, 1978). I am grateful to Laurence Browne for drawing my attention to this reference.
2 For the sake of argument, I will ignore claims that psychic readings are 'cold', 'warm', or 'hot' (for definitions, see footnote 67, Chapter 1; see also Barker, 2022).
3 Jung's other writings almost seem to avoid the subject of imagination, though his 'active imagination' (a type of free-form fantasy with therapeutic intent) is discussed in voluminous detail (see Chodorow, 1997). Where 'imagination' proper could be defined or discussed, he attributes its properties to the unconscious (e.g., Jung, 1953/1966, para. 273). To prove this point, the index entry for "imagination, power of" (1953/1966, p. 328) links to paragraph 273, which does not even mention the word 'imagination'. Oddly, there appears to be a pattern in the Jungian literature where 'imagination' is poorly defined (e.g., Jung, 1964, 1953/1966), or not defined at all (e.g., Jung, 1921/1971, 1963/1970; Samuels, Shorter, & Plaut, 1986/1992).
4 See "imagination" in *Dictionary.com* (https://www.dictionary.com/browse/imagination).
5 See "imagination" in StackExchange: English Language and Usage (https://english.stackexchange.com/questions/335860/why-indefinite-article-with-imagination).
6 Irwin (1979) also says the same of PK—it is not necessarily "a kind of *paranormal output* phenomenon" (p. 117).
7 There is no satisfactory evidence in parapsychology that these information-carrying 'energy forces' can travel forward and backward in time (theories in physics merely allow for the possibility—see Bierman, 2010), and these forces tend to attenuate and dissipate over extreme distances, despite some evidence to the contrary (Shiah, 2012).
8 Warcollier (1938) is most likely using the word perception in the sense of becoming aware or conscious of something; or coming to a realization or understanding, but not in the sense of using the normal perceptual (sensory) organs.
9 In truth, many psi pundits have never really broken free of the 'mental radio' analogy and influence, though they may think they have. The idea is kept alive by psi models that still refer to anomalous *communication* and *transmission*.
10 However, see Thalbourne's Kundalini studies reviewed in the subsection *Is Laboratory Psi Research Eliciting Synchronicity?* in Storm (2025).
11 The year 1974 was a critical time for me as my family moved to a new location, I enrolled in a new high school, and lost touch with my old school friends. Suffice it to say, I did not enjoy those final years in that new school. As a repeated event, the two performances of *Yesterday Once More* are meaningful due to the fact that I profess a nostalgic streak (especially concerning profoundly moving personal issues from the past).

Chapter 4

The Extraordinary Case of Bishop James Pike

"... perhaps I underrate the creative power of my unconscious imagination"
James A. Pike (1969, p. 298)

In this chapter I present a case of ostensible synchronicity in far greater detail than I have provided thus far. This case entails reference to the psychology and parapsychology of Bishop James Pike, which I juxtapose with similar reference to his troubled son Jim. Pike was not overtly psychic, but his crisis was archetypally profound, and originated in a problematized father/son relationship. As his lengthy account reveals, Pike spent an inordinate amount of time chasing the ghost of his son in order to heal a split. I suggest the synchronistic and archetypal aspects tell us much, but I am left with the feeling that Pike did not have access to a complete picture of his situation that might have given him greater solace.

Who Was Bishop James Pike?

The story of Bishop James A. Pike (1913–1969) involves more than just an unexplained series of occurrences in the last chapter of his life; it is an awe-inspiring saga that is tragic in its telling, so much so that it cannot be given a fair treatment without first presenting a brief outline of the man himself. Before I do that, I must add that I have devoted a whole chapter to the Pike case because I see so many coincidences that are clearly synchronistic that the material itself also must be treated with due care and deserves a thorough-going analysis. But more than that, I find it remarkable (and very telling) that absolutely nobody who has written substantially on synchronicity has thought to bring this case to the fore—indeed, the purpose of this chapter is to help make greater sense of all previous chapters. Of course, it is possible that I am mistaken about the renown I attribute to Pike, and that is why he has been overlooked (although he wrote many books, appeared frequently on radio and television; associated with Martin Luther King; and had highly publicised heresy charges brought against him, etc.). Indeed, my discovery of the man may only be synchronicity to me (if not serendipity, which I define as an accidental but fortuitous event), and if not

DOI: 10.4324/9781003561330-5

for that fact, I would be no wiser than any other who has written on synchronicity without mentioning the Pike case.

As I have suggested, most people today would not know of Bishop Pike, yet the character of Timothy Archer, in Philip K. Dick's last book, *The Transmigration of Timothy Archer* (1982), was based on Pike, and E. L. Doctorow (2000) has a fictionalized version of Pike in his novel *City of God*. I came across this extraordinary real-life character as a fan of Leonard Nimoy's television series *In Search Of …* (Landsburg, 1977–1982). It was in an episode from the sixth (and final) season of the series, *In Search Of Bishop Pike*, that the question was asked, "Was Bishop James Pike a minister, a martyr, or a madman?" There is not sufficient room here to try to answer that question, or go into every little early-life detail—there are other sources for that (see Robertson, 2004),[1] but to get an idea of how iconoclastic Pike was, readers might like to visit the website of *The New York Times*, and read columnist Raymond A. Schroth's (1976) article, "The Death and Life of Bishop Pike". Schroth records:

> […] if anyone under 30 remembers Bishop James A. Pike it is as the sad character who "died lost in the desert" or "had that séance on TV." To others he was the most controversial clergyman of his day: Columbia University chaplain, Dean of the Cathedral of St. John the Divine, Bishop of California, social activist, gadfly intellectual, TV personality, then—in a final behavior pattern that led some to question his sanity—ex-bishop, "heretic," worn-out self-publicist and mystic manqué.

In that episode of *In Search of …*, though Nimoy was always sympathetic to people claiming extraordinary experiences, a number of anomalies were presented in a rather matter-of-fact way (those anomalies mentioned are included in the list that follows in the next section). In this chapter, I will show how this bizarre sequence of unusual (perhaps paranormal) events is more than anomalistic, and warrants being classed as a very unique case of recurrent synchronicity.

Born James Albert Pike in Oklahoma City, Oklahoma, USA, Pike was an Episcopal bishop (Church of England), prolific writer, and one of the first mainline religious figures to appear regularly on television. It is ironic that he had many questions about the Church and its dogma, and he was particularly critical of its failure to keep up with the times. For example, he fought with Catholic bishops over their attacks on Planned Parenthood and their opposition to birth control. However, even Pike himself expressed doubts about the afterlife, and other fundamental precepts of Christian belief (e.g., virgin birth and the Trinity), so it is no wonder that he got into so much conflict with Church authorities. Although charges of heresy were brought against him multiple times throughout the 1960s, they were dropped to avoid negative attention against the Church as a respected institution.

Pike was married to Esther Yanovsky (they divorced in 1966) and they had four children, including their eldest Jim. By all accounts, Jim was an average student, with part of his struggle being related to career and other future choices, but that was the least of Jim's worries. In his teenage years, Jim began experimenting with hallucinogenic drugs and conveyed his serious existential concerns to Pike, who (in his 1969 book *The Other Side*) relates these issues to the reader in quite a caring, sympathetic, and understanding manner befitting a responsible father and a man of the cloth. In particular, and forming a major section of the book, Pike describes how he spent a considerable amount of time with Jim in shared accommodation in Cambridge (UK), where Jim's issues constantly came up for discussion—the original aims of the trip to Cambridge (though partly as a sabbatical) was for Pike to engage in professional work there, while Jim continued his studies at the university. Of course, Pike makes it quite clear that he invited his son to join him on the trip as an opportunity to connect with his son.

Late into their lengthy stay in Cambridge, Pike needed to return to the United States due to pressing business concerns, leaving Jim to return at a later date. In the book, Pike's own struggle with Jim, Jim's drug-taking, and Jim's difficulties with studies, friendships, and people generally, is palpable. Jim's psychological pressures ultimately got the better of him—on February 4, 1966, using a rifle purchased at a nearby gun store, Jim took his own life in a hotel room on Thirty-First Street in New York City.

The Evidence

After Jim's suicide, a lengthy series of peculiar (mostly physical) phenomena manifested from February 20, 1966 onwards (16 days after Jim's suicide). Most of these suggest ESP in the form of uncharacteristic thoughts or 'channelled ideas', PK in the form of materializations and out-of-place objects, and 'interferences' and symbolic or 'coded' representations concerning relevant persons and the environment—specifically, these phenomena are:[2]

- two postcards on the floor "lying so as to form a 140° angle with their outer edges" (p. 70);
- "bangs" (front curls) of Pike's secretary Maren Bergrud singed (occurring three times) (pp. 71, 73);
- Maren's bad dream about "archdeacons" (interpreted as "*archdemons*"; pp. 72–73);
- Maren waking up to find her "third and fourth fingernails were injured" as if by a "sharp instrument pressed under them" (p. 72);
- Maren claiming that Pike declared to her that he does not care for people; quoting him as saying: "You can't count on anybody .... Look out for Number 1." (p. 75);

- Reverend David Barr (Pike's friend and colleague) confessing his momentary but inexplicable feelings of worthlessness (pp. 75–76);
- two paperback books lying together on the floor at an angle of 140° (p. 77);
- souvenir picture of Beersheba (Israel) removed from its frame and 'shifted' to the inside of the closet amongst some clothes (p. 78);
- blank stationery and postcards found amongst a messy pile of clothes in the closet on Jim's side, yet the other side of the closet (Pike's side) was neat and tidy (p. 78);
- Jim's alarm clock reading 8:19, corresponding to "around 3.00 a.m., New York time", assigned by the coroner as the time of Jim's suicide (pp. 79–80);
- Venetian blinds closed differently from the usual way (p. 81);
- photo of Pike's daughter Connie shifted from a light fixture to the dresser drawer (p. 81);
- a number of fresh bottles of milk (refrigerated or kept cold) all turned sour (pp. 82–83);
- garbage bag "attached to the disposal device on the wall by the sink" (p. 83);
- Pike, for some unknown reason, deciding to look up at a clock to see the time 8:19 (p. 83);
- the rooms in the flat uncharacteristically warm (p. 84);
- the Bible moved to the same place the postcards and paperbacks had been found earlier (i.e., between the two beds) (p. 84);
- the Church of England Year-book found moved to "behind the electric heater" (p. 84);
- two books found "moved" (p. 88);
- open windows "which had been closed" (p. 88);
- "misplaced clothes" (p. 88);
- safety pins lying open "in several places" (p. 88);
- a "broken Marlboro cigarette" (p. 88);
- "an object [a silver hand mirror, part of a dresser-set] in motion" sliding off a shelf (p. 88);
- a journal missing from the desk but found in Pike's "Samsonite attaché case" (p. 89);
- a lock of Maren's hair found between the two beds (p. 90);
- the same two safety pins (left where they were previously) slightly moved and opened at 140° (p. 90);
- a book (*Armageddon* by Leon Ulrich) found under the bed, with a postcard of Peterborough, a torn piece of paper stuck to it, and a thumbprint, apparently not Pike's, Maren's, or David's (p. 90);
- a book (*The Date of the Last Supper!* by Annie Jaubert), fortuitously found with a Beersheba camel post-card (apparently one of Jim's) stuck inside marking a chapter about John and the other apostles; of timely interest to Pike who was researching the topics (p. 140);
- Jaubert's book (*Last Supper*) found on the floor, fortuitously lying next to a UNESCO book sought by Pike (p. 140);

- an associate of Pike's, John McConnell, recalling being awakened at the time of Jim's suicide with a "terrible sense of dread" that someone outside his "own family" was dying (p. 144);
- On the same night, a female friend of John McConnell seeing "two awful faces of evil" (p. 144);
- John McConnell's female friend phoning an 'upstate' friend of hers who "had known Jim" (p. 144). Jim is mentioned though his suicide was not known at that point in time;
- Miss Anna Zacharias (who later marries John McConnell) reports "a strange episode" involving a 3:00am wake-up on February 4th to a feeling of "great fear" (p. 145);
- two of Jim's friends, Nan and Billie, awakened on the morning of February 4th with a "horrible feeling that tragedy had somehow struck" (p. 145);
- a number of "*open safety pins*" (some in pairs) 'reading' "eight nineteen" in the living room of Pike's friend David Baar's home (pp. 147–148).

Having found no earthly reasons for these 'anomalies', Pike resigned himself to no other possible explanation but that they meant something, and were particularly related to Jim. His reasoning stemmed from a number of facts: Jim liked purchasing postcards, and did so on their travels; Jim did not like Maren's hair-style and thought she should cut off the fringe; Jim did not really care much for people; Jim often felt worthless; Jim was messy with his clothes, often leaving them strewn about the Cambridge flat; Jim had the duty of putting out the garbage; Jim's preferred cigarette brand was Marlboro; and so on.

Of particular import is the fact that the time of 8:19 corresponds to an angle of approximately 140°, the angle at which the postcards, books, and safety pins were said to be found. However, 3:00, New York time (the approximate time the coroner ruled as the time of Jim's death), is actually 8:00, London time; not 8:19. For whatever reason, Pike assumed 8:19 was more accurate.[3] Clearly, Pike thought the physical anomalies indicated the right time, and it would then surely have crossed his mind that the coroner was wrong. However, Pike never discusses this discrepancy. All these rationalizations led Pike to reduce the above anomalies to causal factors relating to Jim—indeed, he thought Jim had perpetrated them from the 'Other Side'. Before I consider Pike's assumptions and conclusions further, I will first consider the various psychological and parapsychological aspects of the case.

The Psychology and Parapsychology of Pike's Experiences

In this section I consider the psychological and parapsychological factors that are evident, or may have had influence in Pike's case. It will become apparent that not all aspects of the case are explained by a purely psychological approach.

Psychological Factors and Explanations

The psychological analyses of Pike's experiences, and those of the other players in the drama, are not offered here to be parsimonious, or reductive, or comprehensive. I merely present conventional viewpoints to give a broader perspective on the case. The experiences do seem to gravitate around a common theme (Jim's suicide). Pike, and Pike's associates (Maren Bergrud, David Barr, etc.), and others, experienced psychological and physical disturbances, and Pike collates these with Jim's mental state before and after his suicide. It should be noted that the emotional responses are the typical reactions and natural reflexes of individuals who find themselves engrossed or enmeshed in tragic circumstances. Recall that most of the players knew of Jim's suicide so their reactions (psychological and/or psychosomatic) are understood and to be expected.

There are, however, others (e.g., John McConnell, Anna Zacharias) who did not know of Jim's suicide, yet they too had similar reactions prior to learning about the tragedy. Pike preferred to regard these unfortunate moods and other emotional states as somehow belonging to Jim who projected them onto others deliberately or unwittingly. But as Pike also wondered, it is not clear why certain people would be 'chosen' by a discarnate Jim to bear his emotions for him, or how Jim's emotions could spill over into the human sphere and just happen to show that degree of selectivity. In fact, most of these people, whether they knew about Jim's suicide or not, were Pike's associates and this fact alone speaks more to Pike's psychology than it does to Jim's, but that hypothesis partly suggests paranormality and must be pursued in the next subsection (that is, while Pike's associates who knew of Jim's suicide might empathize with Pike's loss, and emote accordingly, others who did not know about the suicide, may have responded emotionally after having been triggered telepathically by Pike's state of mind).

It should also be noted that Pike introduced into his account of Jim's suicide (in his book *The Other Side*) only those individuals who were confirmed as having unusual (potentially paranormal) experiences, yet there would have been dozens, or even scores of individuals in Pike's and Jim's social world (e.g., immediate family and other relatives, friends, colleagues, and acquaintances) of whom we learn nothing from Pike, and these individuals include Pike's first wife Jane Alvies, his second wife Esther (Jim's biological mother no less), and Pike's three other children—and let us not forget grandparents, uncles, and aunts, all of whom are conspicuously and surprisingly absent in the telling. We might argue then that, statistically, all the negative mental (emotional) coincidences (the self-doubt, melancholy, unusual dreams) that we do learn about are commonly experienced in all walks of life, so the affected people we do hear about could constitute a single meaningless chance grouping similar to Jung's fish series (thus ruling out the paranormal, and therefore any synchronistic considerations).

But is this argument all too familiar? Does it not bear the hallmarks of the Law of Truly Large Numbers discussed in Chapter 1? However, this Law of convenience is incapable of handling cases on an individual level; thus it rules out any possible assertion of meaning that might genuinely apply, both personally and in the real world. And since (as I also said in Chapter 1) there are those instances for which we *can* determine meaning and meaningfulness, we can abandon the Law of Truly Large Numbers. Yet, sometimes finding something of meaning can be fraught with complications if it is of dubious causality. As will be seen, the psychic and mediumistic material is of questionable worth, but even if the Barnum Effect was at play,[4] some portions of the material may not be dregs, but may be pure distillates of psychological merit (which is to say, Pike might serendipitously have reaped some therapeutic benefit from that material—indeed, it appears he did).

Thus, some psychological explanations are helpful, but not all—in particular, the physical anomalies Pike reported, unless we resort to forgetfulness or carelessness (e.g., the postcards, paperbacks, and safety pins may have been lying there all along, but Pike, in his grief, had not noticed them earlier), human clumsiness (e.g., someone dropped the objects in their respective places), or fraud (i.e., the 'evidence' had been deliberately planted). But otherwise the disappearances or reappearances of books, postcards, photographs, safety pins, and (in particular instances) their peculiar geometrical layouts at 140° angles, are difficult to explain. Indeed, Pike went to considerable effort trying to work out how the various items might have been accidentally left there by the charlady, cleaner, etc., but his inquiries and deductions yielded nothing. Maren's burnt hair and damaged fingernails are not so easily explained either, unless we characterize Maren as a borderline type who could not admit to her own self-harm (not altogether unlikely given that she later proved to be a suicidal type).[5]

Following on from these points, there is one other psychological explanation worth exploring: "apophenia" (see Chapter 1). Apophenia is misperception of images or sounds in random stimuli (e.g., seeing faces in clouds or burnt toast). Milbourne Christopher (an American illusionist and magic historian) holds that Pike and his colleagues may have been victims of apophenia (Christopher, 1975). He reduces the way in which the postcards and safety pins appeared on the floor to indicate the time of Jim's suicide as only having 'meaning' because Pike *et alia* created connections which were never there in the first place (the time of 8:19 might be a case in point since the coroner ruled Jim's time of death was 8:00, London time; perhaps Pike deferred to the time of 8:19 to suit the evidence from the clock, postcards, etc.). The problem with this explanation is that the phenomena repeat themselves multiple times in different settings for different individuals, yet Christopher seems to think this form of mass delusion could maintain itself without Pike *et alia* ever waking up to their folly. In short, there is a point at which a man can protest too much, and then the suspicions backfire. The other problem is we simply do not know that the coroner's estimated time of suicide was accurate; which is to say, the forensic evidence to hand leads a pathologist to construct a 'best fit' scenario. The materials in question, taken collectively, constitute a consistent array of objects; they do not readily form obtuse angles naturally (i.e., by chance, especially the safety pins—see footnote 3); and the postcards and books hold particular relevance (i.e., they belonged to Jim).

Parapsychological Factors and Explanations

Given the inadequacies or uncertainties of the psychological explanations, we are compelled to consider the parapsychological aspects of the case. Pike suggests Jung's two theories about the collective unconscious and synchronicity might explain the personal links, though he seems prepared to class these links as "pure coincidence" (p. 147). Earlier in the book, however, Pike refers to his "lowered guard" and the "reduced effectiveness" of his so-called "selective screen" which enables "psychic communication" (p. 124). Pike is effectively describing a key factor related to synchronicity; namely, *abaissement du niveau mental* (i.e., lowering of the mental threshold; see Chapter 3). The circumstances are indeed pointers to a synchronistic interpretation since the main elements of Pike's accounts—his emotionally-charged and powerful psychological images of a 'discarnate' Jim and associated factors (e.g., Jim's time of death), the tangible and symbolic manifestations, and their meaningful connections to each other—are just about as obviously synchronistic as we can expect.

Prior to Pike's attribution of the above anomalies to Jim from the 'Other Side', Pike entertained the possibility of a "poltergeist" (p. 78); an hypothesis he revisited later in the book, at the suggestion of renowned reincarnation investigator, the late Ian Stevenson of the Virginia School of Medicine. Stevenson told Pike "it's just possible … that you yourself were the source of the poltergeist phenomena" (p. 293). Pike also thought that the 'horrible feelings' reported by John, Anna, Nan, Billie, and the others, "must have been Jim's just before he died … accounted for by ESP" (p. 146). This assumption emerged as a result of seeing a number of psychics or mediums who produced allegedly veridical information that suggested to Pike mainly ESP and occasional postmortem survival.

First, he saw medium Ena Twigg (1914–1984), arranged through a colleague of his (canon John Pearce-Higgins, known for his 'depossession' work). In a series of sessions, Mrs. Twigg produced some intriguing and ostensibly paranormal readings for an impressed Pike; not only were they putatively from Jim's channelled spirit, but they also came from Pike's mentor Paul Tillich (1886–1965), the notable philosopher and theologian. Twigg engaged in both direct clairaudience and trance-like mediumship, the latter of which Pike found "perplexing" (p. 122). Then, Pike followed up his inquiries with medium Reverend George Daisley (1911–2001) of the Spiritual Frontiers

Fellowship. More communications from Jim ensued, including channelling from Edgar Cayce, the famous trance-medium and psychic. Daisley's communications were mostly of a paranormal nature, ostensibly from Jim, but possibly telepathic, as Pike noted.

Finally, one major sitting—a séance of sorts—occurred on a network television program "W-5" ("Who, What, Why, When, and Where"), filmed in Toronto, Canada, in September 1967, and hosted by Allen Spraggett (1967), author of *The Unexplained*. After much discussion about mediumship for the benefit of the host and the audience (pp. 191–196), a special guest medium Arthur Ford, who also happened to be an ordained minister, slipped into an altered state, and thus began an impromptu séance. Through 'Fletcher' (Ford's spirit guide), this event produced a great deal of factual and speculative material from 'Jim' and sundry other characters, including Jim's grandfather Elijah (referred to as 'Elias'), Pike's associates Marvin Halverson, Louis Pitt, George Zabriskie, Donald McKinnon, Karl Block, and others. Curiously, all these individuals (excluding Elijah) were known to Pike, not Jim. (Pike paid a second visit to Ford after the show for further psychic readings, and he took with him Diane Kennedy, his newly-appointed personal assistant.)

Along with Pike's supposition of possible telepathic links that might explain the messages (mostly the standard platitudes, misgivings, regrets, and so forth), Pike "suggests much of the psychic's own understanding is being expressed" in the communications, though he conceded much of it was possibly from "the surviving personality", which is to say Jim (p. 181). Still, he was impressed by all three mediums, and spent a considerable portion of the book attesting to their authenticity. Nevertheless, he did state that much of the psychic content could have been produced by research (he acknowledged "frauds in the field"; p. 195).

In line with Pike's suspicions, skeptical investigator John Booth alleged that Twigg knew a great deal about Pike and his family before the séance (Booth, 1986). And a few years after the televised séance, Ford was exposed for widespread fraud by his biographers Allen Spraggett and William Rauscher (Spraggett & Rauscher, 1973). Ford's files contained many obituaries, newspaper clippings, and other information that enabled Ford to research the background of his clients. Spraggett and Rauscher felt there was sufficient evidence suggesting that Ford had faked the 1967 TV-séance. Clearly at a disadvantage in not knowing about these accusations and exposés (though, as said, he did have his suspicions), Pike remained open to parapsychological explanations.

Taking these factors into consideration, I am not prepared to give any more time to the séance material as I regard it as spurious in this instance. Besides which, it makes little difference whether or not the material was genuine (from Jim, or about Jim), for one is faced with the issue of post-mortem survival vs. 'super-psi' (where 'psi' is ESP/PK; 'super-psi' is also known as 'living agent psi'; LAP), the dichotomy of which one feels compelled to resolve, or at least make an attempt at resolving. The survival solution means there was communication between a discarnate entity (Jim) and various psychics (Twigg/Daisley/Ford) but, in a synchronicity scenario, a communicating discarnate entity is no different than a living person for the simple reason that, *if* an entity (Jim) attempts contact with the living (Pike *et alia*), or (in dispensing with the survival argument, we opt for LAP) *if* the medium is reading the minds of Pike *et alia, then* communication in both cases can be read as *telepathy* (following the Rhinean paradigm), and I interpret telepathy as synchronicity. That is to say, when the right archetype is activated in one person, the same archetype can be activated in other persons/personalities known to that person, at any distance, at any time. As Jung (1952/1969) explains, the archetype is experienced as "affectivity" (para. 846). The archetype behind the outer component in synchronicity is the same archetype behind the 'inner' component that is represented by a pertinent image in the experient's mind. Here the archetype is a uniquely human, inherited 'mode of apprehension' (a way to think, emote, and act) that results in a pattern of behaviour much like a blueprint guides action.

Whichever Rhinean term one may naïvely think settles the issue on the Pike communications (for clairvoyance is also suggested in *The Other Side*), we will see there *is* no way of settling it, as Pike was to discover. More and more, we see Pike grappling with Rhinean terms, *and* the survival question, while simultaneously moving towards a synchronistic turn of mind. Even by the end of the book, Pike never avows that "Jim said …" anything (p. 307), and only admits that he *believed* Jim was "in touch" with him.

Confining myself to the physical evidence, we are left with one other conventional (Rhinean) term (namely, PK), which means we may struggle, as Pike did, with interpretations and apportionments of responsibility to any and all characters in the drama (Jim, Pike himself, his associates, or even the poltergeist that Stevenson suggested), or we label these physical anomalies further examples of synchronicity. Ordinarily, we might opt for one of two possibilities—the phenomena are either materializations of matter (postcards, safety pins, etc.) out of thin air (a prominent theme in poltergeist literature), or they were apported by whomsoever, to be discovered later by Pike *et alia* (for an interesting and comprehensive treatment of these 'material' problems, see Barrington, 2018; Inglis, 1985; Jinks, 2016).

Thus, PK effects seem harder to explain than ESP because (due to cultural prejudice) we allow (in the case of ESP) a certain flexibility to the mind, and give it a transcendental aspect we would never apportion to matter, which we feel must behave itself at all times. But Jung attributed a 'psychoid' aspect to the archetype (see next subsection), which Main (2014) describes very well when he says "archetypes can structure matter as well as psyche – and not just separately but at the same time in respect to the same pattern of meaning" (p. 225). To illustrate this point, and show that Pike's is not an isolated case, there is an oft-cited event given by Jung (1961/1989) in his *Memories,*

Dreams, Reflections, involving his mentor at the time, Sigmund Freud, and a bookcase in Freud's study. In 1909, Jung and Freud were in Vienna having a heated argument over parapsychology.[6] Jung writes that he had a curious sensation:

> It was as if my diaphragm were made of iron and were becoming red-hot—a glowing vault. And at that moment there was such a loud report in the bookcase, which stood right next to us, that we both started up in alarm, fearing the thing was going to topple over on us. I said to Freud: "There, that is an example of a so-called catalytic exteriorization phenomenon."
>
> "Oh come," he exclaimed. "That is sheer bosh."
>
> "It is not," I replied. "You are mistaken, Herr Professor. And to prove my point I now predict that in a moment there will be another such loud report!" Sure enough, no sooner had I said the words than the same detonation went off in the bookcase.
>
> To this day I do not know what gave me this certainty.
>
> (pp. 155–156)

We learn later that Freud (1909, as cited in Fisher, 2011) had his own explanation for the bookcase explosions; indeed, in Jung's absence it happened again and again, and not in the context of thoughts similar to those held by Freud and Jung on the day in question. Fisher takes Freud's side and dismisses the coincidence as mere chance, and is content with Freud's causal account of the explosions. But the causality underpinning the bookcase explosions is irrelevant; we can expect a single cause for that alone. The incident is still synchronicity because the necessary inner and outer components are present—the inner component being particularly cogent in the affectivity and interaction of both players in the drama, and the outer event being the bookcase explosions (we might even propose there were two synchronicities—one for each of the players, with each getting a 'bang' out of it). Inglis (1985) is helpful here for he notes that these sorts of effects tend to carry the same phenomenology: (i) they nearly always involve two people; (ii) the two are usually relatives or friends—"one who observed, or experienced, the effect", and the other usually at a distance and/or "in a state of tension or crisis"; and (iii) they usually involve a "household appliance, like a clock or picture" (p. 104), and we might add to that list, furniture, safety pins, postcards, and paperbacks.

Theoretically, while the events in Pike's experience could equally be attributed to his unconscious, or Jim from the Other Side, or a poltergeist, it ultimately matters not as, invariably, we are playing a kind of identity politics when we go looking for a 'focus' or a culprit, when all-along we may be dealing with archetypal energies, where the psychoid aspect in the psyche/matter dyad becomes evident (here, 'psychoid' means matter *behaves* as if it had a psychological dimension that explains psychophysical events like synchronicity). If Pike unconsciously 'knew' or 'discovered' the time of his son's death, and was psychokinetically instrumental in the 8:19 sequence, he no doubt arrived at it synchronistically as a meaningful, symbolic reminder to come to an awakening—a realization—about himself (some might not be able to resist the pun that it was *about time* too, since the problem was *about* time).[7]

Furthermore, following the afterlife paradigm, only Jim could have known the exact time of his own death, so we can assume that the 8:19 array of evidence does not reduce to interfering, tricksterish poltergeistry, but is more likely Jim's handiwork, though he never admitted to it in the communications. Yet Pike (1969, pp. 293–299), under Stevenson's tutelage, still makes a case for himself being the poltergeist "focus" (p. 295). Ultimately, Pike cannot decide, stating "it is equally plausible to me ... that either my son was the source of the various phenomena or that the source was I myself (or either or both of my companions and I)" (p. 298). One can see that Pike's reasoning reduces the poltergeist to human factors, as proffered by many (e.g., Pratt & Roll, 1958), including D. Scott Rogo, who reduced the phenomenon to RSPK:

> poltergeists focus on unhappy families who tend to repress and sublimate massive amounts of inner aggression and anger. This anger tends to build within the mind of one of the family members until it explodes outward in the form of the poltergeist.
>
> (Rogo, 1986, back-cover)

Australian poltergeist researchers, Tony Healy and Paul Cropper, agree that their vast collection of case studies lends support to Rogo's conclusions as being applicable in most poltergeist cases (Healy & Cropper, 2014). These conclusions are somewhat undermined by recent shifts from a 'disease' model directed at the agent (see, for example, Roll, 1977) to a 'dis-ease' model involving transliminal processes in the agent (Ventola et al., 2019), which fortunately dispenses with past accusations of mental illness on the part of the agent.

All very well, but we see that the creativity, the imagery, the symbolism underlying Pike's physical synchronicities seem uncanny and unfathomable, with attribution as to their causes beyond our ken, so that the poltergeist sneaks back in as a likely candidate, but not solely, for if there is anything like, or anything approximating, a poltergeist influence, whatever that may be, it is more a co-conspirator in the drama than anything else. That is, Pike is in it up to his neck, but in a *relative way*. German parapsychologist Hans Bender (1980) made good effort drawing out this point that the "arranging power" of the individual (albeit unconscious) is far too limited to bring about symbolic messages at a scale recognised as paranormal, and it is better to attribute such occurrences to archetypes. Pike (1969) makes a case for the process being analogous to dreaming:

> [...] in a dream state the full drama is produced unconsciously. For such remarkable plays, where are the producer, the scenario writer, the designer of sets, the wardrobe mistress, the director? Have those who have categorized psychic phenomena and even ESP as incredible nonsense ever pondered *that* mystery? How does the dream get put together into a dynamic production when the dreamer, unconscious, is "out of it"?
>
> (p. 304)

The same question can be asked in relation to synchronicity—indeed, Pike may not have realized just how appropriate his dream analogy was. One must concede that one is truly "out of it" when the symbolic world unfolds and appears to us as paranormal. Even in the case of intentional synchronicity, where there is a degree of conscious involvement, the question concerning how it constructs itself is not fully answered in its details, though Jung's *unus mundus* model that describes psychophysical reality, and echoes the ancient idea of the microcosmic/macrocosmic totality, is a reasonable starting point—reality unfolds like a dream or play, and we are players in it, with our behaviours being shaped by the imaginable and the unimaginable. The answer appears to lie lurking in the depths of the unconscious—in each *individual* unconscious—which in itself resolves the diffusion problem of the 'one' amongst the 'many' implied in a macrocosmic sea of ideas and the people who have them. One's consciousness is quite plainly not flooded by the contents of that sea; rather each navigates in the relatively calm waters of their own mind.

Sure to be a sticking point for some, I have consequently nominated the 'deep imagination' as the creative source and filter (i.e., limiting principle through meaning) of the individual's ideas. This process necessarily involves the psychological domain, the collective unconscious (Jung, 1959/1968). Coming close to this idea, and to Pike's analogy, is the notion that waking-state paranormal events (psi, synchronicity) are structurally isomorphic to dreams, all underpinned by neurological structure like those cognitive processes with which we are more familiar. Only, as is merely suggested in mundane psi, when archetypes manifest in synchronistic situations, the border between self and world collapses as inner (psychological) and outer (physical) are drawn together in meaning. As quoted in Chapter 1 (see *Psychoid Factor*), but worth quoting again, Jung notes:

> You can never say with certainty whether what appears to be going on in the collective unconscious of a single individual is not also happening in other individuals or organisms or things or situations.
>
> (Jung, 1952/1969, para. 912)

However, we do see that imagination is only the link from 'our side'. Imagination *per se* is not (and cannot be) the sole explanation as to how cognitions and perturbations are propagated by the contents of that 'other' realm, and we will not have an answer until we exhaust all possible research avenues in our endeavours to fully fathom the nature of the key to that 'other', which I suggest are the archetypes in the collective unconscious; a realm Bender (1980) calls "nature in its entirety" (p. 24). Thus, when Pike (1969) notes, in reference to dreams and meaningful coincidences, that one finds oneself constantly trying to come to terms with the "totally illogical aspects of it all and the incredible absurdity of it" (p. 284), the way to undo some of the absurdity will probably prove to be archetypal.

Enter the Archetype

Synchronicity was first conceived by Jung to ameliorate the 'triadic' (space-time-causality) limitations of science, but Jung would not have failed to see synchronicity in Pike's tragic circumstances because the *emotional quotient, numinosity*, and *meaningfulness* are so apparent—the emotional quotient we find in the turmoil surrounding Jim's suicide, and the numinosity and meaningfulness we find in the arrays of postcards, books, and safety pins, and the implications inherent in those arrays. And then, of course, there is the archetype: In fact, two archetypes stand out—the first is the problematized father/son relationship that bitterly resolves into the heavy loss of the son, and the subsequent horror of the father, so that this archetype is intricately bound up with a second archetype; death, with all its associations, including trauma and grief.

For good reason we see this same father/son dynamic embodied in the myth of the inventor Daedalus (from the Greek *Daidalos* = 'to work cunningly or artfully') and his son Icarus (whose name possibly derives from the Etruscan *Vikare* = 'a substitute'). As Jung (1959/1968) has noted, these parallels are legitimate because the psychological dynamics we live out in our day-to-day lives are monumentalized in mythology (mythology *is* the first psychology). Human events, behaviours, and interactions are the same stories told over and over again across the eons of time. In the 'Pike drama', the die was already cast: Daedalus and Icarus escape from imprisonment on the island of Crete using feathered wings fashioned by Daedalus. In their flight, Icarus does not heed the pleas of his father; he flies too high, and the sun melts the wax bonding the feathers of his wings. The wings fragment, whereupon Icarus falls into the sea and drowns.

The parallels are all too clear: We can see that, for the pure thrill of it, both sons (Jim and Icarus) 'got high', dangerously and fatally so, and they accomplished this by artificial (unnatural) means. There are other parallels: We get the impression from *The Other Side*, that Pike, an assiduous worker, dedicated and proud (like Daedalus), seems all too caught up in his controversial 'inventions' (his peers called them 'heresies') to play the role of father more fully, thus raising a carefree (some may say undisciplined) son—Ovid described Icarus as lazy, and meddling, and a hindrance while his father worked on the wings, whereas Pike tells us that Jim was lackadaisical about his studies and his friendships. Fathers and sons both seem to wish for escape. After Icarus' death, Daedalus cursed his 'art'; after Jim's death, Pike resigned his position as Bishop of California.

Like Daedalus, who built the Labyrinth that housed the half-man/half-bull hybrid known as the Minotaur, Pike's unconstrained workaholism (very much evident in *The Other Side*), his intuitive flights of fancy, and his dubious (even narcissistic) relationship skills became a maze around which 'darker' (monstrous) psychological aspects of himself were trapped—that is to say, unvented and never given a legitimate outlet. These energies can reach their zenith—all it takes is a tragedy of proportions sufficient to spill over into the world via the unconscious. What ensues is all manner of psychophysical phenomena manifesting as an unbridled series of coincidences and synchronistic occurrences. These 'externalities' can be seen as archetypally co-evolved and conjoined with the 'internalities' until the distinctions blur—the two in conjunction describe an age-old human process, reworked and refined until, ultimately, they bind to become an archetypal human experience that extends beyond the individual's psychophysiological sphere, and become psychophysical. In that sense, the paranormal aspects are normalized. It is as if that psychoid realm just mentioned manifests a connecting tissue between inner and outer; the defining rule in the tenet, 'as above, so below', is that events are bound by meaning, not cause. Meaningful 'outer' occurrences (those 'exteriorizations' Jung mentions) seem almost psychosomatic as opposed to psychokinetic. That is to say, the physical aspects of Pike's experience, given their psychoid nature, have mental counterparts that are accessible only through the mind because the two realms, mental and physical, are not separate and distinct, but are expressions of a single reality (for details, see *Dual-Aspect Monism* in Chapter 1).

Clearly, there is more to be concerned with in psi than the breaking of Broad's (1949) basic limiting principles.[8] The mythological parallels in cases like Pike's that speak to archetypal factors suggest, in no uncertain terms, the likelihood that psi phenomena are synchronistic. In such cases, the archetypes play pivotal roles; they are templates for human behaviour, and once an archetype is constellated, it follows its course to the end—fate, as it may be, takes over: "Archetypes are complexes of experience that come upon us like fate" (Jung, 1959/1968, para. 62). Of course, psi in the laboratory is of a different order; but only in degree, not kind. That being said, although the archetypal soup (the collective unconscious) writ large is psychosocially, psychodynamically, and psychophysically complex, and its contents, the archetypes themselves, are "formal factors responsible for the organisation of unconscious psychic processes" (1952/1969, para. 841), these processes may nevertheless extend sufficiently, and be so organised, they are objectively observable, even in the laboratory.

Summing Up

Pike's biographer David Robertson (2004) noted

> In April of 1969, while Pike and his [second] wife [Diane Kennedy] were driving to Qumran [Israel], they got lost and their car became stuck in the dirt. After ten hours of walking, Diane made it out. Five days later the bishop's body was found.

We also learn that this trip into the desert was poorly prepared (no guide, an inaccurate map, and insufficient water). It took five days to find Pike's decomposing body—he'd fallen to his death about sixty feet off a canyon ridge onto a ledge below. Not just a sad end but an ironic end in the sense that his death was the lonely (archetypal) death of a prophet of old; a wanderer in the wilderness in search of truth, in search of an invisible God, in search of an answer to the ultimate question, Why? We'll never know what Pike discovered in his last moments, and perhaps that is fitting. One's personal voyage remains forever personal and one travels the road of one's personal myth to the end, with much left untold. And perhaps for good reason, for one's life is so often fraught with complications, that even the sincerest and sorriest telling will not prevent judgements of all kinds; and who should judge?

The Other Side does leave much untold, but we learn enough to know of the struggle Bishop James Pike had with his son's suicide. Yet at first blush, one wonders why the last chapter of *The Other Side* waxes tirelessly about the history and the mystery of humankind, the normal (e.g., higher consciousness and dreaming), and the paranormal (including an impressive defense of parapsychology)—even the grandeur of the universe, and our place in it—but with only a brief reflection on his son (only two pages in a 28-page chapter). Even the 'Afterwords', the greater part of which Pike leaves to Ena Twigg, seem perfunctory and platitudinous to my way of thinking, albeit satisfactory to Pike. While Pike had over 300 pages to come to grips with his son's suicide; particularly the horrific nature of its execution, it is possible Pike never really got over the tragedy. Did writing *The Other Side* help give Pike some kind of closure, or did he sink into denial? Was Pike so racked with remorse and guilt that he sought an answer in the way of the prophets? Does Robertson's quote suggest such recourse?

My thoughts on the how and the why of Jim's actions revolve around his drug-taking. Pike describes occasions when Jim had very frightening trips after having taken one drug or another, and Pike tells how he was always there to comfort Jim and help him get through those drug-induced ordeals. Such non-ordinary states of consciousness could be described as being out of one's mind, literally—a kind of madness—the many ghastly types of suicide seem like temporary acts of insanity, and are legally described as such. Jim may have been of a type for whom that 'other' state of mind was, ultimately, a one-way trip. To borrow from mythologist Joseph Campbell, Jim may well have drowned "in the same waters in which the mystic swims with delight" (as cited in Lee, 1985, p. 40), but we must remember: Jim passed; it was Pike who had to struggle day after day in the shadow of Jim's monstrous madness, *and* make sense of it, *and* try to survive. But in trying to make sense of the unusual phenomena listed above, we have seen that psychological and conventional parapsychological explanations do not entirely satisfy. What is missing is a synchronistic turn of mind that pitches from the level of meaning rather than cause. Part of that pitch requires an understanding of archetypes, of which we are perhaps making some progress, that allows us to hazard a guess as to why things happen the way they do.

While we ponder the tragedy, we may take comfort in the greater meaning underlying this declaration from Pike: "extra-sensory perception is a profound and wonderful mystery and gives beautiful evidence of the synchronicity of the universe—the Unus in the universe" (p. 195). And Pike made the following equation: Unus = "God". More generally, we might say that paranormal experiences give us a glimpse of an otherwise ineffable Oneness that many are urged to anthropomorphize to render possible a human connection. Pike expands on these ideas in the final chapter, and one easily discovers that Pike had written Jim's short life into those closing statements which embrace a more holistic view of our universe—a universe that is ultimately better understood with a synchronistic turn of mind.

Notes

1 A brief but comprehensive biography of Bishop James Pike's life by Michael G. Maudlin can be found here: https://www.booksandculture.com/articles/webexclusives/2004/august/040830a.html
2 This list does not include the mediumistic or psychic readings.
3 The time of 8:19 actually corresponds to 135° (not 140°) between two clock hands. Pike may have gone to the effort of measuring this angle accurately with a protractor (same goes for the angles between the postcards, the paperbacks, and the safety pins), and assuming he did, his error was easily an honest mistake being out by only three or four percent each time. The safety pins are an anomaly in their own right—while the postcards and paperbacks may have been 'accidents' (e.g., they 'fell' to the floor that way), safety pins normally open at a mere 30° if left untampered. To form an angle of 140° (or even 135°), safety pins have to be physically bent by hand, all paranormality aside, and they tend not to settle at the desired angle without considerable trial and error.
4 The APA Dictionary of Psychology defines the Barnum Effect as "the tendency to believe that vague predictions or general personality descriptions, … have specific applications to oneself" (https://dictionary.apa.org/barnum-effect).
5 In 1967, at the height of the Pike drama, Maren committed suicide from an overdose of sleeping pills. Pike suggests her cancer contributed to her decision to suicide, but Robertson (2004) points out that Pike and Maren were living together, in a relationship, and she took her own life after an argument between the two of them.

6 Originally a skeptic, Freud later showed himself to be more accepting of 'occult' matters (Freud, 1933).

7 Issues with time—particularly the obsession with clock time as in Pike's case—evoke the *senex* (Old Man) archetype. The counterpart of the *senex* is the *puer eternus* (eternal child or youth). In the section above (*Enter the Archetype*) we can see this two-part complex played out mythologically as father and son (see also Tarnas, 2007, p. 58).

8 Philosopher C. D. Broad (1949) introduced four major basic limiting principles (though other examples are given) thought to be self-evident and generally taken for granted: there can be no backward causation (i.e., no future-telling), no action at a distance (i.e., no mind over matter), no perception unmediated by the senses (i.e., no mind-reading, no distant seeing), and mind depends on brain (i.e., consciousness cannot engage in nonlocal functions).

Chapter 5

Synchronicity Writ Large

> "Human experience, which is constantly contradicting theory, is the great test of truth"
>
> Samuel Johnson (as cited in Boswell, 1799, p. 526)

C. G. Jung (1952/1969) characterized ESP and PK as forms of synchronicity. I have touched upon this subject numerous times throughout the book (indeed, it is a main theme of the book). In this final chapter, I will return to a few key issues pertinent to the idea of a merger of psi and synchronicity, and arrive at some far-reaching conclusions. The reader can visit issues related to this idea in Storm (2025). In that book, I suggest ESP and PK as a unitary process (psi) might shift people to a "synchronistic mode of thought" (p. 17). But I also acknowledged that unification was more a metaphysical endpoint than something that could be demonstrated in practical terms due to the force of the 'complementarity principle' that dominates our experience in many ways (see also the entry *Dual-Aspect Monism* in Chapter 1). We are divided between our minds (*psyche*) and our bodies, or more generally matter (*physis*), and this polarity is even evident in the 'synchronistic dichotomy', where the so-called *unus mundus* ('one world'), or psychophysical reality, or 'common ground', is thought of as neutralizing such dichotomies (see the entry *Unus Mundus* in Chapter 1). Main (2014) describes this reality in a similar way in terms of archetypes as mediating or contingent factors that have unifying properties and "can structure matter as well as psyche" (p. 225).

Going further, it is easy to see how attempts to merge psi with synchronicity can create a flurry of concern, for much is at stake. But confusion has reigned for too long for Jungian scholars and parapsychologists alike—one only has to think of the reaction against synchronicity by Beloff (1990), or its defense by Mansfield (1995), as described in Chapter 2. In the first section below, I will contrast Jung's position with what is best called the Rhinean counter-position, and I will close with a further consideration of the idea of a merger. In subsequent sections, I will show how synchronicity can be misunderstood, but it will be seen that many wide-spread ideas about psi, or

DOI: 10.4324/9781003561330-6

phenomena that *appear* as psi or *could be explained* as psi, are better explained as synchronicity, while others are not paranormal in any sense. I will close with a review of the main points in all preceding chapters.

Synchronicity, Psi, and the Merger

The Jungian Conflation

In the context of synchronicity, the problem with Jung's liberal use of Rhinean terms, which are mainly terms adopted by Rhine (i.e., telepathy, clairvoyance, precognition, retrocognition, and psychokinesis), is that it exposes Jung's dependence on, and satisfaction with, the conventional understanding of paranormal processes. A good example of how contradictions ultimately arise is given in Storm (2025; see *Towards a Synchronistic Understanding of Psi*). Michael Fordham (author of the Editorial Preface to Jung's *Synchronicity*) goes even further in describing Jung's decision to use Rhine's (statistical) findings to support synchronicity as "a puzzling complication" (1973, p. v) because it infers causality. Up to a point, I am in agreement with Fordham—I do not consider synchronicity to be a causal effect in the conventional sense; nor is it an anomalous form of information transmission or energy exchange, but I do allow for a statistical approach to its testing. Jung shows a degree of flexibility in his theory that gives synchronicity a paranormal twist in the Rhinean sense that it could do without (para. 840, 863, 965). Also, he was not wrong to test astrology statistically, and I believe he erred in dismissing that approach not long after his experiments failed to satisfy him. But I have also argued that the wider view of synchronicity does not accommodate other disparities between psi and synchronicity (for a detailed treatment of this problem, see again "The Reach of Synchronicity" in Chapter 2). It is not a matter of making room for two types of paranormal process; put simply, the two are conflicted. But nor is it a matter of only re-envisioning one or the other—both need revision.

Von Franz (1992) does make a bid for unification by talking of "telepathic" perception and implied precognition *as if* both are forms of synchronicity by describing any kind of "causal connection" (via energy or information) as "logically inconceivable" (p. 21). Later, she expresses her opposition to terms like "*telepathy*" and "*telekinesis*" because they imply "transmitting energy" (p. 320). Not far wrong in wishing to strip psi of causal processes free of information or energy transmission, she does seem to have embraced psi phenomena "with certainty" as synchronistic (p. 213). But she makes the same error as Jung, and overlooks the fact that Rhine took a statistical approach to ESP and PK, and thought of them as causal, whereas she sees the statistical accessibility (quantitatively speaking) of synchronicity as impossible, and so a broader approach is out of the question.

Jung goes no further in clearing up the problem. However, he did speak of ESP and PK as the kind of phenomena that indicate transmission (of information or energy) is not possible: There is "good reason to doubt whether it is a question of transmission at all.... I have picked on the term 'synchronicity' ... as a principle of explanation" (Jung, 1952/1969, para. 840; see also para. 837, 976–979). Jung actually means synchronicity would better describe psi, yet Rhineans have never thought that way. But then the road takes another turn—Jung concludes that space and time are "elastic" and can be "reduced almost to vanishing point" (para. 840). Synchronicity is thus a "psychically conditioned relativity of space and time" (para. 840). And thus are psi and synchronicity united again, but for another very wrong reason. Von Franz (1992) agrees with Jung saying of ESP that it "cancel(s) out time, space, and causality" (p. 213). When Jung speaks this way, as if spacetime was in some sense *flexible in the human psyche*, it is very misleading. Some Jungians lead people into believing, of psi *and* synchronicity, that "Knowledge of events at a distance or in the future is possible because, within the unconscious psyche, all events coexist beyond time and space" (Main, 2004, p. 85; see also Haule, 2011b). It is not "all events"—it is only those archetypes that pin themselves (or can be pinned) to those events, but even they are not *beyond time and space.* All indications are that archetypes function perfectly well within the constructs of space and time, and do not warp spacetime.

It surprises me that Jung, von Franz, and others, speak the way they do, for it does seem they really do think spacetime has to be reduced to vanishing point for psi and synchronicity to work. We see the same talk coming from Kauffman and Patra (2022), when they ask "Is mind outside physical Spacetime" (p. 1). In truth, if that were possible, nothing experienced mentally would make sense, and not much else would make sense either if mind enjoys the privilege suggested by Kauffman and Patra (NB: This privileged view is also propounded by many a parapsychologist). There is more to learn about spacetime—certainly Muller (2016) speaks of spacetime creation (see the section "Now and into the Future" in this chapter)—but commentators who entertain the possibility of actual spacetime transcendence or 'violation' need to offer an explanation as to how the mind/brain complex switches the spacetime function on and off (presumably it is in 'off' mode most of the time). We have seen clearly that intention often fails (see *Imagination, Intention, and Pro Attitude* in Chapter 3). My hypothesis is that synchronicity theory is a less ambitious way of comprehending psi, and it does not require a mind-bending, space-warping function or capacity. All conscious experience (even of a paranormal kind) functions within the constraints of spacetime, and within one's frame of reference. I also suggest it is unreasonable and impractical to assume that mind can know what it is looking for outside its frame of reference, and can somehow find (actually pinpoint in a vast universe) something relevant (or know it is relevant) and turn it into coherent information.

To avoid confusion, it is more parsimonious to see the principle of synchronicity (including psi) as being based on an actual, evident archetypal realm such that the idea of literally accessing *future* or *distant* knowledge is redundant. Thus, when Jung and von Franz speak of *absolute knowledge*, it is only accurate when seen as "something like *knowledge* in the form of symbolic images" (von Franz, 1992, p. 25), or "subjective … configuration[s]" (p. 204). Of course, if the true meaning of coincidence is to be understood in its fullest, we must confine these images and configurations to the single source of the collective unconscious. But while Jung, von Franz, *et alia*, want to unify (and even simplify), they yet perpetuate the idea of actual spacetime transcendence, even requiring of science that it re-envision the spacetime concept (Jung, 1952/1969, para. 840). They make such statements because they are still boggled by the Rhinean findings that suggest unlimited access to information and knowledge, despite their other statements to the contrary. This situation is as awkward and confusing as it is untenable. Going *beyond* spacetime might be better understood as a mere dipping into the "timelessness" (and "spacelessness") of the collective unconscious that is underpinned by eternal, unchanging acausal orderedness (von Franz, 1992, p. 297). In this regard, archetypal patterns are repeating patterns such that they take on the semblance of being pre-existent (future or distant) knowledge. I even suggest Nostradamus capitalized on his archetypal experiences (see the subsection below *Nostradamus: Past, Present, and 'Future'*). Through archetypes, the collective unconscious has intricate connections in the mind/brain complex, and it is only due to the fact that our sensed and experienced inner and outer worlds have connections to our archetypal roots, that anything can make sense in consciousness. Failing that connection, all else remains indecipherable. This unifying and extensive (or 'transgressive') aspect of the constellated archetype seems to stretch the fabric of spacetime, when in fact we witness in ourselves and in the environment the ubiquity of the archetype.

Archetypes are like constants or laws of nature, and are all-pervading, persistent, and consistent, and in that sense, only *seem* to transcend spacetime. Yet, as we read his essay, we see Jung (1952/1969) effectively massaging spacetime to make synchronicity and psi mesh. His spin allows synchronicity to be seen by sundry others as a literal drawing of information from the past or the future, and/or from a great distance, thus aligning with Rhinean psi: For example, Main (2004) refers to future knowing as "precognitive coincidence" (p. 86)—a reasonable psychic depiction but arguably an impossible synchronistic hybrid. I suggest Jung's own term "absolute knowledge" has been taken too literally, especially for the correspondences reported in Rhine's studies (see also Jung where he speaks of Swedenborg's "access to absolute knowledge"; para. 912). That is surely one of Jung's biggest oversights. It is very easy to misconstrue Jung, and overlook von Franz's reference to *absolute knowledge* as "symbolic images" and "subjective configurations" that are not depictions of external occurrences.

Due to Jung's (1952/1969) interest in chasing the effect beyond known sources—note, for example, his focus on the psi-based aspects of the scarab case and his similar cases (para. 856–857), and even his outright reference to precognition and other psi phenomena as if their phenomenology is characteristic of synchronicity (Jung, 1951/1969, para. 974–978)—I suggest we do not come away with a clear sense of how synchronicity should be generally understood. Jung essentially advocated a *merging* of psi with synchronicity in such a way that the phenomenology of the former was *transferred* to the latter—thus, we get a *merger with transfer* (henceforth referred to as the 'Jungian conflation'). The evidence is clear that Jung thought this way; for example:

> the innumerable cases of meaningful coincidence that have been observed not only by me but by many others, and recorded in large collections … include everything that goes by the name clairvoyance, telepathy, etc.
>
> (para. 983)

This quote could be read two ways for Jung was not firm enough, or specific enough, and so did not fully clarify, critique, dispute, or even reject, the Rhinean understanding of terms like "clairvoyance, telepathy, etc.", so as things stand, the connotations inherent in the conventional parapsychological postulates idle away in the background of Jung's own synchronistic view. Elsewhere in Jung's essay, Jung did mean psi to be characterized as meaningful and coincidental, but still the sense of the two as one is cloaked in ambiguity. The best we can say is that Jung (and at least one of his followers) made the case for synchronicity clear for the most part (see Jung, 1952/1969, para. 858), but his aim can sometimes be misconstrued (see especially para. 840).

Eisenbud's Solution

We also have the psi/synchronicity merger looked at from another perspective (namely, as a conventional parapsychologist might see it), and we can see this played out by Eisenbud (1975, 1980) using Rhine's rules: By way of example, if we take Jung's scarab case, we see that reducing synchronicity to psi can turn a *coincidence* (albeit a complex and meaningful one) into *precognition* (the dream foretold the appearance of a beetle), or *bio-PK* (the dream became a self-fulfilling prophecy requiring Jung's client and/or himself to exert an unconscious attracting force on the rose chafer; see Haule, 2011b). It is even possible to proffer *clairvoyance* as an explanation (the client intuited the imminent arrival of a beetle so she unwittingly worked her dream into the conversation), or *retro-PK* (the rose-chafer was a future stimulus, or even feedback, at the time of the dream). And so on. All the while, causes are implied in the various interpretations. There is almost no end to the possibilities or the complications, whereas the simple synchronistic solution, which Jung explicated with only reasonably sufficient precision, is that the scarab dream is built on contingent factors that present to us as *coincidental.* And at the risk of labouring the point, the factors that distinguish this kind of coincidence from others are the numinous, archetypal, and meaningful aspects, which provide the 'architecture' for the event.

Eisenbud (1975) confirms that Jung used the term synchronicity effectively as the phenomenological equivalent of "psi". But Eisenbud reminds us of a difference—psi occurrences are thought to be "embedded in a causal matrix", whereas synchronicity is "totally outside the realm of causality", linked only by "meaning" (p. 6). In the wider field of parapsychology, and much to Jung's chagrin (see Jung, 1952/1969, para. 840), these synchronistic distinctions have not moved the other way and become defining aspects of ESP and PK, and how could they, although later theories, borrowing from Jung, suggest there has been an influence, as in von Lucadou's (2015) Model of Pragmatic Information (for a review, see Chapter 4 in Storm, 2025). But, as we have seen, Eisenbud dismisses altogether the idea of synchronicity as a phenomenon in its own right, arguing that it should be *reduced* to psi, while the synchronistic aspects can be abandoned. So, Eisenbud would draw synchronicity over to psi and abandon the Jungian baggage, whereas Jung would pull the other way, but *not* abandon the Rhinean baggage in the case of psi (the 'Jungian conflation').

To elaborate, Eisenbud (1975) points out how some of Jung's examples are of the "strange coincidence" type; "not what are usually thought of as uncomplicated psi" (p. 6). But Eisenbud then naïvely gives telepathy as an example of 'uncomplicated' psi. In fact, psi is often nothing if not complicated. For a start, the failure to prove *pure* telepathy forces us to take it as an article of faith (see Chapter 1 in Storm, 2025), or view it in another light—for example, one of the other psi alternatives, such as clairvoyance or precognition, or possibly inter-brain neural synchronization (IBNS), which may be an archetypal process (mentioned in the two subsections, *Memory Theories* and *Emotion*, in Chapter 3). That aside, it is true we are given to understand that psi is dynamically simple and *causally* traceable to the individual (i.e., people *cause* psi), whereas with synchronicity, people mostly find themselves somehow unwillingly ensnared in meaningfully dynamic, complex situations that they *did not cause*—the latter are, in a sense, headier and contextually broader (as is argued by Mansfield et al., 1998). But in actual fact, the opposite can often be true: synchronicity can be intentional (as in divinatory practice), and psi can be nonintentional as far as conscious agency is concerned, often characterized by complex situational dynamics; consider, for example, the 'Pauli Effect' (see Storm, 2025), whereas some synchronicities are so innocuous they could easily be passed over as mundane (some of my personal examples might spring to mind, though I would maintain they adequately serve as exemplars).[1]

The trick in Eisenbud's approach is that, for any given paranormal event, Eisenbud accepts psi to some degree, but when the event gets complicated and assumes synchronistic proportions, he attributes the complications to chance, the capitalization of chance, and the *normal* (albeit unconscious) machinations of the observer/agent. For Eisenbud (1980), that explanation is "preferable" to an "unknowable matrix of cosmic heavings and settlings", within which are individuals held to be "script-abiding players in an archetypal drama" (p. 26). But who is to say none of us play parts in these dramas at least some of the time? It is true that chance and chance-like events occur all the time but one can easily reject those that lack numinosity and meaningfulness, whereas if one takes parsimony too far, one can end up dismissing all inexplicable encounters by simply appealing to the Law of Truly Large Numbers, which I critiqued in Chapter 1 for its over-use when dealing with such situations as and when they arise.

Reconciliation

To show how these two views are not irreconcilable, consider the opinion of someone who had been deeply immersed in synchronistic experience on a continual basis for many years: none other than Alan Vaughan (1936–2001), famed for his participation in dream-ESP studies at the Maimonides Research Institute in the 1970s (see Ullman, Krippner, & Vaughan, 1973). Eisenbud (1975) says Vaughan believed he could "differentiate those coincidences" that can be classed as psi from those that are "beyond the limits of human psi" (p. 6), the latter of which is reserved the special distinction of being 'synchronistic'. But Vaughan (1979) later clarified his position further by saying that synchronicity would be better classed as "beyond the limits of an *individual's* psi" (p. 223). Of course, that clarification still depicts synchronicity as a grander form of psi "where many people [are] meshed into communal consciousness for production of the event" (p. 223). Earlier, Vaughan (1973) described synchronicity as possibly being the "basic 'particle' of psi" (p. 153). It is not always clear whether Vaughan, in his book *Incredible Coincidence*, does hold that psi and synchronicity are distinct categories, or synchronicity falls somewhere on the continuum of a psi spectrum, or *vice versa*—decades later he shared with me his notion of unification in response to a paper of mine that had just been published (Storm, 1999; for a revised version, see Storm, 2008b):

> I find myself much in agreement with you and would push psi and synchronicity even closer together, as I do in my book INCREDIBLE COINCIDENCE.... My view was much influenced by Jule Eisenbud, who pointed out that for Jung, psi WAS synchronicity.
>
> (A. Vaughan, personal communication, February 19, 2000)

Of course, as argued above, Eisenbud (1975) was hardly trying to convince anyone that psi was synchronicity on Jung's say-so—as pointed out, he argued the opposite, and was merely trying to highlight the folly in Jung's thinking.

Vaughan had asked back in 1979 if "pure synchronicity" is the product of some "out-there" "cosmic order", or is a paranormal phenomenon reducible to psi, "derived from interacting human-consciousness units on a scale far larger than is usually considered in parapsychology" (Vaughan, 1979, p. 239). He even explicitly tried to explain many cases of synchronicity in Rhinean terms, exactly as Eisenbud (1980) recommended. Braude (2007) is of a similar opinion when he likened synchronicity to "large-scale PK", as is Grattan-Guinness (1978) when he, in rather circumspect fashion, entertained the Eisenbudian approach, noting (a) it is "particularly dangerous to seek" a "holistic explanation" (p. 953), and (b) the agent is a causal factor ("it is the aims or stresses which cause the psi faculty to spring into action"; p. 954). Grattan-Guinness (1983) developed the idea further "that coincidences may be related to some of the general theories of psi mediation" (p. 59). As we see here, and as I have said previously, there is a general aversion to synchronicity theory.

In his struggle to reconcile the two, Vaughan was not far from resolving the issue, and only needed to see psi in a way that goes somewhat beyond his *and* these commentators' views on the matter, for I suggest there is some overlap in all the above statements. Psi translates as synchronicity when we see appropriate situational contingencies being met, but these are not dictated by circumstantial random forces (chance), for the circumstances are not random but are only chance-like. Nor do they reflect an *immutable* 'cosmic order'. The expression "interacting human-consciousness units" not only suggests an ongoing and ceaseless inter-connectedness amongst people (and psi is regarded as exactly that), but we also need to recognise our individual bidirectional relationship with a *flexible* cosmic order or macrocosm in the synchronistic sense, that suggests not "a scale far larger" than psi (like 'super-psi'), but a scale that goes *beyond* the psi construct in the sense of not seeing ESP and PK as paranormal thoughts and actions causally stemming from abilities. When synchronicity is seen as psi, it is only because it appears that an individual has expressed a psychic ability, and even a dose of magical thinking.

Vaughan's idea of a "cosmic order" did not go far enough in considering the critical role of archetypal and other synchronistic factors. In fact, the inter-connectedness of which he speaks and the flexibility of that cosmic order are most evident when archetypes are activated or constellated; otherwise nothing changes that cosmic order and it appears immutable. Furthermore, archetypes are not "evoked by a conscious act of the will" (Jung, 1975, p. 541). Like archetypes, personal psychology counts, which is nothing less than the implication made above by Grattan-Guinness (1983), and which all Jung's relevant cases prove, but if we are free to ignore the personal quotient, we should expect to see synchronicity more often than we do because the personal factor would play no part. This we do not see. Having said that, Jung argued that the more astute psychics and mediums, who *seem* to have ready access to their own so-called psychic function, only do so because they actually put themselves in "a state corresponding to an archetypal constellation" (p. 542). It is on that basis that psi and synchronicity can be reconciled. I call this congruence of concepts *merger without transfer* (i.e., it undoes the Jungian conflation by removing the 'complicating' implications fundamental to the psi paradigm while maintaining the holistic implications fundamental to synchronicity).

For Eisenbud (1975), it seems that a *merger without transfer* is too much of a hurdle, with Vaughan in a similar situation for one time in his life. I have mainly juxtaposed the views of a few commentators here, but the similarly expressed views of others have been raised throughout this book and elsewhere (see Storm, 2025), and there is no point repeating them. Most have never reconciled the dilemma—they either maintain the split seeing dissimilarities between psi and synchronicity, or they push for unification, seeing synchronicity as behaving like psi. The latter is a form of denial; if Eisenbud was to have used the word 'unification', it would be to make the problem of synchronicity go away. It has not gone away, yet psi seems to get all the attention. Interestingly, Greatrex (1999) argued that "some such theory as synchronicity … would be staring us in the face, if we had not been taught to label strange events as telepathy, clairvoyance, precognition or mere coincidence" (p. 5). But this is why synchronicity is so revolutionary—it challenges those taken-for-granted assumptions. The Jungian conflation, however, and its connotations must be taken head-on and dissolved.

Both Jung and Rhine, like the rest of us, were preconditioned to long-established (now conventional) ideas about how the paranormal manifests; Greatrex (1999) is clear on this. Indeed, we are still stuck with that problem. Jung's grappling with ESP and PK as classes or types of synchronicity (actually, as *wider* forms of it), while still allowing ESP and PK their Rhinean phenomenology, was a contradiction most likely overlooked based on his 'hand-shake' with Rhine: Mansfield et al. (1998) says as much: "Jung failed to distinguish [synchronicity from psi] … because he wanted the support of Rhine's experiments for his new concept of synchronicity" (p. 20). To put it simply, synchronicity cannot logically be *the* super-ordinate category that subsumes psi phenomena if it includes both acausal *and* causal phenomena, as in (a) acausal meaningful coincidences beyond psi, *and* (b) causal psi with all its phenomenological trappings.[2] But nor can psi be a super-ordinate category (*pace* J. Eisenbud, J. B. Rhine, *et alia*). Even outside synchronicity, it has not given birth to a principle of unification that has any clarity or viability whatsoever or, what is more important, any explanatory power (as highlighted in Chapter 1 in Storm, 2025), so nor does it have the theoretical power that allows synchronicity to be subsumed into a psi-based schema.

In likening psi to synchronicity, Jung should have reminded himself that paranormal correspondence *as coincidences* are not caused (once causes are proposed, they cannot be called coincidences). He accepted that *information transfer* and *energy exchange* have certain limits, but in the case of synchronicity, the two concepts, information transfer *and* energy exchange, are *paranormally* redundant anyway, and so they do not have to be dealt with by putting a spin on spacetime. Ironically, it was surprisingly obvious to Beloff (1977) why synchronicity would be an alternative to psi:

> Once it had become absolutely clear ... that the search for a physical carrier of psi information was leading nowhere and that a mechanistic model of the psi process ... was never going to work, the necessity for a radical rethinking of the whole problem seemed inescapable. The attraction of the synchronicity solution was that it dispensed with the onus of finding a causal nexus for the phenomena without, at the same time, demoting them to the category of mere statistical artefacts.
>
> (p. 573)[3]

We see that the factor of most interest to parapsychologists (i.e., the factor that evokes the mystery in psi and synchronicity) is largely of a spatio-temporal nature. Non-local consciousness is an oft-used albeit rough-and-ready concept that gets around the problem of information transfer and/or energy transmission (or energy exchange), which is why some theorists cannot let go of the associations made between these concepts and psi. Understood that way, we thus see that the mystery is predicated on psychological relativity, which is easily dismissed once we consider the 'transcending' role of archetypes. The archetypal factor works universally and ubiquitously like the fundamental laws of physics; like constants or equations that rein in a universe of hypotheticals. Once this veil of blindness to the facts about archetypes is lifted, we can transcend the paranormal problem. However, if we couch psi and synchronicity in *relative* spatiotemporal terms, the hunt for causes will trap us in a web of deceit manifesting as terminological problems that set up too many interpretive options, but do little to help thin out the density of multiple causes.

Dark Psi and Dark Synchronicity

It seems, from his deeper (more speculative) analyses of the psi and synchronicity concepts, Eisenbud (1970, 1980, 1982, 1983) gives his ideas a solid footing in evolutionary and holistic principles for psi, but simultaneously disavows anything of a kind for synchronicity. He seems certain the "obscure concept" of synchronicity was devised by Jung as an abstract "scapegoat" that would serve to eliminate "every trace of the human will" (1980, p. 26). Ultimately, Eisenbud regards synchronicity as a "cosmic copout" whereby causality is projected way beyond the individual, thus relegating the believer to a primitive state of mind akin to that of our pre-industrial ancestors. By this he means we can avoid dealing with the worst of our "needs and desires" by simply attributing to synchronicity (because it is *acausal*) those events that should ordinarily be 'owned' by us. Yet the psi concept holds good ground for Eisenbud who even proposes, as Main (2007) puts it, that "our aggressive feelings and thoughts may be telepathically and psychokinetically effective" (p. 33). Eisenbud is drawing attention to the fact that human nature leaves a lot to be desired and its deepest darkest stirrings may manifest psychically and destructively, whereas it almost seems as though he puts no onus on synchronicity—quite the opposite; he ultimately repudiates synchronicity for being dishonest in a psychoanalytic sense.

While some synchronicity pundits do have a romantic view of the concept, such that (either by oversight, defence, or denial) they never mention the harmful or fatal cases of synchronicity, I fail to see how such darker aspects undermine the theory. All they do is complicate matters—to use Eisenbud's (1975) example, a driver of a car who accidentally runs over someone he was thinking about moments earlier might, along with the guilt and other consequences pertaining (assuming of course the driver is a morally decent human being), *does* deal with the meaningful aspects of the fatal encounter insofar as there are synchronistic overtones. And Jung's birds case is marked by tragedy, as were Bishop Pike's encounters (see Chapter 4), so it is not as if the issue of 'dark synchronicity' has slipped under the radar. Furthermore, it is asking a great deal to think that one who feels sure they are psychically responsible could assuage his/her guilt by simply calling psi by another name (viz., synchronicity). Of course, that is not to say it could not be done; humans have made a fine art of denial; but equally, we would not have the harrowing and lasting effects of contrition and remorse if ridding ourselves of guilt was that easy.

The most peculiar (indeed contradictory) aspect of Eisenbud's critique is that he can speak so disparagingly and dismissively of synchronicity in some of his writings, yet elsewhere (see Eisenbud, 1990) he proceeds to analyze a client's precognitive dream and associated coincidences in his own life, in a manner not dissimilar to the way Jung would have treated them, yet fails to acknowledge the obvious synchronistic tone of the material. The meaningful aspects are brought to our attention—indeed, these are clearly what prompted the writing of the paper in the first place—but all causes of the coincidental elements are seen as the result of unconscious motivations or chance (begging the question somewhat, but we can let that pass). Only in a footnote does he mention the word synchronicity, again arguing it to be a cosmic copout that displaces "hidden motivations" (p. 353), and therefore rids the individual of all culpability, as if Jung had ever run with that idea.[4]

Going further, Mishlove and Engen (2007), with Eisenbud in mind, talk about the misguided and "self-destructive tendencies" (p. 237) that may be triggered by meanings that are not there in genuine and imagined "synchronicities and other paranormal events" (p. 237). Mishlove and Engen explain:

> [...] mere subjective conviction about allegedly meaningful conjunctions is not evidence of genuine synchronicity, as cases of psychotic delusion and hallucination make apparent.
>
> (2007, p. 237)

Quite correct *and* Mishlove and Engen also "remain unpersuaded that the phenomenon of apophenia can adequately account for all ostensibly paranormal experiences" (p. 237). Rather than dismissing psi experiences and meaningful coincidences out of hand, they tacitly imply that care must be taken to interpret them correctly.

But a broader issue should concern us: While Rhinean and Jungian ideas can lead some unfortunates to disaster, it is through no fault of genuine psi and synchronicity that disturbed people may react in untoward ways and misinterpret their meanings, which is no less true of all great ideas and truths. Not so long ago, mental disorder was a madness caused by possession, the work of supernatural beings, rather than brain disorders, brain damage, excessive drug use (e.g., alcoholism), or even inappropriate diet. Possession is a danger mostly gone nowadays, except in rare instances (see Gauld & Cornell, 1979). It would also seem that psi and synchronicity are the least of our worries, or are we to give serious consideration to the possibility that the world has occasionally fallen into catastrophe *because* a handful of renegades and tyrants let loose their paranormal powers, which Braude (1986) calls "paranormal hostilities" (p. 280). In truth, humankind's worst behaviours appear to stem from more potent instincts than a very occasional and effete occult 'ability'.

There are three main issues concerning synchronicity discussed here: the first is its 'dark' side, the second is its 'cosmic' aspect, and the third is its extent. All three are interwoven and inseparable, so that trying to deal with one very soon means dealing with the others. First, the literature is dotted with synchronistic incidents that indicate synchronicity is no walk in the park; it can be complicated, harrowing, challenging, and even marked by tragedy.

Second, although we might hope that people will have the moral courage to own their own psi, and take remedial steps to become responsible persons, synchronicity is not an excuse to act with impunity—the proven necessity for the concept of intentional synchronicity has made it quite clear where the locus of responsibility is situated (see Chapter 2). On psi, we only have to recall the more reprehensible acts of Ted Owens (Mishlove, 2000) to know that psi ownership and ethical responsibility do not go hand in hand—Owens was quick to claim culpability for his worst deeds but remained unapologetic. Ted Owens (1920–1987) claimed he was the cause of UFO appearances, lightning and thunder, plane crashes, power outages, turnarounds in sporting events, and even the Challenger space shuttle disaster of 1986 (for a review of the Owens case, see Chapter 1 in Storm, 2025). Believing that the source of psi is in oneself does not automatically put one on the road to spiritual enlightenment (indeed, Grof and Grof [1990] point out that psi experience can be a distraction).

On synchronicity, if Owens were to have had an awakening of sorts that might have led him to attribute all his proven paranormal efforts to synchronicity alone, could we really be sure he would usurp his conscience and concede the cosmos was to blame, and he was not responsible? The only concession we can make was that Owens knew there was something more to it than his own motivations at work, yet guilt never left him entirely. Recall the cautionary tales of Jonah and Job of Old Testament fame (Jung, 1958/1969; Lasine, 2017)—their ordeals (i.e., external happenings that parallel inner disorders) only ended because both realized and conceded that they themselves (who they were) were contingent factors in the tragedies that unfolded around them (the modern mind can hardly miss the synchronistic overtones). As Wachtel (1973) has noted, "situations are largely of one's own making and are themselves describable as a characteristic of one's own personality" (p. 330). Yet, strangely, the world is dragged into the drama, or more correctly, we are dragged in.

Thankfully, Owens was a rarity, but more than that, he was oftentimes a psi-misser, and that is an important consideration relevant to the third issue. Owens was certainly no tyrant like the despots of the past; but then the latter never came close to being like Owens either as far as their paranormal 'abilities' go (given they ever had any, and we are even talking about an ability *per se*). Since we have never seen psi wreak untold catastrophe on a global scale, why should we expect worse from synchronicity, intentional or otherwise? Indeed, experience shows both synchronicity and psi run down and exhaust themselves naturally in the individual. Studies featuring lengthy runs of trials attest to that fact; besides which, the meta-analyses on psi illustrate only generally *weak* (i.e., small) effects that span decades, with no sign yet that these effects will ever be unwieldy and dangerous (see Chapter 2 in Storm, 2025).

We can appeal to Vaughan (1979) who captures the more pertinent points raised here: "The cosmic is not an external copout, since we are part of its integral design. The concept of synchronicity might lead us to find the other parts and put them together" (p. 223), implying that synchronicity is its own cure. In cultivating a 'cosmic consciousness', we gain self-knowledge. The more cogent problem facing parapsychologists, and humanity in general, is how to treat the fear, ignorance, and naïveté associated with parapsychological ideas. Paradoxically, Vaughan was optimistic that a natural barrier to extreme psi abilities is our very "fear of the unknown" (p. 223). It is unfortunate that those same fears also manifest as prejudices against the paranormal, its practitioners, its believers, and (let us not forget) psi theories that displease for spurious reasons.

Of Miracles and Misattributions

If we cannot go further than put the paranormal wheels in motion with intention, and even by so doing, can only expect weak (small) effects, or cannot obtain impressive hits on demand, thus dispensing with the ancient (but still current) idea that an individual can potentially have paranormal powers of untold magnitude, what are we to make of those extraordinary cases bordering on the astounding, or even miraculous? We first need to consider whether these exceptions are cases of psi or synchronicity, but since I am arguing that psi is synchronicity, I go further and argue that if a phenomenon is not psi, then it is not synchronicity. Indeed, some may wonder where the synchronicity is in levitation, as exemplified in Franciscan friar St. Joseph of Cupertino who allegedly levitated in the presence of Pope Urban VIII (see Braude, 1986). Where might the synchronicity be in Katie the "gold leaf lady" who exudes from various parts of her body alloys comprised not of gold but of various elements including nickel, silver, cadmium, and even lead (see Braude, 2007)? Some may insist these are clear-cut examples of psi (i.e., PK), thereby differentiating psi from synchronicity, but can we be so sure St. Joseph and Katie produced evidence of psi?

Ordinarily those two people would be regarded as macro-PK stars—they psychically *moved* matter, or spontaneously *manifested* same. Braude (2015) raises the issue of psychokinetic limits, but ultimately that which is to be regarded as macro-PK is a matter of consensus (relatively speaking). For example, the Society for Psychical Research (SPR) states that levitation occurs "without apparent use of orthodox physical or technological means".[5] Materialization *per se* also implies unorthodox means. Provisionally then, the macro-PK attribution appears to have its roots in sheer perplexity (i.e., people cannot find orthodox ways to think about them or explain them)—hence, certain forms of 'PK' are revered as macro-PK because of their *unorthodoxy*. Yet at least one theory avoids dealing with levitation: Decision Augmentation Theory (reviewed in Storm, 2025) is not geared to explain it: "The source of the statistical variation is unrestricted and may be of classical or quantum origin" (May, Utts, & Spottiswoode, 1995, p. 200).[6] So whether or not levitation is paranormal, not every parapsychologist thinks they need explain it, or even feel compelled to regard it as macro-PK, partly because the phenomenon is too rare and cannot be studied, so no firm conclusion can be reached. It is a safer bet not to claim effects as being paranormal too ardently and too quickly for the physical sciences *may* end up explaining some macro-PK in orthodox ways, and QM may be one of those ways!

Somewhat ironically, it seems like over-reaching that comparatively less astounding effects such as "psychosomatic ailments and self-healing through hypnosis might be classed as PK" (Braude, 2015, p. 258). These phenomena are well accepted by the medical profession as psychophysiological effects (self-healing is even dispassionately referred to as 'spontaneous remission' which is not to imply paranormal causation; rather, remission is attributed to changes in diet, introducing an exercise regime and reducing stress, social interaction and support from family and friends, and making meaningful changes in personal beliefs and attitudes). Braude's point is that PK, by at least one definition, is not necessarily confined to "extra-somatic" targets (p. 258), and again all decisions about PK are based merely on what a theory can (or cannot) accommodate anyway—a point I just made. Having said that, I suggest that what we have here are four anomalies (levitation, certain kinds of materialization, psychosomatic ailments, and self-healing) which we cannot confidently label as psychophysical, but they are more likely psychophysiological. In short, these are not convincingly psi. It should also be clear that these four anomalies are thus not any kind of synchronicity as they would not satisfy the pertinent definitions (for definitions, see *Synchronicity* in Chapter 1). That is, since the processes in their entirety occur wholly *within* their respective biological systems (within the organisms), they are psychophysiological and therefore causal (historically, mechanically, and scientifically), even if they are a long way from being understood.

In truth there are other forms of macro-PK that are not psychophysiological at first blush. Whatever the cause of the *physical* components of some 'big-time' macro-PK events (e.g., table-tilting, thoughtography), the events are synchronistic (acausal and psychophysical) if they meaningfully coincide with the *mental* images (and therefore intentions) of the necessarily involved agent or agents. There could be other explanations ("may be of classical or quantum origin"), but as Main (2004) points out, "archetypes can structure matter as well as psyche – and not just separately but at the same time in respect to the same pattern of meaning" (p. 225). Consider the thoughtography of Ted Serios. By his mind alone, Serios was allegedly able to project or 'impress' mostly fuzzy and/or barely discernable images (though many were impressively clear) onto photographic media not sourced in the conventional photographic sense from a physical (external world) subject. Eisenbud (1967) insisted on a certain "meaningfulness" (p. 38) to these images, and he offered psychodynamic (often-times convoluted and arguably spurious) explanations for them (see his Chapter 9, *The Target Situation*). As we expect of synchronicity (though, as we know, Eisenbud resists this concept), most images are sporadic and unpredictable, and Serios usually had much difficulty 'imaging' what was asked of him; only a few capture the literal elements of the predesignated targets, such as the "the clock tower of [Westminster] Abbey" (p. 57), and a ship Serios had been "supposedly aiming to get" (p. 131). Most of the images that are discernable do not seem to have been specifically held in mind by Serios as targets *per se*—at least not in a literal sense, and/or not necessarily consciously. Others are thought by Eisenbud to be symbolic representations (unconsciously imagined re-creations) that he passes as 'corresponding' to ideas held by Serios, announced in advance of creating the product. For the most part then, arguments for meaningfulness—even in a synchronistic sense—must be pitched in the abstract (I have covered this issue of interpretations of meaningfulness and correspondence in Chapter 2). Still, to be parsimonious, it may be convenient not to grapple with psi as an explanation: As long as heavy cases of macro-PK are thought to be paranormal, the parapsychologist of a Rhinean persuasion has the added burden of explaining how the physical aspects are causal expressions of an ability or capability, which is perhaps still a greater challenge than that faced by the synchronist who must grapple with the holistic complexities of meanings associated with archetypes. Indeed, Eisenbud actually draws attention to this two-fold problem, but never really solves it.

We can, however, easily grapple with other rare PK-like phenomena such as fire-walking, which includes handling red-hot and molten metal (Coe, 1958; Tabori, 1950/1974). These high-temperature effects appear to have normal explanations. For example, Mayne Reid Coe, Jr., gave many examples of his successful attempts at fire-walking and related behaviours, but explained all of them naturally and normally; "protection is afforded by the spherical condition assumed by liquids" (Coe, p. 97). Tabori's investigations of two fire-walkers led him to conclude that "the effect was due neither to trickery or paranormal powers" (pp. 192–195).

Then we have psychokinetic metal-bending (PKMB), *so different* in degree and kind from the micro-PK forms (e.g., RNG and arguably dice-throwing), the term "paranormal" may never have been justified (see West, 2012, for a similar argument). They only provisionally fit the PK category for the primary reason that no scientifically acceptable cause has been posited: We have nothing like "a theory of the mechanism of PK on the horizon" (Watkins, 2015, p. 78),[7] and as reliable as eye-witness testimony can be (especially when it is given by professional parapsychologists), even the best (most impressive) cases are still largely anecdotal (see Chapter 19 in Hasted, 1981; see also Watkins, 2015, concerning teleportation and Hasted's experiments with Uri Geller in 1974).

Of course, use of the PK label derives from the assumption that the phenomena are what they are purported to be. For example, experimental physicist and a supposed authority on PKMB, John Hasted (1981) was severely criticised by W. Byers Brown (1981) for writing a book that was "disappointingly inconclusive" (p. 156). Although Hasted admits he did not take a "hard-line" attitude towards the "careful documenting and reliable witnessing" of the "paranormal phenomena" (p. 155), Brown's response may be overly dismissive when we consider Hasted's use of sophisticated measuring instruments in his tests and analyses. Nevertheless, and more to my point, Brown noted that there was "very little explicit discussion … of what characterizes the mental states involved when paranormal happenings occur" (p. 155). Since next to nothing was done by Hasted to demonstrate the metal bending was "psycho-physical" (p. 155), and on whose part (including Hasted's), we cannot assume the effects suggest synchronicity, or even conventional psi (PK) for that matter (an example is given in the next paragraph). PKMB phenomena of this order (that lack meaningfulness) stand in stark contrast to (say) Pike's paperclips that were very much context bound; they were elements of a complex synchronistic situation, and their causality was definitely unresolved to say the least (see Chapter 4).

As we see, we definitely need to give more attention to anomalous effects thought to be paranormal. For example, the impressive "paranormal deformation" effect described in the study by Randall and Davis (1982) is possibly other than a PK effect. The test material was *nitinol* wire (a nickel/titanium alloy) pre-shaped under high temperature (~500°C). The test subject (an 11-year-old school boy) stroked the piece of pre-set straight wire, permanently distorting its shape since the wire did not straighten even after being placed in boiling water which should have re-set the wire (temperatures between 80°C–100°C restore nitinol to its pre-set shape). However, the authors did not take measurements at the boy's finger-tips (e.g., temperature, electrical charge)—electrostatic discharges reaching tens of thousands of volts can be "imperceptible to the human body" (Mini-circuits, 2015), and they can reach temperatures of thousands of degrees Celsius within a very short timeframe, say, in the order of microseconds or nanoseconds. In the boy's case, these events could have occurred at certain places along the wire, thus changing the wire's shape. This proposition is not undermined by the fact that multiple attempts to restore the wire to its original form (even at 600°C) met with failure each time for the boy had irrevocably changed the wire's memory. The boy's capability seems anomalous in itself, more because of its rarity than anything else, but the evident effects of that capability must arguably remain psychophysiological but not psychophysical in the synchronistic sense.

Generally, macro-PK presents problems for parapsychologists because there is little reliable evidence for it in well-controlled studies (Irwin & Watt, 2007), though the best evidence, usually from 'star subjects', sometimes appears compelling (see again Randall & Davis, 1982). Emissions of measurably high electromagnetic radiation, especially from star subjects (meditators, healers) are of this nature, as demonstrated by Joines, Baumann, and Kruth (2012), but these energies are also clearly psychophysiological in origin. Joines et al. (2004) even remarked that it is not very well known that "emission of electromagnetic energy in the form of low-intensity light from biological systems is a common phenomenon" (p. 445; see also the 'lightning' example in Hilleard, 2014). Yet, research of this nature goes back as far as 1920s Russia (for reviews, see Alvarado, 1987; Joines et al., 2012), but as it is Russian research, perhaps it is no surprise that it failed to make a mark in the West.

Similarly, research from Japanese parapsychologist Hideyuki Kokubo (2013) and his colleagues suggest a direct physical explanation for bio-PK healing, showing how "biophotons", which are ultraviolet/infrared photons, are not only emitted by living organisms, but healers appear to be able to induce significantly higher counts of biophotons from vegetable specimens ('white spine type' cucumber) compared to control specimens. As an interactive link involving biophoton exchange is indicated, these effects would be biophysical (not psychophysical). Studies by Roney-Dougal and Solfvin (2002, 2003), that produced significant effects in healer-attended lettuce seeds compared to control seeds, may have also tested the biophysical principle (i.e., the effects may not be paranormal).

Select individuals are also able to produce a measurable wave-like "bio-PK field" (Kokubo, 2013, p. 12) around their person, as recorded on 'bio-sensors', although the term bio-PK may be misapplied in this instance. True to the standard understanding of physical waveforms, combined healers' waves can result in destructive interference if they are out of phase. That the major and particular quality of healing itself is beneficial (a remarkable characteristic of psychic healing generally) rather than detrimental, we may be sure it is associated with healing intention, but no satisfactory explanation is forthcoming. More importantly, none of the effects presented by Kokubo can be considered acausal in the synchronistic sense, but nor can they be regarded as psi effects *per se* (e.g., bio-PK), given that direct biophysical connections are demonstrated between healer and target.

We may need to consider the nature of psychic diagnosis, especially since reliable studies on this phenomenon are few and far between (for a review, see Irwin & Watt, 2007). While such diagnoses have come down to us as clairvoyance, we cannot rule out telepathy-like links, and these might eventually be explained as IBNS (Valencia & Froese, 2020) that may, at its core, depend on archetypal structures that enable connectivity when activated. As I said earlier, the many typically human (social) environments and interactions are potentially archetypal situations within which the same archetype invariably constellates in pairs or even groups (see *Expanded and Extended Consciousness* in the subsection *On Model Building* in Chapter 4 of Storm, 2025). I suggest neural synchronization is a kind of bond between the 'psychic' diagnostician and the patient, and this bond facilitates a direct reading of the ailment that merely suggests telepathy.

There are cases of successful healing intention (for a review, see Cardeña, 2018b) that include DMILS, remote helping, noncontact healing (e.g., intercessory prayer, Reiki), and remote staring, though the jury is still out on remote staring (a.k.a. 'the sense of being stared at'; see Lohr et al., 2013; Radin, 2005; Rock, 2010). But we must ascertain what it means to *intend* healing. IBNS would explain the bond between healer and healee that gives emotional support to the healee, resulting in a positive change in attitude in the latter that triggers a healing effect similar to the effects observed in placebo cases. As such, the healing effect would not be macro-PK or bio-PK from the healer. I submit that any successful healing probably starts as an 'inter-brain' process involving neural synchronization (IBNS), such that the positive emotional component, coupled with the inner image of a caring 'other', initiates the motivation to self-heal, which is a natural internal process (extraordinary cases of this type will follow shortly). Thus the healing itself is a purely neuro-psychological (non-paranormal) process (see also the reviews by Benor, 2001; Jonas & Crawford, 2003).

What is true for some forms of macro-PK may also be true for some extraordinary extrasensory anomalies, which are shown to fit adequately within the mainstream scientific paradigm, as appears to be the case for disaster detection (Bates, 2010), and premonition of death (Barker, 1968). Stokes (2014) gives impressive examples of spontaneous psi, but he offers plausible *normal* explanations (pp. 81–83). Perhaps being critical to a fault, there is doubt about the paranormality of water divining (i.e., dowsing; see Jenkins, 2017), psychometry (Barrington, 2019), and *déjà vu* (Baker, 1992), even though once again there are exceptional cases that unfortunately (and often) do not go beyond anecdote. Psychometry is a good example, and William Bengston describes a case of a star subject and psychometrician (Bennett Mayrick) tested under laboratory conditions who stated "any object they give me for a reading has to be something they know a lot about" (Bengston with Fraser, 2010, p. 19). This condition suggests Mayrick's*modus operandi* was nothing less than IBNS, which requires cross-brain coupling, but has nothing to do with the object. Not only was Mayrick successful at describing the contents of a box, his beta and theta EEG readings were high—similarly found in laboratory studies of IBNS (Valencia & Froese, 2020). Where water dowsing has been successful, evidence indicates that the kidneys, brains, and pineal region of the dowsers are sensitive to electromagnetic fields, with more successful dowsers tending to have low skin resistance (Jenkins, 2017). Although there are a number of theories explaining *déjà vu*, it is commonly thought that new information can go directly into long-term memory but bypasses short-term memory so as to be 'recalled' as an old memory.

We should also be wary of claimed forms of alleged psi manifestation, old *and* new, that are related to the genetic factor. For example, "bio-psychometry" (Roll, et al., 2021, p. 92), a sub-class of psychometry, is based on organ recipients mysteriously taking on the behavioural characteristics of their donors. However, organs like the heart, lungs, liver, and kidney, have independent neurological structure like 'little brains' that hold so-called 'cellular memories' defined as "a sustained cellular response to a transient stimulus" (Harvard Medical School, 2009, as cited in Absi, 2014; see alsoLiester, 2020). Interestingly, the example of cellular memory in Absi (2014) is given as a case of bio-psychometry by Roll et al., who call it "psi entanglement" (p. 93): In this instance, heart/lung recipient Claire Sylvia developed the dubious eating habits of her donor who was a young fast-food fanatic. In other words, the parapsychological claim of bio-psychometry in this instance overlooks the likelihood that it is psychophysiological interaction (not psychophysical entanglement). Despite the quite feasible though still controversial argument for cellular memory, Dossey (2008) uncompromisingly repudiates it for an exclusively paranormal (nonlocal) alternative to explain cellular memory specifically, and reincarnation generally. The research by Liester (2020) suggests more parsimonious explanations including epigenetic memory, DNA memory, RNA memory, and protein memory. He also refers to "intracardiac neurological memory" as a possible cause of personality changes after heart transplantation.

As I said at the beginning of this book, afterlife (post-mortem survival) research may not even belong in parapsychology (see Irwin, 2002, for a similar argument), though I make allowances for LAP. On this issue, there are exceptionally creative cases involving channeling, mediumship, automatic writing, and even possession that do suggest anomalous processes (for example, see the impressive case of Iris Farczady as described by Barrington, Mulacz, and Rivas, 2005). Could there be a synchronistic aspect to these phenomena? As I will argue here, quite possibly not, and in so doing, I also dispense with the ESP assumption (LAP or otherwise). Two outstanding cases will suffice to illustrate this point: (i) American woman, Pearl Lenore Curran (1883–1937), with her impressive output of novels, poems, and prose, attributed to a discarnate entity 'Patience Worth' (Litvag, 1972), and (ii) English woman Rosemary Brown (1916–2001), with her extensive *oeuvre* of musical compositions attributed to the channeled spirits of Liszt, Chopin, Mozart, Bach, Beethoven, and many others (Brown, 1971).[8]

As I proposed in Chapter 4, *if* a discarnate entity attempts contact with a living person, or *if* a psychic or medium is mind-reading an incarnate person, *then* communication in either case can be deemed 'extrasensory' (e.g., *telepathic* to use the Rhinean term), which equates with synchronicity. Of course, given the nature of Curran's and Brown's prodigious talents, we can reasonably regard LAP as implausible, whereas the hypothesis that discarnate entities are involved might serve a synchronistic purpose, but whose? We might, however, be jumping the gun. In these instances, as unlikely as it may seem to some, alternate explanations lie solely in the natural albeit rare processes of the mind/brain complex. Thus, a paranormal explanation is not even warranted. Specifically, *dissociation* and *mimicry* have been proposed to explain Curran's and Brown's extraordinary creations (see Braude, 2003). These processes are now well understood, to the degree that they parsimoniously explain a panoply of creative anomalies of the above-mentioned kind. As a *caveat*, it should be noted that the standard and calibre of these works, literary and musical, are sometimes thought to hold valid sway in the arguments for or against paranormality, but I regard all qualitative determinations as too subjective and biased to be entered into the debate.

Braude (2003) covers these issues quite well, and his argument from dissociation in the Curran case is best presented here in his own words:

> [...] we can explain Pearl's creative facility and anomalous knowledge in terms of latent capacities and (presumably psychic) processes for which we have independent evidence. For that reason, I'm inclined to echo Schiller's comment that "it is...*safer* to credit 'Patience Worth' to the unconscious and to classify her, officially, as Mrs. Curran's 'secondary self' "... the case is a humbling reminder that there's much still to learn about the human mind.
>
> (p. 174)

Braude runs a slightly different line of argument concerning Rosemary Brown's compositional style:

> In my view, the most plausible and parsimonious hypothesis is that Mrs. Brown was a naturally gifted impressionist ... of course, that hypothesis is not undermined by the apparent originality of some of Mrs. Brown's compositions. In fact, it's precisely what one would expect of a good impressionist.
>
> (p. 168)

Braude notes Brown's compositions are examples of "refined (and presumably unconscious) musical mimicry" (p. 168). Clearly the two—dissociation and mimicry—are psychologically and phenomenologically dissimilar (one a more unconscious process; the other, less so). But they are not incompatible states, and my observation of Rosemary's mimicry in action (Slate-writer, 2015), leads me to conclude that she appears sufficiently absorbed or immersed in her work that she might also be in a relatively (mild) dissociated state (along the lines of 'flow' or 'absorption'). Indeed, Braude concedes the pivotal role of the unconscious for both women, which stresses my earlier point about the deeply imaginal dimensions of the human mind that need no recourse to paranormal considerations in these cases (see Chapter 3). Putting aside these finer points about the creative process, if dissociation and mimicry prove to be more reasonable explanations for Curran's and Brown's prodigious talents, respectively, then the arguments from psi and synchronicity subside.

Interestingly, and seemingly with some justification, Vaughan (1979) makes no small claim about the possibility of extraordinary cases of *intentional synchronicity* (though he does not use that term), and he does present quite a few extraordinary examples amongst his "152 stories—the largest collection of coincidence cases ever assembled" (p. 14). My assessment of Vaughan's "stories" is that many could pass as meaningless chance groupings, or (at best) could be classed as 'low-level' synchronicities (often the case with ESP and PK) in the sense that it is difficult to show how they meet all the necessary synchronistic criteria. While many of Vaughan's incidents might be chance-like based on frequency counts and other data that allow for odds calculations, that does not minimize their synchronistic value (see the section "Alternative Explanations of Synchronicity: I. Chance" in Chapter 1).

The majority of cases, however, fall outside this consideration, and tend to take the following form: Vaughan (or someone else) happens to see a long-lost loved-one, whom he (or she) was only just thinking about (or it is a stranger he or she would like to meet without forcing an introduction), and at some future time, going about his (or her) business, he (or she) serendipitously meets that person unexpectedly under genuine (i.e., uncontrived) circumstances. Other examples follow the standard 'I-thought-of-you-and-you-suddenly-phoned-me' type, or the 'I-really-needed-that-to-happen-and-it-did' type, much like PMIR as reviewed by Storm (2025)—for similar serendipities, see Beitman (2016). Vaughan also reports numerous lost-and-found link-ups—that is, finding long-lost things, likely as not in not-so-obvious places.

Even so, people lose and find things everyday and can easily come across them by chance without needing to assume psi helped them. Anecdotes like these are covered elsewhere in great detail (Barrington, 2018; Jinks, 2016). None of Vaughan's many anecdotes help the synchronicity case all that much because the reader is hit with a heterogeneous barrage of incidents, that are indiscriminately or socially categorized, and only occasionally does Vaughan give some thought to them in a meaningful synchronistic sense. At the end of the day, we simply do not know which to take seriously and which to ignore.

One phenomenal exception to Vaughan's (1979) many run-of-the-mill cases is Belgian man, Monsieur Pierre De Rudder, whose leg was seriously crippled from a falling tree. Many pieces of fractured bone had to be removed, and it seemed he was compelled to use crutches for the rest of his life. After eight years of visiting doctors to no avail, and in terrible pain, De Rudder went on a pilgrimage to Our Lady of Lourdes in Oostakker, Belgium. Having seated himself in a little cave where a statue of Our Lady of Lourdes had been erected, De Rudder fervently prayed for healing so he could work again and support his wife and children. Vaughan notes how De Rudder "felt deeply moved, overwhelmed by a strange feeling …" (p. 165), and was suddenly able to get up and walk through the crowd, and from then on "walked normally until his death in 1898" at age 76 (Neiman, 1995, pp. 100–101).

Later examination of De Rudder's leg showed that his wound was completely healed, and his leg was normal. Posthumous examination via physical inspection (autopsy and X-rays) of De Rudder's corpse revealed a piece of healthy white bone over one inch long connecting two sections of original bone that still showed traces of breakage. The case has never been adequately explained by medical authorities (for other miraculous healings with no clear or normal explanations, see Dowling, 1984). Vaughan regarded the De Rudder case as synchronicity on the basis that "miracles" have "no apparent causal agency by which they are produced" (p. 163). But in using the word "miracle", Vaughan set himself up for a hasty conclusion. There is reason to be doubtful here because even though we can acknowledge the presence of intention on De Rudder's part, as well as the subsequent numinosity, and the profoundly meaningful outcome, *there is no acausal, psychophysical correlation*—only a psychophysiological one that suggests causality (which may be true of all miracles of a psychophysiological nature).

We might make comparisons with the extra-ordinary feats and experiences of Ted Owens (Mishlove, 2000), or Bishop Pike (see the previous chapter), but those two cases have profoundly psychophysical components and were accordingly presented as synchronicity. For some people, in spite of the psychophysiological and causal overtones, appeal to paranormality is a satisfactory lead as to how such healing occurred for De Rudder, but calling it a 'psi process' explains very little in the way of mechanism, besides being purely *ad hoc*, whereas other routes are available to us when we consider regeneration in the animal kingdom for a great variety of species. For example, salamanders can regenerate brain tissue, hearts, parts of their eyes, and even their limbs and tails (Sun et al., 2018; see also, Lye, 2018). Similar findings are demonstrated for some species of crab (Patterson, Dick, & Elwood, 2009). Regeneration of amputated limbs using neurosteroids has been achieved in African clawed frogs (Herrera-Rincon et al., 2018). In humans, natural healing abilities already border on the miraculous if one stops to think of common-place examples of natural repair to damaged tissue, organs (e.g., liver, lungs), and even finger tips, cartilage, and bone (Dr. Bell C NDE, 1998–2021; Hsueh et al., 2009; Illingworth, 1974). One study even showed higher rates of *in vitro* bone, tendon and fibroblast cell proliferation compared with controls (Gronowicz et al., 2008). While the impressive rate of healing *implied* in the De Rudder case seems to be in the short-term (seconds, minutes, or hours), it has been suggested that the healing was not "instantaneous" (Nickell, 2010), and going by some eye-witness accounts, we cannot rule out healing onset from as far back as weeks or even months before De Rudder's arrival at Oostakker (Neiman, 1995).

Such considerations based in evolutionary principles, rather than paranormal supposition, give us every reason to assume that a maximal healing capacity could be a genetically inherent factor. Though generally atrophied, and only marginally functional for the vast majority of us, this capacity has been demonstrated to full and profound degrees in rare cases, De Rudder being quite possibly one of them (see also The Miracle Hunter, 2015). To demonstrate such effects successfully in human samples would more than likely require up-scaled testing of intention effects (not possible with animals) along the lines of similarly oriented human healing studies. To illustrate this point, albeit to a lesser extent, Rock, Permezel, and Storm (2012) showed that the "blind" delivery of "subtle energy" (i.e., Quantum BioEnergetics; QBE) on humans resulted in improved psychological effects (measured as self-reported moods), that included significantly less tension, anxiety, anger, and hostility compared with placebo and control groups. More importantly, placebo effects exclusive of any ostensible paranormal healing (QBE) were also indicated, thus suggesting intention effects were solely responsible: Specifically, paranormal believers (a.k.a. 'sheep') in the placebo group were significantly lower in depression and dejection compared to all other groups. The researchers did state that "the placebo effect may contribute towards the healing outcome given the suggestibility of sheep" (Rock et al., 2012, p. 116)—suggestibility would go hand-in-hand with intentionality, and common sense suggests positive intention must aid self-healing in humans. However, they noted that sheep who knew they were getting QBE treatment still had higher levels of depression and dejection after treatment compared to placebo sheep. In other words, the reduced depression/dejection effect could not be entirely attributable to wishful thinking on the part of placebo sheep deluding themselves.

Of course, it probably goes without saying that a favourable healing outcome is most likely when healing is *sought or desired* by the recipient (Berghmans, 2022), and there is mounting evidence that skeptics resist offers of that sort—in fact, skeptics are quite "reactant" when faced with such opportunities (Storm, 2016, 2019a, 2019b; Storm, Ertel, & Rock, 2013; Storm & Rock, 2014b), especially if there is the slightest suspicion the effect might be anomalous. The situation is quite the opposite for believers who, like De Rudder, make a concerted effort to initiate healing, and it is not only psychological change that can be effected through sheer mental effort, as work in hypnosis research has shown. For example, children and adults have been cured of warts in a matter of months when ordinarily it can take years for warts to disappear naturally, if at all (for numerous studies, see Lankton, 2011); hypnosis and guided imagery can help control cancer pain, and there is some evidence that these techniques can affect disease progression and survival (Spiegel & Moore, 1997). Paley (2016) even describes such healing of mind, body, and spirit as "a meaningful experience of self-transformation" (p. 96).

Placebo effects and self-healing, however, are not synchronistic just because they are meaningful (and even though they can involve intention), given they are unquestionably causal and occur *within* the psychophysiological system, which is why it would be just as much a misattribution to call them psi. But it would *not* be a mistake to claim that such effects may kick-start in the imagination which, as we have seen, clearly underpins conscious (and even unconscious) intention, guided imagery, mindful willing, suggestibility, autosuggestion, and hypnosis. These cases, though they may seem anomalous, are of utmost psychological and medical interest (see Bengston with Fraser, 2010; Tausk, Elenkov, & Moynihan, 2008), and justifiably so, but we have to be wary of parapsychological claims that centre on a supposed acausal disconnect between 'idea' and 'physiological response' (for example, see Kelly & Tucker, 2015).

I close this subsection with a few more cases where charges of misattribution may again be warranted. In June 1968, it was officially reported that a disturbed individual Sirhan Bishara Sirhan, a 24-year-old Palestinian, assassinated presidential candidate Robert F. Kennedy. In the previous month of May, Vaughan (1979) had a precognitive dream in which he reported that the assassin would be an American Indian—though Vaughan regarded the ethnicity as symbolic and even thought he may be an "Indian from India" (p. 107). Although Sirhan also has a dark complexion, Vaughan was diplomatic enough to say that an Indian was "involved", which is not exactly how the *National Enquirer* reported it in 1974:

> Vaughan now says his dreams tell him an Indian—not Sirhan Sirhan—fired the fatal shots.
>
> (as cited in Vaughan, 1979, p. 107)

To this day, Sirhan does not recall any of the events of that fateful day, even under hypnosis. Interestingly, a counsellor and hypnotherapist named Bill Cross (later of the Psychic Integration Institute, of which Vaughan was a member, and thus came to know Cross) was one of those who hypnotized the alleged assassin. Working at the San Quentin prison where Sirhan was held, Cross hypnotized Sirhan, whereupon it was revealed that he had been hypnotized in the past by an "East Indian" (Vaughan's Indian?), but Sirhan could not recall the name of the hypnotist, nor the reasons for the hypnotism. Vaughan makes reference to the possibility that Sirhan was a 'Manchurian candidate' (a person hypnotized to carry out the assassination plan of an organization), and that was also Cross's opinion in 1976.

The niggling doubt with this account is that Vaughan seems to identify a 'culpable' person, but we do not learn whether that person is the assassin, or merely a co-conspirator. We are left to speculate, and begin to see that there is no societal advantage in having a psychic experience where only vague and ambiguous information is its product, and that is probably one reason why "the authorities have not yet acted on this information about the East Indian" (Vaughan, 1979, p. 107). Indeed, four decades later, nothing was settled despite much controversy surrounding Sirhan's guilt, and the claims made for and against him (Jackman, 2018; Kujawsky, 2008; Martinez & Johnson, 2012). We can blame psi (its dimness, its weakness) for failing to play a stronger role, but how do we know it was not meant to fulfil its function under a different guise—namely, as synchronicity? Perhaps psi, but only by another name, serves a purpose other than sleuthing and hit-making; especially at an individual level. Let us call it synchronicity. There is no doubt that a dream *could* contain elements of concern to the community, but a weighing up of dream content should first include an assessment of meaningfulness at a *personal* level, just as Vaughan meant when he said: "The ultimate meaning of synchronicity is that we have responsibility for our lives—that we create our own realities" (p. 224). Such a responsibility might scream for attention when it is the only course of action on offer. As it happened, Vaughan does not arrive at a personal solution, and the reason for that seems to be based on his fixation with his experience being public and psychic rather than private and synchronistic.

Then we come to telephone telepathy (e.g., Sheldrake, 2014). IBNS may explain this phenomenon. Parapsychologist Christine Hardy (2011) is an example of someone who extended her consciousness and merged with other people engaged in similar practices (see *On Model Building* in Storm, 2025). Valencia and Froese (2020) have reviewed studies where neural synchronization has been demonstrated under controlled conditions. They note that synchronization occurs "across brains during meaningful social interaction … [and is] associated with subjective reports of social connectedness, engagement, and cooperativeness, as well as experiences of social cohesion and 'self-other merging' " (p. 1). I do not regard the work on telepathy-like activity by

Standish et al. (2003), and Richards et al. (2005), as being much different in principle—the same parameters are present. In their first study (Standish et al., 2003), we see two individuals (a male and a female) well known to each other, isolated from each other, engaged in a single task passively observing checkerboards; the only difference is the black-and-white checks flickered for one (the sender), but were static for the other (the receiver). Prior to the tests proper, both engaged in shared activities (e.g., meditation) in order to encourage a 'connectedness', after which they were isolated. The fMRI scans of the female receiver's visual cortex showed significantly increased brain activity "when the male was visually stimulated with the flashing checkerboard pattern" (Williams, 2015, p. 50). Findings were also significant in a study by Richards et al. (2005) which used a different male/female pair. Synchronization may not only be triggered in two isolated people when engaged in viewing patterned stimuli, but also when they are isolated and sharing (*or are about to share*) a phone call. Thus, meaningful social interactions can bring about synchronization that is essentially telepathy-like.

Of course, we do not yet know the spatiotemporal limits of IBNS, so further experimentation is necessary. For example, anticipation (feeling in advance of knowing) seems to only go so far, and may only work in real time: Sheldrake (2014) failed to find a significant effect for "telephone precognition"—his test subjects could not significantly predict who a phone-caller was *prior* to their being selected to make the call. The average hit rate for phone calls was a non-significant 33.2% (where MCE = 33.3%). Note, however, that for telephone telepathy (i.e., in real time), Sheldrake reported highly significant average hit-rates of 40% to 45% (MCE = 25%), and an even higher average hit rate of 81% for overseas callers ("up to 12,500 miles away"; p. 8). In this design, the test subject ("callee") must "guess who the caller is before the caller says anything" (p. 8). The crux here is that the callee knows the three callers—they "share emotional or social bonds" (p. 8)—and produce hit-rates above 50%, but with strangers, the hit-rate is at chance. In a replication study by Wahbeh et al. (2024),[9] telephone telepathy was also significantly demonstrated (50%; MCE = 33.3%), but telephone precognition produced chance results (32%).

For Sheldrake (2014), the communication anomaly was explained as "telepathy rather than precognition" (p. 7), thus putting some theories at risk that explain psi as a precognitive effect (see "Multiphasic Model of Precognition" in Storm, 2025). However, from the perspective of IBNS, the failure of the 'subject' (percipient/callee) to precognize is understandable because the caller is not pre-selected (random selection being made later in keeping with the protocols of precognition testing), so neither the caller-to-be, nor the callee, could be in a mental state of preparedness that would facilitate neural synchronization—by the time the caller was selected, it would be too late to establish neural synchronization between caller and callee because the callee had already made his/her best guess as to whom the caller might be. But note the difference in the telepathic condition: The pre-selected caller is asked "to please send their positive intention and focused attention to that person [the callee]" (Wahbeh et al., 2024, p. 241). Telephone-precognition cannot offer that advantage.

The more important issue, however, is that in psi research, effect sizes are all roughly the same in strength for telepathy, clairvoyance, and precognition. Under the principle of synchronicity, that is because these three psi modalities are one and the same effect cloaked methodologically under different guises. But Sheldrake's test findings on telephone-precognition, and those of Wahbeh et al. (2024), when contrasted with the highly significant test findings for telephone-telepathy, suggest a disparity. The difference surely lies in the fact that the future targets here are living beings, whereas the more general precognition literature shows that targets are always non-living objects or images, depicting (or depicted in) either static (e.g., photographic) or dynamic (e.g., filmic) scenarios that can easily fit into archetypal categories—people, however, are not archetypes. That difference is paramount.

Note too that the Rhinean model cannot explain this disparity; but IBNS can. As I have argued earlier, certain future possibilities, visualized as images with great effort and focus by participants in real time (as in free response trials), can manifest archetypally; the corresponding (target) image, presented at any time or place, tends to stand out against the decoys provided the archetype has constellated. These images are brought forth via certain practices (prior meditation experience) or conditions (e.g., induced relaxation, ASCs) that stimulate the deep imagination linked to the collective unconscious and therefore the archetypes. On the one hand, those successful (so-called) predictions or readings of the 'future' *per se* are actually 'identified' as such on the strength of their archetypal content—they follow an engrained pattern to the end like a ball about to roll off a table; one can know the outcome even to the extent that one can intervene and prevent (or take advantage of) an anticipated future. On the other hand, a person's (a caller's) future action is not necessarily readable as an archetype. If the above findings persist, and they are not Type II errors in the telephone-precognition case, then we may be inclined to assume that there are thus clear parallels between IBNS and synchronicity: First, the effects defy conventional causal explanations; second, the effects depend on real-time connection (synchronization) with living beings; third, the experience is mutually meaningful; and fourth, *affectivity* (emotional/social bond) is a critical variable.

Finally, we have twin telepathy; a topic touched upon in Chapter 1. Some cases of twin-telepathy (particularly with monozygotic twins) are actually pseudo-telepathic and better explained genetically as similarity of thought (a.k.a. 'thought concordance'),[10] whereas genuine telepathy, according to Playfair (2002), may be a kind of 'entanglement' or 'bonding'—also referred to as "biological entanglement" (Dossey, 2016, p. 321). Later, Playfair (2017) used the term 'macro-entanglement' and described twins "as a single macro-entangled system" (p. 7). But are twins forever entangled from birth? We need clarification on whether macro-entanglement is a 'stand-by' condition—an ongoing state idling in the background of the twins' ordinary lives—or an all-or-nothing condition induced by crisis, but otherwise non-existent. From a genetic point of view, macro-entanglement between monozygotic twins could actually be a kind of archetypal process that replicates (mirrors) an event in one twin once the other has inadvertently acted as the initiator. Either way, macro-entanglement may be conducive of IBNS.

The case for a genetic component underpinning pseudo-psychic and psychic processes is a strong one: Monozygotic (identical) twins split from the same fertilized egg, so they would have been one person before the split, but are fated to become two persons with many shared characteristics after the split. It is as if physically separated identical twins live their lives still conjoined, even without ever having met, but since so many of their cognitions and behaviours are alike (even sleep patterns, dreaming, EEG, etc.), it is easy to fall into the trap of labelling these matches (shared thoughts and deeds, etc.) as being 'telepathic', as if one twin can influence the other psychically. Examples include twins drawing the same picture when asked separately to draw anything they like, choosing the same gifts for each other, knowing when the other is about to telephone, contracting the same congenital disease at the same time without one knowing the other has it, and even dying at the same time. Playfair (2002, 2017) has listed these, and agrees that we are not talking telepathy in such instances (although he has contradicted himself by labelling some of these as "telepathy which operates only at the unconscious level"; 2002, p. 151). But he also argues that the anomalies (matching behaviours) that are *not* explained genetically should be deemed telepathic because they are unpredictable (Playfair gives many examples of one twin emotionally and/or physiologically reacting to the grim fate of the other, unexplainably, unknowingly, and unpredictably). This line of reasoning was made much earlier when Gurney, Myers, and Podmore (1886, as cited in Playfair, 2002) stated that twin coincidences are either "predictable" (genetic) or "unpredictable" (p. 25), the latter provisionally indicating psi.

Taking his cue from quantum physics, Playfair (2002) further suggests these 'coincidences' arise from identical twins being a "correlated or 'entangled' system ever since they split apart" (p. 149), to the degree that twins perform better than non-identicals (even siblings) in psi tasks. He puts up a good case for biological/organic entanglement, his argument supported by ideas and findings from studies by Grinberg-Zylberbaum (1997), and he endorses Zohar's (1990) extrapolation of quantum entanglement to the human sphere (especially identicals). The problems are, first, that we do not know if entanglement at the micro scale of electrons and photons applies at the macro scale for people (see Chapter 5 in Storm, 2025), and second, entanglement in QM refers to instantaneous effects, whereas we do not know if these telepathic effects are instantaneous or are limited by the rules of Einsteinian relativity, which disputes instantaneous information transmission. By convention, the assumption is that psi is not bound by distance or time (it is nonlocal). This finding leads some parapsychologists to the conclusion that psi functions independently of spacetime (i.e., psi is not a classical effect, or a relative effect, but resembles some kind of quantum effect—see Dossey, 2013; Radin, 2006; Schwartz, 2018).

However, since synchronicity involves the constellation of archetypes, we might expect archetypal patterns would more often constellate in entangled systems compared to non-entangled systems, and we might then expect more 'transgressivity' in the former, which would explain the higher rates in identicals of experiences that go beyond the usual understanding of telepathy *per se*, even bringing in the psychoid factor, and showing how fine the line is between ESP and PK. As Playfair (2002) has noted: "Twins have reacted, often quite dramatically [i.e., physically], when the other one is falling downstairs, breaking a leg or a nose, having a painful injection several miles away, … burning a hand, suffocating, giving birth, … or being shot dead" (pp. 148–149).

Archetypes, however, are unpredictable, which may explain why identicals do not always demonstrate these paranormal linkages or biological entanglement (i.e., psi or meaningful coincidence)—in some instances, they even perform *worse* than non-identicals and non-twin siblings (Blackmore & Chamberlain, 1993; Charlesworth, 1975), and even psychics (Bohm, 1984, as cited in Playfair, 2002, p. 106). Generally though, three studies reviewed by Playfair (2017) have shown that dizygotic twins experience only half as many psychic experiences (including shared dreams) as monozygotic twins (p. 5). Nevertheless, exceptions need explaining, and we know there are other psi-conducive factors that could have more marked effects than biological entanglement. Perhaps entanglement is not even entirely necessary, for Charlesworth also found that his best-performing cohort of "fraternal twins were significantly more extraverted than the identical twins" who did not perform as well (p. 88). He argued (as does Playfair) that extraversion—being a positive, confident attitude towards the 'object' (as Jung calls it)—may have an important influence on the results (see also Honorton et al., 1998).

As for psychics, their generally superior psi performances compared to identicals might be expected, but we cannot say if they have an entangled system more extensive or more far-reaching than identicals, or whether other factors are at play. It may be that psychics produce more 'hits' because they have wider access to archetypal situations, which might be a substantive factor of biological entanglement in the human sphere. Perhaps biological entanglement is malleable and/or can be induced (say, through mutual meditation, or mental focus of both psychic and sitter), permitting the psychic to tune-in and tune-out, presumably at will. But unless psychics have good control over this capability, we might expect their lives to be more critically challenged than identicals due to their broad-ranging sensitivity.

Still on other factors, there is evidence that non-genetically related pairs with strong emotional bonds (e.g., married couples) tend to perform better on psi tasks than control pairs of complete strangers with no emotional bonds (Gurney et al., 1886; Sheldrake & Smart, 2003a, 2003b). But two real-time ESP studies found that siblings performed the best, followed by parent-child, strangers, married couples, and friends, in that order (Alexander & Broughton, 2001; Broughton & Alexander, 1997). In terms of reported psi experiences (real-time and precognitive), incidence is highest between people who are biologically related, especially if the experiences concern death or crisis (Roll et al., 2021), so we cannot yet say that emotion trumps biological entanglement. Roll et al. note that there could be a "reporting artifact" as family members are more in touch with each other, and more often confirm their psi experiences (p. 81). Anyway, the point here is that psi (and therefore synchronicity) can be encouraged for a variety of reasons, and we see that biological entanglement is not an entirely necessary condition for telepathy (and psi in general), even if it does seem to give an advantage. For example, Parker (2010) tested 14 pairs of identicals in the ganzfeld condition, and their hit-rate was 36% (where MCE = 25%), whereas the meta-analyses so far show a consistent albeit slightly lower 31% for random pairs (Storm & Tressoldi, 2020). But it does seem that biological entanglement brings with it some extremely undesirable (PK) side-effects, as listed above and below.

While identical twins are under-researched in parapsychology, it may be fair to say that the genetic factor (including thought concordance) seems to be part and parcel of a single biological entanglement system that accounts for pseudo-telepathy and telepathy *per se*, with both factors unique to a subset (arguably "30 percent") of identicals (Playfair, 2017, p. 7). So saying, it is easy to misattribute and assume genetics underpins psi/synchronicity, but we see it is not entirely necessary, and is even a liability. But another problem concerns *unconscious telepathy*, which I raised above. Playfair (2002) is conspicuously silent on its implications. Some staunch parapsychologists might prefer that the standard (conservative) definition of telepathy should not change, and may consider instances like the following to be better relegated to the annals of unexplainable coincidence: In 1987, Romanian twin Romulus Cozma strangled his partner Monica in a park at around the same time his drunken twin brother Remus first strangled and then stabbed his argumentative partner (also called Monica), though neither knew of the other's actions (Playfair, pp. 79–80). Did the image of Remus's actions appear in Romulus's mind, and if so, why did Romulus act on it? Would that make it unconscious telepathy, or is a genetic component at play? Surely the Cozmas inherited the same psychopathic tendency given the entanglement, which in itself may have set the ball in motion for the double murder. Indeed, at the police station, Romulus said he felt "impelled", and "couldn't resist", and perhaps "didn't want to" (p. 80).

Playfair (2002) gives numerous examples of other dark effects, including shared pain, double limb breakages, and double deaths, each involving great distance, but with each tied to a primary event, and Playfair does seem to think they all indicate telepathy. In the case of the Cozmas, he even implies the first event *initiated* the second:

> It may sound improbable to suggest that Romulus picked up his brother's sudden fit of murderous rage and acted on it automatically without knowing why, yet in the absence of any known motive on his part this seems the most likely explanation.
>
> (p. 80)

While this dramatic subset of effects have its *source* in biological entanglement, we must note that telepathy by definition is not about planting ideas or images *as spurs for action*, and it has certainly never been hailed as a form of mind control, but is simply "paranormal acquisition of information concerning the thoughts, feelings or activity of another conscious being" (Thalbourne, 2003, p. 125).

Nevertheless, the sharing of unfortunate (even horrifying) twists of fate may say something about how minds can work when they are strongly entangled or 'melded', which gives ample reason to encourage individuality, and to discourage sameness. Indeed Charlesworth (1975) thought that his identicals performed poorly on the psi task because there was a strong demand on them (from their mothers) to individuate, and on that account, many twins probably cut off their psychic (synchronizing or synchronistic) links with each other, and arguably with good reason. This possibility may solve Playfair's (2017) question as to why only 30% of twins demonstrate telepathy or "experiences suggestive of it" (p. 7).[11] Similarly, the natural bid for healthy independence in relationships might explain why strangers, on occasion, can even do better on ESP tasks than married couples and friends (Alexander & Broughton, 2001; Broughton & Alexander, 1997).

To close, it is argued that categorizing some anomalies as 'psi' or 'synchronicity' may not be warranted. Cases in point include psychophysiological responses, the extraordinary products of dissociation and mimicry, and the psychosomatic character of the placebo effect. And there appears to be no evidence (or possibility) for telephone-precognition in contrast with telephone-telepathy, suggesting the latter is a process linked to IBNS. But there are other kinds of misattribution—some ostensible psi effects (e.g., Vaughan's JFK assassination dream) seem purposeless until they are treated as synchronicity; and some instances of twin telepathy (e.g., thought concordance) have only the patina of psi and synchronicity. We do however need to consider IBNS, archetypal processes, and biological entanglement, as possible explanations for at least some of the mind-melding effects described by Playfair (2002).

The Limits of Synchronicity in Space and Time

Are we sufficiently advanced in our understanding of synchronicity to make claims about how far in space and time it may extend? The synchronicity enthusiast might answer in the affirmative because synchronicity—a re-envisioned psychophysical parallelism—extends the mind/body *harmony* to a mind/matter *matrix* governed by archetypal principles that, in a sense, binds psyche (mind) and world (universe), suggesting spacetime is not relevant to synchronicity *in a theoretical or practical sense*, and therefore does not inhibit or prohibit the effect, but nor does that mean synchronicity somehow overrides or distorts spacetime. Synchronicity is contingent upon the constellation of archetypes which have universal extension; they are ubiquitous, and they manifest in real time but with invariable outcomes. In other words, *spatiotemporal transcendence* could be described as an 'as if' aspect of synchronicity whereby, in practical terms, physical/literal assumptions are drawn from metaphysical/archetypal factors. Interestingly, Rhinean parapsychologists go much further by claiming their experimentally demonstrated effects *do* indicate *spatiotemporal transcendence* (i.e., there are no spacetime limits to psi). In this section, I will review some spatiotemporal claims made of psi, and I will show that tests on the limits of psi can be seen as tests on the limits of synchronicity, but the latter allows us to adopt a completely different and broader viewpoint on psi effects.

The Planets–Metals Paradox

As we will see in subsections to follow, there is very little in the literature that tests psychic functioning beyond Earth-bound distances. When such tests were run, remote viewing (RV) seemed to be the method of choice for the obvious reason that it is a form of clairvoyance,[12] and therefore does not require a sender or agent be placed at an as-yet inaccessible distance. However, we do have a cosmological example with a strong mystical or metaphysical overtone that suggests synchronicity (meaningful coincidence) rather than psi had been effected at distances spanning the solar system, and as far away as Saturn. As Greek chemist Yannis Almirantis (2005) explains the effect, we begin to understand that an archetypal matrix potentially has vast extension. In this regard, Vaughan's (1979) 'cosmic order', and his suggestion that we are at one in that matrix, may be a preferred viewpoint to the ideology behind the psi construct that speaks to the interaction of inner (mind) and outer (world) via an information channel that supposedly bridges the inherent mind/matter gap *and* overcomes astronomical distances, *but* does not factor the cosmic order into any of its modelling.

This hypothesized matrix is well illustrated in the so-called astronomical problem known as the *planets-metals paradox* (Almirantis, 2005). The problem and solution starts with the order of the so-called 'planets' (the ancients included the Sun and the Moon as 'planets' ['wanderers'] since both move across the sky). Dating back to the Hellenistic period (323 B.C.E. until 31 B. C.E.), but no earlier than 300 B.C.E. for this specific issue, the days of the week (still in current use) became associated with the planets:

- Sun—Sunday;
- Moon—Monday;
- Mars—Tuesday;
- Mercury—Wednesday;
- Jupiter—Thursday;
- Venus—Friday;
- Saturn—Saturday.

These names are based on the deities of the given culture. In Teutonic-speaking languages, Teutonic deities were preferred, so the original Latin names for four days of the week (*dies Martis, dies Mercurii, dies Jovis*, and *dies Veneris*) were substituted for their Teutonic equivalents, Tuesday (after Tiu), Wednesday (after Woden), Thursday (after Thor), and Friday (after Frida), respectively.

The planets are then arranged in a circle in their 'traditional geocentric order', from closest to farthest, as derived in Hellenistic times: Moon, Mercury, Venus, Sun, Mars, Jupiter, and Saturn. This sequence is correct even in terms of the contemporary heliocentric system. While Venus does come closer to Earth than Mercury, Mercury is *on average* closest to Earth than Venus (Stockman, Monroe, & Cordner, 2019). Almirantis (2005) points out that "Almost every one of the possible planetary arrangements … had been proposed by someone" (p. 33), yet this order (called the "preponderant arrangement") became final. Using a circle to illustrate the arrangement, and starting with the closest body to Earth (i.e., the Moon), we work clockwise around that circle, so next is Mercury, then Venus, and so on, in terms of ever-increasing distances from Earth. Note, however, the days are only read off in proper order when we follow the star-shaped pattern shown in Figure 5.1. As will become evident, my main focus is on symmetries, and the improbability of these symmetries being established by chance alone. Indeed, symmetry has meaning of its own, and is objectively verifiable when a specific geometrical rule applies. Almirantis (2005) explains the symmetry in Figure 5.1 as being based on beliefs held during the Hellenistic era. I include this figure here to show that this symmetry existed in the mindset of people at that time.

The patterns that emerge get even more interesting: Without changing the order of the planets in Figure 5.1, a new symmetry emerges as illustrated in Figure 5.2, its non-randomness quite evident as an arrangement in the form of a star-shaped heptagon. Only in modern times do we see that ranking each planet against its traditional corresponding metal, and then assigning atomic numbers, gives us this star-shaped heptagon—we start with Mars (its metal, iron, has the lowest atomic number of 26), and then we follow a straight line down to Venus (its metal, copper), and from Venus we move right up to the Moon (its metal, silver), and so on, until we finish with Saturn (its metal, Lead, has the highest atomic number of 82).

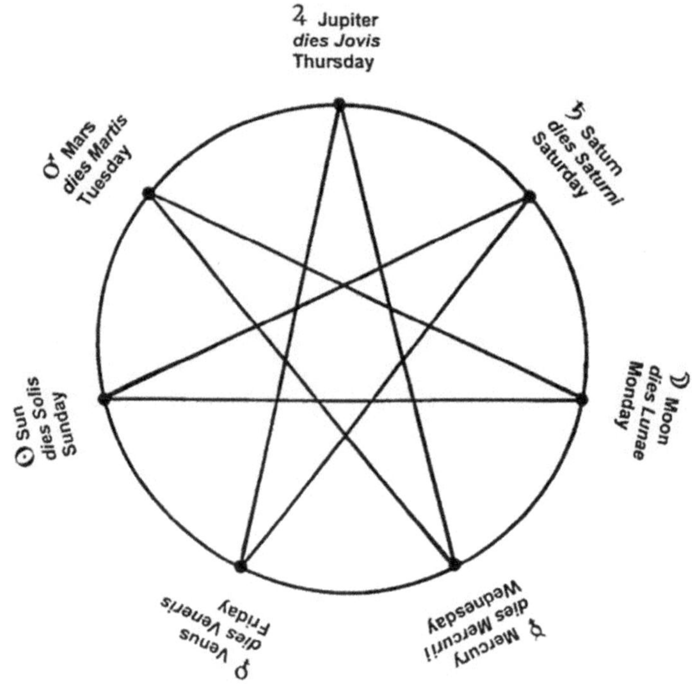

Figure 5.1 The succession of day-names in the planetary week, as derived by the geocentric arrangements of the planets. (*Source*: © 2005, Y. Almirantis; used with permission)

In this preponderant arrangement we see the ancient *affinities* and *correspondences* of the seven 'planets' with their metals (e.g., Mars ↔ iron), as listed here:

- Mars ↔ iron (Fe, atomic number 26);
- Venus ↔ copper (Cu, 29);
- Moon ↔ silver (Ag, 47);
- Jupiter ↔ tin (Sn, 50);
- Sun ↔ gold (Au, 79);
- Mercury ↔ mercury (Hg, 80);
- Saturn ↔ lead (Pb, 82).

This arrangement is "most venerable and long lasting" (Almirantis, 2005, p. 35) and is in fact the only surviving one, and was first mentioned in a sixth-century manuscript. The metals are listed by their atomic numbers in ascending order, though these numbers were unknown to the ancients. The so-called "dogma of the seven metals" (p. 36) prevailed until the 16th century, even though the ancients knew of other metals such as zinc, cobalt, and bismuth. Yet the components that constitute the planets-metals pattern

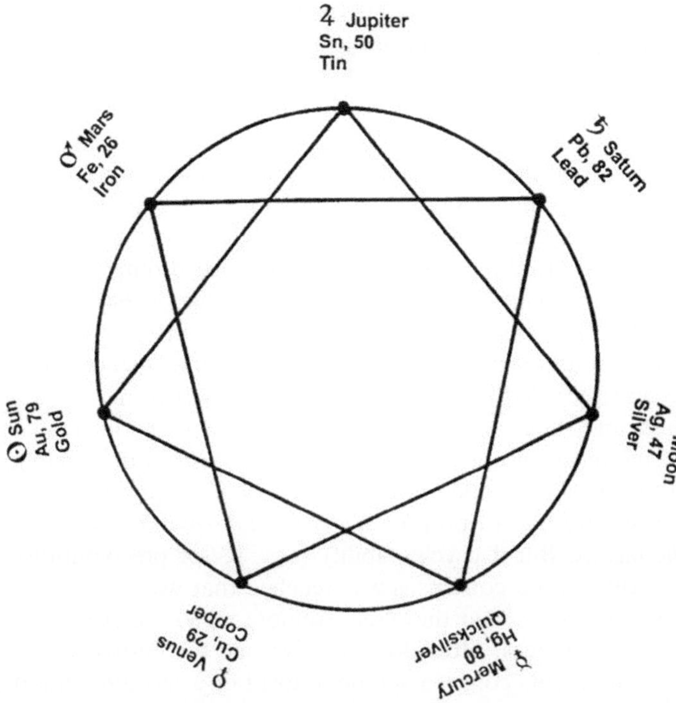

Figure 5.2 "The paradox of planetary metals". The combination of the geocentric arrangement of the planets with the atomic numbers of the planetary metals leads to the formation of this star-shaped heptagon. (*Source*: © 2005, Y. Almirantis; used with permission.)

depicted in Figure 5.2 are ancient—the planetary arrangement *and* the planets-metals correspondences date from the 2nd and 6th century B.C., respectively. And the more sophisticated knowledge about the elements that makes the high-symmetry polygon possible came much later—atomic number was introduced in the early 18th century, and atomic weight was introduced in 1913.

Statistically, the number of other possible configurations, or sequences of any two vertices chosen at random (as in Figure 5.1) are in the hundreds, so to arrive at the final pattern by chance is very unlikely (< 1%)—that is, 120:1 (or to be precise, p =.0083). Almirantis (2005) calls this "probability of obtaining the planetary-metals paradox, the correct quantification for the 'strangeness' of the phenomenon under consideration" (p. 39). He also points out that there are only two other patterns (one star-shaped, and the other a regular heptagon) that are "highly symmetrical" (p. 39), but the key issue here is that the nature philosophers (alchemists) did not care for them. Nor did they care to replace any of the preferred metals with other metals known at the time.

Almirantis (2005) notes that the physical and chemical properties of metals known in antiquity (density, hardness, facility to be oxidized, brightness) could not have served as methods for arranging the metals in the order given above. If this worldview had depended on those properties, the order would be different (effectively random with no symmetry). And in the modern era, relative distances of the planets (following the heliocentric model) cannot produce the same arrangement. This example impresses upon us the notion of a paradox because much of the key information was inaccessible to the ancients yet they arrived at a meaningful result. According to Almirantis the "concept of synchronicity is a possible working hypothesis" (p. 31): "Only nowadays, with a knowledge of atomic quantities, is the paradox evident. It is either meaningful and synchronistic, or it is sheer coincidence" (p. 41).

We have already ruled out "sheer [mere or casual] coincidence" on statistical grounds, and Almirantis (2005) does not regard the arrangement as an artifact or "the result of ancient knowledge of unknown provenance" (p. 31). But it might be worth considering the possibility of "unknown provenance" if, for example, we are free to propose *a psychic information channel to the planets and the metals*. But if psychic ability (e.g., RV or precognition) was used by some ancients, and a consensus was reached that way, there are too many unanswerable questions: Did they 'see' (remote view) the planets to discover their geocentric distances? How does psi give one the desired measurements? Do these measurements come in symbolic form or a more quantitative form? Did they even need actual measurements? Did they 'discover' the atomic numbers of the associated metals up to and including lead, and did those numbers even make sense? Could they see into the atom in order to comprehend what an atomic number might mean? To pre-empt all that, how did they decide which metal (and why metals?) should go with which planet, and which weekday should go with which deity? And on it goes.

It is all very fine to suggest psi can give the information that is needed, in accordance with the appropriate intentions, but that information must resonate and make certain sense to the ancients—in that regard, a conventional psychic explanation of the planets-metals paradox fails here, whereas an "already existing, correct, but unconscious image" (Jung, 1952/1969, para. 857) would not seem out of place, and would have a certain familiarity about it. This 'image' would be multifaceted and have archetypal proportions, suggesting or even indicating synchronicity, which is not to undermine the possibility that psi could give the desired information. However, a psychic process lacks parsimony compared to synchronicity. More than that, the ancients would have no need of psi in this instance. First, they only needed to work with what they already knew using methods they had to hand, and in this instance, they did not need any kind of psi modality scanning for cosmic and local information because normal observation and past discoveries suffice in explaining the *overt* knowledge. Then second, a less overt ('occult') process would follow that can only be described as synchronistic that brings to consciousness the 'image' with its cosmic configurations—

the distances, the associations with the metals—that would no doubt blend with the relevant mythological motifs. These *a priori* configurations on such a cosmic scale cannot be invented, nor could the schema have been a contrivance, or even serendipitous given its complexity, just as it is unlikely the ancients capitalized on chance as Eisenbud might have it.

In the planets-metals paradox, we may be witness to an ordering system triggered by cosmic (archetypal) events established in our evolutionary past. Synchronistically, we can see a mix and refinement of pre-existing observations and irruptions of contents from a deep level of mind that fit certain archetypal parameters—these may well be encoded in the core of our being. When the right match or correspondence (or a series of them) emerges, those breakthroughs even come with a feeling of confidence in the outcome that shores up the cosmos for the ancient mind, even before all the facts are in. A meaningful interconnection (synchronicity) between causally unrelated events seems evident here, suggesting we are attuned to such interconnections via the archetypes.

Remote Viewing

Returning to remote viewing (RV), and considering just the practical work that actually tests the physical range (distance) of workable paranormal effects in real (not metaphysical) terms, we can reasonably start with pioneering remote-viewing experimenter Russell Targ, who is of the opinion "that the accuracy and reliability of remote viewing is independent of distance up to 10,000 km" (Targ, 2019, p. 569). We can extend the compass of the effect much further than that for it is claimed that RV was used to glean information about the gas giant Jupiter, its appearance, its atmosphere, and possibly its faint ring structure. Jupiter is a mere 45 light minutes from our sun, but that translates as a staggering 750 million kilometres from the sun (622 million kilometres from Earth). RVer Ingo Swann 'saw' the planet Jupiter for about 3½ minutes in April 1973, after which time much of his report was validated by evidence from the Pioneer 10 space probe later that year (November/December), Pioneer 11 in 1974, Voyager I in 1979, and Juno in 2016.

It must be said, however, that Swann (1995) was rather coy about the implications of the exercise, stating that his "Jupiter Probe was only an exploratory experiment, and not meant as a 'claim' of anything". His reserve shows in statements such as the following where he describes possible rings around Jupiter:

> Very high in the atmosphere there are crystals … they glitter. Maybe the stripes are like bands of crystals, maybe like rings of Saturn, though not far out like that. Very close within the atmosphere.

At first, Swann refers to 'stripes' and 'bands': "There's a planet with stripes.… I hope it's Jupiter". By "stripes", Swann appears to mean the horizontal bands of mainly earth-toned (red-orange) coloured gases that give Jupiter its stripy appearance; these are the low-altitude gas clouds that shroud the planet. He does not appear to be referring to "rings" like those of Saturn which are "far out", but he *is* saying they are "within the atmosphere". However, Swann then refers to his sketch that does indicate rings in the Saturnian sense of being well clear of the planet's atmosphere (see Figure 5.3). As always, ambiguity begs clarification, for it could be said that Swann merely covers all his bases with as much information as he can muster so that he may be right some of the time.

Six years later, *Time* magazine reported "a thin, flat ring around the great planet" (March 19, 1979, p. 86, as cited in Swann, 1995), and NASA reported that "Jupiter's rings … are composed of small, dark particles … formed from dust kicked up as interplanetary meteoroids smash into the giant planet's small innermost moons" (NASA, 2019). This "dust" might be comparable to the "crystals" (the term Swann uses), but Swann only gave a brief outline about a single ring: "Jupiter has mainly one fat ring. And you will see it when

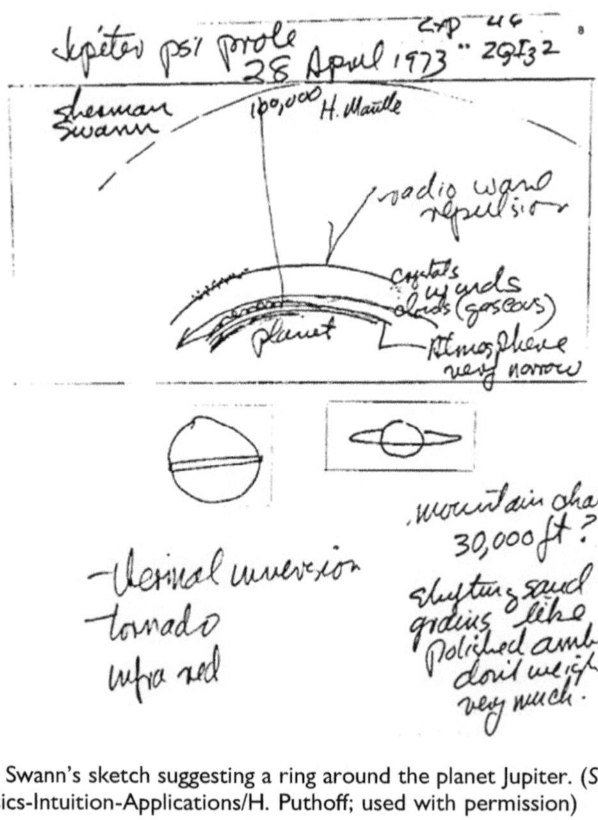

Figure 5.3 Ingo Swann's sketch suggesting a ring around the planet Jupiter. (*Source*: © 2003, Physics-Intuition-Applications/H. Puthoff; used with permission)

you get there" (Targ, 2019, p. 577). There are, however, other rings he either did not see, or he simply did not bother to report, for we now know that Jupiter has a set of four rings: "the halo ring, the main ring, the Amalthea gossamer ring, and the Thebe gossamer ring" (Cain, 2009).

It is possible to spot other hits and misses in Swann's (1995) report. For example, in 2016, the Juno mission found that Jupiter has an "enormous, fuzzy core that might be partially dissolved" (Weitering, 2018), whereas Swann said it had a "solid core". However, Swann proved some astronomers wrong in saying the core was "tens of masses the size of Earth's own mass." Astronomers had once thought Jupiter would either have "a very small and dense core, or perhaps no core at all."

It must be said that Swann (1995) is acceptably (if not convincingly) accurate overall about Jupiter's general physical appearance, its gaseous surface, its hydrogen "mantle" and atmospheric phenomena (e.g., water and ice crystals, storms, high-velocity winds, etc.), as well as Jupiter's magnetic/electromagnetic radiation and gravitational phenomena, although some of this information was known prior to 1973 from telescopic and radiotelescopic research (see Elkins-Tanton, 2006). And Swann admitted to Targ (2019) that "he had been looking at the solar system his entire life" (p. 577). To my way of thinking, and given the claim made in the previous subsection that describes a very different process from conventional psi modelling, this admission speaks volumes—Swann's rich mental storehouse of facts and ideas is ripe for synchronistic exploitation. And let us not forget, normal human intuition and creativity puts pieces together as in a jigsaw puzzle, thus giving a whole that is more than the sum of its parts.

We must be willing to accept that anything ostensibly *psychic* implies the mental construction of parallels (correspondences), and that gives rise to the idea that *information sources* may be anomalous: Thus, either literal information perception via nonlocal consciousness explains the result, or it comes down to previous learning combined with *a priori* 'knowing' based on archetypal prompting. In regard to our solar system, which is comprised of impersonal and universal factors, Jacobi (1973) notes: "the cosmos itself is built on a few simple principles" (p. 45), so the archetypal content will be simple but may possibly be blurred, thus explaining both the *sharpness* as well as the *fuzziness* of detail in Swann's (1995) depiction. This is why I propose such a pivotal role for the deep imagination in paranormal functioning, but in this instance of Swann's Jupiter RV, I suggest synchronicity describes the effects more appropriately. Swann seemed not entirely confident in his RV; perhaps he suspected he had engaged in an exercise whereby his imagination played a major part—all he had to do, frankly and honestly, was tell all he knew and all he could surmise.

Still on the subject of distance, in 1971, Edgar Mitchell (1930–2016), NASA astronaut and founder of the Institute of Noetic Sciences, gives us a different framework to ponder in his controlled ESP study conducted onboard his Apollo 14 return flight from the moon. Although "unofficial" (Mitchell, 1971, p. 89),[13] the study was loosely based on a standard forced-choice design using Zener card symbols (actually, instead of physical cards, and only out of convenience, Mitchell used self-generated random number tables as a source for digits to which he assigned the five symbols). He set up a team of four perceivers back on Earth, while he assumed the role of sender/agent in outer space. Psi testing was conducted over a six-day period (February 1, 2, 3, 4, 7, & 8), though only four days of actual testing ('sending') eventuated. Extravehicular activities on the lunar surface were conducted on February 5 and 6, so there was no testing on those days, but Mitchell's distances from Earth at the time of the runs would still have ranged from many tens of thousands, to hundreds of thousands of kilometres.

Mitchell (1971) reported significant deviations (positive and negative) in scoring, oddly referred to as a "psi-differential response" (p. 89), in which perceivers first scored in one direction (i.e., psi-hitting), and then in another (i.e., psi-missing), all in accordance with how the data was assessed, and whose data was to be included in the count. Elsewhere, Mitchell only reports significant psi-hitting from the first of four analyses (51 hits in 200 trials, where MCE = 40 hits), and he does not mention the other three (Mystery Wire, 2021). Carroll (2009) opines that ESP was *not* demonstrated because he does not accept the "psi-differential response" as evidence, and he believes some runs were inappropriately excluded from that "First Analysis" (these runs were omitted for spurious methodological reasons; see Mitchell, pp. 96–97). It should be noted, however, that the term "psi-differential response" (Mitchell, p. 101; a.k.a. 'psi-differential effect') properly refers to significant scoring differences between *two contrasting conditions* (e.g., 'forced-choice' vs. 'free-response'; or clairvoyance vs. precognition; see Carpenter, 1977, pp. 207–208); not the scoring differences between runs in the *same* condition (run-score variance),[14] or in Mitchell's case, where the term is used rather loosely to describe different outcomes derived by different statistical treatments on *different subsets of the same (or largely the same) data.*

Another critic weighed in: Ulivi (2004) made the point that the rest period was delayed, so that the perceivers on Earth "attempted to catch Mitchell's thoughts 40 minutes before their actual 'transmission'" (p. 151). Ulivi's complaint undermines the fact that those runs were legitimately reframed as "most like tests of precognition" (Mitchell, 1971, p. 96), because "subjects' guess runs did not actually coincide with the sending time" (p. 95). Thus, it is debatable whether and when telepathy was actually tested, though Mitchell thought it possible (p 105). Mitchell also points out that "the experiment was not designed to test the effect of distance" (p. 105). His aim was to see what "psi ability" might do "in flight", but he then concludes that "neither time nor space seems to limit … the function tested here" (p. 105). So not only were time *and* space relevant in this ESP test, but also the "function" is left unexplained; in fact, Mitchell avoided the issue by claiming that a variety of

ESP "manifestations" were tested as "one basic ... psi ability" under the hypothesized "unitary psi process" (p. 105). I have dealt with this so-called unitary psi construct and psi nomenclature (see Chapter 1 in Storm, 2025) and found them to be largely conceptual frameworks with little to speak of in terms of their pragmatic worth. In truth, a less equivocal albeit nominal label for Mitchell's effects would be 'distal synchronicity' with a possible 'asynchronous' component. If we accept that the various analyses taken as a whole indicate, or at least suggest, some kind of anomalous effect, since the type of psi tested remains ambiguous, we are still free to claim that synchronicity was effected *between people* separated by greater than Earth-bound distances, but we can only speculate about 'psi ability' and the 'unitary psi process'.

Nostradamus: Past, Present, and 'Future'

As far as the time factor is concerned (e.g., how far into the future psi may extend), Mossbridge (2023) reports "lead times" (the gap between "the precognitive experience and the related future event"; p. 10) at the 'short' end of the time scale (i.e., microseconds, seconds, minutes) as in presentiment effects (a.k.a. predictive physiological anticipation; see *General Acausal Orderedness* in Chapter 2). Mossbridge also notes that lead times for precognitive RV and precognitive dreaming can extend from minutes to years. One research team reported the following:

> Spontaneously occurring precognitive dreams are most likely replays of biographical, unforeseeable, future dangers, and roughly 50% of them correlate with events occurring within a temporal window of 12 hours after waking up.
>
> (De Pablos, Sabater, & Liarte, 2011, p. 138)

Targ (2019) reported longer spans than the 12-hour average reported by De Pablos et al. (2011); times up to several days into the future were not unusual. For precognition generally (RV and dreams), Dean's (1974) earlier review reported time spans ranging from weeks to years. As examples, remote viewer Sandra Hilleard gives a time-frame of two weeks from her professional experience (S. Hilleard, personal communication, March 2, 2022), whereas Paquette (2011) allegedly dreamed of the September 11 tower strikes of 2001 some eleven years before the event. Schwartz (2022) believes lead times can be extended to decades: He even hypothesized that future events in the year 2060 were remote viewed in 2020. We must wait until 2060 to have our proof.

When considering temporal distance, we must keep in mind that the accuracy of precognition is related not just to *time*, but also to the *magnitude* of the event. Events that are urgent or stressful, and have great emotional (shock) value such as accidents and disasters, appear to be more often reported than happy events (Dean, 1974; Vaughan, 1973).

Thus, modern research and anecdotal accounts tell us 'future telling', 'future seeing', prophecy, or precognition, via dreaming or RV, can extend hours, days, years, or even decades into the future, but the older records suggest that verification sometimes has to wait until centuries have elapsed: Case in point, the prophecies of Nostradamus. My opinion is that a large number of Nostradamus's predictions, taken at face value, contribute markedly to the debate about the possibility of so-called seeing the future, *paranormally/synchronistically*, for a good number of them seem to have been confirmed on specific details; even names and dates, and specific places of historical significance (see Appendix D for examples). By induction, we may infer that Nostradamus's unconfirmed future-oriented predictions may one day be successfully interpreted. We can make of that what we will, but in the preface to the first publication of his *Prophecies* of 1555, he expressly states that his predictions extend to the year 3797A.D.

Importantly, Nostradamus is regarded as an astrologer, who also practiced other divinatory techniques, by which we may conclude he had a synchronistic sensibility. He followed astrological principles (which he called "celestial science"; Cheetham, 1976, p. 6) by drawing charts to help make many of his prognostications. However, in my evaluation of the full volume of *The Prophecies*, the percentage of predictions directly and overtly attributable to astrology, as expressly indicated by astrological references in the verses, is only 6.4% of the total count of relevant quatrains (i.e., 60 out of 939). The rest (93.6%) are arguably devised by other means, including the practices espoused in the two opening quatrains I.1 and I.2. Cheetham describes these methods as "divination" (referring to his technique; not to seeking guidance from divine or supernatural agency). As we shall see, if certain claims made about Nostradamus are true (that he borrowed from astrologers of the past), the figure of 6.4% is not necessarily inaccurate, but it could be a gross under-estimation if he refrained from inserting key astrological references in some or many quatrains for tactical reasons.

The reason I raise the astrological issue here is partly because Tarnas (2007) describes a work ethic and overview Nostradamus appears to have practiced whereby

> the insights that *archetypal astrology* [emphasis added] makes possible retrospectively into the dynamic patterns of human experience can be precise, nuanced, and consistently far more revealing than the always problematic and often inept attempts at concrete prediction of a literalistic astrology.
>
> (p. 462)

It is claimed that Nostradamus borrowed from past astrological records and checked them against past outcomes; a practice known as *comparative horoscopy* (Brind'Amour, 1993; and see Appendix D). The charge against Nostradamus, if legitimate, actually supports synchronicity theory (irrespective of what little damage it could do to Nostradamus's reputation) for this technique hones the craft and provides reliable (explicit and therefore useful) content insofar as its motifs are trans-temporal (archetypal) and can therefore refer to future times. Archetypal astrology focuses on the same archetypal ideas which are represented in the same motifs: the planets, the signs, and so on. Crucially in her analyses, Cheetham (1976, 1989) is of the opinion, which I share, that Nostradamus may have included a number of "retroactive predictions" (i.e., retrocognitions) among his prophecies. As we have seen, however, this subset of quatrains may not have been derived by an unsuspecting Nostradamus, but may have been borrowed. Given the points just made about comparative horoscopy, it makes sense to borrow since some future predictions can be made simply because they are repetitions of the past based on repeated astrological/archetypal patterns.

Insofar as astrological technique was used to divine some number of quatrains, bearing in mind that some can and do pinpoint specific dates, even these may still be re-hashed works of past masters *as well as* Nostradamus's own work. When it comes to such complex procedures, *repetition* is built into astrology—terms like *cycle, phase, retrograde, waxing*, and *waning*, suggest it—so while we accept (and expect) Nostradamus may have 'borrowed' from past astrological works, we cannot be sure to what extent. These points contribute to the claim that 'seeing' the so-called 'future' *synchronistically* is possible, though they do not suggest a mechanism of precognition as conventionally understood.

Nostradamus may also have experienced the problem of *temporal ambiguity*, which is based in the *temporal fuzziness* of synchronicity. Temporal uncertainty is to be expected in divinatory practice (and psi studies) whenever temporal fuzziness manifests because no tell-tale chronological markers or clues are available for clarification. Archetypes, as contingent factors in synchronistic experience, are temporally transcendent (chronologically independent) and therein lies their temporal ambiguity—they do not carry a time-stamp, meaning there will tend to be no identifying factors that can be used to distinguish an event's chronology as belonging in the past, present, or future. Archetypes act like physical laws that maintain ongoing and persistent effects across time. (In the next subsection, it will be seen that temporal ambiguity is evident in the RV experiences of Pat Price that resulted in temporal uncertainty.)

Nostradamus's predictions contribute to the debate about the possibility of *synchronistically* 'seeing the future'—an idea which is not new, for in the introductory remarks for October in his 1565 Almanac, Nostradamus says: "But the certainty of things past and present gives us confidence in things to come, as definite indications of events".[15] He means detailed observation and analysis of some past events reveal certain replicable (astrological/archetypal) patterns that tend to repeat (occur in much the same way) in some future events (which is the whole point of Jung's astrological studies in a nutshell), thus making prediction *only look like* precognition. The giveaway is that predictions often fail, and oftentimes we may expect to see that in huge compendiums like *The Prophecies*. Of course, at the very least we can allow for the fact that being forewarned is being forearmed and, given the nature of these prophecies *per se* (i.e., they are potentials; not absolutes), we are not bound by them. Thus, we can turn prophecy to our advantage. This point leads to another reason for failure of some quatrains—not because a specific quatrain could apply to multiple events in history (which we see is natural anyway), or the details are contradictory, but because history has taken a turn that makes the eventuality of those quatrains improbable or even impossible.

It also bears noting that the greater prevalence of failure (compared to success) is expected as an inherent problem in meaningful coincidence formation, either because no archetype has been constellated (even forcing some psychics to 'wing it' and produce Barnum statements), or an inappropriate archetype has been constellated (and there can be good reason for that), which therefore does not align with the archetypal content of the target—hence, little to no correspondence. But even when an appropriate archetype has been constellated, the interpretation may be wrong. This situation very much depends on the psychic or participant and very little can be done to put it right. Consider Alan Vaughan's failed prediction of a New York City smogbank on Thanksgiving Day 1967, which he then decided was a "thick cloud of smoke" caused by "burning leaves" (cited in Rawlette, 2019b, p. 570).

Thus there is not just one kind of failure in synchronicity and therefore in psi, most often thought to be due to a failure to initiate the psi function, or its complete shut-down. Equally, when it is operating, there can be contamination due to irrelevant content ('noise'), much like 'analytical overlay' in RV (see next section), though let us not forget occasional displacement. Conventionally, parapsychologists want to eliminate noise as it obscures or distorts correct details, but calling it noise, and attempting to enhance the psi signal by the elimination of that noise, is a default position based on ESP being naïvely thought of as a communication anomaly (see Chapter 3). In fact, the parapsychologist's contention concerning noise is not fully justified. Under synchronicity theory, no yet-to-be-determined sensory apparatus or modality is necessary, targets are not actually *perceived*, and ESP is simply a misnomer for meaningful coincidence. When synchronicity is discernable, it is primarily because appropriate archetypal correspondences between the target and the participant's mental state come to the fore. Fortunately, these alignments do occur more often than chance can explain, and are statistically determinable despite failures due to (i) no constellated archetype, (ii) misinterpretation of a relevant archetype, or (iii) a constellated irrelevant archetype. The resultant effects are conventionally interpreted as 'no signal', 'noise', and 'displacement', respectively, though these terms are misleading in themselves.

In that context, I return to this section's heading and ask: What are the limits of synchronicity in space and time? Arguably, there can be no virtual limits, but in another sense the question is meaningless given the ubiquity of archetypes. We would do well to appreciate the fact that limitations in our knowledge also limit our understanding of synchronicity. Does synchronicity, as a single mechanism, explain the planets-metals paradox just as well as it explains the anomalous effects produced by Swann, Mitchell, and Nostradamus, or do we struggle with a multiplicity of terms and convoluted explanations? Again the problem with terminology arises, and it will come up again in the next section.

Remote Viewing and the Rashomon Effect

Although I have just focused on the future to test the assumption of temporal transcendence (for want of a better term), I do note that retrocognition lends effective support to the same assumption (see Lamont, 2016; Stevenson, 1977; Targ & Katra, 1998). Although the notion is plausible within the constraints of the psi hypothesis, how do we confirm the effect is truly retrocognitive, especially in a remote-viewing scenario? Besides the verification problem, paranormal information acquisition (e.g., via clairvoyance) of (say) ancient ruins, or undiscovered or forgotten records of past events, or even precognition of records that will become available, must be controlled rendering the task difficult, if not impossible. As we shall see, the general problem with the Rhinean model is that we cannot have complete confidence in claims that real-time RV (i.e., clairvoyance) furnishes information *only* about real-time (current) events (this issue is discussed in the subsection *Laboratory Psi and Parapsychological Nomenclature* in Chapter 1 of Storm, 2025).

As before, I present material in a Rhinean vein *as if* past and future (like the present) are fluid (not fixed) as far as psi is concerned, and the psychic individual can access information from these temporal domains. However, by the end of this section, I will argue that time-boundedness has an archetypal dimension that puts a different slant on temporal transcendence, or more broadly *spatio*temporal transcendence—either way, 'transcendence' *per se* is questionable. I shall show how the psychic capacity to draw past and future information into the present is an obsolete and unworkable framework that ultimately obfuscates our understanding. To do that, I re-visit an RV case discussed in Chapter 1 of Storm (2025) that was described as having a mix of trans-temporal elements.

The case concerns URDF-3 (Unidentified Research and Development Facility 3) that notably featured the gantry crane and sphere-fabricating activity at Semipalatinsk, Kazakhstan (formerly of the Soviet Union), and the claimed construction of "a containment vessel for a particle-beam weapon to shoot down US satellites that were taking pictures" (Targ, 2012, p. 53). I will present my own analysis (observations and comments) but not exclusively, as

I will include components of cultural anthropologist Eric Wargo's (2020) dissection of the case. Two major findings will become evident: First, it will be seen that real-time and trans-temporal elements in RV are context-bound constructs. Second, although it starts quite simply as session work between renowned remote-viewer Patrick H. Price and an experimenter (Russell Targ with some involvement from Hal Puthoff), overall understanding and interpretation of the case material is complicated by the direct influence of a number of other key personalities in the drama. Consequently, Wargo believes the so-called "Rashomon effect" came to be a crucial contaminating element in the effort to uncover the truth about the remote viewing of URDF-3.[16] I suggest the Rashomon effect refers as much to results and outcomes as it does to influential elements in social situations, and on that account it is no less akin to Trickster phenomenology. Wargo means there is no telling whose account reliably indicates what transpired in those sessions in the same sense that *Rashomon* (the Japanese tale) is a convoluted "Whodunit" comprised of four conflicting eye-witness accounts of a murder or possible suicide. The Rashomon effect in the present context comprises the construction of viewpoints concerning ostensible real-time and trans-temporal RV effects, as well as a few assumptions made about URDF-3's purpose.

As I said in Storm (2025), Price described possible bomb construction at the site. This remote viewing was in 1974; Price died *without ever receiving personal feedback* on his performance. In 1977, the publication *Aviation Week & Space Technology* gave a report on 'sphere-fabricating activity at Semipalatinsk'. Targ (2012) regarded the whole RV session as feedback-free "*direct experience of the site*" (p. 55), but seven years later, he opted for an RV effect caused by "direct access to *any point in space-time* [emphasis added]" (Targ, 2019, p. 590).

Wargo (2020) recognises hits in Price's RV (such as a rail-mounted gantry crane that Price sketched), but very obvious and important details were not reported by Price (e.g., four derricks), as indicated in a CIA satellite photograph of the site shown to Price. A great number of other details supplied by Price were simply wrong. There are a few versions that tell of the events that transpired over that period of Price's RV (July 9, 10, 11, and 15, 1974), and years later, but these do not always align. Wargo points out that the Rashomon effect kicks in here, the key players being: (i) Russell Targ who paints a picture of Price as "effortlessly journeying halfway around the planet to spy on a remote Soviet test site with his roving consciousness" (p. 11); (ii) CIA contract monitor Ken Kress, who noted "the preponderance of false or useless information despite one or two clearly impressive psychic hits, such as the famous crane" (p. 11); (iii) Los Alamos physicist and expert on Semipalatinsk, Danny B. Stillman, who reviewed the case for the CIA in 1975, and "found little of real intelligence value in what Price described … the crane notwithstanding" (p. 11); and (iv) Pat Price himself. (Wargo acknowledges Hal Puthoff's involvement in the saga, but that seems incidental to the Rashomon effect.)

Starting with Price, as we move through the material (only a small portion presented here, but suffice to illustrate my point), it becomes evident to me that there was considerable noise in Price's RV, which might be explained as coming from a mix of sources including feedback (e.g., CIA photography, and other information/intelligence told or made available to Price), Price's informed guesswork, analytical overlay (to be discussed shortly), and his keyed-up imagination. The RV itself, to take a Rhinean approach, might be claimed as a mix of telepathy, clairvoyance, and precognition—the lines of demarcation become so blurred it is difficult to differentiate the worthwhile information from the worthless. And then there are the interpretations and expectations of Targ, Kress, and Stillman, respectively.

On Price's first day of testing, Stillman's CIA report noted:

> He [Price] said the military complex looks like it's been there for two to three years when in fact it's been there for over a decade.... He sees some [at least nine] landmark-type items that simply don't appear at or near URDF-3.... Price accurately described the location and type of target (but that was given) but failed on the layout and type of buildings. He tended to spend too much time on specifics only to say, "I'll come back to that," but seldom did. He successfully evaded drawing a perimeter of the area even though he was asked to do so twice.
>
> (1975, pp. 12–13)

Stillman concluded that "nothing positive to validate remote viewing resulted from this first day's session" (p. 13).

Price did a little better on the second day—the day he supplied the sketch for the gantry crane (though he remote viewed it the day before)—thus furnishing "the most positive evidence yet of Price's remote viewing" (Stillman, 1975, p. 18). Although these are Stillman's words, we are informed that the "CIA already knew about it from their surveillance" (Wargo, 2020, p. 13). In addition, Price does mistakenly say the crane was "so heavy that it left tracks in the ground", but he corrects himself, noting the railroad track, and referring to the target as a "riding gantry" (Stillman, 1975, p. 14). Targ does not mention the error; instead it as though, in the very same breath, Price mentions the crane for the first time and straight away notes how "it seems to be riding on a track" (Targ & Katra, 1998, p. 47).

After Price drew the crane, Targ and Katra (1998) say that "several days" *after* the "remote viewing", both Targ and Price "were astonished" to learn that the site was a "super-secret Soviet atomic-bomb laboratory at Semipalatinsk" (p. 47). That may be so, but clearly the original satellite photo and the derived sketch, *both showing the crane*, had to have existed *before* the sessions (see Figure 5.4). Kress (1999) confirms the satellite photography was already to hand:

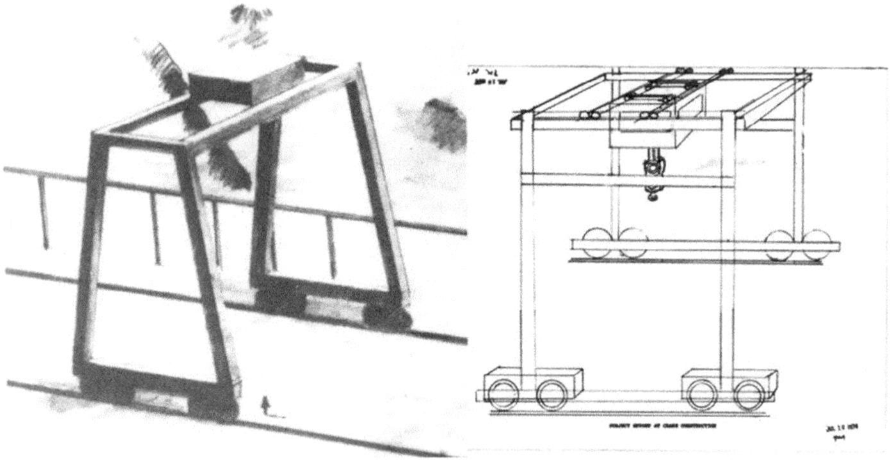

Figure 5.4 On the left is the CIA's rendition of the gantry crane (derived from a CIA satellite photo), and on the right is Pat Price's RV-session drawing of the crane at the Semipalatinsk Test Site, Kazakhstan. (*Source*: © 1996, H. Puthoff; used with permission)

> I reviewed the photos of URDF-3 and chose two features … if Price described these structures ["the tall crane and the four structures resembling oil well derricks"], I would be prepared to … collect more relevant intelligence details.
>
> (p. 74)

On the strength of Price's crane sketch, and according to Targ's (2012) account, Kress confirmed with satellite imagery that Price was looking in the right area (Wargo, 2020, p. 13). However, none of the key players, then or since, have commented on the possibility that Price accessed this material (not the actual URDF-3 site) using some other psi modality besides RV. One highly-decorated officer did surmise that Price's hits may have been due to "mental telepathy" (Targ & Katra, 1998, p. 53). Targ, however, was convinced Price had "*direct experience of the site*" (p. 49), but there is simply no way of knowing this can be true for every detail, and it does not explain Price's many misses.

Stillman's (1975) report also reproduced illustrations of a "dome-shaped building" and a "cement silo-like building", about which Stillman says "there is nothing at URDF-3 that looks like the dome-shaped building or the silo-like building" (p. 18). While these same silos are identified as "a cluster of gas cylinders" by Targ and Katra (1998, p. 49), these only "capture a gestalt" to use Wargo's (2020, p. 19) expression.

On the third day Price was incorrect again about a few main features (e.g., distance to the nearest railroad from the site in question). More importantly, there-and-then, Kress quizzed Price on his failure to spot the four derricks (a.k.a. 'headframes'): "with two more days of work, we never heard about the derricks" (p. 75). Kress accepted Price's explanation (Price thought only one derrick was still standing), but given Kress's "data was three or four months old" (p. 75), he did not know better, and nor did Price. In fact, all four derricks were "still intact at the time of the session and thus should have been visible" (Wargo, 2020, p. 13; see also Stillman, 1975, p. 27). To be accurate, Kress says: "Two derricks were partially disassembled, but basically all four were visible" (p. 75). Targ never even mentions the derricks (Targ, 2019; Targ & Katra, 1998).

Little of practical value emerged on the fourth day—Price even regarded his "feeling" as incorrect because "he had been trying to force-fit a space-oriented situation to the target location" (Stillman, 1975, p. 27). Stillman's report for the four days rather sweepingly concluded that the RV experiment was a "failure" (p. 27), and was "unsuccessful" (p. 29).

Then we come to the so-called 'gores' (a.k.a. 'segments' or 'wedges'), supposedly to be welded together to make a giant sixty-foot diameter metal sphere. Its purpose is a main selling point of RV in Targ's popular accounts of that four-day session (e.g., Targ, 2012, 2019; Targ & Katra, 1998). Targ says Price described the goings-on inside a building that could not be seen by satellite (Targ & Katra, 1998, p. 47). Apparently the sphere was being assembled there from thick metal 'gores' that look like sections of an orange peel. The sphere itself was supposedly to be used "to capture and store energy from nuclear-driven explosives or pulse power generators" (Robertson, 1977, as cited in Targ & Katra, 1998, p. 49). Wargo notes a host of problems in the reporting: Price did not talk about sphere construction. He described a room like an iron foundry which housed "an enormous—60-foot-long—impeller turbine hanging from a crane" (p. 15). Price does mention "some segments" that are "wedge-shaped" (not 'gores') that "look like segments of an orange" (Price, 1974, as cited in Wargo, 2020, p. 15). Wargo states "There is no sense, nor even possibility, that they are as big as the 60-foot impeller", and Price never specified their size, and apparently never used the word "sphere" (p. 15).

> The bottom line is that the famous 60-foot steel sphere appears to be mythical, a chimera reflecting various disparate impressions Price mentioned on July 11 and 15, 1974 and distorted in hindsight by that attention-getting *Aviation Week* article.
>
> (Wargo, 2020, p. 16)

That *Aviation Week* article claimed "the Soviets were probably developing charged particle beam technology, which would involve the capture of energy from small nuclear explosions inside huge steel spheres" (Wargo, 2020, p. 14). To Price's credit, he did say: "what they're constructing in the overall, is a nuclear powered generation system of quite a magnitude. I feel pretty goddamn confident" (Price, 1974, cited in Wargo, p. 16). Price later corrected himself saying: "the wedge shaped pieces that originally I felt were an electrical application are in fact enriched material laid in a particular pattern fit together sequentially in segments. That goes together and in fact does make a bomb" (Price, 1974, cited in Wargo, 2020, p. 15). Unfortunately Price had erred again:

> […]in 1992, following the collapse of the Soviet Union, when Russian scientists invited their Western colleagues for a tour of Semipalatinsk…. It became immediately apparent to the visitors that … Baikal-1 facility [URDF-3] did house nuclear reactors … but their purpose was to develop technology for nuclear-powered spaceflight, atomic rockets that could potentially be used on a Mars mission.
>
> (Wargo, 2020, pp. 17–18)

And then some years later it came out that everything about the gores and the spheres, and other intelligence about Baikal-1, were known about as early as the 1960s (Dobbs, 1999; see also Wargo, 2020, p. 18). Michael Dobbs of the *Washington Post* noted: "in the late '60s … satellite pictures showed Soviet workers assembling several steel spheres nearly 60 feet in diameter."

Interestingly, Wargo (2020) himself enters as a player in the Rashomon effect with his own interpretation of what might have happened by noting that Price's RV was not accurate if we regard it as clairvoyance (real-time RV), but if we take it as precognition on Price's part (whether he knew it or not), then that "feedback could well have consisted of, or been informed by, inaccurate beliefs or hypotheses about the purpose of the site, possibly even an early draft of the *Aviation Week* article" (p. 18). The "feedback" theory only holds if the "early draft" *actually existed* two years earlier before Price died in 1975, but a true Rhinean cannot rule out conventional precognition, nor retrocognition of intelligence that was available dating back to the 1960s. Here we have a clear case of modality conflation in RV (discussed in Chapter 1 of Storm, 2025); under the assumption, of course, that we are talking about psi modalities *per se.* Just the scanty sampling of intelligence discussed above is enough to suggest it. As I said above, Targ no longer exclusively refers to Price's RV as "direct experience of the site" (Targ, 2012, p. 55), having realized how spatiotemporally flexible RV can be, and later implied that RVers can have "direct access to *any point in space-time* [emphasis added]" (Targ, 2019, p. 590). Accepting that possibility as a reality about RV now makes RV a more complicated process than ever, though the process can be simplified when taking a synchronistic point of view.

Another issue also becomes pertinent as is evident from Price's testimony: Remote viewers must be watchful of "analytical overlay [AOL], … the analytic response of the viewer's mind to signal line input" (Smith, 1998, p. 17):

> AOLs may be recognized in several ways. First, if there is a comparator present ("it looks like…", "it's sort of…", etc.) the information present will almost inevitably be an AOL, and should always be treated as one. Secondly, a mental image that is sharp, clear, and static—that is, there is no motion present in it, and in fact it appears virtually to be a mental photograph of the site—is also certainly AOL.
>
> (p. 17)

Smith gives other indicators of AOL, such as hesitation, "out of structure" responses, voice inflections from the viewer, and similar micro-behaviours (p. 17). These can all be regarded as sources for unwarranted conscious input; a kind of confabulation beyond the role of the deep imagination and what it can legitimately furnish. A good example of how AOL could come about is in Price's admitted attempt "to force-fit a space-oriented situation to the target location" (Stillman, 1975, p. 27).

While some of Price's remote viewing definitely indicates AOL, Price had mainly been susceptible to three primary processes: (i) putative psi in apparently very indistinct forms (actually synchronicity due to a mix of archetypal forms), (ii) memory (personal knowledge), *and* (iii) pure fantasy (including guessing and changing his mind). As Stillman (1975) warns: "If the user of Price's remote-viewing talents has no way of checking, how could he differentiate the fact from the fiction?" (p. 25). In fact, the same goes for Swann regarding Jupiter's rings. Price and Swann could not control any of these processes because RV (or what is understood to be RV) is such an 'open' process, and crucial details about the targets were not (and could not be) made sufficiently explicit. It is the price one pays for believing RV is an effect that takes place nonlocally (i.e., outside time and space). Thus, the examples I have given for both Swann and Price—generally recognised as two of the most outstanding RVers to date that therefore fully justifies this critique—do suggest that even expert RVers may be uncertain about the processes operative at any given time during their session work, and (to repeat) uncertainty about process (and content) translates as lack of control. As a result, spurious and not so spurious in-session material comes through, so that clarity and understanding is compromised; hence, the Rashomon effect. As noted earlier, the high fail rate in psi research is a natural consequence of intentional synchronicity and the downside of psi testing. Evidently, the problem is not rare; the acclaimed trance-medium and psychic Edgar Cayce (also referred to as a remote viewer) may have produced some successful readings under trance (e.g., Cayce, 1974), but we find these are mixed in with some spurious claims that were also produced during trance states. If the right archetypes do not constellate when a psychic goes into trance, the psychic may depend on that aspect of the imagination responsible for fantasy, thus producing not only inaccuracies, but Cayce-like readings in the form of prognoses, predictions, treatments, etc., not all of which stand up to close scrutiny (Nickell, 1998, Stollznow, 2014).

Wargo (2020) reports that remote viewers claim "that it ultimately does not matter where the information comes from or exactly how they get it" (p. 20). In one sense, he and they are right because only results count, and RVers do get results (seeMcMoneagle, 1997, 2000; Schwartz, 2000, 2005). However, conflations of fact with fiction, and present-events with past-occurrences and possible-futures, are problematic because investigators (agencies, researchers) may come to depend on those distinctions for the sake of interpretation, the planning of strategies, retaliatory actions, interventions, and so on. With this kind of research, and from the perspective of agencies trying to harness paranormal 'powers of the mind' for whatever purpose, or theoreticians and laboratory researchers aiming to understand the process, we seem to be in a bind. As Wargo quite correctly states, "Not being absolutely clear about the nature of psi leaves it wide open to error" (p. 20). As I have just intimated, asserting that spatiotemporal factors play a part in RV (and ESP generally) can create serious misunderstandings that can lead to false interpretations.

From Wargo's point of view, the problem is nested in an ambiguous process filtered through memories and "feedback experience in the viewer's future that could be mistaken …" (p. 20), and to top it all off (at least in some cases) selective reporting and personal testimony from well-meaning or over-enthusiastic others does not help; once again, the Rashomon effect. But even if we cleared away all the misinformation that resulted from that effect and had what appeared to be pure effects, there might still be the occasional lucky guesswork buried amongst the legitimate RV.

In previous chapters, I commented on the inadequacy of Rhinean nomenclature (see also Storm, 2025); the terms themselves are conceptually fuzzy and do little to identify the process beyond a schematic view (for an example, see Chapter 4). It is just possible the Rashomon effect in the above parapsychological episode was, in a rather tricksterish manner, propagated by the burgeoning need to identify psi modalities and keep parapsychologists believing these effects had been nailed. This is not to argue the *efficacy* of RV; my focus is mainly on *terminology*—while Wargo has identified a cluttering social process, even he does not seem to be aware of the pointless use of terminology, as indicated by the interpretations. Let us not forget that modality is only important *if we work within the Rhinean paradigm*, but we have seen no real progress there (again see Chapter 1 in Storm, 2025).

Psi modality is a non-issue in synchronicity.[17] In fact, in synchronicity, there are no psi modalities, whereas to assume that unreliable psi modalities inform us as to source can only be misleading due to the flexibility of the terminology. Yet, we are not left with holes in our knowledge even if we do not seek causes in terms of modality. In an experimental situation, one can still think in terms of past events, or immediate (current) events, or possible future events, and then design the study with those theoretical parameters in mind, but with a synchronistic purview. That is, while the experimenter may ask 'What happened and where?', 'What is happening now at some distance and/or to whom?', or 'What will happen?', we must think holistically, realizing that spacetime parameters are not the issue when it comes to archetypes so we must suspend our spatiotemporal notions and focus on archetypal situations. If the right archetype constellates (which is more likely than the wrong archetype because of the contributing influence of intention *as a frame of mind with a subsequently cogent link to the appropriate archetype*), the result is much better than a guess. Or if a system of divination is to be used, one proceeds much as before, bearing in mind that one is looking for an archetypal solution exemplified in age-old patterns and human situations (e.g., as laid out in the *I Ching*, Tarot, astrology, and the like). But in these cases, even when they are synchronicity, one cannot expect the process to yield a literal portrayal; a detailed, blow-by-blow account of actual reality (as it was, is, or will be). Instead, one should see the outcome as a representation of a *probable* (even likely) event.

Psi is regarded by some theoreticians as more than a problem couched in semantic wordplay around a unitary psi process, for those theoreticians hold that the modalities differ from each other in radically different ways and are mutually exclusive. For example, German parapsychologist Eberhard Bauer has stated:

> It is safe to assume that this [psi] dilemma is not simply a semantic one. It reflects principally different theoretical models which have of course consequences for the empirical testability of the hypotheses derived therefrom.
>
> (Bauer, 1984, p. 143)

I argue that is a pseudo-problem, but Wargo (2020) has whipped up the crisis again for psi pundits who need to know which modality is operative. Yet he very nearly makes my point: "the psychic captures some distinct shape or perhaps an overall gestalt, but elements may be transposed or displaced, and a clear sense of identity or function of objects is often lacking" (p. 19). Of course, he does not raise these elements to an archetypal level because his approach is entirely non-synchronistic. But neither does he allow for the fact that even an 'unclear sense' can still be efficacious. And this is true of synchronicity; the examples we have seen show there was on occasion sufficient precision, not just in spotting correspondences, but also to garner useful and meaningful information from them.

Synchronicity, as a single, unitary process involving coincidence formation, can be complicated by the number of archetypes that may be constellated, but still it renders redundant the idea that parapsychology should concern itself with modality discernment. In the case that Wargo (2020) presents, Price was wrong sometimes *and* right sometimes, but so much was left to (mis)interpretation because modality was so important. We need only concern ourselves with archetypes (which ones were activated for Price and why). Some might say the archetype may imply a psi source and therefore a modality. Archetypes, however, are sources that merely *suggest* psi modalities—the difference is key. Identifying the source (archetype) can only come from inquiry into the meaningfulness of the arrangement that Price had set up via his intentional efforts, and via his nature and his being. A researcher working with the Rhinean model would very probably not frame the problem that way, but the same researcher could never explain why a psychic might seem to have a preference for one modality over another; nor explain the apparent chopping and changing of modality (if and when it is spotted), and some may be better at this than others. Consider, for example, how some of us are grounded in the present, whereas nostalgic types dwell on the past and intuitive types prefer to know what the future holds. In that sense, source only *becomes* an issue (where is the target in spacetime?) insofar as it speaks to the archetypal arrangements unique to RVers like Pat Price, and delving into that issue is simultaneously seeking an answer to the question, Who is Pat Price? The same question can be asked of Ingo Swann, or Ted Owens, or anyone; indeed everyone. Hence, the paradigm within which the parapsychologist works governs the questions asked, how those questions are answered, and the conclusions reached. Researchers failed to understand their 'star subject'—they merely assumed a capacity on Price's part, and gave Price a task, and Price himself got to work, doing what he does best, which (take it or leave it) included letting his imagination run wild. Some may say this was early days of RV research, and lessons were learned. One only hopes so.

These days, researchers may suggest there are cases of (say) an RVer's capacity for clairvoyance exhausting itself, so they unconsciously slip into (say) precognition (or retrocognition) mode in the interests of garnering fresh information. But perhaps RVers (like any psychic) are not aware that, during their self-induced ASC, this 'slipping' is actually switching out of one archetypal situation into another. That is to say, psi is synchronicity, and is not about conjuring up images from past, or present, or future, via the relevant modality; it is about working with archetypes that happen to present themselves, and whenever possible allowing themselves to switch from one *amenable* archetype to another and gleaning that experience of its information. The process is not necessarily fruitful; archetypes may have limited use even when they do constellate—this is why we see Price excusing himself even when he hits on something and, in trying to be specific, ultimately says "I'll come back to that".

Still, we cannot rule out the possibility that we can infer a source from an archetype—it is really a matter of identifying the target *in the archetypal content*, and that may be sufficiently unique to render a match. Many an RVer may see their situation as seeking meaningful (target) content in the archetypal soup. In this matter we are still very much in the dark, for the parapsychological agenda has not been to seek archetypes—we have been committed (perhaps overcommitted) to seeking out targets in time and space to prove psi and benefit from it. Nevertheless it follows that the target is our link to the archetype, which we will know by deriving it once we verify the target. Are parapsychologists doing that?

Much is made of the Semipalatinsk case, but if there ever was a case that shows RV in its best light, it is not this one. Indeed, I have been more impressed by work shown to me by RVers I know personally. However, this review is not to denigrate Price, his RV work, or other official RV investigations—for example, Lieutenant Colonel Brian Buzby, project manager at the United States Army Intelligence and Security Command, commented on the success of CENTER LANE (a code name and forerunner of STAR GATE), noting that “about 350 missions out of 700 (50%) were deemed to possess intelligence value, and 85% showed positive evidence for remote viewing” (May & Marwaha, 2018, p. 17). Other reviews and meta-analyses (Baptista et al., 2015; May & Marwaha, 2018), and even my own successful dabbling (Storm, 2003b) supports RV in principle. This foray has been about the Rashomon effect as it pertains to psi modalities and subsequent interpretations: As Wargo (2020) has shown, we need to be wary of first-person and collaborative accounts of past events (e.g., Kress, 1999; Targ, 2012, 2019; Targ & Katra, 1998; Targ & Puthoff, 1977; Stillman, 1975). Given the degree of flexibility in interpretation, and the perennial difficulty of implementing suitable controls that rule out seemingly logical but misleading deductions, uninformed speculation, guesswork, misinformation, misreading, and misunderstanding, as well as multi-faceted spin from sincere but highly motivated individuals (the core of the Rashomon effect), many psi effects become ripe for the picking, though not in the best sense of that expression.

While not entirely about method either, criticisms about modalities became necessary. Certain kinds of psychic process, and especially the environments *in which* and *about which* they take place, along with hidden agendas, can facilitate deception and self-deception, so that everyone in the game has to be mindful. As Wargo (2020) states quite plainly, “It is not enough to prove psi exists—which has already been done” (p. 20). Of course, the question of psi has not been answered, but the paradigm that has grown out of the psi hypothesis sits too much on its own, and many do much to keep it that way. I suggest it is not enough to go on and on about the ‘powers of the mind’ until we know what ‘power’ is supposed to mean in terms of its limits, its purpose, and (most importantly) how to control (subdue) its influence and influencers, so we do not fall into the hands of the Trickster (see Chapters 2 and 3 in Storm, 2025), as has been shown in the Price case where we saw the Rashomon effect in full force. We would be better off accepting that we can be fooled by claims of modalities, or to put it another way, by archetypes, but only to the extent that we do not understand them sufficiently well (or even know) when they appear. In the following section, these ideas are explored further.

Electronic Voice Phenomena: False Positives or Synchronicity?

The idea of spirit (discarnate-entity) contact through electronic media is intriguing; of course it is also a relatively new and controversial phenomenon having emerged out of advancements in technology over the last century or so. Even the inventor and telephone pioneer, Thomas Alva Edison (1847–1931), thought spirits might try to communicate with us via the 'modern' media. These communications have come to be known as electronic voice phenomena (EVP; I will also use the acronym EVP in singular form). Latvian author and student of C. G. Jung, Konstantin Raudive (1906–1974), was a pioneer in the field of EVP, which are best characterized as sounds on electronic recordings, usually interpreted as the voices of discarnate entities. I bring EVP into the synchronicity arena because they illustrate well the inherent difficulty of sorting out genuine meaningful coincidences (synchronicity) from meaningless chance groupings. I must add that even when EVP might seem genuine, it is not the role of synchronicity theory to help settle the afterlife question by taking EVP as proof of post-mortem survival. Synchronicity theory's focus is on correspondences and establishing whether they have value based on a sufficient accumulation of detail that enables one to reach an informed and satisfactory conclusion in terms of their meaningfulness.

Raudive's approach to EVP recording resulted in *microphone voices* (from leaving the tape recorder running), and *radio voices* and *diode voices* (off-tuned radio and crystal-set recordings, respectively). An EVP message, "*Vadormir, Margarete*" ("Go to sleep, Margaret") spurred Raudive (1971) to remark in his landmark book *Breakthrough*:

> These words made a deep impression on me, as Margarete Petrautzki had died recently, and her illness and death had greatly affected me.
>
> (p. 16)

The reader may already spot a possible discrepancy here in that the meaningfulness is apparent but the physical (outer) event came prior to its recognition as an inner (psychological) fact, which introduces the possibility of front-loading (i.e., priming). However, Jung's (1952/1969, para. 850) definition of synchronicity allows for this reversal, and Main (2004) acknowledges its validity. I dealt with this reversed order in a previous chapter (see *The Two Spatial Forms of Synchronicity* in Chapter 2). Raudive's book is based on his work with over 400 EVP experients, who produced a grand total of some 70,000 audiotape recordings. The last ten years of Raudive's life were spent in further exploration of EVP. He even collaborated with noted German parapsychologist Hans Bender.

In his book, Raudive made particular points about the voices, noting that voice-entities speak "very rapidly, in a mixture of languages, sometimes as many as five or six in one sentence"; "They speak in a definite rhythm, which seems to be forced upon them"; "The rhythmic mode of speech imposes a shortened, telegram-style phrase or sentence"; and "grammatical rules are frequently abandoned and neologisms abound" (Raudive, 1971, pp. 31–32). Of course any kind of short telegraphic "phrase" or "sentence", poor grammar, and "neologisms"—in whatever context—are to be expected given what we know of the technical realities of random (usually unwanted) noises that fire off in brief and indiscriminate bursts from radios and other such electronic equipment. The EVP pundit could turn this short-coming around and argue that the technology, no matter how advanced, is always limited, and never really designed for the task at hand anyway, so it only *inhibits* or *lowers the quality* of the voices, but it never *causes* them.

On the face of it, however, the better quality cases of psi correspondences have a far greater capacity for objective verification compared to EVP. Put simply, giving an 'auditory moment' (i.e., a spontaneous, unexpected sound) a meaning, just because it sounds familiar, is not a proof of anomalous communication—it is the result of a matching exercise, but with a crucial and distinctive difference if we compare it to target identification in a free-response trial. In EVP, even when the voices seem familiar or are identifiable, the pool of interpretations is vast, which maximizes the possibility of a match with an undefined target that the subject is free to 'identify' for meaning; not so in free response, which has a defined target amongst decoys that comprise a limited set. The 'free' response, therefore, is not so *free*, but such a constraint at least makes statistical evaluation possible. Consider the following short passages listed by EVP researcher David Ellis (1975) as utterances a group of volunteers thought they heard when presented with a single Raudive EVP: "make beans my lovely", "late sleep I'm serviette ong", "lately mikye bien", "late leave Mike shairries", "let's leave Michael here Kevin", "nimst die Michael as yet", "make me quite clear gemmell", "methylene Mike is here" (pp. 36–37). Yet Raudive had interpreted the voice as saying "may dream, my dear yes!"

It has been claimed that many EVP recordings were made under 'strict laboratory conditions', but it should be noted that under the circumstances, as is also the case with many spontaneous phenomena, no amount of laboratory control can guarantee the elimination of chance occurrences, or necessarily allow one to differentiate the false from the true positives. German-Australian parapsychologist Jürgen Keil (1980) noted other methodological weaknesses in this kind of research. For instance, he observed that Raudive edited his tapes afterwards, and his EVP subjects were *told what to expect to hear*. On this point, Nees and Phillips (2015) have shown that a paranormal prime "increased the proportion of trials for which participants perceived voices in both EVP stimuli and degraded speech" (p. 129). This is where David Ellis comes in. Ellis was the first recipient of a Perrrott-Warrick grant which funded his EVP research in the 1970s that culminated in a book and a peer-reviewed paper (Ellis, 1975, 1978). He regarded the so-called 'voices' as static (e.g., random electrical signals from power lines or electric motors) or other technologically induced aberrations that mimic the human voice. As already noted, EVP recordings were also proved to be degraded radio broadcast signals that interfere with the recording devices (Barušs, 2001, 2007; Boccuzzi & Beischel, 2011; Ellis, 1975), but they can also be background conversation and utterances of the operators handling the recording equipment (Ellis, 1978).

Nees and Phillips (2015) have noted that when voices are detected, there is "low agreement" in regard to "content of EVP messages" (p. 129). Cardoso's (2012) assortment of acoustic abnormalities, described as EVP, tended to need confirmation by other EVP researchers. Indeed, EVP can easily be offered as examples of apophenia (see Chapter 1), in the sense that meaning can be conjured out of ambiguous static of the forms just described, and shaped by primes and context.

While we cannot entirely rule out the claim that EVP can be false positives, none of the following four factors—schizotypy, fantasy-proneness, hallucination-proneness, and paranormal belief—have been shown to predict EVP experiences (Drinkwater et al., 2020). So, it does not appear that the typical EVP-experient is delusional, or hallucinating, or fantasizing, or suggestible due to their belief. Given the dubious sources of these 'sound bites' and given their ambiguity; what then drives the EVP experient? In most cases there is a need to make contact with a departed loved-one as a way of dealing with grief and loss, which is why the EVP can have such emotional impact for the experient. And if some people feel they do hear the voice of a departed loved-one in a given EVP, and the coincidence can result in a change of attitude, mood, or mindset, or consolidate a belief in the afterlife, might EVP be more like meaningful coincidence (e.g., serendipitous) under some circumstances? I shall consider that possibility next.

The skeptic might like to regress to earlier criticisms (see Chapter 1) and insist EVP are meaningless chance events, and perhaps the same goes for all other cases of synchronicity and psi, and the experient merely draws a subjectively validated, self-generated meaning from these experiences. But it was already established that this kind of conclusion is not only unlikely, it misses the point. Synchronistically, it is not a matter of deciding whether a paranormal phenomenon is (a) a convenient (serendipitous) accident that we happen upon, or generate purely as a wish-fulfilment, or (b) the product of a living mind/brain non-locally meshing (i.e., communicating or opening an information channel) with something 'other' outside the aid of the normal sensory modalities (a current favourite with most parapsychologists). For many, (a) and (b) might be *the* two antithetical ways of viewing these phenomena, but a third option sees EVP (like psi and synchronicity) as events that could possibly have archetypal significance. That does seem to leave a lot to chance, but we can do much to encourage the synchronistic circumstance—starting with intentions, attitudes, and emotional states—so that an archetype may have opportunity to constellate. If and when that happens, EVP becomes as meaningful an experience as any other described as synchronicity thus far, though I suggest the outcome could be obscure (leaving much room for interpretation), as the so-called 'match' (correspondence) is actually to a general sentiment or hope, but not a specific idea or image held in consciousness. Nevertheless, the archetype's 'connecting potential' and its "transgressivity" (Jung, 1952/1969, para. 964) work, in a sense, like the extension of consciousness, taking the individual beyond psychological (inner) experience to psychophysical (inner/outer) experience, that can be 'relational' in human terms, and even go beyond that. To support the 'relational' case, I give two examples from Ellis (1978), showing how EVP can be crucial and timely utterances.

First, when Ellis and parapsychologist Manfred Cassirer visited Raudive, and their morning's work had gone "well past lunch-time", Raudive played a voice which (in Latvian) said "We are slaves of hunger" (Ellis, 1978, p. 149). Ellis argued the voice was an example of Raudive "unconsciously sensing the unvoiced thoughts of those present and expressing them in one of his interpretations" (p. 149). We do not know if Raudive's choice was random or deliberate, but Ellis implied a telepathic link may have governed Raudive's selection. But it may also have been IBNS given the shared sentiments of those present. In synchronicity, this link is a timely correspondence; it holds relevance, numinosity, and meaning, and a very basic, felt instinct, lies at the core of the experience, so a feeling-toned archetype is suggested (Jung, 1987).[18] But that proposition says nothing about the ultimate source.

Similarly, in a second example, the EVP word "tactful" was voiced, and all three agreed on its interpretation because, prior to that moment, Ellis noted there had been "disagreement" about when to conduct formal analyses on their experimental sessions, and as a result, relations had "become rather strained" (p. 149). Crucially, after hearing the word "tactful", Ellis added that the "desired result of improving relations" had been achieved as if to say the voicing of the word "tactful" had been taken as instructional, and was duly noted by all. And yet, it was later conceded (not by Ellis alone) that the word "tactful" was "no more than a mechanical noise" (p. 149). This later insight thus dispenses with any kind of transmission model, but it does not eliminate the synchronistic assumption, and again it says nothing about the ultimate source.

Both examples might be false positives, but I have stressed all along that in synchronicity, the focus is primarily on the correspondences, and no absolute claims can be made that information was communicated. Also in both cases, emotion was key. Interestingly, the conclusion Ellis draws suggests a synchronistic twist in that he says EVP interpretations must take into consideration the "unvoiced feelings of those present", and recognise that the voices can be very "fitting" of the moment (p. 150). This viewpoint goes beyond points (a) and (b) just given, to yield cases of EVP that have emotional overtones, numinosity, and meaningful elements suggestive of synchronicity.

Now and into the Future

The concept of *now*—the idea of an eternal present—has perplexed philosophers and theologians throughout history. Some cultures (the Hopi) do not even give representation to it, seeing only a manifested past and an imminent future (von Franz, 1992). Robert A. Muller (2016) notes how Aristotle tied himself up with his own words: "the 'now' which seems to bind the past and the future—does it always remain one and the same or is it always other and other?" (p. 17). Augustine dismissed past and future, and opted for three kinds of 'present': "a present of things past, memory; a present of things present, sight; a present of things future, expectation" (p. 18). Even physicists struggle: "In his book *A Brief History of Time*, Stephen Hawking doesn't even mention the now conundrum" (Muller, p. 20). Einstein may have noted that "the separation between past, present and future has only the importance of an admittedly tenacious illusion" (Venning, 2019), but everything has a context, and while it certainly appears in the context of his General Theory of Relativity that the rate at which time flows very well depends on wherever and whenever one is, one can only have one perspective; the *now* one is in.

Muller and Maguire (2016) give us a new perspective: "the future does not yet exist; we are not moving into the future, but the future is being constantly created" (p. 2). They argue that space and time are so closely bound under relativity theory that "any change in the amount of local space will result in a corresponding change in the local time" (p. 3). Muller and Maguire make these propositions under the rubric of their so-called "Now Theory". In their paper, they give an example of how new space and new time were created by the observed merging of two black holes. The data for this calculation came from the Laser Interferometer Gravitational-Wave Observatory (LIGO; Abbott et al., 2016). LIGO was originally set up to verify the general theory of relativity, but Muller and Maguire see potential for work aimed at investigating Now Theory.

As a specific example, Abbott et al. (2016) reported the two black hole masses as initially being of the order of 36 and 29 solar masses ($M_{\odot}$)—total: 65 $M_{\odot}$—but the final combined mass reduced to approximately 62 $M_{\odot}$ due to the loss of about 3 $M_{\odot}$ radiating as gravitational waves. Abbott et al. note that "this is the first direct detection of gravitational waves and the first observation of a binary black hole merger" (p. 1). Muller and Maguire (2016) go further with this revelatory finding by noting that space *and* time were created out of the merger. By observing that black holes have a considerable effect on space, and by applying dimensional analysis, they calculated that space increased by 180 km in radius, and the time created was about one millisecond as indicated by the delay "in the end of the pulse vs the beginning" (p. 5). Apparently, the extra space and time caused by the merger resulted in a time delay evident as a growing lag in the emission of the gravitational wave. Thus, Muller and Maguire show that Now Theory is falsifiable because in measuring the expansion (creation) of space, we are able to measure the extension (creation) of time. And Muller (2016) holds that spacetime is not static but is continuously generated by cosmic events, especially expansion of the universe, and he also points out that time will not go into reverse as the result of a hypothetical Big Crunch. The Big Crunch Theory was disproved by Saul Perlmutter and his colleagues, Brian P. Schmidt and Adam G. Riess, who won the 2011 Nobel Prize in Physics for their work on this problem. From multiple observations of distant galaxies, it was determined that the universe was not slowing down due to mutual gravity, but "the expansion of the universe was accelerating" (Muller, 2016, p. 156).

Muller (2016) regards as incorrect and back-to-front Eddington's idea that time emerges as a result of an entropic universe: "the entropy explanation of the arrow of time is deeply flawed" (p. 161). Even Hawking thought that "disorder increases with time because we measure time in the direction in which disorder increases" (cited in Muller, p. 182). *Ipse dixit*! Someone in authority has spoken. Rather, entropy is only possible *because* time is constantly being created. Muller notes that "microwave radiation and the remote surfaces of black holes and the distant edge of the observable universe" are the "dominant reservoirs of entropy", but "civilization depends on local decreases in entropy" (p. 303). This decrease in entropy creates order but there is no sign of time reversal. This "now" we experience is continually advancing and is "the leading edge of time" (p. 293).

While Now Theory has caused a wave of resistance in the physics communities, at least one physicist has no clue as to whether Muller and Maguire are right or wrong (Neil deGrasse Tyson, as cited in Science Daily, 2016). And the impact Muller's brand of spacetime creation might have on our understanding of psi and synchronicity is also uncertain, but when it comes to precognition, there may be considerable impact on conventional understandings. Logically and crucially, Now Theory would have it that one cannot see or learn about unmanifested (future) events *ahead of time*—they can only unfold *in real time.* While some parapsychologists argue that forward causal chains suffice in explaining precognition as an effect unfolding in the present (i.e., in real time; see Braude, 1979), precognition as conventionally understood conflicts with Now Theory. Other parapsychologists will not be deterred—the so-called evidence for precognition is all parapsychologists need to claim that the future is more than a probable realm of the unmanifested and unfolding.

Observational theorists—proponents of Observational Theories (OTs)—go further by proposing an explanation for precognition based on QM principles (e.g., nonlocality, backward causation), which characterize precognition as retrocausation (i.e., retro-PK), or "trans-temporal coupling" to be precise (a "diffuse probability-based phenomenon akin to Einstein's 'spooky action at a distance'"; Millar, 2019). Rather than suggest that effects can precede causes, Brian Millar (2019) proposes the successful outcome in a 'precognition' task is a 'quantum correlation'. Feedback and target selection are all part of a single event across the span of time, even into the future. If future feedback supposedly influences choices in the present, how can we view that feedback other than as something *pre-existing in the future*? "What can be affected/seen by psi is curtailed to the feedback available" (Millar, 2019). Under the OTs, since feedback and selection supposedly constitute one event, one cannot change a thing; not the future, not the world, and not the feedback.

We can infer from the OTs the shaky premise that some future events are just as much locked in as those of the past, as is proposed in teleological theories involving block universes, which are deterministic, and imply no freewill (see also Ellis, 2006, for a similar critique). Now Theory does not allow for determined futures and multiple (concurrent) futures; Muller (2016) is quite clear that now theory ensures freewill. Now Theory would be the final nail in the coffin for ideas in physics and parapsychology that make too much of time symmetry and precognition. And for a detailed argument on the futility of retrocausation, see Braude (1986).

As for synchronicity, I have argued that none of the psi modalities, including precognition, have any relevance to it, so it cannot be in conflict with Now Theory. Precognition *per se* (as asynchronous synchronicity) is resonant endopsychic correspondence with a constellated archetype, and it is expressed *within* spacetime—that is, *now*—in short, synchronicity does not violate spacetime principles. Jung may have linked his synchronicity theory with QM insofar as both describe phenomena that are part of the general acausal orderedness, but he never spoke of feedback being a necessary (instrumental) component of meaningful coincidence. So while Millar (2019) denies the process underpinning OT is causal, it still seems strange that he brings in synchronicity as relevant to OT by calling synchronicity "a near precursor of OT thought". I suggest it is more or less the other way around: OT is "wanna-be" synchronicity theory that depends on convoluted QM science with all its contradictions, lack of consensus, and mythological dimensions (see Chapter 5 in Storm, 2025; see also Becker, 2019, for a critique on QM).

Muller's (2016) "now" connotes a real present; a continuously unfolding present—it shores up the conception in most people's minds that past events can be recalled, future events can be anticipated but are *for the most part* uncertain and undetermined, and both can be integrated and mediated in the 'now'. It is only in the now that creation becomes manifest, whereas the future is not yet manifest; the 'realm' of possibilities. I suggest Now Theory allows us to re-envision the entire parapsychological substrate with greater parsimony than before, which means dispensing with ambiguous nomenclature and paradoxical modalities, and taking as our working model the idea that correspondences in parapsychology are actually meaningful coincidences; not indefinable psi.

Conclusion

This book, in conjunction with Storm (2025), endeavoured to demonstrate that (i) most psi theories, and the parapsychological nomenclature that goes with them, are to some degree ambiguous and may therefore impede scientific progress; (ii) a number of philosophical premises that underpin the various psi theories tend to be taken for granted; (iii) synchronicity has not been given the attention it deserves by parapsychologists; but (iv) in a few best case scenarios, theoreticians have 'reinvented the wheel' of synchronicity; and (v) synchronicity theory is a comprehensible and comprehensive model that reinterprets so-called 'psychic' functioning. While I have tried to cover these five points thoroughly, the question remains as to whether my coverage taken as a whole can have a positive and much-needed effect on parapsychology.

Broadly speaking, change in society often follows change in our scientific institutions, though the reverse is also true. And often, a consensus must be reached (or something approximating a consensus); otherwise, even the best ideas may impress only a limited few who may even be compelled to wonder why their ideas did not catch on. In those instances, either the ideas were not as good as they seemed, or the world just was not ready for them. Clearly there must be a powerful social component behind the acceptance of, or resistance to an idea, but every so often, even an iconoclastic idea does not meet with resistance: As 19th-century French novelist Victor Hugo (1802–1885) once said, "there is nothing more powerful than an idea whose time has come!" Either parapsychology has never had that timely idea—for if Hugo is right, society would have made way for it—or alternatively, anything that comes out of parapsychology itself is viewed with suspicion and excluded from Hugo's dictum. But that alternative cannot be true: Hugo's notion of the timely idea implies that on occasion a change is so badly needed that the new idea will be greeted with open arms, no matter its source, *even if* it happens to be parapsychological. But still we wait.

Many parapsychologists have made continued efforts to reach the wider masses through their theories and ideas, but it has been a many-decades-long struggle with little showing for it when weighed up against the time and energy that has been put into the field. That is not to say there has been no progress, but we know psi phenomena do not get a fair treatment by academia and mainstream media. Are they entirely at fault, or is it possible the problems within parapsychological circles are a contributing factor to non-acceptance? There are two key issues—the findings *and* the theories that explain them. If the problem is to do with the findings, we cannot simply fault the parapsychologists for there are blocks on both sides of the debate between believers and skeptics. Stalemate exists partly because skeptics do have a case in some instances. In other instances, the skeptics are just plain wrong and maybe a little humility might help (see also Chapter 3 in Storm, 2025). If the problem is to do with the theoretical ideas circulating in the field, we can address that issue from the perspective of the five points I just raised above. Taking all the *relevant* findings into consideration (for the more salient of them are indisputably critical to science), surely the theory of choice will be the one that explains them the best but makes the least demands on our credulity (on these points, see Parapsychological Association, 2022). Let us consider synchronicity in that light.

The very first advantage in synchronicity is that there is no serious challenge to the precepts of modern science, the basic limiting principles, spacetime, and even consciousness; none of these are violated. Only the assumption of archetypes and its associated phenomena (numinosity and meaningfulness) are the called-for fundamentals here; like gravity, archetypes are ubiquitous; they are constant and consistent in their influence (or sufficiently so); they never cease to function across spacetime but do not violate or transcend spacetime, though it might appear they do so. Archetypes are an intrinsic part of our being and the world; most times we are not aware of their functioning, while at other times we get hints of a kind of presence of something 'other' merely influencing our experience, and still at other times they may seem quite obvious to us. Empirical evidence is slowly accumulating, and I make this statement in reference to research on archetypes: For example, see Bradshaw and Storm (2013), Gibson (2010), Grof (1985), Rosen et al. (1991), and Sotirova-Kohli et al. (2011, 2013). (See also the entry for *Individuation* in Chapter 1.) The challenge for parapsychology is that experimentation needs to incorporate archetypal representations and other synchronistic factors into its designs if the field is to make progress.

Synchronicity is a mystery in its own right, but fortunately nothing to the order and magnitude of what we now call psi, the interest of which to the parapsychologist today (as it was to the ancients) has been generated naturally and entirely out of its phenomenology. And it is not at all naïve to say so. To be critical, the very premise that psi or psychic phenomena is *paranormal* has emerged from (and is founded on) a superficial understanding of its correspondences. This understanding works as a rule that has overlooked the deeper value of those correspondences that would have helped limit the psi construct to a more modest conceptualization. It is an unfortunate observation, but nothing less than literal-mindedness has reigned supreme for a very long time. That 'rule' is now long past its 'use-by' date.

To be specific, explanations of the various psi anomalies, these days primarily attributable to human mental factors, were initially sought in terms of powers of the person (magic) or outside forces (spirits, discarnate entities), but the thinking changed to materialist (physicalist) modes of explanation, and psi became a signal via some kind of information transmission (ESP), or it became an influence via some kind of energy exchange (PK)—electromagnetism, fields, waves, particles (e.g., neutrinos, antimatter, tachyons) were proposed. Now we seek explanations from quantum mechanics, space-warping, time-warping, time travel, time symmetry, spacetime transcendence, multi-dimensionalism ('many worlds'), block universes—the list goes on (see Stokes, 1987, for reviews and criticisms; see also Irwin & Watt, 2007; Mitchell, 2004; May & Marwaha, 2015a, 2015b). Theoretical examples and reviews of some of these approaches can be found in Chapter 4 of Storm (2025). And since hardly any of these theories give *sufficient* credence to meaningful coincidence as an independent factor and solution (let alone a replacement for psi), it seems the ancient idea of the individual and his/her holistic links to nature are 'old-hat' and not to be entertained.

Starting in the 1930s, J. B. Rhine's parapsychological research brought with it some advanced ideas, but these were not explored to the fullest, and especially in the last decades of the 20th century since Rhine left us, psi proponents have mostly championed paradigms that drew from only the more overt or cogent Rhinean ideas (or ideas of that ilk). However, the subtler of Rhine's ideas have not taken root and are not sufficiently scrutinized these days (for details, see Chapter 1 in Storm, 2025). Rhine virtually laid out an agenda that could have changed parapsychology's direction for the better, but it seems to have been marginalized by his own personal pursuit to isolate a subset of psi modalities that have stuck with us ever since. But his aversion to Jung's synchronicity could not have helped.

Having set a synchronistic theme, it is in that light that I now present my responses to the above-listed five points:

In the case of (i), ambiguous nomenclature and the psi theories that use those terms are problematic. Rhine (1947) and others drew attention to the former (e.g., the subcategories of psi are interchangeable provided we can 'rethink' the psi mechanism), but the broader implications were overlooked as many new theories merely revamped ESP and PK, and even valorised one psi modality over the other. We could make excuses for that—in a postmodern age, we are supposed to embrace ambiguity and celebrate diversity via relative ways of seeing. Maybe social scientists think so, but there is nothing praiseworthy or helpful or insightful about sloppy terms when precision is required. And only a postmodernist could have a problem with Einstein's famous equation because "it privileges the speed of light over other speeds that are vitally necessary to us" (Irigaray, 1987, p. 102). But Bauer (1984) hit the nail on the head:

> This picture of parapsychological diversity makes it rather easy for critics to compile from the literature a collection of widely varying statements and opinions … which can be used to paint a livid picture of the most absurd consequences from research in this area …
>
> (p. 142)

There might still be hope for the term 'psi', although I did say it is "unworkable as a construct" (Storm, 2025, p. 18),[19] but that is because many go beyond its nominal value and wish to see it as an explanation. The term 'psi' unites ESP and PK as variants of a single process, and they do often seem to be inseparable (as Rhine argued), but no one has demonstrated the two working in unison. I would argue that the two are in a *complementary* relationship, but even Rhine conceded that psi was merely a "device of convenience and does not imply that it is *known* that there is only one basic underlying type of process" (Rhine & Pratt, 1957/1974, p. 9). But psi cannot be "known" in the way an experimenter might suppose which, to be fair, is unavoidable from an epistemological point of view (see the entry *Unus Mundus* in Chapter 1). It is ironic that in his statement Rhine undermines the importance of the complementarity that he helped establish and which is implied in the term psi. The ESP/PK dichotomy represents an empirical gap that can only be bridged by philosophical outlook. It is the same for mind and matter in dual-aspect monism (see the entry *Dual-Aspect Monism* in Chapter 1); one simply has to discover something meaningful in the paradox. I wager the broader parapsychology community would never accept the *unity* of ESP and PK (psi) in quite the way as I have argued (i.e., as a complementarity) for current conventional usage sees the term psi most often applied out of convenience (as Rhine said), such as in cases where it is not certain whether ESP or PK took place. Ordinarily, when such a critical situation arises, one assumes ESP (supposedly afferent) or PK (supposedly efferent) took place, which means psi is not seen as a unitary process.

In the case of (ii), I refer to 'philosophical premises' in the plural, but there is one major assumption made in all the psi theories—namely, that spacetime is not inviolable, and psi via human consciousness can transcend distance and time, thus making ESP and PK what they are. This conclusion is still current: "if *psi does exist*, it means that human consciousness can interact with its environment beyond the usual boundaries of space and time" (Rabeyron, 2020, p. 7). Of course, there is another philosophical issue I will touch on (i.e., acausality), but the current understanding in parapsychology about spacetime begs greater attention. Theoreticians insist that anomalous communication and anomalous perturbation (i.e., information acquisition and energy exchange) lie at the heart of psi and so spacetime must be transcended in order for them to work. And the 'transcending' itself is done by a reified version of consciousness which has never been clarified or had its parameters formally outlined. Alternatively, in the synchronicity concept, a constellated archetype works within the spacetime framework, and the acausal (synchronistic) connection between 'inner' and 'outer' means no causal factor, only meaning, explains the connection.

On the causality issue, on the one hand, some parapsychologists (now considered 'old-school') treat psi as a causal process suggesting information transfer is possible, as in telepathic communications. On the other hand, doubt has slowly emerged about information transfer as largely illusory, and insufficiently demonstrated in peer-reviewed studies (Irwin & Watt, 2007; Millar, 2015). That is to say, transfer of information or energy is not the only explanation for the various psi anomalies—the Model of Pragmatic Information speaks to that issue (see von Lucadou et al., 2007), as does synchronicity theory. This lack of evidence that might have led us to specify the *actual process* is particularly noted by modern theorists who embrace the various

Observational Theories (OTs) that are based on discoveries in QM. OT theorists even refer to *trans-temporal coupling*. Again, we only have correlations (or if one prefers, correspondences) that might lead some to make misleading claims about functional causation (mentioned in Chapter 1). Thus, it is no surprise that OT theorists reject 'over-simplified' explanations for the causal transfer of information that retro-PK and precognition naively suggest, which is why Millar (2019) even compares the OTs to synchronicity. By dismissing the causal approach, the observer cannot be *exclusively* instrumental in the psi effect. The individual is merely contingent in the effect via intention or mere presence (see *The Two Agentive Forms of Synchronicity* in Chapter 2). Millar (2015) has said, "the most disturbing consequence of OT is that, if true, psi is nearly useless" (p. 175; see also Society for Scientific Exploration, 2020). More generally, if all the *causal* psi theories are incorrect, the fate of psi as *functionally causal* is sealed if it is the single expression of a host of nonlocal correlations under differing experiential circumstances and methodological scenarios.

I mentioned bridging the gap between ESP and PK by way of a philosophical outlook. That outlook works in other ways: Atmanspacher (2014b) said "dual-aspect monism merges an ontic monism, reflected by a psychophysically neutral background reality, with an epistemic dualism of the mental and the physical as perspectival aspects of the underlying ontic reality" (p. 181). That is, one single and unified reality underpins the duality we experience. I cited Benovsky (2016) earlier (Chapter 1): He asks us to imagine our experience *ontologically* as a two-part event in our brains and in our minds. Jung (1977) has said a similar thing when he points out that observing the psyche is simultaneously observing an aspect of matter. The reason for the underlying self-deception—seeing it as one or the other—appears to be phenomenological in nature. In other words, subjective experience—the *as ifs*, and *what it is like*—has decided the matter. Our experience has been split in two, but I suggest that a change in mindset might shift people to a synchronistic mode of thought in which unification is a metaphysical endpoint. However, a revealing statement by Rhine (1947) demonstrates the underriding difficulty in imagining such a shift to a unitary perspective (which is one reason we end up with complementary viewpoints): "no one can conceive of the interaction of the two systems [mind and body], except by supposing that there are properties common to both" (p. 178). That interaction is either almost material, as represented by an "underlying order of neutral substituent energetics … a substrate", or it is conceptual in the form of a "transition point, an abstraction" (p. 179).

In the case of (iii), I am confident in saying that synchronicity has not been given the attention it deserves by parapsychologists. While this may be so, it is at least a good step forward for the field to know that (a) some theorists are (sometimes inadvertently) giving heed to the synchronistic notion that our effect of interest is a psychophysical correlation (and if we recall that correlation does not imply causation, we would find it much easier to dump misleading notions like *functional causation*); (b) synchronicity is a more neutral (less loaded) term than psi (taken as ESP and PK and their sub-types) since it does not make assumptions about paranormal abilities; (c) synchronicity is a less intellectually taxing concept as there is no need to grapple with the spacetime construct and the paradoxes that emerge when we contemplate, for example, baffling concepts like precognition, retro-PK, and so on; and (d) synchronicity can be sensibly investigated.

In the case of (iv), the idea of a synchronistic world is as old as the search for knowledge; yet few in the modern era pick up on that. Very early in this book I said it was probably the scale and scope of synchronicity theory that put off parapsychologists. Yet the eight theories reviewed in Chapter 4 of Storm (2025) all borrow from Jung (1952/1969), and exhibit signs that theoreticians are 'reinventing the wheel' of synchronicity, though only to varying degrees. Some aspects of those theories, however, are fundamentally synchronistic: Stanford's (1990) Psi-Mediated Instrumental Response, Gatlin's (2008) meaningful information creation, von Lucadou's (2015) Model of Pragmatic Information (MPI), Archetypal Synchronistic Resonance (ASR; Mishlove & Engen, 2007), and Carpenter's (2012) First Sight Theory (FST), all count meaning/meaningfulness as a crucial element of psi. Only ASR speaks of archetypes, only FST (Carpenter, 2012) questions psi as an ability, and only MPI (von Lucadou, 2015) shows a direct theoretical influence of the synchronicity principle. But next to none of them make reference to a broader viewpoint bordering on the holistic beyond the limited need-serving agenda of the individual.

In the case of (v), I have argued that synchronicity theory is a comprehensible and comprehensive model that reinterprets 'psychic' functioning. From the outlines of the psi theories in Chapter 4 of Storm (2025), readers would have noted how they can be quite complex, and in some cases, I have even refrained from going into details to spare the reader. However, synchronicity is not a difficult theory to understand, yet I have been quite thorough in covering all its aspects. Some theories have reduced psi to a single function (e.g., precognition) that might seem to simplify the mechanics of psi (the process), but they still do not cover all aspects, or all manifestations, of psi.

I see synchronicity as comprehensive in that the many and varied manifestations of psi (so-called) can be properly understood as meaningful coincidences, but synchronicity speaks to all types of coincidences by strict inclusion of one form as meaningful, according to definitions, so that others are meaningless by default (see Chapters 1 & 2). Apart from the archetypal factors and related numinosity, the methodological issues, and the testability of synchronicity, the typical case of synchronicity is distinguished from the *casual* coincidence by being a *meaningful* coincidence. Meaningfulness can become a bug-bear in its own right, and it does not help that some theorists define the term rather rigidly (Aziz, 1990; Mansfield, 1995); others less formally (Beitman, 2016; Vaughan, 1979). But meaning holds its own against the often-times scrambling incoherence of real-world events, and despite those complications, we can see in the synchronistic event its utility for personal growth. With a sufficient degree of objectivity, given the human-wide presence of archetypes, we can draw out a meaning in a synchronistic experience and act on it, even necessarily going beyond the correspondences, because archetypal patterns repeat and we are born with the capacity to see those patterns for what they are without others having to infer delusional states in those who practice personal interpretations. I emphasize too the point that other advantages (even quite profitable ones) can be taken provided we can take appropriate action based on the perceptual cues of those sufficiently fortuitous spatial (distal) and/or temporal (asynchronous) separations between events that make up the synchronicity—these gaps can give time for the person to act in a favourable (even profitable) manner, but I stress only on occasion. The workings of the archetypes are fickle to say the least. Indeed, in Chapter 2, I furthered that point by discussing the unlikely extension of synchronicity to an all-embracing scientific principle. My sense of the concept of synchronicity is governed by certain parameters that specifically limit synchronicity to human experience, yet the concept necessarily places the individual in a framework beyond the self centre. But not so far beyond the human framework that I would be compelled to describe *as synchronistic* the fundamental workings of the universe; its laws, its principles.

In earlier sections of this final chapter, I attributed causal factors to psychosomatic and psychophysiological effects, thus ruling these out as candidates for psi and therefore synchronicity by their respective definitions—many of these effects are known to medicine (e.g., psychiatry). Also in this chapter, I critiqued the idea of consciousness as an *unaided* (isolated) independent entity. Consciousness must necessarily be in-tune and aligned with its brain and physical body, or to put it another way, the mind/brain complex is better understood as a functionally organised unitary organism rather than a dichotomous or split entity at odds with itself (for considerable research to that effect, see Valencia & Froese, 2020; Williams, 2015). Along similar lines of thought, archetypes may extend to the psychoid realm as a bridge between psyche and matter and, as a part of the collective unconscious, they might thus be seen as going beyond the human psyche *per se*, or they facilitate an extension of it—that is why I suggested in this chapter that IBNS is an as-yet unspecified archetypal process. We must give heed to the possibility that some seemingly anomalous phenomena and experiences (not necessarily paranormal but suggestively synchronistic at this stage) can be brought about by those same evolutionary processes that have shaped our generally accepted natures and behaviours.

My final point, made earlier but bears repeating: As far as *experiencing* synchronicity is concerned, one may get a sense that archetypes are boundless, which again might propagate the idea that spacetime can be transcended by the mind/brain complex. As I said above, Muller's (2016) "now" connotes a real present, and it is only in the ever-unfolding present that the universe becomes manifested, while the future is unmanifested; the 'realm' of possibilities. And bizarre as it may sound, Muller has been beaten to the punch for that idea is not new: "There was no time before time but time was created with the world" (Anon, cited in Jung, 1952/1969, para. 967, n17). As I also said, to be beguiled by terms like 'boundlessness' and 'transcendence' more likely only helps to create our own special illusion, even opening us up to the mistaken idea that the hard sciences (i.e., those that study matter) can be built on synchronistic principles, and we must infuse it with our psyche as if we must now embrace a special form of projection (not at all what I have been saying). That is why I could not go so far as agreeing entirely with Donati (2008) in her original statement that synchronicity as a principle would "grant privilege to a unitary worldview in which both science and philosophy (including metaphysics) together should help to create a fertile ground for the emergence of scientific theories" (p. 60). In short, even though we can be sure archetypal forms extend to (and emerge from) matter (e.g., in the configurational properties of numbers), nothing synchronistic emerges until a living being becomes meaningfully engaged or enmeshed by way of the relevant archetype (one may even choose to grapple with the paradox that we are in the experience and part of it, but independent of it; consciousness gives us that privilege). Then we might speak of psychophysical or parapsychological factors.

To quote Grattan-Guinness (1978), synchronicity "is more modest in its existential claims" (p. 954), when compared to the paranormal claims made in parapsychology, though that enlightened view actually comes from a synchronicity skeptic. When a 'big picture' (holistic) idea of the human world is given credence, humans discover themselves as players in world events where the occasional paranormal dimension can be seen as only apparent—where there is no need to invoke notions of the presence of extra-sensory or super-sensory abilities and powers potentially bordering on omnipotence. A special kind of coincidence explains much of it, but without the need to multiply entities beyond necessity. The fabric of the human world need only have woven into it repeating and recurring archetypal threads throughout that hold it together and give it a certain pattern often conveyed in human experience as meaning.

For the most part, synchronicity (like psi) is fickle and uncontrollable, but it is not altogether sporadic and unpredictable, for we can often determine those archetypal patterns that manifest as meaningful outcomes and events—laboratory findings give us good reason to make the claim for an extrachance phenomenon like synchronicity. This synchronistic view vanquishes the skeptic's dismissive nonsense whereby anything paranormal must necessarily be nothing more than chance co-occurrence of non-related events. But nor are these coincidences to be reduced to magic requiring a special knack or skill; an innate or learned ability. And above all, we still have influence for human intention can work in unexplainable ways. Even though our normal, everyday aims and subsequent successes constantly and convincingly suggest authorship lies buried in our very own agency, we should not be so absolute.

Throughout this book I have argued for primordial (archetypal) processes that set the agenda for how scenarios will play out: Jung proposed that *archetypes* are core elements of synchronicity, and he argued that when they *constellate*, conventional spacetime rules (those with which we are familiar) seem to 'bend' and we get effects that look paranormal (more correctly, they are synchronistic). What we might say is that we can have direct experience of ubiquitous and universal archetypal patterns when they constellate by going beyond their inner (mental) reference frame. We are swimming in a sea of these possibilities, but still remain within spacetime constraints—archetypal experience gives only the suggestion of a lifting of the spacetime veil.

For our purposes, 'now' is perpetually created anew, giving a psychological and entropic sense of an arrow of time moving forward, so that for us 'now' exists at the razor's edge of eternity. Our focus then, even though we are forever placed as finite beings on that precipitous edge, is 'here' and 'now' on *process*—how it all works. I have suggested that end is achieved via the deep imagination, which is often an interactional process of conscious intention with the elements (archetypes) of a stratum of the psyche that Jung (1959/1968) called the collective unconscious. Though not an entirely reliable function, the deep imagination is sufficiently serviceable and workable in a range of applications still under-researched. The findings in parapsychology have hinted as much, so we must now look to that deeper realm of the imagination.

Notes

1 It is a common understanding that other people's stories and coincidences are never thought to be as surprising or impressive as one's own (Falk, 1989; Moore, Thalbourne, & Storm, 2010) See also Chapter 4 for examples.

2 Note that the "A" in GAO (standing for "acausal") undermines the parapsychologist's (and Jung's) claim for a cause-based psi, which has led to no end of confusion. I dealt with the causality/acausality issue in Chapter 1 (*Causality and Acausality*), and Chapter 2 (*Categorical Problems: V. Causality vs. Acausality*). See also, 'The Trick of the Cause in Parapsychology' in Chapter 3 of Storm (2025).

3 This quote can also be found in a reprinted article (Beloff, 2008, pp. 99–100).

4 Eisenbud (1990) mentions Jung by name, but does not reference him.

5 See "Levitation" in the Society for Psychical Research Glossary (https://www.spr.ac.uk/research/glossary).

6 May et al. (1995) proposed that "humans integrate information obtained by anomalous cognition [e.g., precognition] into the usual decision process" (p. 195). Decision Augmentation Theory therefore is paranormally acquired efficacious

information incorporated unconsciously so as to influence the organism's mental and behavioural decisions.

7 In the context of his chapter, I take Watkins (2015) to mean macro-PK primarily.

8 The anomalies associated with Pearl Curran and Rosemary Brown are too numerous and detailed to go into here, so I refer interested readers to Braude (2003).

9 Wahbeh et al. (2024) review telephone-telepathy and telephone-precognition studies dating back to 2003.

10 Recall from Chapter 1 that Blackmore and Chamberlain (1993) demonstrated superior "thought concordance" in their identicals without needing to posit that it was psi (ESP or meaningful coincidence).

11 That figure of 30% comes from a 1981 survey (Rosambeau, 1981). However, percentages can range up to 60% in reference to experiences "judged to be of a telepathic nature" (Brusewitz et al., 2013, p. 220), although "frequent telepathic experiences" can be as low as 14% for identical twins (p. 231).

12 Besides RV as clairvoyance, other RV work involves 'dyads', or agent/viewer pairs, to prove RV in telepathic mode.

13 Mitchell (1971) never sought, and did not have, prior approval from NASA to conduct his experiment.

14 For a discussion of *run-score variance*, see "Alternative Explanations of Synchronicity: I. Chance" in Chapter 1.

15 These words appear to have been borrowed from 12th century Italian theologian Abbot Joachim of Fiore.

16 As it happened, I watched Kurosawa's (1950) classic film *Rashomon* on the night of June 25, 2020, only to find in my email the following morning, an e-version of #42 of the magazine *Edgescience* that features Wargo's (2020) article on the Rashomon effect. *Rashomon* means "Main City Gate" which has nothing to do with the effect.

17 I suspect there will be much dispute over this claim as indeed Jung himself, in his *Synchronicity* essay and elsewhere, accepted Rhine's terms in principle, but not for the right reasons, as I have argued at the beginning of this chapter.

18 In particular, see the full quote from Jung (1955/1987, p. 116) in the entry *Archetypes* in "Some Synchronistic Terms" in Chapter 1. Also, as Jung explains elsewhere, the archetype becomes conscious in the expectation or hope of effects that carry with them "affectivity", which "rests to a large extent on the instincts, whose formal aspect is the archetype" (1952/1969, para. 846).

19 For a more informed understanding of the points made here, I encourage readers to visit Chapter 1 of Storm (2025).

Appendix A: The Birthday Paradox

Calculating the probability that at least two people have the same birthday in a group of n people.

First, it is simpler to calculate the probability $\bar{p}(n)$ that all n birthdays are *different*.

Thus, $\bar{p}(n)$ is zero when $n > 365$. When $n \leq 365$:

$$\begin{aligned}\overline{p}(n) &= 1 \times (1 - 1/365) \times (1 - 2/365) \times \cdots \times (1 - [n-1]/365) \\ &= \frac{365 \times 364 \times \cdots \times (365 - n + 1)}{365^n} \\ &= \frac{365!}{365^n(365-n)!} = \frac{n!.\binom{365}{n}}{365^n} = \frac{{}_{365}P_n}{365^n}\end{aligned}$$

where ! is the factorial operator, $\binom{365}{n}$ is the binomial coefficient, and ${}_kP_r$ (i.e., ${}_{365}P_n$ in the equation) denotes permutation.

The equation means the first person's birthday cannot be the same as anyone else's in the group, the second person's birthday cannot be the same as the first person's (364/365); the third person's birthday cannot be the same as the first or second person's (363/365), and so on to the nth birthday, which cannot be the same as any of the $n - 1$ preceding birthdays.

Second, the probability of at least two of the n persons having the same birthday is complementary to all n birthdays being different. Therefore, its probability $p(n)$ is

$$p(n) = 1 - \overline{p}(n)$$

Appendix B: Experiments on Meaningful Coincidence

Braud's Experiments with Meaningful Key Words

Braud (1983) conducted two experiments to assess meaningful coincidence quantitatively, and in both cases he achieved significant results. In the first experiment, Braud selected ten *key* words on the basis of a "special feeling" or "anomalous attention". Ten *control* words were selected from a compilation of spoken English frequency norms. Both key and control word-pairs were matched on frequency. The experiment was run over a 24-hour period for each pair. Occurrences of the key words were found in the environment, casual conversation, radio dialogue, etc.

Braud did not count the occurrences of the key word in its initial context, since it was over-represented there. Braud also conducted his day-to-day routine as per usual, so as to avoid seeking out "confirmatory contexts" where the key word might appear with greater than usual frequency. Upon statistical analysis, the "key (synchronistic) instances occurred significantly sooner than the matched control instances" (1983, p. 6).

In a second experiment, Braud used a "limited newspaper record" (1983, p. 7) to source his key and control words (selection was as per the first experiment). Again ten trials were run. The newspaper, the *San Antonio Express*, was preselected, as was the issue for the day if "a possible meaningful coincidence was identified on a particular day" (p. 7). Braud read the articles column by column, and readings were timed. The two words were timed from the moment they appeared in the text. Again there was a significant result. The key words were encountered sooner than the matched controls. These results suggested that not only does "a *tool* for the study of synchronicity" exist (p. 8), but also that synchronicity is at least as regular and predictable as parapsychological phenomena.

Experiments with the *I Ching*

Storm and Thalbourne (1998–1999) conducted an initial study using the *I Ching* in a somewhat unorthodox manner, though one of the traditional techniques (i.e., coin-throwing) was used as the means by which hexagram lines were generated (there were six studies using this design up to 2014). Participants were required to pre-select 16 "descriptors pairs" out of the complete set of 64 descriptors that corresponded to 64 *I Ching* readings. The divinatory process kicks in when three coins are tossed six times to produce a so-called hexagram (a symbol comprised of six lines that is linked to a reading that gives a forecast). Though seemingly chosen at random, the forecast is argued by Jung to be derived as part of a process that is synchronistic—"the psychic process itself is just as much 'arranged' as the coinciding representation which anticipates the external physical process" (Jung, as cited in Greatrex, 1999, p. 6). In other words, in these early studies up to 2014, it was reasoned that some of the sixteen choices—if not all of them—may resonate for the participant at various emotional levels and at least one of these inner (psychological) process would meaningfully connect with the physical (outer) arrangement of the coin outcomes that determine the symbol and subsequent reading.

In the first two studies, Storm and Thalbourne (1998–1999, 2001) found significant effects—outcome hexagrams were matched to descriptor-pairs more often than could be explained by chance (32% and then 35%, where chance is only 25%). Although other *I Ching* studies have produced mixed results on the hexagram outcome variables (fluctuating around chance), the overall trend has been towards above-chance hitting at 27% (see Storm, 2001, 2002, 2006a, 2008a; Thalbourne & Storm, 2014). Besides the aggregate effect being weak (though weak does not mean unimportant), the effects have been inconsistent from study to study.

Storm (2008a) conducted a follow-up study to test perceptions of meaningfulness of hexagram readings (these were rated on scale of "0% meaningful" to "100% meaningful"). He found significant differences between (i) believers (77.24%) and non-believers (53.26%), and (ii) "hitters" (participants who correctly preselected the outcome hexagram; meaningfulness score = 72.53%) and "missers" (participants who failed to preselect the outcome hexagram; meaningfulness score = 64.70%). Also, the believer/non-believer difference on hitting was also significant (30.1% vs. 19.4%, respectively, where MCE = 25%), which is also known as a sheep–goat effect (for a definition of sheep-goat effect, see footnote 47 in Chapter 1).

Palmer (2016) pointed out that the hitting/missing meaningfulness difference is "most likely an artifact" (p. 194) given that some participants could tie their outcome readings to one of their 16 pre-selected (i.e., meaningfully selected) descriptor pairs and therefore possibly rate the readings high on meaningfulness, while all other participants who made no relevant pre-selections could therefore possibly rate their readings low. Ordinarily, when we have an artifact, we withdraw the claim for a genuine effect but, in this case, that would be unreasonable. For a start, whether or not *some* participants might refer back to their pre-selections (assuming the parallel even dawned on them), nothing will stop *all* participants reviewing their genuine mental (psychological) states as they read, so the content has every chance of resonating meaningfully, and with integrity in either case. Note too that "Participants were not told whether their hexagram was a hit or not" (Storm, 2008a, p. 112). This fact adds emphasis to my previous point. Also, the sheep/goat × hitting/missing interaction effect was not significant, so it is unlikely that (a) getting a hit resulted in disproportionately high meaningfulness ratings given by some hitters who were sheep, *OR* (b) getting a miss resulted in disproportionately low meaningfulness ratings given by some missers who were goats. Since sheep scored significantly more hits than goats, either of these two, (a) or (b), would only have been a likely scenario *if there was a significant interaction effect.*

Roe, Martin, and Drennan (2014) used cards with short statements (synopses) to paraphrase the hexagram readings, and these cards were slotted into a triangular grid-like framework (a Q-Sort grid) of 64 cells, which amounts to a rating or ranking process. The *I Ching* methodology was computerized so that the entire procedure involved no manual steps (i.e., no ticking off 16 of 64 descriptor pairs, and no coin-throwing). Participants were guided by on-screen instructions and electronic read-outs, with all data-entry by keyboard, and an RNG was used to generate hexagram lines. Graphically and statistically, an ostensible psi effect in a sample is indicated by a significant shift from a mean score of zero to some higher mean score. In two randomization methods (pseudo and "true"), Roe et al. reported positive mean shifts in the hypothesized direction, and one negative mean shift (method: random number tables)—all shifts were small and nonsignificant. The major problem with the study was that the small sample of only 33 participants did not have sufficient power for the small effects to reach significance.

In 2014, Storm and Rock (2014a) borrowed the Q-Sort protocol designed by Roe et al. (2014), but modified it, thus allowing participants the chance to rank all 64 two-word descriptor-pairs (ranging from –7 to +7; with a mean of zero), instead of selecting only 16 from the pool of 64. This procedure also dispensed with the 64 lengthy statements Roe et al. used. Some significant effects were found for paranormal believers with believers producing stronger *I Ching* effects than nonbelievers.

Houran and Lange (2012) investigated combinations of Paranormal Belief (high-scoring vs. low-scoring as measured on Tobacyk's, 1988, Revised Paranormal Belief Scale) and Transliminality (high-scoring vs. low-scoring) in the context of an *I Ching* task. The authors reported a statistically significant hexagram hit rate of 45% for the overall sample, where MCE = 25%. As hypothesized, the high/high group produced the highest hit rate. In a follow-up study, Lange and Houran (2013) again hypothesized that experimenters and participants scoring high on both Paranormal Belief *and* Transliminality (i.e., high-participant/high-experimenter) would produce a higher hexagram hit rate than their low scoring participant/experimenter counterparts (i.e., low-participant/high-experimenter; high-participant/low-experimenter, and low-participant/low-experimenter). The "First Hexagram" hit rate for both the overall sample and the high-high group was statistically significant, but at chance level for the other three groups.

The Author's Synchronicity Tests on the Melbourne Cup

The Melbourne Cup, Australia's biggest horse race, held in Melbourne, Victoria, every year on the first Tuesday of November, has a long and illustrious history going back to 1861. It has achieved worldwide fame, and Alice Johnson (1899) noted how it was not surprising that there have been many dream-ESP cases that describe successful predictions of Melbourne Cup winners. She does appeal to the Law of Truly Large Numbers ("… as the dreams must be numbered by thousands, one or two of the dreams occasionally come true"; p. 317), but she gives one example that is out of the ordinary: Some four months before the Melbourne Cup of 1895, a Redfern resident dreamed of the horse *Auraria* winning, but he also dreamed he would die before the race was run. He backed the horse for a £200 win, and gave the ticket to his wife. Although he enjoyed good health at the time of the dream, he took ill and died (as predicted) some weeks before the race, but *Auraria* did win (as also predicted). His wife collected the winnings. Johnson makes light of the win on statistical grounds giving odds against dreaming of a winning horse at "not more than about 100 to 1" (p. 319), and she presumes that the dreamer may have been aware (even subliminally) that a life-threatening malady was imminent, but she was never able to prove her theory.

The following four studies do not depend on the arbitrary and effectively nonintentional nature of dreams, but were conducted to test the proposition that synchronicity can be intentional.

Study One (2013). On the Monday night before the Melbourne Cup race, I attempted intentional synchronicity to see if it might yield the Cup winner (reported in Storm, 2014). It happened to be the case that I wanted to watch a classic Japanese movie *Gate of Hell* (Nagata & Kinugasa, 1953) that I had never seen, and had been putting off for almost a week. Monday night before the big day Tuesday, I finally did watch the film, which was set in feudal Japan. Two rivals were out to prove themselves in an annual horse race, and I found it most intriguing that the horse of one rival was draped in a bright purple sash, for I wondered if the horse and colour purple were clues to the identity of the Cup winner. The other rival's horse sported an orange sash. The horse in purple won. Come Tuesday morning, before the main race at 2:30 p.m., I checked the newspaper for information about the horses. The Cup was running three horses with jockeys in purple (*Fiorente, Hawkspur*, and *Simenon*). Come Tuesday morning, I put "win and place" bets (i.e., each-way bets) on three horses: *Fiorente* (a favourite), *Hawkspur*, and *Voleuse de Coeurs* (based on a tip from a self-proclaimed psychic friend). For reasons not clear to me, I did not bet on *Simenon*, which ultimately came fourth. *Fiorente* was the winner, and I made a small profit.

Study Two (2014). I set about my evening (Monday night before the race on Tuesday) in the usual way—by sitting down to an evening in front of the TV (reported in Storm, 2015). I watched a re-run of *Agatha Christie's Marple* (an episode called "Murder Is Easy"). I was looking for a "sign", but the only thing that jumped out at me repeatedly were blue wild flowers. I kept blue in mind. Interestingly, I had a dream the day before (early Sunday morning) about my riding a brown horse, but there are many brown and "brownish" (i. e., bay, chestnut) horses in the Melbourne Cup, so the colour "brown" was of little help. My clues thus far: blue flower, and brown (or chestnut, or bay!) horse. As was the case in 2013, I expected the blue to associate with the jockey's silks (in particular, one jockey riding the favourite, *Protectionist*, which was to win), but there were at least six other jockeys in blue silks—I had no exclusion criteria to get a reasonable shortlist of (say) three or four horses to bet on. But I was in the ball-park. In fact, I found an online ABC NEWS article confirming that (a) bays win the Cup most often, and (b) "runners with predominantly blue jockey silks" also win most often.[1] This outcome could therefore be regarded as synchronistic. As it happened, I did not have time nor inclination to make an official bet anyway—without some additional criteria, and extra time for a little more "homework" on colour combinations, I did not fancy my chances.

Study Three (2015). On the Monday night before the Melbourne Cup race, I watched an episode of *The Saint* (Charteris et al., 1964), which happened to feature a horse race. Unfortunately, this episode was in black and white, and only a brief scene of the horse race was shown, so I could not make out any distinguishing features (colours or numbers) that would be of help to me in preparing a short list of jockeys/horses.

Study Four (2018). I did not follow the Melbourne Cup in 2016 and 2017, and had very nearly ignored the race in 2018. In fact, I had forgotten about the race up until the Tuesday morning of race day, having been preoccupied with more pressing matters. At around 12:30 p.m. (two hours before the race, Adelaide time), I wondered what activity I could engage in that might create an opportunity for intentional synchronicity. I was actually driving to the beach intending to have lunch on the foreshore, and on the way I thought to play some music in the car, and listen for clues in the lyrics of whatever song came up, though I cannot say why I thought that might create the first half of the synchronicity (the corresponding second half being the future target—i.e., the winning jockey/horse). In the car, I *thought* of playing some music by Swedish pop group ABBA (which I did not do), but at that moment a particular album cover of theirs, Voulez-Vous, came to mind which features a mainly blue cover, with Agnetha Fältskog wearing a blue dress—note point (b) in *Study Two* above about jockeys wearing "predominantly blue jockey silks" winning most often *as of 2015*. However, only later that day (after the race) did I discover that the website Races.com.au noted that more "winning jockeys have worn black as their main colour than any other colour", followed by "navy blue and royal blue" as the next more popular colour in recent Melbourne Cup history.[2] So, I was to go against the trend for when I arrived back home at 2:00 p.m., I did not play any ABBA music, but (with so little time left) I decided instead to check a list of all 24 jockeys and single out those jockeys wearing purely blue silks for my shortlist. I found three jockeys who wore only blue silks—their horses were *Best Solution, Avilius*, and *Cross Counter*. The winning horse was *Cross Counter*. There was no time for betting, but my usual strategy (when there are not too many horses on my shortlist) would have been to bet "each-way" (i.e., bet for a win and a place) on all short-listed horses. The odds (win, 9:1; place, 3:1) would have assured a profit.

Study Five (2019). Going about my usual routine on the night prior to the race, I felt somewhat compromised as I was working my way through the 1960s TV drama series *Peyton Place*, and did not think any particular episode could produce much that was reliable in the way of colour clues (the series ran from 1964 to 1969, and went to colour in 1966). Very old videotape copies of the episodes were obviously recorded directly from television, and years later were converted to digital format, and then uploaded to Youtube channel "SoapsNthings", but with much colour degradation and/or alteration (some of the worst copies were awash in shades of grey and purple, with only occasional splashes of colour here and there). On the Monday night before the race, I had nearly completed watching the entire five seasons on YouTube. That night, I viewed a few of the remaining episodes, including episode #490, although all that came to my attention in that episode was the elderly widow, Maggie Riggs, wearing a woollen scarf alternately coloured red and black (or perhaps *orange* and black, given the colour distortion). There were no jockeys wearing red and black, or orange and black, although three jockeys did feature orange in their silks—they rode *Il Paradiso, Vow and Declare*, and *Magic Wand*. The winner was *Vow and Declare* whose jockey wore mainly orange (much more orange than the other two). Only two jockeys wore red: *Prince of Arran*'s jockey wore red and blue silk; *Steel Prince*'s jockey wore silk featuring a red cross—these two ran second and third, respectively. With five horses on the shortlist, and not knowing which to eliminate, the best gambling option would have been to make "each-way" or "place" bets on all five horses.

Discussion and Conclusions

William Braud's successful experiments were simple, straight-forward attempts to see if his unique selection of key words would pop up externally somewhere (e.g., in media), thus forming matched pairs with greater than chance frequency. Braud called these matches "meaningful coincidences", but he also deferred to the word "synchronicity". It was never clear to me whether he thought the two were different somehow, perhaps with meaningful coincidence, in his mind, being a lesser form of synchronicity. It would seem so, as the coincidence factor is definitely there, but his examples do not seem to express any great level of meaning for him personally—at least, not beyond that "first level" described by Aziz (1990).

The author's experiments with the *I Ching* tried to overcome that limitation by making possible a meaningful experience for participants, which is the crux of the *I Ching* philosophy. The ancient Chinese were interested in how and why things in nature and human experience that occur together might be related, and whether there was some way of deliberately capturing that in a humanly devised process or system. The development of the *I Ching* came to be particularly focused on higher principles not dependent on temporal or spatial parameters, but were universal and forever true. Ideally, these "truths" could or would be addressed and presented in philosophical contexts, manifesting as meanings generated and represented in pertinent readings. The author's studies were encouraging in that respect—it seemed that chance could not explain how some participants were able to produce readings that anticipated or spoke to their feelings *a priori*. Two different approaches to testing the *I Ching* were taken, but outcomes bore similarities that supported (though only somewhat) the general assumption that the *I Ching* system can offer perspectives on, or solutions to unanswerable or unresolvable questions, without the outcome necessarily being wholly attributable to chance factors.

Generally, the results of a series of Melbourne Cup races suggest that intentional synchronicity may be a viable means of predicting future outcomes in a gambling scenario, and could even prove lucrative (as in *Study One*). However, questions relating to source (or better, priming) material, especially its quality, need addressing (as was the case in *Study Three* and *Study Five*). Basically, good-quality source material is not always available, though that will depend on the practitioner's lifestyle (e.g., his/her media and entertainment preferences and interests). That is to say, clues do not always appear in the stimulus material, but that is due to choices and capacity to spot clues if they are there in the material (which is hopefully of good quality), so various natural limits come into play. On the one hand, a major part of the protocol (i.e., identifying and evaluating the cogency of the stimuli) seems more like art than science requiring training (as in remote viewing) to filter out nonessential details. On the other hand, it may be that essential details are lacking so that a shortlist cannot be prepared as was evident in *Study Two* and *Study Four*.

Many more trials are needed that test a range of participants (e.g., both amateur and professional gamblers), to see how well the protocol performs in the long run, and for whom. In the meantime, strategic betting is advised, although opinion is divided as to which form of betting is going to be more fruitful and/or profitable when shortlists do result from the protocol—e.g., *place betting* or *each-way betting*. That may depend on the odds, as every race is different. Of course, the author's Melbourne Cup studies were tests of synchronistic intention; not betting strategies (if the former is consistent, the latter will have to be devised by those with a basic understanding of statistics, and/or a good knowledge of the betting world).

Notes

1 https://www.abc.net.au/news/2015-11-02/melbourne-cup-2015-how-the-runners-compare-to-past-champions/6891238
2 http://www.races.com.au/melbourne-cup/melbourne-cup-history/facts-and-statistics/

Appendix C: The I Ching and the Binary System—Comparisons

Origins of the *I Ching*

The *I Ching* is an ancient Chinese system of divination, consisting of a book of 64 hexagrams (six-line symbols) and their corresponding readings that supposedly enlighten in practical and philosophical ways, and even provide forecasts of future events in response to questions posed by the user. The *I Ching* then, as the so-called "Book of Changes", was both didactic and oracular. The 64 hexagrams symbolize human, social, and cosmic "situations". Hellmut Wilhelm (1905–1990)—son of Richard Wilhelm (1873–1930), both of whom were noted German sinologists—argued in his book *Changes* that these situations addressed "primary needs", "evolution of personality", "character traits", "social life", and "images of suprapersonal significance" (Wilhelm, 1960, pp. 4–5).

Legend has it that King Fu Hsi (2953–2838 B.C.E.) laid down the basics of the *I Ching* system. King Wên, the founder of the Chou dynasty (1150–249 B.C.E.), wrote most of the original text, and his son Chu Kung, the Duke of Chou, expanded the text further. Buddhist and Taoist philosophies are evident in the *I Ching*, as is the influence of Confucius, who authored the commentaries that supplement the readings.

The *I Ching* was first introduced into the English-speaking world in 1899 through James Legge's (1971) book *I Ching*, which was a translation of the original Chinese text. The "emblematic representations" (the hexagrams) were a mystery to Legge, and his skepticism, and the fact that he did not use the *I Ching* personally, is evident throughout the text. Richard Wilhelm's book *I Ching or the Book of Changes* (1987) and Ritsema and Sabbadini's (2005) book *The Original I Ching Oracle*, are two of the most in-depth works to date on this enigmatic divinatory system. In common use today, the standard practice requires the throwing of three coins six times to generate a hexagram reading, which depicts a scenario (with commentary) that ostensibly describes the past, present, and even future life situation of the user.

Structure of the *I Ching* as a Binary System

The major principle of the *I Ching*, which instils it with a meaningful structure, is the binary or yin/yang philosophy, and it is this philosophy that activates that meaningful structure, in the sense that change is inevitable and comes about as a result of the resonance between two polar opposites, yin and yang. Capra (1988) describes this resonance as the dynamic interplay of these archetypal opposites: Yin represents the principles of Earth, passivity, the "feminine", the negative, and darkness, while yang represents the principles of Heaven, activity, the "masculine", the positive, and light. These two are indispensable as they hold the universe in balance. Therein lies the principle of "twoness" or duality. The two elements of the yin/yang binary system are represented as "broken" and "unbroken" lines (see Figure C.1).

By various combinations of yin and yang (yin/yin, yin/yang, yang/yin, and yang/yang) the four duograms or bigrams are formed (see Figure C.2). The duograms represent a four-step continuum, moving from old yin to old yang—a gradual shift from one polar opposite to the other.

By the addition of a yin or a yang line to each of the duograms, eight trigrams (the *pa kua*) are formed (see Figure C.3).

The trigrams also represent a continuum, but in eight steps, from Heaven through to Earth.[1] The individual trigrams are magnified in meaning above and beyond the simple degrees of yin and yang, or the duograms. For example, Heaven (≡) symbolizes creativity, masculinity, activity, and the Father. Finally, pairing the

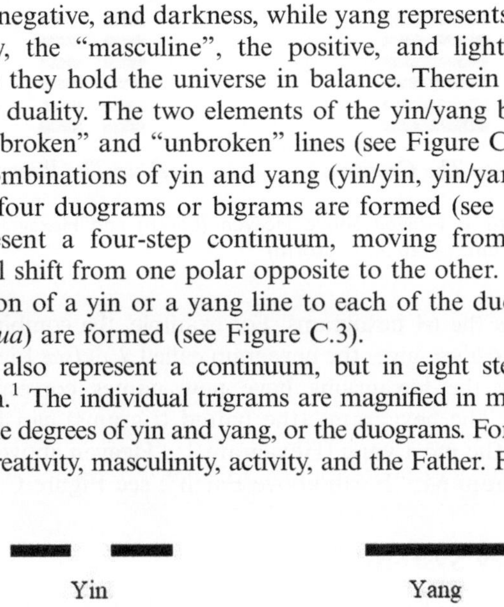

Figure C.1 The yin and yang lines. (© 2024, L. Storm)

Figure C.2 The four duograms. (© 2024, L. Storm)

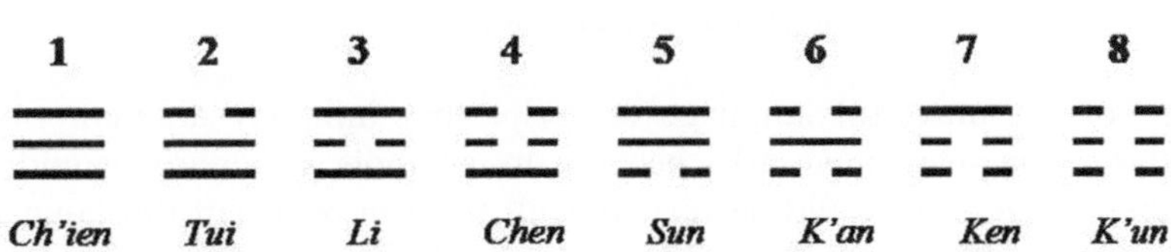

Figure C.3 The eight trigrams (*pa kua*). (© 2024, L. Storm)

Figure C.4 Constructing hexagram #11: "Earth above Heaven" (*T'ai*). (© 2024, L. Storm)

Figure C.5 Hexagram 1: Heaven above Heaven (*Chi'en*) and Hexagram 64: Earth above Earth (*K'un*). (© 2024, L. Storm)

trigrams produces the 64 hexagrams. For example, the combination of two trigrams, *K'un* plus *Ch'ien*, gives the hexagram called *T'ai* (*see* Figure C.4).

In most cases the hexagrams have new names corresponding to their unique qualities. The hexagrams (the paired trigrams) can be arranged as a continuum from the most yang (Hexagram 1: "Heaven above Heaven") to the most yin (Hexagram 64: "Earth above Earth"; see Figure C.5).[2]

Leibniz's Binary System

The binary system familiar to us today is generally believed to have been invented by Gottfried Wilhelm Leibniz (1646–1716). Just as the Chinese saw the Principle of Two at work in everyday (unscientific, unmathematical) life events bound up in meaningful scenarios, governed by the rule of archetypal principles (though they did not use such terms), Leibniz too recognised the same principle embodied in the various dyads, such as 'on-off', 'yes-no', 'dark-light', and so on (see Storm, 2008e, for more on dyads). Taking these ideas further, "Leibniz believed logic, or 'the laws of thought' could be moved from a verbal state – which was subject to the ambiguities of language, tone and circumstance – into an absolute mathematical condition" (Redshaw, 1996). In *De Arte Combinatoria* (*On the Art of Combination*), Leibniz envisioned

> a sort of universal language or script, but infinitely different from all those imagined previously, because its symbols and words would direct the reason.... It would be very difficult to form or invent this language or characteristic, but very easy to understand it without any dictionaries.
>
> (Leibniz, 1666, cited in Maracchia, 2013, p. 139)

Here we have Leibniz's problem in a nutshell. While Leibniz's aim was to find a simple (binary) system to make mathematics and problem-solving easier, he did not have a practical, conceptually broader information-processing system in mind at the time (the 17th century), the main reason being that the appropriate technology, and the fields of information theory, electronics, and computing, were nonexistent. Though virtually impossible then, due to the difficulty in manually managing and analysing binary data, it became possible in the computer age (the 20th century) to convert logical verbal statements into purely mathematical statements, manage, store, and analyse the resulting data, and generate solutions.

As I just mentioned, the binary system underpins the basic principles of modern computing, and therefore plays a pivotal part in the functioning of modern electronic devices. The main reason binary adapted so well in modern computing is a practical and simple one: "off" (no electrical charge) can represent 0, while "on" (electrical charge) can represent 1. From there, zeroes and ones (i.e., binary digits or "bits") can be combined to represent numbers, 0, 1, 2, 3, 4, 5, etc., as 0, 1, 10, 11, 100, 101, etc., respectively. Going further, alphabets, and therefore text, and therefore information in any written language, can be converted to meaningful information in the form of 0s (zeroes) and 1s (ones)—for example, A = 01000001. Being represented as a "charge" or "no-charge", the 0s and 1s can be stored/recorded digitally in electronic memory circuits, not only as numbers and text, but also as images and musical notation. The binary numeral system is also referred to as the base-2 numeral system (in our everyday lives, we use the base-10 numeral system).

Though I mention Leibniz's problem of not being able to realize his ideas fully, my purpose in this appendix was to show how the modern binary system dates back more than a few centuries to Leibniz, and is basically a rediscovery of principles far older, and already applied, albeit in a culturally different manner. Another key point here is that Leibniz arrived at his binary system without the aid of the *I Ching* and its underlying philosophy, which he discovered after he developed his system. But he did see the *I Ching* as backing up his ideas about the binary system. The reader may see that I have touched upon these points in the above-described *I Ching* system, but I need to elaborate further as there is more than a mere 'yin'/'yang' → 'zero'/'one' exchange involved here. All hexagrams can be converted to binary numbers. Figure C.5 gives an example—we simply convert *K'un* to 000000 = 0, and *Chi'en* to 111111 = 63. The conversion follows a simple rule effectively given above except that off/on is replaced with yin/yang: hence, broken line = 0; unbroken line = 1. Figure C6 shows how all 64 *I Ching* hexagrams can be converted to binary numbers (NB: hexagrams have been rotated 90° clockwise to better illustrate the binary equivalent).

A number of points need to be made here regarding Figure C.6. First, there are only 64 possible configurations of six hexagram lines given various combinations of yin and yang lines. Second, the two non-binary hexagram numbering systems—King Wên's and Richard Wilhelm's (Wilhelm, 1987, pp. 730–731)—purposefully follow different rules so that there is a disparity: King Wên's system aids in hexagram searches for divinatory purposes, whereas Wilhelm's "moving line sequence" presents as a book of wisdom. Third, in Figure C.6, we see that the hexagrams are re-ordered following the rule of step-by-step increases (and decreases) in the number of unbroken lines replacing broken lines so that numbering (counting upwards) can then occur in accordance with base 2 rules.

Hexagram	Base 2 → 10	King Wên #	Name	Hexagram	Base 2 → 10	King Wên #	Name
䷁	000000 = 0	2	The Receptive	䷗	100000 = 32	24	Return
䷖	000001 = 1	23	Splitting Apart	䷚	100001 = 33	27	Corners of the Mouth
䷇	000010 = 2	8	Holding Together	䷂	100010 = 34	3	Difficulty at the Beginning
䷒	000011 = 3	19	Approach	䷩	100011 = 35	42	Increase
䷏	000100 = 4	16	Enthusiasm	䷲	100100 = 36	51	The Arousing
䷢	000101 = 5	35	Progress	䷔	100101 = 37	21	Biting Through
䷬	000110 = 6	45	Gathering Together	䷐	100110 = 38	17	Following
䷋	000111 = 7	12	Standstill	䷘	100111 = 39	25	Innocence
䷎	001000 = 8	15	Modesty	䷣	101000 = 40	36	Darkening of the Heart
䷳	001001 = 9	52	Keeping Still	䷕	101001 = 41	22	Grace
䷦	001010 = 10	39	Obstruction	䷾	101010 = 42	63	After Completion
䷴	001011 = 11	53	Development	䷤	101011 = 43	37	The Family
䷽	001100 = 12	62	Preponderance of the Small	䷶	101100 = 44	55	Abundance
䷷	001101 = 13	56	The Wanderer	䷝	101101 = 45	30	The Clinging
䷞	001110 = 14	31	Influence	䷰	101110 = 46	49	Revolution
䷠	001111 = 15	33	Retreat	䷌	101111 = 47	13	Fellowship with Men
䷆	010000 = 16	7	The Army	䷓	110000 = 48	20	Contemplation
䷃	010001 = 17	4	Youthful Folly	䷨	110001 = 49	41	Decrease
䷜	010010 = 18	29	The Abysmal	䷻	110010 = 50	60	Limitation
䷺	010011 = 19	59	Dispersion	䷼	110011 = 51	61	Inner Truth
䷧	010100 = 20	40	Deliverance	䷵	110100 = 52	54	The Marrying Maiden
䷿	010101 = 21	64	Before Completion	䷥	110101 = 53	38	Opposition
䷮	010110 = 22	47	Oppression	䷹	110110 = 54	58	The Joyous
䷅	010111 = 23	6	Conflict	䷉	110111 = 55	10	Treading
䷭	011000 = 24	46	Pushing Upward	䷊	111000 = 56	11	Peace
䷑	011001 = 25	18	Work On What Has Been Spoiled	䷙	111001 = 57	26	Taming Power of the Great
䷯	011010 = 26	48	The Well	䷄	111010 = 58	5	Waiting
䷸	011011 = 27	57	The Gentle	䷈	111011 = 59	9	Taming Power of the Small
䷟	011100 = 28	32	Duration	䷡	111100 = 60	34	Power of the Great
䷱	011101 = 29	50	The Cauldron	䷍	111101 = 61	14	Possession in Great Measure
䷛	011110 = 30	28	Preponderance Of The Great	䷪	111110 = 62	43	Break-through
䷫	011111 = 31	44	Coming To Meet	䷀	111111 = 63	1	The Creative

Figure C.6 The 64 hexagrams converted to binary numbers. (© 2024, L. Storm)

Therefore, in Figure C.6, Hexagram #2 (King Wên) starts the sequence, but it is converted to 0 in base 2 (not 1);[3] therefore, the binary count can only go up to 63 (Hexagram #1). We can see, therefore, that the ordinal values carry no express meaning. Fourth, the reason the ordinal hexagram values impart no specific meaning is because two trigrams are combined to form a hexagram, with its name, commentary, and interpretation being derived on the basis of the coupling; not the ordinal values which can change.

As it happened, Chinese scholar and philosopher Shao Yung developed this same method, though apparently the arrangement was not intended, and he had not devised a use for it beyond the same basic principles that Leibniz was to put forward centuries later. Ryan (1996) described these principles as "proto-scientific", with Shao and Leibniz both espousing the view "that the cosmos was created according to the binary system, which is reflected in all things and discoverable by human beings" (p. 59). But Leibniz could go no further. Redshaw (1996) even claims that for Leibniz

> the long strings of binary numbers that replaced single decimal digits must have seemed daunting. Actually, they must have seemed overwhelming, because Leibniz seemed to lose the plot towards the end of his life, endowing his binary system with a kind of quasi-religious mysticism.

Just as Yin and Yang represent the opposing forces in the universe, the two principles also represent inner psychological forces of the mind. In fairness, Leibniz (1698) *did* see that much—he proposed that the "power, knowledge, and will" of the individual "varied according to different combinations of unity and zero" (as cited in Ryan, 1996, p. 68). Ryan notes that Leibniz (and Shao Yung) came close to a schema whereby:

> […] the human mind played a central role in the world by utilizing reason and sensory input. Thus, knowledge was meant to serve the human spirit and, as Leibniz emphasized, the human body.
>
> (p. 82)

Of course, the key question was how to codify 0s and 1s to show how information could be specified (encrypted/encoded) beyond two broad concepts, yin and yang. But three centuries later, the reverse was found. Instead of seeking ways to convert information into binary form, Hu, Petoukhov, and Petukhova (2017) discovered that nature had already done the encoding:

> The ancient Chinese did not know about the genetic code of protein sequences of amino acids but this code is organized in accordance with the I-Ching: particularly, the genetic code is constructed on DNA molecules using 4 nitrogenous bases, 16 doublets, and 64 triplets.
>
> (p. 354)

> By analogy with the alphabet of 4 nitrogenous bases (adenine, cytosine, guanine and thymine) in the genetic DNA-molecules, the Yin–Yang system uses 4 bigrams with their conditional names: Old Yang, Old Yin, Young Yang and Young Yin.
>
> (p. 355)

These duograms, Old Yang, Old Yin, Young Yang and Young Yin, are given above, in Figure C.3. Petoukhov and Petukhova (2018) are in agreement with Jung about archetypes:

> An ancient principle of a fractal type is known: the cosmos and the microcosm repeat each other. Each person is a microcosm. The doctrine of the parallelism of the macrocosm and the microcosm is one of the oldest philosophical concepts. The Ancient Chinese statement that the Yin-Yang tables of I-Ching are fundamental archetypes of Nature belongs to this direction of thoughts.
>
> (p. 46)

In the West, it seems these ideas have not been fully embraced, but on this point, Wilhelm (1960) notes:

> [...] we may well permit ourselves to try to understand the experiment of the Chinese as a consummation to which we in the West have not been able to bring ourselves.
>
> (p. 98)

The Binary System—Some Personal Thoughts

Binary forces interact and form combinations. Their interactions moderate and modify each other and give each other place (i.e., new meanings or relationships are formed). Just as 0s and 1s are represented in computers and accumulate to represent information (as numbers, letters, etc.), the lines in the hexagrams represent concepts; they are binary in the yin and yang principles, which build up from basic units. The binary forces are not just conceptually elevated in the psyche; they also have real but opposed values in the universe and in the virtual world of the computer.

In the natural world, the conflation of deep ideas (as given above) must be unravelled if Leibniz is right that "mechanical laws" have "metaphysical reasons" underpinning them (Leibniz, as cited in Ryan, 1996, p. 82). In Chapter 2, I endeavoured to make a point about Jung's and Pauli's aims, whereby Donati (2008) thought it possible "to grant privilege to a unitary worldview in which both science and philosophy (including metaphysics) together should help to create a fertile ground for the emergence of scientific theories" (p. 60). As long as any idea remains philosophical or metaphysical, it has no place in science, or at least there will be a struggle to find a place for it as advocates of various persuasions continue to argue the points for and against. That is partly why Leibniz was flummoxed—he lacked the means by which the two opposing principles, the physical and the metaphysical, could be assimilated. Often the world has to catch up (sometimes technologically) with advanced thoughts that have come seemingly before their time, often only speculatively.

In conclusion, it is generally thought that a binary system of sorts dates back to ancient China where it was gainfully employed in the system of wisdom and divination, the *I Ching* (Ryan, 1996). Ryan notes that the derivations of the *I Ching* system and Leibniz's binary system were both based on mathematical techniques, each inspired by metaphysical worldviews. However, hexagram symbols (even as binary strings) are one thing; "long strings of binary numbers" necessary to code complex information are quite another, and they would naturally boggle the 17th-century mind. Either way, these strings, simple and complex, represent the archetypal properties of the binary/dualistic principle magnified, bit by bit, pair by pair, dyad by dyad, to form many diffuse, disparate, and fused states. With advancements in science and technology, we may find ways to give physical (manifest) form to such metaphysical ideas.

***

Notes

1 The great master of Sung Confucianism, Shao Yung (1012–1077) added yin and yang lines beneath each trigram to form 16 "complexes of four", and the process was repeated twice; first to give 32 complexes of five, and again to give 64 hexagrams (H. Wilhelm, 1960, p. 90).

2 In Figure C.5, the numbering (ordering) is based on successive additions of broken (yin) lines replacing unbroken (yang) lines, with hexagrams numbered 1 to 64. However, in the King Wên sequence, *K'un* is Hexagram 2 (not 64). Hexagrams are derived from the *pa kua* (trigrams; see Figure C.3) arranged in an 8×8 grid, from which the King Wên hexagram number can be determined (e.g., Figure C.4).

3 It is thought that 0 (zero) had not been invented in China, so King Wên's sequence starts at 1 (one).

Appendix D: Nostradamus and His Critics

French physician and seer Michel de Nostredame (a.k.a. Nostradamus, the Latinized variant of his name), was born in 1503 in Saint-Rémy-de-Provence, and he died in 1566 in Salon-de-Provence. He was a much-travelled physician, treating and healing plague victims in towns across France by regularly administering a highly potent medicine, the recipe of which included rose petals (for Vitamin C), Florentine iris (as an expectorant and decongestant), and cloves (to relieve pain and reduce fever). He also published a recipe book and many almanacs, but he is most famous for his major work of 1568, *Les Prophéties* (*Prophecies*), which presented predictions or prophecies in the form of quatrains (four-line poems of alternate rhyming verse). The posthumous 1568 edition contained ten "Centuries", so-called because each contained 100 quatrains (except for Century VII). While Nostradamus had planned to publish ten centuries in a single volume, two shorter versions were released in advance (1555: Centuries I to IV only, with 53 quatrains in IV; 1557: Centuries I to VII only, with IV by then complete, but only 42 quatrains in VII).

It is unfortunate that the original French texts differ from publication to publication in the early editions, several of the oldest editions are undated or falsely dated, and there have been many forgeries over the centuries (Cheetham, 1976, 1989). Added to those problems, Nostradamus deliberately cloaked his quatrains in ambiguity, he used obscure phraseology, with codified names (e.g., anagrams), and he presented them in anything but chronological order, all of which was done mainly to avoid prosecution by the authorities of the day. If that was not enough, interpretations of the quatrains vary from translator to translator. Critics therefore argue that it is impossible to muster a consensus as to what Nostradamus meant in his quatrains, and they especially doubt their alleged prophetic elements. Of course, this outcome is ideal if one's aim in the first place was to avoid the charge of being an heretic and practitioner of magic since proof is needed before such charges can be laid: In a dedicatory letter to King Henri II included in the 1558 edition of his *Prophecies*, Nostradamus says:

> If I had wanted to date each quatrain, I could have done so. But this would not have been agreeable to all, least of all to those interpreting them, and was not to be done until Your Majesty granted me full power to do so, lest calumniators be furnished with an opportunity to injure me.[6]

Nevertheless, convincing interpretations seem to have been made, and according to Cheetham (1976), no critic has managed "wholly to dismiss out of hand the small hard core of Nostradamus's accurate predictions" (p. 13).

Apart from the ambiguity in most of the quatrains, the authenticity of many of them is doubted. It has been claimed that Nostradamus used *comparative horoscopy* (i.e., recycling past planetary configurations that accompany known past events to make future predictions) to derive his predictions—implied by some as plagiaristic (Brind'Amour, 1993). One claimant, Laurens Videl (an astrologer and contemporary of Nostradamus) even labelled Nostradamus incompetent for depending on comparative horoscopy. Given his established astrological expertise, Nostradamus's use of an ancient and highly regarded procedure hardly makes him incompetent, and certainly, any kind of so-called plagiarism would be of a very low order; besides which, the scholarship of the day cannot be judged against modern standards.

To continue this charge of plagiarism, it is also claimed that an alleged major source of material for the quatrains is the *Mirabilis Liber* (a compilation of prophecies from a host of unwitting contributors over periods ranging from the 7th to the 16th century). This claim, made by Lemesurier (2003a, 2003b, 2010), is undermined by the fact that the bulk of the *Mirabilis* material clearly refers to events in the ancient past (not the future), which actually justifies *comparative horoscopy* (as just mentioned). But the *Mirabilis* material also happens to be mostly generic and non-specific (even as to the vicissitudes of the Church over the centuries), whereas Nostradamus is not as vague as we have been led to believe—he is often specific, even giving names and dates, as in the following examples:

- **Names:** "*Pasteur*" (I.25); "*Franco*" (IX.16); "*De Gaule*" (IX.33);[7]
- **Dates:** "*three times twenty and six*" (II.51) for 1666, the year of the great fire of London; "*1727 in October*" (III.77), for October, 1727, the Treaty of Hamedan, whereby the Ottoman Empire ("*people of Egypt*") gained sovereignty over major parts of Iran ("*Persia*").

Other dates (so-called "index dates") appear before our very eyes in the quatrain numbers themselves, as noted by Hogue (1997), and Reading (2010). For example, Reading gives numerous examples of "events surrounding King Charles I's life and predicted death, the English Civil War, and also the life and death of Charles's nemesis, Oliver Cromwell" (p. 10), all set in the 17th century:

- Quatrain I.44: The First English Civil War (1644);
- Quatrain III.44: Matthew Hopkins Witch-finder General (1644);
- Quatrain VIII.44: Queen Henrietta Maria flees England (1644);
- Quatrain IV.45: Prince Rupert surrenders Bristol (1645);
- Quatrain II.48: Oliver Cromwell and the thirty tyrants (1648);
- Quatrain IX.49: The execution of King Charles I (1649);
- Quatrain III.50: The Stuart Restoration – False Start (1650);
- Quatrain I.53: Oliver Cromwell becomes Lord Protector of England (1653).

While Nostradamus implies that he went into a trance-like or visionary state (Quatrains I.1 and I.2), critics argue that he never actually stated that he personally used such techniques, but only indulged in contemplation, meditation, and incubation (Lemesurier, 2003b). Yet Cheetham's (1976) research concludes that Nostradamus "believed himself to possess certain powers" (p. 14). And clearly Nostradamus did more than cogitate. In the same letter to Henri II, Nostradamus stated he "made computations for events …", and calculated all his prophecies by "astronomical doctrine modified by … [his] natural instinct".[8]

Lemesurier (2003b) would have us believe that Nostradamus was a conventional scholar (and/or perhaps a fraudster) who had no sincere or personal interest in divinatory practice. Quatrain VI.100, for instance, is used to attack astrologers ("*Let all astrologers … stay far off …*"), and is given as proof that Nostradamus was never an occultist. Such statements easily offend professional astrologers (for example, in 1558, Laurens Videl wrote a pamphlet declaring Nostradamus ignorant and poorly trained).[9] Logically, however, Cheetham (1989) notes that Nostradamus was only admonishing amateur astrologers—those who "did not make it a lifetime study" (p. 374). His own words prove Cheetham's point, for Nostradamus adds to his warning: "*He who does otherwise, let him be priest to the rite*" (p. 374), which can only mean that if one should wish to practice, they must do it within a professional and ethical framework.

But the accusations do not stop there: Lemesurier (2003b) claims that the letter to Henri II states that the prophecies "were about Europe, North Africa and part of Asia Minor" (p. 145), but *not the rest of the world.* We see first, however, that Nostradamus actually said: "And in the most part [et la pluspart] they … are in accord with astronomical calculations corresponding to … the regions, countries and most of the towns and cities of all Europe, including Africa and part of Asia",[10] implying that some number of quatrains refer to other parts of the world not mentioned in the letter. Second, the letter is clearly intended for future humanity to see (or why else publish it?), and in that letter, Nostradamus invites the whole world to beware of three apocalyptical figures who would cause catastrophe on a global scale (all evidently detailed in his quatrains).

To go further, some quatrains are thought to be about the New World and other parts of the globe, as suggested in the "*new city*" (IX.92), and the "*garden of the World near the New City*" (X.49; Cheetham, 1989, p. 521), which allegedly refer to New York City (and Central Park?), with X.49 also mentioning "*the road of the hollow mountains*", taken to mean a "street lined with skyscrapers" (Cheetham, p. 521). Cheetham notes that "New City" ("*Cité neusue*") was New York City's "contemporary name during Nostradamus's lifetime" (p. 373). Cheetham also infers the Russian Revolution in regard to the "*evils committed by the great Red one [grand Roge]*" (VIII.80; p. 436). While many quatrains are open to interpretation due to their ambiguity, reasonable doubt precludes absolute declarations that these quatrains are not geographically or geo-politically pertinent to countries beyond Europe, North Africa and parts of Asia Minor. Both Cheetham and Hogue (1997) make numerous references to countries beyond the limited scope set by Lemesurier (2003b).

To summarize, critics seem loathe to make the concession that cloaking predictions in ambiguity was an effective means by which Nostradamus safeguided himself. Equally, the issue of duplication seems to be a problem for critics. Where borrowing from predecessors may seem evident, critics overlook the underlying principle of *comparative horoscopy*, whereby past astrological patterns tend to repeat and correlate with real-world events, so that the charge of plagiarism seems rather heavy, and is hardly justified given medieval standards.

Some critics do not allow for the possibility that Nostradamus arrived at his predictions independently through his own divinatory endeavours, which is to say he did not have an aversion to occult practices (a conclusion supported by various sources). Most predictions have a style unique to Nostradamus, and a good number of them make very specific allusions not found elsewhere, despite oftentimes being paradoxically couched in metaphor. Some predictions clearly have global relevance, thus putting paid to the charge that Nostradamus only applied his art to his part of the world.

***

Notes

1 For an English translation of Nostradamus's letter to Henri II, see https://www.sacred-texts.com/nos/epistle.htm
2 Sometimes names were masked anagrammatically with meaningful purpose. For example: "*Hister*" (IV.68) = Hitler, who came from Braunau am Inn (Austria) near the Danube, the ancient Latin name of which is *Ister*; "PAU NAY LORON" (VIII.1) = NAPAULON ROY (French = Napoleon the "King" or Emperor).
3 See https://www.sacred-texts.com/nos/epistle.htm
4 See https://www.history.com/news/5-things-you-may-not-know-about-nostradamus
5 See http://nostradamuscode.com/Henry_Epistle.htm

References[1]

Abbott, B. P. et al., (2016). Observation of gravitational waves from a binary black hole merger. *Physical Letters Review, 116*, 061102. doi:10.1103/PhysRevLett.116.061102..

Absi, G. (2014, November 11). Is the brain the only place that stores our memories? *The Nerve Blog*. https://sites.bu.edu/ombs/2014/11/11/is-the-brain-the-only-place-that-stores-our-memories/.

Alcock, J. E. (1981). *Parapsychology: science or magic? A psychological perspective.* Pergamon Press.

Alexander, C. H. & Broughton, R. S. (2001). Cerebral hemisphere dominance and ESP performance in the autoganzfeld. *Journal of Parapsychology, 65*, 397–416.

Almirantis, Y. (2005). The paradox of the planetary metals. *Journal of Scientific Exploration, 19*(1), 31–42.

Alvarado, C. S. (1987). Observations of luminous phenomena around the human body: A review. *Journal of the Society for Psychical Research, 54*, 38–60.

Andreasen, N. C. (2011). A journey into chaos: Creativity and the unconscious. In A. R. Singh & S. A. Singh (Eds.), *Brain, mind and consciousness: An international, interdisciplinary perspective, MSM, 9*(1), 42–53.

Arminjon, M. (2011). The four postulates of Freudian unconscious neurocognitive convergences. *Frontiers in Psychology, 2*, 1–13. doi:10.3389/fpsyg.2011.00125.

Atmanspacher, H. (2012). Dual-aspect monism á la Pauli and Jung. *Journal of Consciousness Studies 19*(9/10), 96–120.

Atmanspacher, H. (2014a). 20th century variants of dual-aspect thinking. *Mind and Matter, 12*(2), 245–288.

Atmanspacher, H. (2014b). Notes on psychophysical phenomena. In H. Atmanspacher & C. A. Fuchs (Eds.), *The Pauli-Jung conjecture and its impact today* (pp. 181–199). Imprint Academic.

Atmanspacher, H. & Fach, W. (2016). Synchronistic mind-matter correlations in therapeutic practice: A commentary on Connolly (2015). *Journal of Analytical Psychology, 61*, 79–85.

Atmanspacher H. & Fuchs, C. A. (Eds.). (2014). *The Pauli-Jung conjecture and its impact today.* Imprint Academic.

Aziz, R. (1990). *C. G. Jung's psychology of religion and synchronicity.* State University of New York Press.

Bainbridge, W. S. (1978). Chariots of the gullible. *Skeptical Inquirer, 3*(2), 33–48.

Baker, R. A. (1992). *Hidden memories: Voices and visions from within.* Prometheus Books.

Bancel, P. A. & Nelson, R. (2008). The GCP event experiment: Design, analytical methods, results. *Journal of Scientific Exploration, 22*(3), 309–333.

Baptista, J., Derakhshani, M., & Tressoldi, P. (2015). Explicit anomalous cognition: A review of the best evidence in ganzfeld, forced-choice, remote viewing and dream studies. In E. Cardeña, J. Palmer, & D. Marcusson-Clavertz (Eds.), *Parapsychology. A handbook for the 21st century* (pp. 192–214). McFarland.

Barker, J. C. (1968). *Scared to death: An examination of fear, its cause and effects.* Frederick Muller.

Barker, J. E. (2021). *Paranormal 101: Fact versus fantasy.* Independently published (James Barker).

Barker, J. E. (2022). *Rating psychics: Eight famous psychics reviewed!* Goodhand Press.

Barrington, M. R. (2018). *JOTT. When things disappear – and come back or relocate – and why it really happens.* Anomalist Books.

Barrington, M. R. (2019, April 6). Psychometry. *Psi Encyclopedia.* https://psi-encyclopedia.spr.ac.uk/articles/psychometry.

Barrington, M. R., Mulacz, P., & Rivas, T. (2005). The case of Iris Farczady. *Journal of the Society for Psychical Research, 69*, 49–77.

Barušs, I. (2001). Failure to replicate electronic voice phenomenon. *Journal of Scientific Exploration, 15*(3), 355–367.

Barušs, I. (2007). An experimental test of instrumental transcommunication. *Journal of Scientific Exploration, 21*(1), 89–98.

Bates, J. (2010). Are Rover, Tabby and other animals more in tune with the universe than we think? *THE A.I.P.R. NEWS, 4*(1), 1–3.

Bauer, E. (1984). Criticism and controversy in parapsychology: An overview. *European Journal of Parapsychology, 5*, 141–166.

Beck, J. (2016, February 23). Coincidences and the meaning of life. *The Atlantic.* https://www.theatlantic.com/science/archive/2016/02/the-true-meaning-of-coincidences/463164/.

Becker, A. (2019). *What is reality? The unfinished quest for the meaning of quantum physics.* John Murray.

Beitman, B. D. (2011). Coincidence studies. *Psychiatric Annals, 41*(12), 561–571.

Beitman, B. D. (2016). *Connecting with coincidences: The new science for using synchronicity and serendipity in your life.* Health Communications.

Beitman, B. D. (2017a, May 1). Categorizing coincidences: Different strokes for different coincidences. *Psychology Today.* www.psychologytoday.com/au/blog/connecting-coincidence/201705/categorizing-coincidences.

Beitman, B. D. (2017b). CCBB: Laurence Browne – The many faces of coincidence. Connecting with coincidence with Dr. Bernie Beitman [audio file]. www.spreaker.com/user/xzoneradiotv/ccbb20170921ep36nfblaurenecbrowne.

Beitman, B. (2022). *Meaningful coincidence: How and why synchronicity and serendipity happen.* Park Street Press.

Beitman, B. D., Celebi, E., & Coleman, S. L. (2010). Synchronicity and healing. In D. A. Monti & B. D. Beitman (Eds.), *Integrative psychiatry* (pp. 445–483). Oxford University Press.

Beitman, B. D. & Shaw, A. (2009). Synchroners, high emotion, and coincidence interpretation. *Psychiatric Annals, 39*(5), 280–286.

Beloff, J. (1977). Psi phenomena: Causal versus acausal interpretation. *Journal of the Society for Psychical Research, 49*, 573–582.

Beloff, J. (1990). *The relentless question: Reflections on the paranormal.* McFarland.

Beloff, J. (2008). Psi phenomena: Causal versus acausal interpretation. In L. Storm (Ed.), *Synchronicity: Multiple perspectives on meaningful coincidence* (pp. 99–108). Pari Publishing.

Bender, H. (1980). Transcultural uniformity of poltergeist patterns as suggestive of an "archetypal" arrangement. In W. G. Roll (Ed.), *Research in parapsychology 1979* (pp. 23–25). Scarecrow Press.

Bengston, W. with Fraser, S. (2010). *The energy cure: Unraveling the mystery of hands-on healing*. Sounds True.

Benor, D. J. (2001). *Spiritual healing: Scientific validation of a healing revolution*. Vision Publishing.

Benovsky, J. (2016). Dual-aspect monism. *Philosophical Investigations, 39*(4), 335–352. doi:10.1111/phin.12122.

Berghmans, C. (2022). The concept of the "Thought-Form" in esoteric and spiritual therapeutic traditions, and its complementarity with the process of visualization and symbolic efficacy: A working hypothesis. *Australian Journal of Parapsychology, 22*, 131–152.

Bierman, D. J. (2010). Consciousness induced restoration of time symmetry (CIRTS): A psychophysical theoretical perspective. *Journal of Parapsychology, 74*, 273–299.

Bierman, D. J. & Rabeyron, T. (2013). *Can psi research sponsor itself?* Simulations and results of an automated ARV-casino experiment. Paper presented at the 56th Annual Parapsychological Association Convention, Viterbo, Italy.

Billows, H. & Storm, L. (2016). Believe it or not: III. Further analyses on predictors of paranormal belief. *Australian Journal of Parapsychology, 16*, 41–61.

Blackburn, S. (1994). *The Oxford dictionary of philosophy.* Oxford University Press.

Blackmore, S. (J.) (1991). Correspondence regarding "probability and the psyche". *Journal of the Society for Psychical Research, 58*, 116–177.

Blackmore, S. J. (1997). Probability misjudgment and belief in the paranormal: A newspaper survey. *British Journal of Psychology, 88*, 683–689.

Blackmore, S. J., & Chamberlain, F. (1993). ESP and thought concordance in twins: A method of comparison. *Journal of the Society for Psychical Research, 59*, 89–96.

Blackmore, S. J., & Rose, N. (1997). Reality and imagination: A psi-conducive confusion? *Journal of Parapsychology, 61*(4), 321–335.

Block, S. (Writer) & Young, R. (Director). (2002). Well schooled in murder [Television series episode]. In S. Haynes (Producer), *The Inspector Lynley mysteries.* BBC One.

Boccuzzi, M. & Beischel, J. (2011). Objective analyses of reported real-time audio instrumental transcommunication and matched control sessions: A pilot study. *Journal of Scientific Exploration, 25*(2), 215–235.

Bohannon, J. (2016, March 3). About 40% of economics experiments fail replication survey. *Science.* https://www.sciencemag.org/news/2016/03/about-40-economics-experiments-fail-replication-survey.

Bohm, D. (1957). *Causality and chance in modern physics.* Routledge & Kegan Paul.

Booker, C. (2004). *The seven basic plots: Why we tell stories.* Continuum.

Booth, J. (1986). *Psychic paradoxes.* Prometheus Books.

Boswell, J. (1799). *The life of Samuel Johnson.* Bigelow, Brown & Company. (Published by Baldwin & Son).

Bottoms, B. L., & Davis, A. L. (1999). The anthropic coincidences. A natural explanation. *The Skeptical Intelligencer, 3*(3), 2–17.

Bradshaw, S. & Storm, L. (2013). Archetypes, symbols, and the apprehension of meaning. *International Journal of Jungian Studies, 5*(2), 154–176.

Braud, W. G. (1983). Toward the quantitative assessment of "meaningful coincidence". *Parapsychological Review*, *14*(4), 5–10.

Braud, W. G. & Schlitz, M. A. (1991). Consciousness interactions with remote biological systems: Anomalous intentionality effects. *Subtle Energies*, *2*, 1–46.

Braude, S. E. (1979). *ESP and psychokinesis: A philosophical examination*. Temple University Press.

Braude, S. E. (1986). *The limits of influence: Psychokinesis and the philosophy of science*. Routledge & Kegan Paul.

Braude, S. E. (2003). *Immortal remains: The evidence for life after death*. Rowman & Littlefield.

Braude, S. E. (2007). *The gold leaf lady and other parapsychological investigations*. University of Chicago Press.

Braude, S. E. (2015). Macro-psychokinesis. In E. Cardeña, J. Palmer, & D. Marcusson-Clavertz (Eds.), *Parapsychology. A handbook for the 21st century* (pp. 258–265). McFarland.

Brehm, J. W. (1966). *A theory of psychological reactance*. Academic Press.

Bressan, P. (2002). The connection between random sequences, everyday coincidences, and belief in the paranormal. *Applied Cognitive Psychology*, *16*, 17–34.

Brian Josephson. (2018, January 31). *Incorporating meaning into fundamental physics* [Video]. YouTube. https://www.youtube.com/watch?v=-Bv5vsZzX6Q

Brind'Amour, P. (1993). *Nostradamus astrophile: Les astres et l'astrologie dans la vie et l'œuvre de Nostradamus*. The University of Ottawa Press.

Broad, C. D. (1949). The relevance of psychical research to philosophy. *Philosophy*, *24*, 291–301.

Brooks, R. M. (2011). Un-thought out metaphysics in analytical psychology: A critique of Jung's epistemological basis for psychic reality. *Journal of Analytical Psychology*, *56*, 492–513.

Broughton, R. S. (2006). Memory, emotion, and the receptive psi process. *Journal of Parapsychology*, *70*, 255–274.

Broughton, R. S. & Alexander, C. H. (1997). Autoganzfeld II: An attempted replication of the PRL autoganzfeld research. *Journal of Parapsychology*, *61*, 209–226.

Brown, J. A. C. (1971). *Freud and the Post-Freudians*. Penguin.

Brown, R. (1971). *Unfinished symphonies: Voices from the beyond*. William Morrow and Company.

Brown, W. B. (1981). [Review of the book *The metal-benders*, by J. Hasted]. *Journal of the Society for Psychical Research*, *51*, 154–156.

Browne, J. (2003). *Charles Darwin: The power of place*. Alfred A. Knopf.

Browne, L. (2017). *The many faces of coincidence*. Imprint Academic.

Brusewitz, G., Cherkas, L., Harris, J., & Parker, A. (2013). Exceptional experiences amongst twins. *Journal of the Society for Psychical Research*, *77*(4), 220–235.

Cain, F. (2009, August 22). How many rings does Jupiter have? *Universe Today: Space and Astronomy News*. https://www.universetoday.com/38059/how-many-rings-does-jupiter-have/.

Cambray, J. (2009). *Synchronicity: Nature and psyche in an interconnected universe*. Texas A&M University Press.

Capra, F. (1988). *The tao of physics*. Flamingo/Fontana.

Cardeña, E. (2018a). Editorial: Four score (plus) years ago. *Journal of Parapsychology*, *82*(Supp.), 5–8.

Cardeña, E. (2018b). The experimental evidence for parapsychological phenomena: A review. *American Psychologist, 73*(5), 663–677.

Cardeña, E., Iribas, A. E., & Reijman, S. (2012). Art and psi. *Journal of Parapsychology, 76*(1), 1–25.

Cardeña, E., Palmer, J., & Marcusson-Clavertz, D. (2015). *Parapsychology: A handbook for the 21st century.* McFarland.

Cardoso, A. (2012). A two-year investigation of the allegedly anomalous electronic voices or EVP. *NeuroQuantology, 10*(3), 492–514.

Carhart-Harris, R. L., Leech R., Hellyer, P. J., Shanahan, M., Feilding, A., Tagliazucchi, E., Chialvo, D. R., & Nutt, D. (2014). The entropic brain: A theory of conscious states informed by neuroimaging research with psychedelic drugs. *Frontiers in Human Neuroscience, 8*(20), 1–22.

Carpenter, J. C. (1977). Intrasubject and subject–agent effects in ESP experiments. In B. B. Wolman (Ed.), *Handbook of Parapsychology* (pp. 202–272). Van Nostrand Reinhold.

Carpenter, J. C. (1991). Prediction of forced-choice ESP performance. Part III: Three attempts to retrieve coded information using mood reports and a repeated-guessing technique. *Journal of Parapsychology, 55*, 227–280.

Carpenter, J. C. (2012). *First sight: ESP and parapsychology in everyday life.* Rowman & Littleman Publishers.

Carpenter, J. C. (2014, November 16). Some gist of first sight. http://firstsightbook.com/wp/.

Carpenter, L., Cannard, C., Wahbeh, H., & Radin, D. (2021). Psychophysical interactions with photons: Three exploratory studies with unexpected results. *Journal of the Society for Psychical Research, 85*, 31–48.

Carroll, R. T. (2009, February 22). [Review of the book *Entangled minds: Extrasensory experiences in a quantum reality*, by D. Radin]. The skeptic's dictionary. http://skepdic.com/refuge/entangledreview.html.

Carson, C., Laham, D., & Moddel, G. (2014). Stock market prediction using associative remote viewing by inexperienced remote viewers. *Journal of Scientific Exploration, 28*(1), 7–16.

Cayce, H. L. (Ed). (1974). *The Edgar Cayce reader.* Warner.

Charlesworth, E. A. (1975). Psi and the imaginary dream. In J. D. Morris, W. G. Roll, & R. L. Morris (Eds.), *Research in Parapsychology 1974* (pp. 85–89). Scarecrow Press.

Charteris, L. & Forrester, L. (Writers), & Carstairs, J. P. (Director). (1964). The romantic matron [Television series episode]. In R. S. Baker & M. Berman (Producers), *The Saint.* ITC/Granada Television Network.

Charteris, L., Kelsey, G., & Sharples, D. (Writers), & Ainsworth, J. (Director). (1962). The careful terrorist [Television series episode]. In R. S. Baker & M. Berman (Producers), *The Saint.* ITC/Granada Television Network.

Cheetham, E. (1976). *The prophecies of Nostradamus.* Corgi Books.

Cheetham, E. (1989). *The final prophecies of Nostradamus.* Bramley Books.

Chodorow, J. (Ed.). (1997). *Jung on active imagination.* Princeton University Press.

Christopher, M. (1975). *Mediums, mystics, and the occult.* Thomas Y. Crowell.

Coe, Jr., M. R. (1958). Fire-walking and related behaviors. *Journal of the American Society for Psychical Research, 52*, 85–97.

Coleman, S. L. & Beitman, B. D. (2009). Characterizing high-frequency coincidence detectors. *Psychiatric Annals, 39*(5), 271–279.

Coleman, S. L., Beitman, B. D., & Celebi, E. (2009). Weird coincidences commonly occur. *Psychiatric Annals, 39*(5), 265–270.

Collins, H. M. & Pinch, T. (1982). *Frames of meaning: The social construction of extraordinary science.* Routledge.

Collins, R. (2009). The teleological argument: An exploration of the fine-tuning of the universe. In W. L. Craig & J. P. Moreland (Eds.), *The Blackwell companion to natural theology* (pp. 202–281). Wiley-Blackwell.

Colman, W. (2011). Synchronicity and the meaning-making psyche. *Journal of Analytical Psychology, 56*, 471–491.

Colman, W. (2012). Reply to Wolfgang Giegerich's "A serious misunderstanding: Synchronicity and the generation of meaning". *Journal of Analytical Psychology, 57*, 512–516.

Combs, A. & Holland, M. (1996). *Synchronicity: Through the eyes of science, myth, and the trickster.* Marlowe & Company.

Connolly, A. (2015). Bridging the reductive and the synthetic: Some reflections on the clinical importance of synchronicity. *Journal of Analytical Psychology, 60*, 159–178.

Conrad, K. (1959). Gestaltanalyse und Daseinsanalytik [General analysis and shape analysis]. *Nervenarzt* [Neurologist], *30*, 405–410.

Coudert, A. P. (1980). *Alchemy: The philosopher's stone.* Wildwood House.

Crandall, J. E. (1985). Effects of favourable and unfavourable conditions on the psi-missing displacement effect. *Journal of the American Society for Psychical Research, 79*, 27–38.

Croft, W. A. & Cruse, D. A. (2004). *Cognitive linguistics.* Cambridge University Press.

Currey, R. (2017). Can Extraversion [E] and Neuroticism [N] as defined by Eysenck match the four astrological elements? *Correlation, 31*(1), 5–33.

Currey, R. (2018). Can western tropical interpretations apply to the sidereal zodiac? *Correlation, 32*(1), 47–61.

Dagnall, N. A., Drinkwater, K., Parker, A., & Clough, P. (2016). Paranormal experience, belief in the paranormal and anomalous beliefs. *Paranthropology, 7*, 4–15. doi:10.3389/fpsyg.2016.01045.

Dalton, K. (1997). Exploring the links: Creativity and psi in the ganzfeld. *Proceedings of the presented papers of the Parapsychological Association 40th Annual Conference* (pp. 119–134). Parapsychological Association.

Darwin, C. (2004). *On the origin of species.* Collector's Library. (Original work published in 1859)

Dean, D. E. (1974). Precognition and retrocognition. In E. Mitchell (Ed.), *Psychic exploration: A challenge for science* (pp. 153–177). Putnam.

Dekking, M. (2005). *A modern introduction to probability and statistics.* Springer.

Delin, P. (2002). Scepticism and credulity. *Australian Journal of Parapsychology, 2*, 28–36. (Reprinted from *Search*, 3, 247–249, by P. Delin, 1972).

Delin, P. (2003). The concept of coincidence. *Australian Journal of Parapsychology, 3*, 94–104.

De Marchi, J. (1952). *The true story of Fatima.* Catechetical Guild Entertainment Society.

De Pablos, F., Sabater, R. L., & Liarte, L. M. (2011). Incorporation of future events into dream content: An experimental study. *Australian Journal of Parapsychology, 11*(2), 138–153.

Diaconis, P. & Mosteller, F. (1989). Methods for studying coincidences. *Journal of the American Statistical Association, 84*, 853–861.

Dick, P. K. (1982). *The transmigration of Timothy Archer.* Simon & Schuster.

Dobbs, M. (1999, October 17). Deconstructing the death ray. *Washington Post*. https://www.washingtonpost.com/wp-srv/inatl/feed/a5067-1999oct17.htm.

Doctorow, E. L. (2000). *City of God.* Thorndike Press.

Don, N. S., McDonough, B. E., & Warren, C. A. (1998). Event-related brain potential (ERP) indicators of unconscious psi: A replication using subjects unselected for psi. *Journal of Parapsychology, 62*, 127–145.

Donati, M. (2008). Beyond synchronicity: The worldview of Carl Gustav Jung and Wolfgang Pauli. In L. Storm (Ed.), *Synchronicity: Multiple perspectives on meaningful coincidence* (pp. 42–63). Pari Publishing.

Dossey, L. (2008). Transplants, cellular memory, and reincarnation. *Explore: The Journal of Science and Healing, 4*(5), 285–293.

Dossey, L. (2013). Unbroken wholeness: The emerging view of human interconnection. *Explore: The Journal of Science and Healing, 9*(1), 1–8.

Dossey, L. (2016). Brains and beyond: The unfolding vision of health and healing. *Explore: The Journal of Science and Healing, 12*(5), 314–324.

Douglas, G. (2020). Is the Gauquelin Effect born at conception? Michel Gauquelin's intuition on geomagnetic micro-pulsations. *Correlation, 33*(1), 10–39.

Dowling, J. (1984). Lourdes cures and their medical assessment. *Journal of the Royal Society of Medicine, 77*, 634–638.

Dr. Bell C NDE. (1998–2021). Experience description. *Near-Death Experience Research Foundation*. https://www.nderf.org/Experiences/1bell_c_nde.html.

Drewes, A. A. (2002). Dr. Louisa Rhine's letters revisited: The children. *Journal of Parapsychology, 66*, 343–370.

Drinkwater, K. G., Dagnall, N., Denovan, A., & Williams, C. (2021, June 28). Paranormal belief, thinking style and delusion formation: A latent profile analysis of within-individual variations in experience-based paranormal facets. *Frontiers in Psychology, 12*, Article 670959. doi:10.3389/fpsyg.2021.670959.

Drinkwater, K., Denovan, A., Dagnall, N., & Parker, A. (2020). Predictors of hearing electronic voice phenomena in random noise: Schizotypy, fantasy proneness, and paranormal beliefs. *Journal of Parapsychology, 84*(1), 96–113.

Duncan, D. (1911). *The life and letters of Herbert Spencer.* Williams and Northgate. (Original work published in 1908)

Dunne, J. W. (1927). *An experiment with time.* Faber & Faber.

Dunning, B. (2020, December 29). The 1994 Ruwa Zimbabwe alien encounter. *SKEPTOID*. https://skeptoid.com/episodes/4760.

Edinger, E. F. (1986). *Ego and archetype.* Penguin.

Edwards, T. (Producer & Writer). (1983). *The case of ESP* [Television documentary]. British Broadcasting Corporation.

Eisenbud, J. (1967). *The world of Ted Serios: "Thoughtographic" studies of an extra-ordinary mind.* Morrow.

Eisenbud, J. (1970). *Psi and psychoanalysis.* Grune & Stratton.

Eisenbud, J. (1975, September/October). Seduction by synchronicity. *Psychic, 6*(4), 6, 61.

Eisenbud, J. (1980). Synchronicity, psychodynamics and psi. In W. G. Roll (Ed.), *Research in parapsychology 1979* (pp. 25–26). Scarecrow Press.

Eisenbud, J. (1982). *Paranormal foreknowledge: Problems and perplexities.* Human Sciences Press.

Eisenbud, J. (1983). *Parapsychology and the unconscious.* North Atlantic Books.

Eisenbud, J. (1990). Of mice and men, or the sorcerer's apprentice: A cautionary tale. *Journal of the American Society for Psychical Research, 84*, 345–364.

Elkins-Tanton, L. T. (2006). *Jupiter and Saturn*. Chelsea House.

Ellis, D. J. (1975). Listening to Raudive voices. *Journal of the Society for Psychical Research, 48*, 31–42.

Ellis, D. J. (1978). *The mediumship of the tape recorder: A detailed examination of the Raudive voice phenomenon of voice extras on tape recordings.* D. J. Ellis.

Ellis, G. F. R. (2006). Physics in the real universe: time and spacetime. *General Relativity and Gravitation, 38*(12), 1797–1824.

Ernst, B. (1978). *The magic mirror of M. C. Escher*. Taschen.

Ertel, S. (1988). Raising the hurdle for the athlete's Mars effect: Association co-varies with eminence. *Journal of Scientific Exploration, 2*(1), 53–82.

Ertel, S. (1992). Update on the "Mars Effect". *Skeptical Inquirer, 16*, 150–160.

Ertel, S. (2003). The Mars effect cannot be pinned on cheating parents. *Skeptical Inquirer, 27*(1), 57–58.

Ertel, S. (2007). Hopeful findings, unduly neglected, on stars and human affair. *Australian Journal of Parapsychology, 71*, 52–71.

Escolà-Gascón, A., Houran, J., Dagnall, N., Drinkwater, K., & Denovan, A. (2023). Follow-up on the U.S. Central Intelligence Agency's (CIA) remote viewing experiments. *Brain and Behavior, 13*(6), e3026.

Eysenck, H. J. (1967). Personality and extrasensory perception. *Journal of the Society for Psychical Research, 44*, 55–71.

Eysenck, H. J. & Nias, D. K. (1982). *Astrology: Science or superstition?* Temple Smith and St Martin's.

Falk, R. (1989). Judgment of coincidences: Mine versus yours. *American Journal of Psychology, 102*, 477–493.

Filk, T. (2014). Quantum entanglement, hidden variables, and acausal correlations. In H. Atmanspacher & C. A. Fuchs (Eds.), *The Pauli-Jung conjecture and its impact today* (pp. 109–123). Imprint Academic.

Fisher, L. (2011, September 20). Jung's explosive visit to Freud: Did Jung cause Freud's bookcase to explode by mental force? *Psychology Today*. https://www.psychologytoday.com/au/blog/untangling-lifes-complexities/201109/jungs-explosive-visit-freud.

Flew, A. (1953). Coincidence and synchronicity. *Journal of the Society for Psychical Research, 37*, 198–201.

Fordham, M. (1973). Editorial preface. In C. G. Jung, *Synchronicity: An acausal connecting principle* (pp. v–vii). Princeton University Press.

Fordham, M. (1993). *The making of an analyst: A memoir*. Free Association Books.

Fowler, R. E. (1974/2001). *UFOs: Interplanetary visitors*. Authors Choice Press.

Freud, S. (1933). *New introductory lectures on psycho-analysis*. W. W. Norton & Company.

Freud, S. (1988). *Case histories 2*. Penguin.

Froese, T., Iizuka, H., & Ikegami, T. (2014). Using minimal human–computer interfaces for studying the interactive development of social awareness. *Frontiers in Psychology, 5*, Article 1061, 1–13.

Fuchs, C. A. (2014). Quantum Bayesianism for the uninoculated. In H. Atmanspacher & C. A. Fuchs (Eds.), *The Pauli-Jung conjecture and its impact today* (pp. 69–91). Exeter, UK: Imprint Academic.

Gadway, J. F. (2013). *Here be angels: Sojourn in a different world.* KaneBeGone Inc.

Gatlin, L. L. (1977). Meaningful information creation: An alternative interpretation of the psi phenomenon. *Journal of the American Society for Psychical Research, 71*, 1–18.

Gatlin, L. L. (2008). Meaningful information creation: An alternative interpretation of the psi phenomenon. In L. Storm (Ed.), *Synchronicity: Multiple perspectives on meaningful coincidence* (pp. 195–211). Pari Publishing.

Gauld, A. (1976). ESP and attempts to explain it. In S. C. Thakur (Ed.), *Philosophy and psychical research* (pp. 17–45). George Allen & Unwin.

Gauld, A. & Cornell, A. D. (1979). *Poltergeists.* Routledge & Kegan Paul.

Gauquelin, M. (1983). *The truth about astrology.* Basil Blackwell.

Gelman, A. (2008). Objections to Bayesian statistics. *Bayesian Analysis, 3*, 445–450.

Gelman, A (2011, April 28). What are the open problems in Bayesian statistics? *The Statistics Forum.* https://statisticsforum.wordpress.com/2011/04/28/what-are-the-open-problems-in-bayesian-statistics/.

Gibson, L. (2010). Ontology of the shadow. Presented at The Jungian Society for Scholarly Studies, VIIth Annual Conference, Burlington, VT, August 2008. http://www.stanislavgrof.com/wp-content/uploads/2015/02/Ontology-of-the-Shadow-full-paper.pdf.

Giegerich, W. (2012). A serious misunderstanding: Synchronicity and the generation of meaning. *Journal of Analytical Psychology, 57*, 500–511.

Gieser, S. (2005). *The innermost kernel: Depth psychology and quantum physics. Wolfgang Pauli's dialogue with C.G. Jung.* Berlin: Springer.

Glass, G. V., McGaw, B., & Smith, M. L. (1981). *Meta-analysis in social research.* Sage.

Goodwyn, E. (2022). The origins of psyche: From experience to ontology. *International Journal of Jungian Studies, 14*(2), 127–146.

Grattan-Guinness, I. (1978). What are coincidences? *Journal of the Society for Psychical Research, 49*, 949–955.

Grattan-Guinness, I. (1983). Coincidences as spontaneous psychical phenomena. *Journal of the Society for Psychical Research, 52*, 59–71.

Greatrex, D. (1999). A note on synchronicity and seriality. *Paranormal Review, 9*, 5–7.

Grinberg-Zylberbaum, J. (1997). Ideas about a new psychophysiology of consciousness: The syntergic theory. *Journal of Mind and Behavior, 18*(4), 443–458.

Grof, S. (1985). *Beyond the brain: Birth, death and transcendence in psychotherapy.* SUNY.

Grof, C. & Grof, S. (1990). *The stormy search for the self.* Jeremy Tarcher.

Gronowicz, G. A., Jhaveri, A., Clarke, L. W., Aronow, M. S., & Smith, T. H. (2008). Therapeutic touch stimulates the proliferation of human cells in culture. *Journal of Alternative and Complementary Medicine, 14*(3), 233–239.

Gurney, E., Myers, F. W. H., & Podmore, F. (1886). *Phantasms of the living.* Trübner.

Hacking, I. (1975). *The emergence of probability: A philosophical study of early ideas about probability, induction and statistical inference.* Cambridge University Press.

Haraldsson, E. (1981). Some determinants of belief in psychical phenomena. *Journal of the American Society for Psychical Research, 75*, 297–309.

Haraldsson, E. (1993). Are religiosity and belief in an afterlife better predictors of ESP performance than belief in psychic phenomena? *Journal of Parapsychology, 57*, 259–273.

Haraldsson, E. (2011). A perfect case? Emil Jensen in the mediumship of Indridi Indridason, the fire in Copenhagen on November 24th 1905 and the discovery of Jensen's identity. *Proceedings of the Society for Psychical Research, 59*, 195–223.

Haraldsson, E. & Houtkooper, J. M. (1995). Meta-analysis of ten experiments on perceptual defensiveness and ESP: ESP scoring patterns, experimenter and decline effects. *Journal of Parapsychology, 59*, 251–271.

Harary, K. & Targ, R. (1985). A new approach to forecasting commodity futures. *PSI Research, 4*(3–4),79–88.

Hardy, C. H. (2011). *The sacred network: Megaliths, cathedrals, ley lines, and the power of shared consciousness.* Inner Tradition.

Hassin, R. R., Uleman, J. S., & Bargh, J. A. (2005). *The new unconscious.* Oxford University Press.

Hasted, J. (1981). *The metal-benders.* Routledge & Kegan Paul.

Haule, J. R. (2011a). *Jung in the 21st century. Volume 1: Evolution and archetype.* Routledge.

Haule, J. R. (2011b). *Jung in the 21st century. Volume 2: Synchronicity and science.* Routledge.

Hazel, R. (1990). *Consulting the coins: A new age interpretation of the I Ching.* Lothian.

Healy, T. & Cropper, P. (2014). *Australian poltergeist: The stone-throwing spook of Humpty Doo and many other cases.* Strange Nation.

Hefner A. G., & Arnold, D. (2018). Numinosity. *The MYSTICA.* https://www.themystica.com/mystica/articles/n/numinosity.html.

Henry, J. (1993). Coincidence experience survey. *Journal of the Society for Psychical Research, 59*, 97–108.

Herrera-Rincon, C., Golding, A. S., Moran, K. M., Harrison, C., Martyniuk, C. J., Guay, J. A., Zaltsman, J., Carabello, H., Kaplan, D. L., & Levin, M., (2018). Brief local application of progesterone via a wearable bioreactor induces long-term regenerative response in adult *Xenopus* hindlimb. *Cell Reports, 25*(6), 1593–1609.

Hilleard, S. (2014). *Anomalies.* Createspace Independent Publishing Platform.

Hogue, J. H. (1997). *Nostradamus: The complete prophecies.* Element.

Holt, N. (2007). *Creativity, altered states of consciousness, and anomalous cognition: The role of epistemological flexibility in the creative process.* [Unpublished doctoral thesis]. University of Northampton.

Holt, N. (2013). Comparing artists with controls on a free-response experience-sampling task: Creativity and anomalous cognition. *Journal of the Society for Psychical Research, 77*, 1–18.

Honorton, C., Ferrari, D. C., & Bem, D. J. (1998). Extraversion and ESP performance: A meta-analysis and a new confirmation. *Journal of Parapsychology, 62*, 255–276.

Houran, J. & Lange, R. (2012). I Ching outcomes from experimental manipulations of transliminality and paranormal belief. *Australian Journal of Parapsychology, 12*, 39–58.

Hsueh, M.-F., Önnerfjord, P., Bolognesi, M. P., Easley, M. E., & Kraus, V. B. (2009, October 9). Analysis of "old" proteins unmasks dynamic gradient of cartilage turnover in human limbs. *Science Advances, 5*, 1–9.

Hu, Z., Petoukhov, S. V., & Petukhova, E. S. (2017). I-Ching, dyadic groups of binary numbers and the geno-logic coding in living bodies. *Progress in Biophysics and Molecular Biology, 131*, 354–368.

Hubbard, D. W. (2010). *How to measure anything: Finding the value of "intangibles" in business* (2nd ed.). Wiley & Sons.

Hume, D. (2007). *A treatise of human nature*. Clarendon Press. (Original work published in 1738)

Hyde, M. (1992). *Jung and astrology*. Aquarius Press/HarperCollins.

Ioannidis, J. A. (2005). Contradicted and initially stronger effects in highly cited clinical research. *Journal of the American Medical Association*, *294*(2), 218–228.

Illingworth, C. M. (1974). Trapped fingers and amputated finger tips in children. *Journal of Paediatric Surgery*, *9*, 853–858.

Inglis, B. (1985). *The paranormal: An encyclopedia of psychic phenomena*. Granada.

Inglis, B. (1990). *Coincidence: A matter of chance – or synchronicity?* Hutchinson.

Irigaray, L. (1987). Sujet de la science, sujet sexué? In (Eds.), *Sens et place des connaissances dans la sociéte – Tome III* (pp. 95–121). Centre National de Recherche Scientifique.

Irwin, H. J. (1979). *Psi and the mind: An information processing approach*. Scarecrow Press.

Irwin, H. J. (2002). Is scientific investigation of postmortem survival an anachronism? The demise of the survival hypothesis. *Australian Journal of Parapsychology*, *2*, 19–27.

Irwin, H. J. (2009). *The psychology of paranormal belief: A researcher's handbook*. University Of Hertfordshire Press.

Irwin, H. J. & Watt, C. A. (2007). *An introduction to parapsychology* (5th ed.). McFarland.

Jackman, T. (2018, June 5). Who killed Bobby Kennedy? His son RFK Jr. doesn't believe it was Sirhan Sirhan. *The Washington Post*. https://www.washingtonpost.com/news/retropolis/wp/2018/05/26/who-killed-bobby-kennedy-his-son-rfk-jr-doesnt-believe-it-was-sirhan-sirhan/.

Jacobi, J. (1973). *The psychology of C. G. Jung*. Yale University Press.

Jacobi, J. (1974). *Complex/archetype/symbol in the psychology of C. G. Jung*. Princeton University Press.

Jaffé, A. (1967). C. G. Jung and parapsychology. In J. R. Smythies (Ed.), *Science and ESP* (pp. 263–280). Routledge & Kegan-Paul.

James, W. (1997). *The meaning of truth*. Amherst, NY: Prometheus. (Original work published in 1909)

Jenkins, H. (2017). Dowsing. *Psi Encyclopedia*. https://psi-encyclopedia.spr.ac.uk/articles/dowsing.

Jinks, A. L. (2016). *Disappearing object phenomenon: An investigation*. McFarland.

Johansen, M. K. & Osman, M. (2015). Coincidences: A fundamental consequence of rational cognition. *New Ideas in Psychology*, *39*, 34–44.

Johnson, A. (1899). Coincidences. *Proceedings of the Society for Psychical Research*, *14*, 158–330.

Joines, W. T., Baumann, S. B., Kim, J., Zile, J. M., & Simmons, C. (2004). *The measurement and characterization of charge accumulation and electromagnetic emission from bioenergy healers*. Paper presented at the 47th Annual Parapsychological Association Convention, Vienna, Austria.

Joines, W. T., Baumann, S., & Kruth, J. G. (2012). Electromagnetic emissions from humans during focused intent. *Journal of Parapsychology*, *76*(2), 275–294.

Jonas, W. B. & Crawford, C. C. (2003). *Healing, intention and energy medicine: Science, research methods and clinical implications*. Churchill Livingstone.

Jung, C. G. (1954). On the nature of the psyche. *CW8* (pp. 159–234). (Original work published in 1947)

Jung, C. G. (1964). Approaching the unconscious. In C. G. Jung (Ed.), *Man and his symbols* (pp. 18–103). Doubleday/Anchor.

Jung, C. G. (1966). Two essays on analytical psychology (2nd ed.). *CW7*. (Original work published in 1953)

Jung, C. G. (1968). Individual dream symbolism in relation to alchemy. *Psychology and alchemy* (2nd ed.). *CW12* (pp. 39–224). (Original work published in 1936)

Jung, C. G. (1968). Religious ideas in alchemy. *Psychology and alchemy* (2nd ed.). *CW12* (pp. 225–472). (Original work published in 1937)

Jung, C. G. (1968). The archetypes and the collective unconscious (2nd ed.). *CW9i*. (Original work published in 1959)

Jung, C. G. (1968a). Letters on synchronicity. *CW18* (pp. 502–509).

Jung, C. G. (1968b). The Tavistock lectures: On the theory and practice of analytical psychology. *CW18* (pp. 5–182).

Jung, C. G. (1969). Appendix: On synchronicity. *CW8* (pp. 520–531). (Original work published in 1951)

Jung, C. G. (1969). Synchronicity: An acausal connecting principle. *CW8* (pp. 417–519). (Original work published in 1952)

Jung, C. G. (1969). *Answer to Job* (2nd ed.). (Original work published in 1958)

Jung, C. G. (1969). The structure and dynamics of the psyche (2nd ed.). *CW8*. (Original work published in 1960)

Jung, C. G. (1970). Civilization in transition. *CW10*. (Original work published in 1964)

Jung, C. G. (1970). Mysterium coniunctionis: An inquiry into the separation and synthesis of psychic opposites in alchemy (2nd ed.). *CW14*. (Original work published in 1963)

Jung, C. G. (1971). Psychological types. *CW6*. (Original work published in 1921)

Jung, C. G. (1975). *C. G. Jung Letters 2: 1951–1961* (R. F. C. Hull, Trans.). Routledge & Kegan Paul.

Jung, C. G. (1977). *C. G. Jung speaking*. Princeton: Princeton University Press.

Jung, C. G. (1987). *Synchronicity: An acausal connecting principle.* Ark Paperbacks. (Original work published in 1955)

Jung, C. G. (1989). Foreword to the I Ching or book of changes. In R. Wilhelm, *The I Ching or book of changes* (pp. xxi–xxxix). (C. F. Baynes, Trans.). Princeton University Press.

Jung, C. G. (1989). *Memories, dreams, reflections* (A. Jaffe, Ed., R. Winston & C. Winston, Trans.). Vintage Books. (Original work published in 1961)

Kant, I. (1781). *The critique of pure reason*. Encyclopedia Britannica (1952).

Katz, D. (1960). The functional approach to the study of attitudes. *Public Opinion Quarterly, 24*, 163–204.

Katz, D. L., Grgić, I., & Fendley, T. W. (2018). An ethnographical assessment of Project Firefly: A yearlong endeavor to create wealth by predicting FOREX currency moves with associative remote viewing. *Journal of Scientific Exploration, 32*(1), 21–54.

Katz, D. L., Grgić, I., Tressoldi, P., & Fendley, T. W. (2021). Associative remote viewing projects: Assessing rater reliability and factors affecting successful predictions. *Journal of the Society for Psychical Research, 85*, 65–90.

Kauffman, S. & Patra, S. (2022). A testable theory for the emergence of the classical world. *Entropy, 24*, 1–15.

Kaufman, G. D. (2001). On thinking of God as serendipitous creativity. *Journal of the American Academy of Religion, 69*(2), 409–425.

Keil, H. H. J. (1980). The voice on tape phenomena: Limitations and possibilities. *European Journal of Parapsychology, 3*, 287–296.

Kelly, E. F., Crabtree, A., & Marshall, P. (2015). *Beyond physicalism: Toward reconciliation of science and spirituality.* Rowman & Littlefield.

Kelly, E. W. & Tucker, J.B. (2015). Research methods with spontaneous case studies. In E. Cardeña, J. Palmer, & D. Marcusson-Clavertz (Eds.), *Parapsychology. A handbook for the 21st century* (pp. 63–76). McFarland.

Keutzer, C. S. (1984). Archetypes, synchronicity and the theory of formative causation. *Journal of Analytical Psychology, 27*(3), 255–266.

Koehler, J. (2009, June 15). *A very lucky wind* [Audio file]. Radiolab. http://www.radiolab.org/story/91686-a-very-lucky-wind/.

Koestler, A.(1974). *The roots of coincidence.* Picador.

Kokubo, H. (2013). Biophysical approach to psi phenomena. *NeuroQuantology, 11*(1), 8–15.

Kolodziejzyk, G. (2012). Greg Kolodziejzyk's 13-year associative remote viewing experiment results. *Journal of Parapsychology, 76*, 349–368.

Korzybski, A. (1941). *Science and sanity: An introduction to non-aristotelian systems and general semantics.* The International Non-Aristotelian Library Publishing Company. (Original work published in 1933)

Kress, K. A. (1999). Parapsychology in intelligence: A personal review and conclusions. *Journal of Scientific Exploration, 13*(1), 69–85.

Krippner, S. (1984). Parapsychological methodology and shamanistic studies. *Psi Research, 3*(3/4), 4–16.

Krippner, S., Bogzaran, F., & de Carvalho, A. P. (2002). *Extraordinary dreams and how to work with them.* SUNY Press.

Krippner, S., Saunders, D. T., Morgan, A., & Quan, A. (2019). Remote viewing of concealed target pictures under light and dark conditions. *Explore: The Journal of Science and Healing, 15*(1), 27–37.

Kruth, J. G. (2019). An exploration of the effects of mood and emotion on a real-world working computer system and network environment. *Journal of Parapsychology, 83*(2), 232–247.

Kuhn, T. S. (1962). *The structure of scientific revolutions.* University of Chicago Press.

Kujawsky, P. (2008, May 29). Palestinian terror stretches back to RFK. *The Jewish Journal.* https://jewishjournal.com/commentary/opinion/63834/.

Kurosawa, A. (Director). (1950). *Rashomon.* [Motion picture]. Daiei Film.

Kutz, M. (2017). *Contextual intelligence: How thinking in 3D can help resolve complexity, uncertainty, and ambiguity.* Palgrave.

Lamont, M. (2016). *The mysterious paths of Versailles: An investigation of a psychical journey back in time.* Xlibris Corp.

Landsburg, A. (Producer). (1977–1982). *In search of …* Alan Landsburg Productions.

Lange, R. & Houran, J. (2013). Towards a replicable formula for significant *I Ching* outcomes. *Australian Journal of Parapsychology, 13*, 9–25.

Lankton, S. (2011). Psychotherapeutic intervention for numerous and large viral warts with adjunctive hypnosis: A case study. *American Journal of Clinical Hypnosis, 49* (3), 211–218.

Lasine, S. (2017). Jonah's complexes and our own: Psychology and the interpretation of the Book of Jonah. *Journal for the Study of the Old Testament, 41*(2), 237–260.

Laszlo, E. (2003). *The connectivity hypothesis: Foundations of an integral science of quantum, cosmos, life and consciousness.* SUNY.

Laughlin, K. (2015, October 7). The spectrum of consciousness: Color symbolism in the typology of C. G. Jung. *Typology Central: A Personality Type Indicator Community.* https://www.typologycentral.com/threads/the-spectrum-of-consciousness.79462/.

Laveman, D. (2014). Business leadership, synchronicity, and psychophysical reality. In H. Atmanspacher & C. A. Fuchs (Eds.), *The Pauli-Jung conjecture and its impact today* (pp. 275–305). Imprint Academic.

Legge, J. (1971). *I Ching.* New American Library.

Lee, V. (1985). Spiritual emergencies. *Yoga Journal, July/August* 39–41.

Leja, M. (1990). Jackson Pollock: Representing the unconscious. *Art History, 13*(4), 542–563.

Lemesurier, P. (2003a). *Nostradamus: The illustrated prophecies.* John Hunt Publishing.

Lemesurier, P. (2003b). *The unknown Nostradamus: The essential biography for his 500th birthday.* John Hunt Publishing.

Lemesurier, P. (2010). *Nostradamus, bibliomancer: The man, the myth, the truth.* Career Press.

Liester, M. B. (2020). Personality changes following heart transplantation: The role of cellular memory. *Medical Hypotheses, 135*(3), 109468 (1–7).

Link, D. (2020, June 6). Fact check: A 1964 conspiracy theory misrepresents Lincoln and Kennedy's similarities. *USA Today.* https://www.usatoday.com/story/news/factcheck/2020/06/06/fact-check-1964-lincoln-kennedy-comparisons-only-partly-accurate/5311926002/.

Littlewood, J. E. (1953). *A mathematician's miscellany.* Cambridge University Press.

Litvag, I. (1972). *Singer in the shadows; The strange story of Patience Worth.* Macmillan.

Lohr, J. M., Adams, T. G., Schwarz, M., & Brady, R. E. (2013). The sense of being stared at. *Skeptic, 18*(1), 51–55.

Lorenz, H. S. (2006). Synchronicity in the 21st century. *Journal of Jungian Scholarly Studies, 2*(2), 1–13.

Lufityanto, G., Donkin, C., & Pearson, J. (2016). Measuring intuition: Nonconscious emotional information boosts decision accuracy and confidence. *Psychological Science, 27*(5), 622–634.

Luke, D. P. (2008). Psychedelic substances and paranormal phenomena: A review of the research. *Journal of Parapsychology, 72*, 77–107.

Luke, D. & Zychowicz, K. (2014). Comparison of outcomes with nonintentional and intentional precognition tasks. *Journal of Parapsychology, 78*(2), 223–234.

Lumsden-Cook, J. (2005a). Affect and random events: Examining the effects of induced emotion upon mind–matter interactions. *Journal of the American Society for Psychical Research, 69*(3), 128–142.

Lumsden-Cook, J. (2005b). Mind–matter and emotion. *Journal of the American Society for Psychical Research, 69*(1), 1–17.

Lye, H. (2018, November 25). Five animals that can regenerate. *The Guardian.* https://www.theguardian.com/technology/2018/nov/25/five-animals-that-can-regenerate-salamander-starfish.

Mackie, J. L. (1980). *The cement of the universe: A study of causation.* Clarendon Press.

Maimonides, M. (1956). *The guide for the perplexed* (M. Friedländer, Trans.). Dover. (Original work published in 1904)

Main, R. (2004). *The rupture of time: Synchronicity and Jung's critique of modern western culture.* Routledge.

Main, R. (2007). *Revelations of chance: Synchronicity as spiritual experience.* State University of New York Press.

Main, R. (2014). Synchronicity and the problem of meaning in science. In H. Atmanspacher & C. A. Fuchs (Eds.), *The Pauli-Jung conjecture and its impact today* (pp. 217–239). Imprint Academic.

Malthus, T. R. (1998). An essay on the principle of population. *Electronic Scholarly Publishing Project.* http://www.esp.org/books/malthus/population/malthus.pdf (Original work published in 1798)

Mansfield, V. (1995). *Synchronicity, science, and soul-making: Understanding Jungian synchronicity through physics, Buddhism, and philosophy.* Open Court.

Mansfield, V., Rhine-Feather, S., & Hall, J. (1998). The Rhine-Jung letters: Distinguishing parapsychological from synchronistic events. *Journal of Parapsychology, 62*, 3–25.

Maracchia, S. (2013). The importance of symbolism in the development of algebra. *Lettera Matematica International, 1*, 137–144.

Maraldi, E. O. (2017). The scientific investigation of anomalous self and identity experiences. *Journal of Nervous and Mental Disease, 205*(11), 900.

Marks-Tarlow, T. & Shapiro, Y. (2021). Synchronicity, acausal connection, and the fractal dynamics of clinical practice. *Psychoanalytic Dialogues, 31*(4), 468–486.

Martin, M. & Augustine, K. (Eds.). (2015). *The myth of an afterlife: The case against life after death.* Rowman & Littlefield.

Martinez, M. & Johnson, B. (2012, March 13). Attorneys for RFK convicted killer Sirhan push "second gunman" argument. *CNN.* https://edition.cnn.com/2012/03/04/justice/california-rfk-second-gun/index.html.

Marwaha, S. B. & May, E. C. (2015). Rethinking extrasensory perception: Toward a multiphasic model of precognition. *SAGE Open, January/March*, 1–17.

Marwaha, S. B. & May, E. C. (2019). Signals: A mechanism to understand psi phenomena. *Zeitschrift für Anomalistik* [*Journal of Anomalistics*], *19*, 73–112.

Matthew, P. (1831). *On naval timber and arboriculture: With critical notes on authors who have recently treated the subject of planting.* Adam Black.

May, E. C., Faith, L. V., Blackman, M., Bourgeois, B., Kerr, N., & Woods, L. (2012). A target pool and database for anomalous cognition experiments. *Journal of the Society for Psychical Research, 76*, 94–103.

May, E. C. & Marwaha, S. B. (2015a). *Extrasensory perception: Support, skepticism, and science, volume 1 – History, controversy, and research.* Praeger.

May, E. C. & Marwaha, S. B. (2015b). *Extrasensory perception: Support, skepticism, and science, volume 2 – Theories of psi.* Praeger.

May, E. C. & Marwaha, S. B. (Eds.). (2018). *The star gate archives: Reports of the United States government sponsored psi program, 1972–1995. Volume 1: Remote viewing, 1972–1984.* McFarland.

May, E. C., Utts, J. M., Humphrey, B. S., Luke, W. L. W., Frivold, T. J., & Trask, V. V. (1990). Advances in remote-viewing analysis. *Journal of Parapsychology, 54*, 193–228.

May, E. C., Utts, J. M., & Spottiswoode, S. J. P. (1995). Decision augmentation theory: Toward a model of anomalous mental phenomena. *Journal of Parapsychology, 59*, 195–220.

Mayer, G. (2018). A walk through the manifold world of coincidences [Review of the book *The many faces of coincidence*, by Laurence Browne]. *Journal of Parapsychology, 82*, 204–207.

Mayer, G. (2019). Editorial: To the heart of the matter – Carl Gustav Jung, synchronicity, and the struggle with empirical data. *Zeitschrift für Anomalistik, 19*(3), 291–299.

McDonough, B. E., Don, N. S., & Warren, C. A. (2002). Differential event-related potentials to targets and decoys in a guessing task. *Journal of Scientific Exploration, 16*(2), 187–206.

McDonough, B. E., Warren, C. A., & Don, N. S. (1990). Precognition and real-time ESP performance in a computer task with an exceptional subject: A replication attempt. *Journal of Parapsychology, 54*, 141–149.

McMoneagle, J. (1997). *Mind trek: Exploring consciousness, time, and space through remote viewing*. Hampton Roads.

McMoneagle, J. (2000). *Remote viewing secrets*. Hampton Roads.

Meier, C. A. (Ed.) (2001). *Atom and archetype: The Pauli/Jung letters, 1932–1958*. Routledge.

Melas, A. (2013). The shape of absolute coincidences: Salmon's Interactive Fork Model as shape of coincidental processes. *Proceedings of 4th World Congress and School on Universal Logic, Rio de Janeiro, Brazil, April 3 & 4, 2013*. http://ceur-ws.org/Vol-1007/paper8.pdf.

Meyer, M. B. (1989). *Role of personality and cognitive variables in the reporting of experienced meaningful coincidences or "synchronicity"*. [Unpublished doctoral thesis]. Saybrook Institute.

Mill, J. S. (1846). *A system of logic: Ratiocinative and inductive*. Harper & Brothers.

Millar, B. (2015). Quantum theory and parapsychology. In E. Cardeña, J. Palmer, & D. Marcusson-Clavertz (Eds.), *Parapsychology. A handbook for the 21st century* (pp. 165–180). McFarland.

Millar, B. (2019, June 25). Observational theories of psi. *Psi Encyclopedia*. https://psi-encyclopedia.spr.ac.uk/articles/observational-theories-psi.

Mills, J. (2013). Jung's metaphysics. *International Journal of Jungian Studies, 5*(1), 19–43.

Mills, J. (2014). Jung as philosopher: Archetypes, the psychoid factor, and the question of the supernatural. *International Journal of Jungian Studies, 6*(3), 227–242.

Mills, J. (2023). Archetype, psyche, world: From experience to cosmopsychism, *International Journal of Jungian Studies, 15*, 32–51.

Mini-circuits. (2015). Application note: The prevention and control of electrostatic discharge (ESD). *Mini-circuits*. https://www.minicircuits.com/app/AN40-005.pdf.

Miracle Hunter, The. (2015). List of approved Lourdes miracles. MiracleHunter.com. www.miraclehunter.com/marian_apparitions/approved_apparitions/lourdes/miracles1.html.

Mishlove, J. (2000). *The PK man: A true story of mind over matter*. Hampton Roads.

Mishlove, J. & Engen, B. C. (2007). Archetypal synchronistic resonance: A new theory of paranormal experience. *Journal of Humanistic Psychology, 47*(2), 223–242.

Mitchell, C. (2004). Avoiding the intervention paradox. *Australian Journal of Parapsychology, 4*, 81–104.

Mitchell, E. (1971). An ESP test from Apollo 14. *Journal of Parapsychology, 35*, 94–111.

Moore, T., Thalbourne, M. A., & Storm, L. (2010). A study on coincidences. *Australian Journal of Parapsychology, 10*, 154–176.

Mossbridge, J. A. (2023). Precognition at the boundaries: An empirical review and theoretical discussion. *Journal of Anomalous Experience and Cognition*, *3*(1), 5–41.

Mossbridge, J. A. & Radin, D. (2018b). Precognition as a form of prospection: A review of the evidence. *Psychology of Consciousness: Theory, Research, and Practice*, *5*(1), 78–93.

Mossbridge, J., Tressoldi, P. & Utts, J. (2012). Predictive physiological anticipation preceding seemingly unpredictable stimuli: A meta-analysis. *Frontiers in Psychology*, *3*, 1–18.

Muller, R. A. (2016). *Now: The physics of time*. W. W. Norton.

Muller, R. A. & Maguire, S. (2016, June 25). Now and the flow of time. *Cornell University*. https://arxiv.org/pdf/1606.07975.pdf.

Mystery Wire. (2021, February 18). Apollo 14 astronaut Edgar Mitchell secretly conducted psychic experiments after walking on the moon. *Oklahoma's News 4*. https://kfor.com/news/apollo-14-astronaut-edgar-mitchell-secretly-conducted-psychic-experiments-after-walking-on-the-moon/.

Nagata, M. (Producer) & Kinugasa, T. (Director). (1953). *Gate of hell*. [Motion picture]. Daiei Film.

NASA. (2019, December 19). Jupiter. *NASA Science: Solar System Exploration*. https://solarsystem.nasa.gov/planets/jupiter/in-depth/#rings_otp.

Nees, M. & Phillips, C. (2015). Auditory pareidolia: Effects of contextual priming on perceptions of purportedly paranormal and ambiguous auditory stimuli. *Applied Cognitive Psychology*, *29*, 129–134.

Neiman, C. (1995). *Miracles: The extraordinary, the impossible and the divine*. Viking Studio Books.

Nelson, R. D. & Bancel, P A. (2011). Effects of mass consciousness: Changes in random data during global events. *Explore: The Journal of Science and Healing*, *7* (16), 373–383.

Nelson, R. D., Jahn, R. G., Dunne, B. J., Dobyns, Y. H., & Bradish, G. J. (1998). FieldREG II: Consciousness field effects: Replications and explorations. *Journal of Scientific Exploration*, *12*(3), 425–454.

Newton, R. G. (1967). Causality effects of particles that travel faster than light. *Physical Review*, *162*, 1274.

Newton, R. G. (1970). Particles that travel faster than light? *Science*, *167*, 1569–1574.

Nickell, J. (1998). *Looking for a miracle: Weeping icons, relics, stigmata, visions & healing cures*. Prometheus Books.

Nickell, J. (2010). Belgian miracles. *Skeptical Inquirer*, *34*(1), 12–15.

O'Connor, C. (1985). Was the Washington University ESP lab a waste of a half a million dollars?*St. Louis*, September issue.

Olio, K. A. (2004). The truth about "False Memory Syndrome". In L. Cosgrove & P. J. Caplan (Eds.), *Bias in psychiatric diagnosis* (pp. 163–168). Jason Aronson.

Orzel, C. [TED-Ed]. (2014, October 16). *Einstein's brilliant mistake: Entangled states* [Video]. YouTube. https://www.youtube.com/watch?v=DbbWx2COU0E.

Orzel, C. (2015, August 13). What has quantum mechanics ever done for us? *Forbes*. https://www.forbes.com/sites/chadorzel/2015/08/13/what-has-quantum-mechanics-ever-done-for-us/#558321d40468.

Paley, V. (2016). *Healing the mind, body and spirit with imagery hypnosis and mindful meditation at a cancer support center*. [Unpublished master's thesis]. University of California.

Pallikari, F., Boller, E., & Bösch, H. (2000). Jungian synchronicity sheds light on the micro-PK mechanism. In *Proceedings of the 43rd Annual Convention of the Parapsychological Association* (pp. 210–223). Parapsychological Association.

Palmer, J. (1972). Scoring in ESP tests as a function of belief in ESP: Part II. Beyond the sheep–goat effect. *Journal of the American Society for Psychical Research, 66*, 1–25.

Palmer, J. (2006). Memory and ESP—A review of the experimental literature. *European Journal of Parapsychology, 21*, 95–121.

Palmer, J. (2008). Synchronicity and psi: How are they related? In L. Storm (Ed.), *Synchronicity: Multiple perspectives on meaningful coincidence* (pp. 175–192). Pari Publishing.

Palmer, J. (2016). Psi and synchronicity: A controlled comparison. *Journal of the Society for Psychical Research, 80*, 193–213.

Paquette, A. (2011). *Dreamer: 20 years of psychic dreams and how they changed my life*. Winchester, UK: O-Books.

Parapsychological Association. (2022, July 22). *What do we want from a theory in parapsychology?* [Video]. YouTube. https://www.youtube.com/watch?v=WeNuma5DvFY.

Parker, A. (2010). A ganzfeld study using identical twins. *Journal of the Society for Psychical Research, 74*, 118–126.

Patterson, L., Dick, J. T. A., & Elwood, R. W. (2009). Claw removal and feeding ability in the edible crab, Cancer pagurus: implications for fishery practice. *Applied Animal Behaviour Science, 116*(2), 302–305.

Paulos, J. A. (1991). *Beyond numeracy*. Penguin.

Peat, F. D. (1987). *Synchronicity: The bridge between mind and matter*. Bantam.

Penrose, R. (2010). *Cycles of time: An extraordinary new view of the universe*. Vintage Books.

Perez, R. (1998). *Garabandal: The village speaks*. The Workers of Our Lady of Mount Carmel, Inc.

Petoukhov, S. V. & Petukhova, E. S. (2018). *"I-Ching", binary systems in modern science and new algebraic approaches in bioinformatics*. Complementum: XXIst Interdisciplinary Medical Congress of Natural Medicine, Šamorín, Slovak Republic, 46–54.

Physics-Intuition-Applications. (2003, October-December). The 1973 remote viewing probe of the planet Jupiter: Rings around Jupiter. *Connections Through Time, 21*. http://www.p-i-a.com/Magazine/Issue21/Applications_21.htm.

Pickover, C. A. (2005). *The Möbius strip: Dr. August Möbius's marvelous band in mathematics, games, literature, art, technology, and cosmology*. Thunder's Mouth Press.

Pike, J. A. (1969). *The other side: An account of my experiences with psychic phenomena*. W. H. Allen.

Playfair, G. L. (2002). *Twin telepathy*. Vega.

Playfair, G. L. (2017). Monozygotic twins and macro-entanglement. *Journal of Nonlocality, 5*(1), 1–10.

Plume, A., & van Weijen, D. (2014, September). *Publish or perish? The rise of the fractional author… Research Trends*. https://www.researchtrends.com/issue-38-september-2014/publish-or-perish-the-rise-of-the-fractional-author/.

Powell, D. H. (2009). *The ESP enigma: The scientific case for psychic phenomena*. Walker & Company.

Pratt, J. G. & Roll, W. G. (1958). The Seaford disturbances. *Journal of Parapsychology, 22*, 79–124.

Pratt, J. G., Rhine, J. B., Smith, B. M., Stuart, C. E., & Greenwood, J. A. (1966). *Extra-sensory perception after sixty years.* Bruce Humphries. (Original work published in 1940)

Progoff, I. (1973). *Jung, synchronicity, and human destiny: Noncausal dimensions of human experience.* Julian Press, Inc.

Purdue OWL. (1995–2017). Reference list: Electronic sources (web publications). https://owl.english.purdue.edu/owl/resource/560/10/.

Puthoff, H. E. (1984). ARV (Associational Remote Viewing) applications [Abstract]. In R. A. White & J. Solfvin (Eds.), *Research in Parapsychology 1984* (pp. 121–122). Metuchen, NJ: Scarecrow Press.

Puthoff, H. E. (1996). CIA-initiated remote viewing program at Stanford Research Institute. *Journal of Scientific Exploration, 10*(1), 63–76.

Rabeyron, T. (2020). Why most research findings about psi are false: The replicability crisis, the psi paradox and the myth of Sisyphus. *Frontiers in Psychology, 11*: 562992. doi:10.3389/fpsyg.2020.562992.

Radin, D. I. (2005). The sense of being stared at: A preliminary meta-analysis. *Journal of Consciousness Studies, 12*(6), 95–100.

Radin, D. I. (2006). *Entangled minds: Extrasensory experiences in a quantum reality.* Paraview/Pocket Books.

Radin, D. I. & Nelson, R. D. (2003). Research on mind-matter interactions (MMI): Individual intention. In W. B. Jonas & C. C. Crawford (Eds.), *Healing, intention and energy medicine: Research and clinical implications* (pp. 39–48). Churchill Livingstone.

Randall, J. L. & Davis, C. P. (1982). Paranormal deformation of nitinol wire: A confirmatory experiment. *Journal of the Society for Psychical Research, 77*, 347–349.

Raudive, K. (1971). *Breakthrough: An amazing experiment in electronic communication with the dead.* Colin Smythe Ltd.

Rawlette, S. H. (2019a). Coincidence or psi? The epistemic import of spontaneous cases of purported psi identified post-verification. *Journal of Scientific Exploration, 33*(1), 9–42.

Rawlette, S. H. (2019b). *The source and significance of coincidences: A hard look at the astonishing evidence.* Sharon Hewitt Rawlette.

Reading, M. (2010). *Nostradamus: The top 100 prophecies.* Watkins.

Redshaw, K. (1996). *Gottfried Wilhelm Leibniz (1646–1716).* http://www.kerryr.net/pioneers/leibniz.htm.

Reichenbach, H. (1956). *The direction of time.* University of California Press.

Rhine, J. B. (1947). *The reach of the mind.* William Sloane Associates, Inc.

Rhine, J. B. & Pratt, J. G. (1974). *Parapsychology: Frontier science of the mind* (5th ed.). Charles C. Thomas. (Original work published in 1957)

Richards, T. L., Kozak, L., Johnson, L. C., & Standish, L. J. (2005). Replicable functional magnetic resonance imaging evidence of correlated brain signals between physically and sensory isolated subjects. *Journal of Alternative and Complementary Medicine, 11*, 955–963.

Richo, D. (2007). *The power of coincidence: How life shows us what we need to know.* Boston, MA: Shambhala.

Ritsema, R. & Sabbadini, S. A. (2005). *The original I Ching oracle.* Watkins.

Robb, A. (2018). *Why we dream: The science, creativity and transformative power of dreams.* Picador.

Robertson, D. M. (2004). *A passionate pilgrim: A biography of Bishop James A. Pike*. Vintage Books.

Rock, A. J. (2010). Is the "sense of being stared at" an artefact of response bias? *Australian Journal of Parapsychology*, *10*(2), 140–152.

Rock, A. J. (Ed.). (2013). *The survival hypothesis: Essays on mediumship*. McFarland.

Rock, A. J., Permezel, F. E., & Storm, L. (2012). Randomized expectancy-enhanced placebo-controlled trial of the impact of Quantum BioEnergetic distant healing and paranormal belief on mood disturbance: A pilot study. *Explore: The Journal of Science and Healing*, *8*, 107–117.

Rock, A. J. & Storm, L. (2015). Testing telepathy in the medium/proxy-sitter dyad: A protocol focusing on the source-of-psi problem. *Journal of Scientific Exploration*, *29* (4), 565–584.

Rock, A. J., Storm, L., Harris, K., & Friedman, H. (2012). Shamanic-like journeying and psi-signal detection: I. In search of the psi-conducive components of a novel experimental protocol. *Journal of Parapsychology*, *76*, 321–347.

Roe, C. (2020). What have we learned from case collections? *Paranormal Review*, *96*, 4–5.

Roe, C. A., Martin, H., & Drennan, S. (2014). Effects of participant and target system lability upon PK performance using an I Ching task. *Journal of the Society for Psychical Research*, *78*, 219–238.

Rogers, D. P. (1966). Negative and positive affect and ESP run-score variance. *Journal of Parapsychology*, *30*, 151–159.

Rogo, D. S. (1986). *On the track of the poltergeist*. Prentice-Hall.

Rogo, D. S. (1988). The psychic warriors. In J. White & M. Rosenbaum (Eds.), *Psychic warfare: Fact or fiction?* (pp. 194–200). Aquarian Press.

Roll, W. G. (1966). ESP and memory. *International Journal of Neuropsychiatry*, *2*, 505–521.

Roll, W. G. (1977). Poltergeists. In B. B. Wolman (Ed.), *Handbook of parapsychology* (pp. 382–413). Van Nostrand Reinhold.

Roll, W. G., Alexander, C. H., Williams, B. J., & Persinger, M. A. (2021). Parapsychology, quantum theory and neuroscience. In S. Krippner, A. J. Rock, H. L. Friedman, & N. L. Zingrone (Eds.), *Advances in parapsychological research 10* (pp. 70–166). McFarland.

Roney-Dougal, S. M. & Solfvin, J. (2002). Field study of enhancement effect on lettuce seeds: Their germination rate, growth and health. *Journal of the Society for Psychical Research*, *66*, 129–143.

Roney-Dougal, S.M. & Solfvin, J. (2003). Field study of an enhancement effect on lettuce seeds: A replication study. *Journal of Parapsychology*, *67*(2), 279–298.

Rosambeau, M. (1981). *How twins grow up*. The Bodley Head.

Rose, N. & Blackmore, S. J. (2001). Are false memories psi-conducive? *Journal of Parapsychology*, *65*(2), 125–144.

Rosen, D. H., Smith, S. M., Huston, H. L., & Gonzalez, G. (1991). Empirical study of associations between symbols and their meanings: evidence of collective and unconscious (archetypal) memory. *Journal of Analytical Psychology*, *36*, 211–228.

Roth, R. F. (2002). Introduction to Carl G. Jung's principle of synchronicity. Remo F. Roth. http://paulijungunusmundus.eu/synw/synchronicity_jung.htm.

Roxburgh, E. C., Ridgway, S., & Roe, C. A. (2015). Exploring the meaning in meaningful coincidences: An interpretative phenomenological analysis of synchronicity in therapy. *European Journal of Psychotherapy & Counselling*, *17*(2), 144–161.

Rubin, L. & Honorton, C. (1971). Separating the yins from the yangs: An experiment with the I Ching . *Journal of Parapsychology, 35*, 313–314.

Rubin, L. & Honorton, C. (1972). Separating the yins from the yangs: An experiment with the *I Ching*. In W. G. Roll, R. L. Morris, & J. D. Morris (Eds.), *Proceedings of the 15th Annual Convention Parapsychological Association* (pp. 6–7). Parapsychological Association.

Russell, B. (1953). *Mysticism and logic*. Pelican. (Original work published in 1917)

Russell, P. (2005, December 1). How to be a wizard. *Peter Russell: Spirit of Now*. http://www.peterrussell.com/PassingThoughts/Wizardry.php.

Ryan, J. A. (1996). *Leibniz's binary system and Shao Yong's Yijing. Philosophy East and West, 46*(1), pp. 59–90.

Sacco, R. G. (2017). The Fibonacci life chart method as a predictor of spiritual experience. *Journal of Educational and Developmental Psychology, 7*(2), 1–13.

Sacco, R. G. (2019). The predictability of synchronicity experience: Results from a survey of Jungian analysts. *International Journal of Psychological Studies, 11*(3), 46–62.

Sagan, C. (1997). *The demon-haunted world: Science as a candle in the dark*. Random House Group.

Saklani, A. (1988). Preliminary tests for psi-ability in shamans of Garhwal Himalaya. *Journal of the Society for Psychical Research, 55*, 60–70.

Samuels, A., Shorter, B., & Plaut, F. (1992). *A critical dictionary of Jungian analysis*. Routledge and Keegan Paul. (Original work published in 1986)

Saunders, P. & Skar, P. (2001). Archetypes, complexes and self-organisation. *Journal of Analytical Psychology, 46*, 305–323.

Schellinger, U., Wittmann, M., & Anton, A. (2019). "Das ist alles so eigentümlich verschachtelt" – Hans Bender und Carl Gustav Jung im Gespräch über Synchronizität ["It's all so strangely convoluted" – Hans Bender and Carl Gustav Jung in conversation about synchronicity]. *Zeitschrift für Anomalistik* [*Journal of Anomalistics*], *19*, 420–467.

Schlitz, M. J. & Honorton, C. (1992). Ganzfeld psi performance within an artistically gifted population. *Journal of the American Society for Psychical Research, 86*, 83–98.

Schmeidler, G. R. (1964). An experiment on precognitive clairvoyance. Part II. The reliability of the scores. *Journal of Parapsychology, 28*, 15–27.

Schmeidler, G. R. (1988). *Parapsychology and psychology: Matches and mismatches*. McFarland.

Schmidt, S., Müller, S., & Walach, H. (2004). Do you know who is on the phone? Replication of an experiment on telephone telepathy. In *Proceedings of the 47th Annual Convention of the Parapsychological Association* (pp. 245–254). Parapsychological Association.

Schroth, R. A. (1976, August 1). The death and life of Bishop Pike. *The New York Times*. http://www.nytimes.com/1976/08/01/archives/the-death-and-life-of-bishop-pike-looking-for-god-in-the-wrong.html.

Schwartz, B. E. (2008). Synchronicity and telepathy. In L. Storm (Ed.), *Synchronicity: Multiple perspectives on meaningful coincidence* (pp. 67–77). Pari, Italy: Pari Publishing.

Schwartz, S. A. (2000). *The Alexandria project*. Author's Guild.

Schwartz, S. A. (2005). *The secret vaults of time*. Hampton Roads.

Schwartz, S. A. (2014). Through time and space: The evidence for remote viewing. In D. Broderick & B. Goertzel (Eds.), *Evidence for psi: Thirteen empirical research reports* (pp. 168–212). McFarland.

Schwartz, S. A. (2018). Nonlocal consciousness and the anthropology of religion. *Explore: The Journal of Science and Healing*, *14*(6), 402–404.
Schwartz, S. A. (2022). 2060 visions of the future. *Venture Inwards*, *38*, 36–40.
Science Daily. (2016, September 21). In exploring the "now", new theory links flow of time with Big Bang. *University of California, Berkeley.* https://www.sciencedaily.com/releases/2016/09/160921121234.htm.
Sender, R., Fuchs, S., & Milo, R. (2016, August 9). Revised estimates for the number of human and bacteria cells in the body. *PLOS Biology*, *14*(8), 1–14: e1002533.
Shamdasani, S. (Ed.). (2009). *The red book: Liber novus* (M. Kyburz, J. Peck, S. Shamdasani, Trans.). Philemon Foundation & W. W. Norton.
Sheldrake, R. (1994). *Seven experiments that could change the world.* Fourth Estate.
Sheldrake, R. (2014). Telepathy in connection with telephone calls, text messages, and emails. *Journal of the International Society of Life Information Science*, *32*(1), 7–10.
Sheldrake, R., Godwin, H., & Rockell, S. (2004). A filmed experiment on telephone telepathy with the Nolan sisters. *Journal of the Society for Psychical Research*, *68*, 168–172.
Sheldrake, R. & Smart, P. (2003a). Experimental tests for telephone telepathy. *Journal of the Society for Psychical Research*, *67*, 184–199.
Sheldrake, R. & Smart, P. (2003b). Videotaped experiments on telephone telepathy. *Journal of Parapsychology*, *67*, 147–166.
Shen, D., Shen, R.-S., & Li, G. (2021). Laboratory investigations of extrasensory identification of concealed 5-character codes by a presumably gifted teenager in China. *Journal of Scientific Exploration*, *35*(3), 570–589.
Shiah, Y.-J. (2011). A proposed process for experiencing visual images of targets during an ESP task. *Journal of Parapsychology*, *75*, 129–143.
Shiah, Y.-J. (2012). A possible mechanism for ESP at the initial perceptual stage. *Journal of Parapsychology*, *76*, 147–159.
Shiel, W. C., Jr. (2020, August 11). Medical definition of apophenia. *Medicine.net.* https://www.medicinenet.com/apophenia/definition.htm.
Shields, C. J. (2007). *Aristotle.* Routledge.
Shin, Y.-W., Lee, J.-S., Han, O.-S., & Rhi, B.-Y. (2005). The influence of complexes on implicit learning. *Journal of Analytical Psychology*, *50*, 175–190.
Silvia, P. J. (2005). Deflecting reactance: The role of similarity in increasing compliance and reducing resistance. *Basic and Applied Social Psychology*, *27*, 227–284.
Sinclair, U. (1930/1962). *Mental radio.* Charles C. Thomas.
Skrbina, D. (2005). *Panpsychism in the west.* MIT Press.
Slate-writer. (2015, March 21). *Music from the beyond?* [Video]. YouTube. https://www.youtube.com/watch?v=mX477Zo7otg.
Smith, C. C., Laham, D., & Moddel, G. (2014). Stock market prediction using associative remote viewing by inexperienced remote viewers. *Explore: The Journal of Science and Healing*, *28*(1), 7–16.
Smith, P. H. (1998). *Coordinate remote viewing training manual.* SRI International.
Sober, E. (2012). Coincidences and how to reason about them. In H. W. de Regt, S. Hartmann, & S. Okasha (Eds.), *EPSA philosophy of science: Amsterdam 2009* (pp. 355–374). Amsterdam: Springer.
Society for Scientific Exploration. (2020, February 21). *Garret Moddel | Quantum mechanics does not explain psi … So far* [Video]. YouTube. https://www.youtube.com/watch?v=QwV4Zmn7sLk&t.

Sotirova-Kohli, M., Opwis, K., Roesler, C., Smith, S. M., Rosen, D. H., Vaid, J., & Djonov, V. (2013). Symbol/meaning paired-associate recall: An "archetypal memory" advantage? *Behavioral Science*, *3*, 541–561.

Sotirova-Kohli, M., Rosen, D. H., Smith, S. M., Henderson, P., & Taki-Reece, S. (2011). Empirical study of Kanji as archetypal images: Understanding the collective unconscious as part of the Japanese language. *Journal of Analytical Psychology*, *56*, 109–132.

Spiegel, D. & Moore, R. (1997). Imagery and hypnosis in the treatment of cancer patients. *Oncology*, *11*(8), 1179–1189.

Spraggett, A. (1967). *The unexplained*. New American Library.

Spraggett, A. & Rauscher, W. V. (1973). *Arthur Ford: The man who talked with the dead*. W. W. Norton & Company.

Standish, L. J., Johnson, L. C., Kozak, L., & Richards, T. (2003). Evidence of correlated functional MRI signals between distant human brains. *Alternative Therapies in Health and Medicine*, *9*, 122–125, 128.

Stanford, R. G. (1974). An experimentally testable model for spontaneous psi events: I. Extrasensory events. *Journal of the American Society for Psychical Research*, *68*, 34–57.

Stanford, R. G. (1990). An experimentally testable model for spontaneous psi events: A review of related evidence and concepts from parapsychology and other sciences. In S. Krippner (Ed.), *Advances in parapsychological research 6* (pp. 54–167). McFarland.

Stanford, R. G. (2006). Making sense of the "extrasensory"—Modeling receptive psi using memory-related concepts. *European Journal of Parapsychology*, *21*, 122–147.

Stanford, R. G., & Stanford, B. E. (1969). Shifts in EEG alpha rhythm as related to calling patterns and ESP run-score variance. *Journal of Parapsychology*, *33*, 39–47.

Stanford, R. G., & Stein, C. (1994). A meta-analysis of ESP studies contrasting hypnosis and a comparison condition. *Journal of Parapsychology*, *58*, 235–269.

Stevens, P. (2002). Can we differentiate between ESP and imagination? *Journal of the Society for Psychical Research*, *66*, 239–246.

Stevenson, I. (1977). Reincarnation: Field studies and theoretical issues. In B. B. Wolman (Ed.), *Handbook of Parapsychology* (pp. 631–663). Van Nostrand Reinhold.

Stillman, D. (1975, December 4). An analysis of a remote viewing experiment of URDF-3. *Central Intelligence Agency*. https://www.cia.gov/library/readingroom/document/cia-rdp96-00791r000200240001-0.

Stillwell, J. (1993). *Classical topology and combinatorial group theory* (2nd ed.). Springer-Verlag.

Stockman, T., Monroe, G. & Cordner, S. (2019, March 12). Venus is not Earth's closest neighbor. *Physics Today*. https://physicstoday.scitation.org/do/10.1063/PT.6.3.20190312a/full/.

Stokes, D. M. (1987). Theoretical parapsychology. In S. Krippner (Ed.), *Advances in parapsychological research 5* (pp. 77–189). McFarland.

Stokes, D. M. (2014). *Reimagining the soul: Afterlife in the age of matter*. McFarland.

Stollznow, K. (2014). *Language myths, mysteries and magic*. Palgrave Macmillan.

Storm, L. (1999). Synchronicity, causality, and acausality. *Journal of Parapsychology*, *63*, 247–269.

Storm, L. (2001). Technical Note: Effect size in "The Transliminal Connection Between Paranormal Effects and Personality in an Experiment with the *I Ching*" by Storm & Thalbourne (1998–1999). *European Journal of Parapsychology*, *16*, 107–108.

Storm, L. (2002). A parapsychological investigation of the *I Ching*: Seeking psi in an ancient Chinese system of divination. *Australian Journal of Parapsychology, 2*, 44–62.
Storm, L. (2003a). Research note: The pro attitude and the "sheep–goat" effect in the *I Ching* database. *Australian Journal of Parapsychology, 3*, 147–152.
Storm, L. (2003b). Remote viewing by committee: RV using a "multiple agent/multiple percipient" design. *Journal of Parapsychology, 67*, 325–342.
Storm, L. (2005). A socioempirical perspective on skepticism about psi. In M. A. Thalbourne & L. Storm (Eds.), *Parapsychology in the twenty-first century: Essays on the future of psychical research* (pp. 275–304). McFarland.
Storm, L. (2006). A parapsychological investigation of the *I Ching*: The relationships between psi, intuition, and time perspective. *Journal of Parapsychology, 70*, 121–141.
Storm, L. (2008a). Investigations of the *I Ching*: I. Relationships between psi, time perspective, paranormal belief and meaningfulness. *Australian Journal of Parapsychology, 8*, 103–127.
Storm, L. (2008b). Synchronicity, causality, and acausality. In L. Storm (Ed.), *Synchronicity: Multiple perspectives on meaningful coincidence* (pp. 153–174). Pari Publishing.
Storm, L. (Ed.). (2008c). *Synchronicity: Multiple perspectives on meaningful coincidence.* Pari Publishing.
Storm, L. (2008d). Synchronicity, science, and religion. In L. Storm (Ed.), *Synchronicity: Multiple perspectives on meaningful coincidence* (pp. 249–258). Pari Publishing.
Storm, L. (2008e). *The enigma of numbers.* Pari Publishing.
Storm, L. (2014). At my desk. *THE A.I.P.R. NEWS, 8*(1), 2.
Storm, L. (2015). At my desk. *THE A.I.P.R. NEWS, 9*(1), 2.
Storm, L. (2016). Conformity and reactance in the *I Ching* using a Q-Sort/RNG-PK method: A pilot study. *Australian Journal of Parapsychology, 16*, 133–162.
Storm, L. (2019a). Imagination and reactance in a psi task using the imagery cultivation model and a fuzzy set encoded target pool. *Journal of Scientific Exploration, 33* (2), 197–212.
Storm, L. (2019b). Reactance in a picture-identification task using a fuzzy-set encoded target pool. *Journal of the Society for Psychical Research, 83*, 129–143.
Storm, L. (2022). The effects of imagery-cultivation on mood and psi performance. *Journal of the Society for Psychical Research, 86*, 95–113.
Storm, L. (2025). *A new approach to psi: Re-envisioning paranormal experience as meaningful coincidence.* Routledge.
Storm, L., Drinkwater, K., & Jinks, A. L. (2017). A question of belief: An analysis of item content in paranormal belief questionnaires. *Journal of Scientific Exploration, 31*(2), 187–230.
Storm, L., Ertel, S., & Rock, A. J. (2013). The sheep–goat effect as a matter of compliance vs. noncompliance: The effect of reactance in a forced-choice ball selection test. *Journal of Scientific Exploration, 27*(3), 393–411.
Storm, L. & Goretzki, M. (2020). Spiritual emergency and psi: Testing the psychic opening hypothesis. *The Journal of Transpersonal Psychology, 52*(1), 142–162.
Storm, L. & Goretzki, M. (2021). The psychology and parapsychology of spiritual emergency. *Journal of Scientific Exploration, 35*(1), 36–64.
Storm, L. & Rock, A. J. (2009a). Imagery cultivation vs. noise reduction: Shamanic-like journeying as a psi-conducive alternative to the Ganzfeld protocol. *Australian Journal of Parapsychology, 9*, 5–31.

Storm, L. & Rock, A. J. (2009b). Shamanic-like journeying and psi: I. Imagery cultivation, personality, and the picture-identification task. *Australian Journal of Parapsychology, 9*, 165–192.

Storm, L. & Rock, A. J. (2014a). An investigation of the *I Ching* using the Q-Sort Method and an RNG-PK design: I. Four possible psi predictors. *Australian Journal of Parapsychology, 14*, 29–67.

Storm, L. & Rock, A. J. (2014b). An investigation of the *I Ching* using the Q-Sort Method and an RNG-PK design: II. The effect of reactance on psi. *Australian Journal of Parapsychology, 12*, 163–190.

Storm, L. & Thalbourne, M. A. (1998–1999). The transliminal connection between personality and paranormal effects in an experiment with the *I Ching*. *European Journal of Parapsychology, 14*, 100–124.

Storm, L. & Thalbourne, M. A. (2000). A paradigm shift away from the ESP–PK dichotomy: The theory of psychopraxia. *Journal of Parapsychology, 64*, 279–300.

Storm, L. & Thalbourne, M. A. (2001). Studies of the *I Ching*: I. A replication. *Journal of Parapsychology, 65*, 105–123.

Storm, L. & Thalbourne, M. A. (2005a). The effect of a change in pro attitude on paranormal performance: A pilot study using naïve and sophisticated skeptics. *Journal of Scientific Exploration, 19*(1), 11–29.

Storm, L. & Thalbourne, M. A. (2005b). The effects of intuition and attitudes towards gambling on ESP performance during a gambling task. *European Journal of Parapsychology, 20*, 22–49.

Storm, L. & Thalbourne, M. A. (2018). Research note: Demonstrating the concurrent validity of two coincidence measures. *Australian Journal of Parapsychology, 18*, 57–69.

Storm, L. & Tressoldi, P. E. (2017). Gathering in more sheep and goats: A meta-analysis of forced-choice sheep–goat studies, 1994–2015. *Journal of the Society for Psychical Research, 81*, 79–107.

Storm, L. & Tressoldi, P. E. (2020). Meta-analysis of free-response studies 2009–2018: Assessing the noise-reduction model ten years on. *Journal of the Society for Psychical Research, 84*, 193–219.

Storm, L., Tressoldi, P. E., & Di Risio, L. (2010). Meta-analysis of free-response studies 1992–2008: Assessing the noise reduction model in parapsychology. *Psychological Bulletin, 136*(4), 471–485. doi:10.1037/a0019457.

Storm, L., Tressoldi, P. E., & Di Risio, L. (2012). Meta-analysis of ESP studies 1987–2008: Assessing the success of the forced-choice design in parapsychology. *Journal of Parapsychology, 76*, 243–273.

Stubenberg, L. (2016, October 3). Neutral monism and the dual aspect theory. *Stanford Encyclopedia of Philosophy.* https://plato.stanford.edu/entries/neutral-monism/#9.4.

Sudduth, M. (2016). *A philosophical critique of empirical arguments for postmortem survival.* Palgrave Macmillan.

Sun, A. X., Londono, R., Hudnall, M. L., Tuan, R. S., & Lozito, T. P. (August 28, 2018). Differences in neural stem cell identity and differentiation capacity drive divergent regenerative outcomes in lizards and salamanders. *Proceedings of the National Academy of Sciences (PNAS),115*(35), E8256–E8265. doi:10.1073/pnas.1803780115.

Surprise, K. (2012). *Synchronicity: The art of coincidence, choice, and unlocking the mind.* Career Press.

Swann, I. (1995, December 12). *The 1973 remote viewing probe of the planet Jupiter.* http://u2.lege.net/biomindsuperpowers.com/site_retrieved_by_wget-20130206/Pages/1973JupiterRVProbe.html.

Tabori, P. (1974). *Harry Price ghost hunter.* Sphere Books. (Original work published in 1950)

Targ, R. (2012). *The reality of ESP: A physicist's proof of psychic abilities.* Theosophical Publishing House.

Targ, R. (2019). What do we know about psi? The first decade of remote-viewing research and operations at Stanford Research Institute. *Journal of Scientific Exploration, 33*(4), 569–592.

Targ, R. & Katra, J. (1998). *Miracles of mind: Exploring nonlocal consciousness and spiritual healing.* New World Library.

Targ, R. & Puthoff, H. E. (1977). *Mind-reach: Scientists look at psychic ability.* Hampton Roads.

Targ, R., Katra, J., Brown, D., & Wiegand, W. (1995). Viewing the future: A pilot study with an error-detecting protocol. *Journal of Scientific Exploration, 9*(3), 367–380.

Tarnas, R. (2007). *Cosmos and psyche: Intimations of a new world view.* Penguin/Plume.

Tart, C.T. (1988). Effects of electrical shielding on GESP performance. *Journal of the American Society for Psychical Research, 82*, 129–146.

Tart, C. T. (2008). Causality and synchronicity: Steps towards clarification. In L. Storm (Ed.), *Synchronicity: Multiple perspectives on meaningful coincidence* (pp. 109–126). Pari Publishing.

Tausk, F., Elenkov, I., & Moynihan, J. (2008). Psychoneuroimmunology. *Dermatologic Therapy, 21*, 22–31.

Taylor, S. E. (1983). Adjustment to threatening events: A theory of cognitive adaptation. *American Psychologist, 38*, 1161–1173.

Thalbourne, M. A. (1981). Some experiments on the paranormal cognition of drawings with special reference to personality and attitudinal variables. [Unpublished doctoral thesis]. Department of Parapsychology, University of Edinburgh.

Thalbourne, M. A. (1994). Postscript to an experiment with the *I Ching*: How many changing lines? *European Journal of Parapsychology, 10*, 130–145.

Thalbourne, M. A. (2003). *A glossary of terms used in parapsychology.* Puente.

Thalbourne, M. A. (2004). *The common thread between ESP and PK.* The Parapsychology Foundation.

Thalbourne, M. A. (2010). Transliminality: A fundamental mechanism in psychology and parapsychology. *Australian Journal of Parapsychology, 10*, 70–81.

Thalbourne, M. A. & Storm, L. (2014). *A further study of psychopraxia using the I Ching. Australian Journal of Parapsychology, 14*, 115–142.

Tobacyk, J. J. (1988). *A Revised Paranormal Belief Scale.* [Unpublished manuscript]. Ruston, LA: Louisiana Tech University.

Toksvig, S. (1948). *Emanuel Swedenborg: Scientist and mystic.* Yale University Press.

TopPop. (2017, December 23). *The Carpenters - Yesterday once more • TopPop* [Video]. YouTube. https://www.youtube.com/watch?v=_CXU6Q4gMeo.

TriumphantGeorge. (2015, April). When I wasn't looking for it, I was surrounded by synchronicity. Now that I'm looking, it's nowhere to be found [comment]. *Glitch in the Matrix.* https://www.reddit.com/r/Glitch_in_the_Matrix/comments/33hmnj/when_i_wasnt_looking_for_it_i_was_surrounded_by/cqkygat/.

Tversky, A. & Kahneman, D. (1974). Judgment under uncertainty: Heuristics and biases. *Science, 185*(4157), 1124–1131.

Ulivi, P. (2004). *Lunar exploration: Human pioneers and robotic surveyors.* Springer-Verlag.

Ullman, M., & Krippner, S., with Vaughan, A. (1973). *Dream telepathy: Experiments in nocturnal ESP.* McFarland.

Utts, J. (1991). Replication and meta-analysis in parapsychology. *Statistical Science, 6*, 363–378.

Utts, J. (1999). The significance of statistics in mind-matter research. *Journal of Scientific Exploration, 13*(4), 615–638.

Valencia, A. L. & Froese, T. (2020). What binds us? Inter-brain neural synchronization and its implications for theories of human consciousness. *Neuroscience of Consciousness, 20*(1), 1–12. doi:10.1093/nc/niaa010.

Vaughan, A. (1973). *Patterns of prophecy.* Hawthorn Books.

Vaughan, A. (1979). *Incredible coincidence: The baffling world of synchronicity.* Ballantine.

Venn, J. (1866). *The logic of chance: An essay on the foundations and province of the theory of probability.* Macmillan.

Venning, T. (2019, June 5). Time's arrow: Albert Einstein's letters to Michele Besso. *Christie's.* https://www.christies.com/features/Einstein-letters-to-Michele-Besso-8422-1.aspx.

Ventola, A., Houran, J., Laythe, B., Storm, L., Parra, A., Dixon, J., & Kruth, J. G. (2019). A transliminal 'dis-ease' model of 'poltergeist agents'. *Journal of the Society for Psychical Research, 83*, 129–171.

Vigorito, T. (2012). Chaos, synchronicity, and the technology of magic. In D. Pinchbeck & K. Jordan (Eds.), *Exploring the edge realms of consciousness: Liminal zones, psychic science, and the hidden dimensions of the mind* (pp. 211–219). Evolver Editions.

Von Däniken, E. (1969). *Chariots of the gods: Unsolved mysteries of the past.* Souvenir Press.

Von Franz, M.-L. (1980). *On divination and synchronicity.* Inner City.

Von Franz, M.-L. (1992). *Psyche and matter.* Shambhala.

Von Franz, M.-L. (1995). *Shadow and evil in fairy tales.* Shambhala.

Von Franz, M.-L. (1997). *Projection and recollection in Jungian psychology: Reflections of the soul.* Open Court.

Von Lucadou, W. (2015). The model of pragmatic information. In E. C. May & S. B. Marwaha (Eds.), *Extrasensory perception: Support, skepticism, and science, volume 2 – Theories of psi* (pp. 221–242). Praeger.

Von Lucadou, W., Römer, H., & Walach, H. (2007). Synchronistic phenomena as entanglement correlations in generalized quantum theory. *Journal of Consciousness Studies, 14*(4), 50–74.

Voracek, M., Rieder, S., Stieger, S., & Swami, V. (2015). What's in a surname? Physique, aptitude, and sports type comparisons between Tailors and Smiths. *PLOS ONE, 10*(7), 1–11.

Wachtel, P. L. (1973). Psychodynamics, behavior therapy, and the implacable experimenter: An inquiry into the consistency of personality. *Journal of Abnormal Psychology, 82*, 324–334.

Wahbeh, H., Cannard, C., Radin, D., & Delorme, A. (2024). Who's calling? Evaluating the accuracy of guessing who is on the phone. *Explore: The Journal of Science and Healing, 20*(2), 239–247.

Walach, H. (2020). Inner experience–direct access to reality: A complementarist ontology and dual aspect monism support a broader epistemology. *Frontiers of Psychology, 11*, 1–14. doi:10.3389/fpsyg.2020.00640.

Walsh, R. (1989). What is a shaman? Definition, origin and distribution. *The Journal of Transpersonal Psychology, 21*, 1–11.

Walton, T. (1996). *Fire in the sky: The Walton experience*. Marlowe. (Original work published in 1979)

Warcollier, R. (1938). Experimental telepathy (trans. by J. B. Gridley from *La telepathie*, 1921). Boston Society for Psychical Research.

Wargo, E. (2020). Pat Price, precognition, and "Star Wars": A reexamination of a historic remote viewing case. *Edgescience, 42*, 10–23.

Warner, J. L. (Executive Producer), & Daves, D. (Director). (1947). *Dark passage* [Motion picture]. Warner Brothers.

Warren, C. A., McDonough, B. E., & Don, N. S. (1992a). Event-related brain potential changes in a psi task. *Journal of Parapsychology, 56*, 1–30.

Warren, C. A., McDonough, B. E., & Don, N. S. (1992b). Partial replication of single subject event-related potential effects in a psi task. In *Proceedings of the 35th Annual Convention of the Parapsychological Association* (pp. 169–181). Parapsychological Association.

Watkins, G. (2015). Macro-psychokinesis. Methodological concerns. In E. Cardeña, J. Palmer, & D. Marcusson-Clavertz (Eds.), *Parapsychology. A handbook for the 21st century* (pp. 77–82). McFarland.

Watson, J. D. & Crick, F. H. C. (1953). A structure for deoxyribose nucleic acid. *Nature, 171*, 737–738.

Watt, C. A. (1990–1991). Psychology and coincidences. *European Journal of Parapsychology, 8*, 66–84.

Weaver, W. (1963). *Lady luck: The theory of probability*. Dover Publications.

Weitering, H. (2018, January 10). "Totally wrong" on Jupiter: What scientists gleaned from NASA's Juno mission. *Space.com*. https://www.space.com/39348-juno-jupiter-mission-planet-revelations.html.

West, J. A. (1992). *The case for astrology*. Penguin/Arkana.

West, D. (2012). Awkward questions. *Journal of the Society for Psychical Research, 76*, 204–209.

Westerlund, J., Parker, A., Dalkvist, J., & Hadlaczky, G. (2006). Remarkable correspondences between ganzfeld mentation and target content: A psychical or psychological effect? *Journal of Parapsychology, 70*, 23–48.

White, R. (2000). Fine-tuning and multiple universes. *Nous, 34*, 260–276.

Wilhelm, H. (1960). *Change: Eight lectures on the I Ching* (trans. C. F. Baynes). Princeton Legacy Library.

Wilhelm, R. (1987). *I Ching or the book of changes* (trans. C. F. Baynes). Princeton University Press. https://archive.org/details/ichingorbookof00bayn/page/n11/mode/2up (Original work published in 1924 in German; and 1950 in English)

Williams, B. J. (2015). *Psychic phenomena and the brain: Exploring the neuropsychology of psi*. Australian Institute of Parapsychological Research, Inc.

Wilmer, H. (1987). *Practical Jung*. Chiron.

Winther, M. (2012). Critique of synchronicity. *Depth Psychology and Spiritual Tradition*. http://mlwi.magix.net/synchronicity.htm.

Wolman, B. B. (Ed.). (1977). *Handbook of parapsychology*. Van Nostrand Reinhold.

Wooffitt, R. (2021). The anomaly that isn't: Poetic confluence, social interaction, and psi. *Edgescience, 48*, 13–16.

Wooffitt, R. (2022). Poetic confluence: The social organization of a telepathic experience. *Journal of Anomalous Experience and Cognition, 1(*1), 80–110.

Wuthnow, R. (1976). Astrology and marginality. *Journal for the Scientific Study of Religion, 15*, 157–168.

Yiassemides, A. (2011). Chronos in synchronicity: Manifestations of the psychoid reality. *Journal of Analytical Psychology, 56*, 451–470.

Yong, E. (2018, November 20). Psychology's replication crisis is running out of excuses. *The Atlantic*. https://www.theatlantic.com/science/archive/2018/11/psychologys-replication-crisis-real/576223/.

Yu, B., Chen, X., Rich, S., Mo, Q., & Yan, H. (2021). Dynamics of the coronavirus disease 2019 (COVID-19) epidemic in Wuhan City, Hubei Province and China: A second derivative analysis of the cumulative daily diagnosed cases during the first 85 days. *Global Health Journal, 5*(1), 4–11. doi:10.1016/j.glohj.2021.02.001.

Zohar, G. (1990). *The quantum self.* Bloomsbury.

Zollo, E. (1978). *The uses of imagination and the decline of the West.* Golgonooza Press.

Zusne, L. & Jones, W. H. (1982). *Anomalistic psychology: A study of extraordinary phenomena of behaviour and experience.* Lawrence Erlbaum Associates.

Zusne, L. & Jones, W. H. (1989). *Anomalistic psychology: A study of magical thinking* (2nd ed.). Lawrence Erlbaum Associates.

Zwart, H. A. E. (2019). Archetypes of knowledge: The relevance of Jung's psychology of scientific discovery for understanding contemporary technoscience. *International Journal of Jungian Studies, 5*(2), 154–176.

Note: CW = The Collected Works of C. G. Jung (20 volumes). Edited by Gerhard Adler, Michael Fordham, and Herbert Read; William McGuire, Executive Editor; translated by R. F. C. Hull. New York and Princeton (Bollingen Series XX) and London, 1953–1979.

Note

1 [*CW* = The Collected Works of C. G. Jung (20 volumes). Edited by Gerhard Adler, Michael Fordham, and Herbert Read; William McGuire, Executive Editor; translated by R. F. C. Hull. New York and Princeton (Bollingen Series XX) and London, 1953–1979.]

Index

For Product Safety Concerns and Information please contact our EU representative GPSR@taylorandfrancis.com Taylor & Francis Verlag GmbH, Kaufingerstraße 24, 80331 München, Germany

* 9 7 8 1 0 3 2 9 0 2 3 8 8 *

T - #0084 - 160425 - C0 - 234/156/20 - PB - 9781032902388 - Matt Lamination